In *Our Name is Mutiny*, Umej Bhatia has created a definitive and engrossing account of the 1915 Singapore Mutiny. Bhatia distinguishes his work from the glossed-over imperial narratives of the mutiny by focusing on the "lived reality" of the revolt. He seamlessly blends eyewitness accounts of violence, heroism, and tragedy with broader analyses of the mutiny's ties to themes of holy war and revolutionary fervor against British imperialism. Though the event took place over 100 years ago, Bhatia's captivating examination of this pivotal moment in Singaporean history is key to understanding how insurgency and mutiny feed into the geopolitical events of the world today.

~ Ali Soufan, author of *Anatomy of Terror*

The Singapore Sepoy Mutiny is not intelligible in itself. It was an event in a great drama – the rise and fall of the Raj in Greater India. British rule was achieved by a relatively small number of white men, first, by officers of the East India Company, later, by officers of the British Government. Sustained by awe, it was established and maintained by violence. It could not last because the subjects far outnumbered their masters. The Empire itself was on the wane in the latter half of the 19th century as other powers waxed. The Indian Mutiny of 1857 was a blow from which the Raj never fully recovered.

Singapore's history is inextricably bound to that history on the sub-continent and beyond. By setting the story of the Singapore Sepoy Mutiny against the backdrop of British India, the involvement of a growing overseas Indian movement fighting British rule and intrigues by Germany and Turkey to subvert Muslim sepoys during the First World War, Umej Bhatia gives a wider significance to what might otherwise be viewed as a minor local insurrection. It was not. The mutineers died for a much larger cause which was the overthrow of British rule and the liberation of India. From the Sepoy Mutiny of 1915 to the establishment of the Indian National Army by Imperial Japan in 1942 was only a short hop in time. Without the threat of widespread violence, the British would not have left India. The sacrifice of the mutineers along with that of many others made possible the success of Gandhi's peaceful struggle for freedom.

~ George Yeo, Former Foreign Minister of Singapore

The dramatic story of Singapore's sepoy rebellion of February 1915 deserves a wider audience. In *Our Name is Mutiny*, Umej Bhatia provides an engaging and readable account of this bloody colonial-era mutiny, while also explaining carefully the wider significance of a revolt whose conspirators spanned the globe, whose aftershocks shaped Singapore's history, and whose aims foreshadowed the eventual decline of the mighty British Empire itself.

~ James Crabtree, author of *The Billionaire Raj*

In investigating the forgotten Sepoy Mutiny of 1915, Umej Bhatia offers deep insights into Singapore's history and encourages us to reflect on the impact of international political turbulence on the structural vulnerability of the global city state today. *Our Name is Mutiny* is a rewarding read.

~ Prof C. Raja Mohan,
Director, Institute of South Asian Studies,
National University of Singapore

A century ago, Singapore was merely a cozy colony, as Umej Bhatia harkens in this masterful study of the city's pivotal role in the east's uprising against colonialism. Far from the central theatre of World War I, the 1915 mutiny there provides an uncanny foreshadowing of the rising intrigue against empire across South, East and Southeast Asia at the intersection of port cities and revolutionary hubs. An essential portrait of the colonial era that provides lasting lessons for the region's multicultural present.

~ Dr Parag Khanna, author of *The Future is Asian*

OUR NAME IS MUTINY

On the front cover:
Captain Moira Francis Allan Maclean who was killed in the
Singapore mutiny, with men of the Mountain Battery of the
Malay States Guides who stoked the 5th Light Infantry to
mutiny.

Lithograph of the assassination attempt of Lord Hardinge,
Viceroy of India, from Look and Learn History Picture Library.

On the back cover:
The SS *Komagata Maru* in Vancouver being watched over by the
tugboat SS *Sea Lion*.

Text © 2019 Umej Bhatia

Published by
Landmark Books Pte Ltd
5001 Beach Road
#02-73/74
Singapore 199588

Landmark Books is an imprint of
Landmark Books Pte Ltd

ISBN 978-981-14-2917-0
Printed in Singapore

OUR NAME IS MUTINY

The Global Revolt against the Raj and the
Hidden History of the Singapore Mutiny
1907 - 1915

◦LANDM△RK◦BOOKS◦

To my father and my mother

*The only known photograph of 5th Light Infantry officers
in uniform serving at the time of the mutiny.
Subedar Sharaf-ud-din, Pathan H Company Commander
and British loyalist, is third from left.*

If someone asks our identity
Tell them our name is Mutiny
We are bound to end tyranny
Rising up is our destiny

That is our *namaz*, our *sandhya*
Our *puja*, our worship
This is our faith
Our work
This our only Khuda, our only Rama.

Kartar Singh Sarabha,
Ghadar revolutionary

Sepoys on parade at Tanglin Barracks

CONTENTS

Acknowledgements

I have so many to thank for helping bring this work to fruition.

Wendy Ang and her team at the National Archives of Singapore and the team at the reference section of the National Library of Singapore. The phenomenal archivists at the India Office Library in London. The Bhojani family, the Fab Four, Avi, Poonam, Aahan and Amay for their love, friendship and support. Robert Clark for so generously sharing with me the war diaries and confidential reports of the 5th Light Infantry after I wrote to him out of the blue. Chng Kai Fong for the invigorating exchanges and James Crabtree who sped through a near cooked version of the manuscript. Parag Khanna for sound advice. Darryl David for always looking out for me. Bilahari Kausikan for his no nonsense encouragement. Hector Kothavala for kindly making available biographical details of his great grand-uncle and namesake. Yogi and Falguni Mehta for their support and kindness. Prof C Raja Mohan for his useful perspectives. Iskander Mydin for help in picture research. Tony and Annette Patel for their support and Stefan and Azizah Piringer for their mentorship. Ken Siah for reading the earliest chapters and urging me on through the years. Jeevan Singh for being a judicious sounding board, and Satvinder Singh and Sharon Kaur for their faith. Ali Soufan for being an intellectual comrade, a brother-in-arms and always il miglior fabbro. Professor Tan Tai Yong for the Foreword and affirming the value of the research. Raf Wober for being witness and whisperer through the ages. Mr George Yeo for intuiting both the macro and micro-history of this work and for his support in this project. My publisher, Goh Eck Kheng, with whom I reunited on this particular book project 18 years after our first collaboration. Stacey Foo for help with archives in London, Shalini Lalwani for her ideas and long friendship, and Ng Teck Hean for his guidance and support.

And last but not least my extended family, firstly the memory of my grandparents Gurnam Singh Soin and Satwant Kaur Medan, survivors of the Partition. Apart from my outstanding and brilliant parents – professionals, scholars and pioneer Singaporeans Amarjit Singh (my first reader) and Dr Kanwaljit Soin, from whom I have learned so much with love, also my children Khalista and Armahn who have taught me patience and the joy of loving what grows and blossoms, my ever-constant brother-in-law Afzal Khushi who has always got my back and his three sons, Amran, Ameer and Aman. Not least but last, my darling wife, Shireen, who has seen me through writing campaigns from the crusades to a mutiny, packed and unpacked in seven cities and never gave up hope.

FOREWORD

In *Our Name is Mutiny: Revolt against the Raj and the Hidden History of the Singapore Mutiny, 1907-1915*, Umej Bhatia presents a thorough and penetrating account of a series of globally connected events that led to the Singapore Mutiny in February 1915, and its denouement. With its layered and nuanced narrative, which situates the causes and consequences against the broader contexts of imperialism, nationalism, revolution and geopolitics, the author has made a significant contribution to the historiography of the attempted revolt against the British Raj from 1907.

The author builds his story patiently. In the first half of the book, he takes the reader away from Singapore to the Punjab in northwestern India, Europe, North America, Canada and Japan. The narrative is replete with rich biographical accounts of a wide cast of characters who were to feature in nationalist debates and revolutionary conspiracies in different parts of the British Empire. Their stories are told with empathy, as individuals who grappled with anxieties and anger as they faced exclusion and repression in their home country, and racism and discrimination in places where they had tried to build new lives. The story, which tells of the international reach of the Ghadar, an underground movement that aimed at the violent overthrow of the British government in India, has all the entangled drama of international "spies, propagandists and revolutionaries" whose activities and conspiracies eventually spilled over into Singapore during the momentous months of 1915.

This latest version of the Singapore Mutiny is to be commended for giving voice to the subalterns, the protagonists who were often forgotten and nameless. By turning our attention to the ordinary soldier, the author gives poignant glimpses into the world of the rank-and-file sepoy and their Indian officers. He explains the combination of attitudes, outlook, aspirations, fears and feelings of isolation as colonial subjects that led them to turn against their British officers and the order to which they had earlier sworn loyalty. By capturing the thoughts of the sepoys, as well as testimonies of local eyewitnesses, this volume has given us a welcome "history from below", providing perspectives we do not often get through official narratives that tend to focus on the viewpoints of the elites.

Finally, while the mutiny appeared to be a local affair, triggered by personal and regimental concerns, this study shows convincingly that the political geography of the event went far beyond the island colony. The 1915 Mutiny had its roots in the Punjab, geographically and culturally very far from colonial Singapore. That it eventually erupted in Singapore, in the midst of a major, global conflagration, involving players from many nations, highlighted the global dimensions of what had previously been seen as a local affair. Umej Bhatia's account of the mutiny underscores the idea that the British Empire was an interconnected structure, linked by networks and flows of personnel, capital and ideas. This is not merely the story of an individual colony; it is a story of empire.

This is a compelling account, elegantly written in vivid and evocative prose. It is admirable that Umej Bhatia, a career diplomat, has found time and intellectual energy to undertake what is obviously a labour of love. Thanks to him, the history of Singapore, and its interconnectedness with events in the world, has been considerably enriched.

Professor Tan Tai Yong
Yale NUS College

PREFACE

In 1915, a new cocktail called the Singapore Sling was served in the Long Bar of the Raffles Hotel. According to hotel legend, a Hainanese barman took up a British Colonel's challenge to mix a drink for European ladies too demure to be seen sipping standard slings. As the soft-pink gin sling was poured for the first time, other hands elsewhere on the island were mixing a far more lethal combination – a cocktail of revolt meant to challenge the Governor and his Colonels maintaining order on the tropical island. Blending heady ideas of insurrection and holy war, the Singapore Mutiny snapped the settlement out of its long afternoon snooze.

By 1915, England was dreaming no longer but mired in the fever nightmare of the First World War. The brutalities of war had yet to disrupt life on the slumbering settlement of Singapore. The compact island served as the capital of the Straits Settlements, a cosy Crown Colony spanning the British controlled territories of Penang and Malacca right down to the Cocos-Keeling and Christmas Islands northwest of Australia. With a population of 760,000 in 1914, the island-settlement assumed an outsize role as a defence base and administrative hub for the Malayan hinterland. Steamers from over 50 shipping lines called at Singapore, making it a key node on the network of trans-imperial submarine telegraph cables and shipping routes. Straddling the approaches to a sea, a pair of oceans and a trio of straits, Singapore was already the world's seventh busiest port by 1914.

Just south of the equator, the diamond-shaped island glistened as a strategic pendant on the British-controlled chain of trade connecting Calcutta in India to Guangdong in China. But the settlement's connectedness also exposed a soft and vulnerable bosom, especially after all its erect British manhood joined the war in Europe. The violent nightmare descended one afternoon when the settlement's protective garrison of British Indian soldiers (also known as sepoys) rose up in revolt. The mutinous men were mostly Muslims, with a handful of Sikhs. Driving the uprising were ideas of *jihad* (holy war) along with a nationalistic, mutiny movement preaching freedom from British rule. The Singapore sepoy mutiny pointed to the future of Britain's weakening grip on its far-flung Eastern Empire.

Coincidentally, the 1915 mutiny erupted on 15 February – on the day and month of Singapore's fall to the Japanese exactly 27 years later. The invasion and occupation of the Singapore during the Second World War is imprinted firmly in its national memory, marked by more than a dozen war memorials across the island. At the Civilian War Memorial off Beach Road, a remembrance service is held every year on 15 February, designated as Singapore's Total Defence Day. Nine kilometres to the west, Reflections at Bukit Chandu commemorates the Singapore Malay Regiment's last stand against the Imperial Japanese Army.

A stone's throw away from Reflections stands an all but forgotten colonial bungalow. With a red roof, dark timber beams and white-washed walls, the house sits in splendid isolation atop a cul-de-sac off the busy Ayer Rajah Expressway. In 1915, the black-and-white "tudor tropical" bungalow was home to one of the island's British Colonels – the Commanding Officer of the 5th Native Light Infantry battalion of sepoys. In mid-February, the island's Chinese New Year festivities were in full swing when a series of loud cracks interrupted the Colonel's afternoon nap. These were not celebratory fire-crackers ushering in the Year of the Rabbit, but the crackle of gunfire of sepoys in full mutiny.

Today, the Colonel's bungalow is nestled in secluded tranquillity frozen in another era. Known as Bukit Damai (Peaceful Hill in Malay), the house preserved at No. 7 Royal Road is approached by the same narrow, one-way lane along which the mutineers once walked and plotted. Next door at No. 6 Royal Road stands a smaller bungalow occupied then by a Major, the battalion's deputy commander. Raised on concrete stilts to keep out floods, large insects and tigers, the space under its floorboards once sheltered the Major's wife from marauding mutineers. A quick crawl under the structure after a century's passage uncovered only old, discarded colonial furniture – history swept under the rug.

Time warps aside, past artefacts rarely lie at rest in land-scarce Singapore. Even old bones must move. Long gone along with the old Bidadari Cemetery are graves of the mutiny's civilian fatalities. The remains of its uniformed dead lie under tombstones at the Kranji War Memorial cemetery, with their fading names inscribed also on Singapore's Cenotaph memorial. Poke around in colonial hangovers like St Andrew's Cathedral, Victoria Memorial Hall, the Singapore Cricket Club or St George's Church and old mutiny momentoes will come to light. Polished plaques reflecting British names but mute on the story of the sepoys, or the trauma of Asians swept up in sudden violence. Much of the event's history was suppressed and buried long ago. Roland Braddell, a once prominent colonial-era Singapore lawyer, predicted in 1932 that the mutiny's secret history would remain untold:

> Round Alexandra Road and Ayer Raja Road many ghosts must walk, for these roads formed the scene of the terrible mutiny of 1915, when over forty white people were done to death. The true story of that outbreak will probably never be written, since there are possibly not more than four or five people alive today who know it. I am one of them.[1]

An eyewitness to the mutiny, Braddell examined the evidence and prosecuted several sepoys in open courts martial. Taking a forensic approach, the lawyer was convinced that the mutiny was master-minded from India, where a broader rebellion had also been planned at the same time. Sensitive to the security concerns of a slowly expiring Empire, Singapore's colonial administrators quickly spun some founding facts to establish the traditional account. According to the standard history, the mutiny was an isolated event of little significance. Effectively reducing the event to a morality tale, this simplistic "Cowboys and Indians" and "Saved by the Cavalry" narrative usually unfolds in four neat acts, culminating with justice served and a vindication.

Act One: Singapore enjoyed security and tranquility until the outbreak of war followed by a mutiny out of the blue. Act Two: the mutineers did heinous acts with a few loyal, ineffective sepoys and a hapless majority melting away. Act Three: despite initial blunders, the British Empire's stalwarts prevailed with acts of pluck and heroism. Act Four: the evildoers were punished, scapegoats shamed, residents of Singapore pledged loyalty and new security measures were introduced along with warnings against sedition or complacency.

It is tempting to draw from the established narrative and shoe-horn some lessons for contemporary Singapore in the process. After all, key Indian revolutionaries operated globally from Europe to Asia to America, linking up with other agents of "counter-empire" and anti-imperial globalization. For some, the mutiny in Singapore can be read ultimately as a story of how revolutionary ideas are spread, and the vulnerability of global hubs to the virus and venom of non-state actors with an extremist agenda. But reading back into history to project retrospectively what we wish to see is a low-hanging fruit which loses flavour fast.

The fact is that the imperial myth of the mutiny and the lived reality of the revolt may as well have been two separate historical episodes. Barring inconvenient realities from troubling its pristine account, the imperial story-line glossed over the deeper forces that detonated and drove the Singapore mutiny, its links to the broader revolt in British-controlled India and the failure of the overall uprising. This unfiltered history may have been deemed unfit for consumption in the colonial era, but the pieties of expired historiography should be discarded as Singapore completes its bicentennial commemoration. Questions long left hanging, including the following, should be posed and answered:

What were the political events, ideas and geopolitical interests that helped to shape the uprising against Britain's Empire in the East?

Who were the men and women who lay the seeds of the revolt in Singapore?

What was the ideology of these Indian revolutionaries and what inspired them to challenge a mighty Empire?

Were the mutinous sepoys in Singapore mere pawns or active agents of revolt, and what were their thoughts, hopes, fears and fates?

What was the colonial government in Singapore's response and the quality of its leadership?

Was the mutiny a holy war, part of an uprising against the British Raj in India or an outburst of collective insubordination?

Was the mutiny a one-off episode or does it hold lessons for the security and vulnerabilities of globally connected city-states like Singapore?

Answers to these questions require an understanding of how the seeds of the anti-imperial Mutiny movement were planted, how and why the movement sprouted so quickly and grew tentacles that triggered a sepoy revolt in Singapore, lying as it did on the path towards a broader uprising in India. The story of the mutiny reveals how larger historical forces interact in unpredictable ways to produce unexpected effects that can alter the destiny of the small, vulnerable and unprepared. More than just an excursion into the past, it is an effort to recover lost links, names and actions. These buried markers touch our lives in ways we barely register. The settlement of Singapore and its global connections in 1915 appear to be part of a now-vanished world. But we still share space with that past, whether we like it or not. In tracing its contours, we will find that certain historical continuities still affect and may even define us.

INTRODUCTION:
Facts and Fictions

Location has always been Singapore's greatest invisible asset, and liability. Singapore as a geographical fact is a key actor in this story, as it interacts with passing personalities and historical forces over time. Colonial Singapore's land-based defence focused on protecting its harbour, which boasted a world-class dockyard. In 1914, the city-settlement's military garrison included two full infantry battalions, one British and the other Indian led by Hindustani speaking British officers. Detachments of Royal Engineers and the Royal Garrison Artillery operated from the southern islands of Pulau Brani and Pulau Blakang Mati (Sentosa Island) respectively. A 200-strong Sikh Police Contingent, quartered in Pearl's Hill near Chinatown, served as a strong reserve force. Providing auxiliary support was a lightly trained civilian volunteer infantry divided into European, Chinese and Malay companies.

In the summer of 1914, the all-British battalion of the King's Own Yorkshire Light Infantry (KOYLI) occupied the European barracks at Tanglin, while the Indian sepoys of the 5th Native Light Infantry (hereafter known as the 5th) were garrisoned at Alexandra Barracks. The 808 sepoys of the 5th were primarily Muslims from the Eastern Punjab (today known as Haryana), Delhi and its surroundings. One half of the battalion were ethnic Pathans. The other half were Ranghars (Muslim Rajputs). Mixed in were a few other clans like Mula Jat Muslims and a small handful of Hindus in support functions. Race and religion aside, the sepoys of the 5th were professional soldiers. Singapore was their first posting outside India. To avoid serving overseas, a few resigned before the battalion left India. There were discipline problems among its Ranghar half, but no military unit lacks trouble-makers. Those who agreed to sail to Singapore were willing volunteers. They were expected to uphold the reputation of the "Loyal Fifth", one of only a dozen regiments that had stayed loyal during the 1857 Indian Rebellion.

The 1857 uprising had been a major trauma for the British Empire. The armed movement by Hindus and Muslims to regain their freedom and dignity began with a mutiny of sepoys in the army of the British East India Company in the Meerut garrison near Delhi. With 6,000 British soldiers and civilians killed and nearly one million Indian casualties, 1857 shook the foundations of Britain's autocratic rule in India. Indian nationalists considered the revolt 1857 *Ka Swatantrya Sama* or "The 1857 Indian War of Independence", as conceived in the title of a 1907 book by Vinayak Damodar Savarkar. Better known as Veer Savarkar, the precocious 24-year-old, London-based Indian revolutionary published his work on the fiftieth anniversary of the 1857 Revolt. Savarkar dreamed of inspiring a second and more successful uprising against British rule.

After 1857, India's British rulers had a care to avoid being caught napping again. Control of India was transferred from the mercantile East India Company to British Crown rule better known as the British Raj. India's administrative and security apparatus was overhauled in an effort to safeguard the Crown Jewel of Britain's colonies. The soldier and scholar General George MacMunn warned that it was "only necessary for a feeling to arise that it is impious and disgraceful to serve the British, for the whole of our fabric to tumble like a house of cards without a shot being fired or a sword unsheathed."[2] India's sepoy army was recruited from fresh regions, with the construction of new "martial races" like the Sikhs, Kumaonis or Gurkhas who had stayed loyal in 1857. Also considered faithful fodder were the Ranghars, Pathans from Hindustan and Punjabi Muslims. Under the British Raj, the sepoys swore allegiance to the *sirkar* (authority) or *badshah* (monarch), the King-Emperor of Britain.

The Ranghars and Pathans of the 5th Light Infantry settled in quickly after their arrival at Singapore's P&O Wharf in April 1914. The sepoys assumed the duties of a typical garrison force, supporting the British battalion at Tanglin Barracks. The Muslims of the 5th had relieved a predominantly Hindu battalion of the 3rd Brahmans. Ironically, it was a Brahmin sepoy who fired the first shot of the Indian Rebellion against British rule in 1857. But the men of the 5th had little clue of a wider uprising against British rule, or any notion of holy war at the command of the Sultan-Caliph of Islam. That was still to come, imminent but unexpected, like the start of the First World War.

With the war's outbreak in August 1914, the sepoys of the 5th found themselves reinforced by a battalion of Sikh and Muslim sepoys from the Malay States Guides regiment. Based in the city of Taiping in the Malayan state of Perak, the Guides were recruited from the Malay States or directly from British India as a military force for the internal defence of the Federated Malay States. Accompanying the Guides' three infantry companies was a small 97-strong, three-gun mountain artillery battery.

As the Western front in Europe turned into a merciless meat-grinder, a manpower-hungry War Office in London scoured its colonies for fresh troops. It was agreed that the British garrison at Tanglin could be safely redeployed from Singapore, leaving behind some British gunners and engineers, the Sikh Police Contingent and civilian volunteer infantry. Singapore's security was now in the hands of two Indian sepoy battalions, the Guides and the 5th. Their British commanders were convinced that the sepoys would willingly volunteer for combat when called upon and do so without questioning why. But they had misread their men's loyalties. Not all were ready to do or die, not for the British Raj at least.

Conflict on the Western front had now spread beyond the shores of Europe to become a global war. Britain faced not only a determined European foe in Imperial Germany, but a Muslim enemy state with the power to declare war as well as holy war. The Ottoman Sultan, Mehmed V, allied with Berlin's eccentric Kaiser Wilhelm, cousin to the King of England. Together, the Germans and Turks conspired to exploit a major vulnerability of British India. More than a quarter of the world's 270 million Muslims were subjects of the British Empire. The Germans persuaded the Ottomans to issue a series of *fatwa* or religious opinions. The purpose was to turn Britain's Muslim subjects against their colonial masters. An opinion issued by the Ottoman Empire's highest Islamic authority made it a ruling for all Sunni Muslims. One *fatwa* read:

> Question: The Muslim subjects of Russia, of France, of England and of all the countries that side with them in their land and sea attacks dealt against the Caliphate for the purpose of annihilating Islam, must these subjects, too, take part in the Holy War against the respective governments from which they depend?
> Answer : 'Yes.'[3]

The *fatwa* was the definition of a loaded question, which the Germans hoped to explode in British faces. Other Ottoman *fatwa* banned Muslims subjects of the British and their allies from fighting Ottoman soldiers. The British issued a counter *fatwa* through a loyalist, Indian Muslim cleric. Permitting sepoys to kill their fellow Muslim Turks in combat, the cleric argued that Ottomans had no legitimacy as guardians of Islam as they did not hail from the tribe of the Prophet Muhammed. These quasi-religious arguments, stoked by rival empires for political and strategic reasons, were treading on dangerous ground. The conflicting messages confused the sepoys then, with repercussions that continue to haunt Islamists today. But Germany's short-term, cold calculation was that:

[T]he sultan-caliph's call to jihad might stir religious fanaticism among colonial Muslims in Asia and Africa and turn Europe's conflict into a world war. The Germans applied endless pressure on their Ottoman allies to provoke global jihad, while the British and French sought by all means to discredit the sultan-caliph and undermine his religious authority in their imperial possessions. In the process, the Allies were drawn ever deeper into the Great War in the Middle East, as much to contain the perceived threat of Islam to their colonies as to defeat the Ottoman Empire as one of the Central Powers.[4]

As both sides fostered geopolitical ideas of Islam, the battle was drawn on a canvas without borders in globalisation's first true era. As the "rival *jihads*" became entangled in the gathering movement of a pan-Indian mutiny uprising, matters became even more confused. The British Empire pressed on in this battle of hearts and minds, determined to maintain its advantage in this global fight. After all, Britannia ruled not only the waves, but controlled crucial infrastructure under the seas, which helped it to connect and control a far-flung empire in a form of telegraphic imperialism. To evade suppression by the British Raj, Indian nationalists planted overseas bases across Europe, while the emerging militant movement planted revolutionaries in key Asian ports including Singapore, Manila, Rangoon and Hong Kong and despatched its activists to the Pacific West Coast of the USA and Canada.

In North America, exiled Hindu radicals, disgruntled Indian students, Sikh and Muslim farmers and lumber-mill workers formed a cross-faith alliance of convenience that also dissolved class lines. San Francisco, then a global revolutionary hub, was where the Indian diaspora established the Hindustan Association of the Pacific Coast. In 1913, as the Governor of Singapore toasted the opening of the world's second largest dry dock, the Indians in San Francisco published a revolutionary newspaper called the *Ghadar*. Calling on Indians to unite, rise and throw the British out of India, *ghadar* meant mutiny or revolt. Derived from Arabic, and absorbed into Urdu and Punjabi, the newspaper's name was inspired by the revolutionary Veer Savarkar's revisionist history of the 1857 Indian Rebellion. Printed in four Indian languages, the *Ghadar* newspaper played up episodes of racism and repression in British India and various outposts of Empire. As its readership expanded, the *Ghadar* soon became synonymous with the militant, anti-British movement it helped to foster – the Ghadar or Mutiny movement.

The *Ghadar*'s founding editor was a talented but mercurial revolutionary and anarchist named Har Dayal. For a brief time just before the

First World War, the Delhi-born Punjabi became the movement's main ideologue in North America. Fluent in a dozen languages, Har Dayal collaborated in London with revolutionaries like Veer Savarkar, instigator of a second great mutiny. Har Dayal abandoned his Oxford University scholarship and a promising career in the Indian Civil Service to oppose British rule. Hunted by the imperial police, Har Dayal sought refuge in the Americas. Between seasons of meditation in a Hawaiian cave and heavy socializing in San Francisco, he dabbled in open marriage and conducted a disastrous affair with his blonde Swiss student.

It took a sensational assassination attempt on the life of the Indian Viceroy in Delhi in 1912 to reawaken Har Dayal and return him to the path of revolution. Henceforth, Har Dayal deployed his compelling rhetoric of freedom to rouse expatriate Indian workers and students in the United States. Har Dayal's protege Gobind Behari Lal, later the first Indian to win the Pulitzer Prize, explained his mentor's method and the significance of the Ghadar "experiment" he helped to launch:

What kind of an experiment was THE G(H)ADAR? It was based upon a theory, which had to be tested… (c)rudely stated the theory was even that the pre-learned Indians can be instructed politically, and become motivated by modern freedom. The idea of self-government, which is political freedom, can be transmitted from the learned to the unlearned common people, farmers, factory and other sorts of routine workers….[5]

German agents encouraged and supported the growth of the Ghadar movement in order to subvert the British Raj. This Mutiny movement soon stretched outwards from the Pacific seaboard states of the USA and Canada across the ocean to the South China Sea, past the maritime cross-roads of Singapore and through the Bay of Bengal right up to India's Punjab. Spurred by incidents of racism in North America and Britain's Eastern Empire covered graphically in the *Ghadar*, the Mutiny movement attracted a growing following. A key flashpoint was the harsh enforcement of regulations against non-white immigration to the Dominions of the British Empire. Canada was one of several of these newly self-governing white-settler communities of the Empire. With imperial connivance, these white-ruled outposts erected barriers to entry by brown-skinned British subjects who theoretically should have enjoyed equal rights and freedom of movement.

Matters came to a head during the *Komagata Maru* incident of 1914. The SS *Komagata Maru* was a Japanese passenger steamer chartered by a Malayan Sikh businessman named Gurdit Singh. Roving between Singapore and the Malayan states of Selangor and Perak, Gurdit had picked up Hokkien Chinese, Malay and some English. More importantly, the itinerant Sikh businessman imbibed ideas from the *Ghadar* newspaper. The shrewd, socially conscious and scrappy Sikh decided to launch a paid, migrant boat journey. The goal was to challenge Canada's colour bar promoted by white Canadian nationalists and their populist politicians against non-white immigrants. Gurdit's enterprise attracted dreamers, migrants, revolutionaries and ex-sepoys battling for equal rights in a white man's world. Bound for Vancouver from Hong Kong via several East Asian ports, the ship was denied entry to Vancouver port and chased away by a Canadian warship. Forced to sail back to Calcutta, a number of passengers were shot and killed after disembarking in an encounter with British security forces. The ship's fate became a rallying cry for propagandists of the *Ghadar*, now widely distributed in India and across North Indian diaspora communities.

With a world war on the horizon, the stretched British Empire's vulnerability to seaborne attacks also emboldened the revolutionaries. Facing the combined might of the German, Austro-Hungarian and Ottoman empires, Britain sought help from Japan, its Asian alliance partner, to police its vast Eastern waters, together with allied Russian and French navies. The closest German fleet was based in Tsingtao, then a German settlement in Northern China. With the outbreak of war, the commander of Britain's China Station moved from Hong Kong to Singapore to supervise his fleet's sprawling operations.

It was a timely move. In the war's opening months, a sole Imperial German naval cruiser and commerce raider known as the SMS *Emden* terrorised allied shipping across the Indian Ocean. After bottling up Singapore's western approaches, the *Emden* created panic with its brazen shelling of Madras (Chennai) port in India. A month later in October 1914, the *Emden* carried out an equally daring raid on Penang harbour, sinking two allied ships under British noses. The German lone wolf then targeted isolated island relay stations in Britain's global "All Red" telegraph cable network. British shipping and imperial prestige suffered several more blows before the *Emden* was finally sunk in a climatic battle off the Cocos-Keeling Islands. Part of its captured crew were then interned in Singapore, where the sailors plotted further damage on British interests by befriending and swaying the loyalties of their sepoy guards. Recalling the raider's rampage on the Indian Ocean, the word 'emden' is still used today in several South Indian languages to denote swaggering mischief.

The *Komagata Maru* incident and the exploits of the *Emden* played on the minds of the Singapore sepoys who formed the island's largest armed force in 1915. Impressed by German naval superiority and appalled by

British racial discrimination, the Sikh and Muslim sepoys of the Malay States Guides refused to deploy overseas. Packed off back in disgrace to their Perak headquarters, the near-mutinous sepoys took pride in standing up for their rights. Only a single section of Guides artillery remained in Singapore with the sepoys of the 5th. These men now pulled double duty guarding Singapore's docks and wharves. Passing through were a steady stream of arrivals and departures with news that undermined official British accounts of the war. German prisoners-of-war from the *Emden* befriended their guards and told them of the brutal conditions in Europe – of armies of the British Empire in desperate trench warfare of gas and bayonets, the terrible conditions, the sickness and damp weather and how they would have to kill fellow Muslims.

The overworked sepoys were open to any number of agents of influence with appeals to faith or nationalism. In their spare time, the sepoys could roam the town of Singapore or visit local Indian socialite businessmen. Discipline-eroding distractions were aplenty in the brightly lit brothels of Singapore's Malay Street, where obliging Japanese *karayuki-san* were also openly patronised by British officers and other ranks. The pious visited mosques where some were exposed to pan-Islamist and revolutionary propaganda.

At about the same time, Indian revolutionaries in America seized the opportunity to strike at the British Raj while its armies were bogged down in Europe. The rolling-stone revolutionaries of the Mutiny movement had once crossed oceans in search of a better life. Now from their bases in California, Vancouver and Oregon, the Indian revolutionaries were returning to launch their uprising against British rule. Under the flag of revolt, the Ghadar revolutionaries devised a make-shift plan with three parts. One, rouse politically conscious Indians in North America and Asian port cities on the Pacific-Indian Ocean steamer route. Two, ship these men in insurgent cells back to the Punjab in India. Three, trigger sepoy mutinies in the Empire's overseas garrisons and India in co-ordination with home-grown and recently imported insurgents. Properly executed, the plan would produce a general uprising in the homeland to topple the Raj and to secure India's independence. The immediate goal was a second and successful revolt, sixty years after the 1857 Indian Sepoy Mutiny.

Steamers operated by Japanese-owned shipping lines unloaded revolutionaries, weapons or propaganda in transit ports of Singapore, Penang, Manila, Rangoon and other outposts of Britain's Eastern Empire. Returning to India via these ports, Ghadar Party conspirators encouraged sepoys in the garrisons of the Eastern Empire to mutiny. Pan-Islamist supporters and German agents coordinated stealthily across bases in Southeast Asia via trade and shipping routes and the regional consular network. Connections enabled by open borders and new forces of communications allowed them to effectively foment revolt.

The target was the allegiance of hundreds of millions of Indian Muslims. The Central Powers of Germany and Ottoman Turkey stepped up their pan-Islamic propaganda to turn Indian Muslims against the British Empire. Muslim sepoys, recognising the Ottoman Turkish Sultan as Caliph of Islam, acknowledged him as the spiritual head of all Sunni Muslims. Sikh sepoys may have heard reports of India's budding revolutionary movement, which used bombs, terror, protests and rallies to achieve its aims. But as contracted military labour of the British Empire, all sepoys – regardless of their faith – owed allegiance to their colonial paymasters.

The men of the 5th landed in Singapore with little inkling of the radical ideas washing so quickly over them in the middle of the war. Stoked by German and Turkish intrigue and carried along by the tides of conflict, some of the sepoys were now primed to make a fateful choice – to embrace a cocktail of *jihad* and the Ghadar mutiny.

The Singapore mutiny took place a week before the larger revolt in India. Locally driven but also one of the string of planned mutinies in India, the Singapore incident can be considered a spill-over mutiny arising from the wider uprising. The exodus of Indian revolutionaries from the North America on a stop-over in Singapore encouraged the disaffection stoked through earlier pan-Islamic agitation and Ghadarite activism in the region. Hence, it was a "*jihad*-mutiny", one with repercussions for the entropying power of the British Empire.

Intriguers latched on to pre-existing grievances in the troubled garrison. The sepoys' British officers quarrelled with their Commanding Officer. Morale in the ranks was low over the high cost of living, the additional mobilisation duties and sepoy factionalism in the bubble of barracks life. The volatile chemistry of uncertainty, fear and powerlessness was stirred by the work of spies, propagandists and revolutionaries. As they prepared to redeploy from Singapore, uncertainty over their destination deepened fears and tensions to breaking point. Under the pressure of these various forces and influences, half the battalion rose up in mutiny on the eve of their transfer from Singapore to Hong Kong.

A Ranghar sepoy, Ismail Khan, fired the first shot that signalled the start of the mutiny on 15 February 1915. Joined by a few Sikhs from the Guides Artillery, the mutineers at Alexandra Barracks ended up killing 44 on the island, including British officers, soldiers, Singapore civilians as well as members of the Johor Military Force. Two Malays and three Chinese were counted among the fatalities. But the number of casualties does not tell the full story of the damage to imperial prestige. Consider that an embarrassed, global sea power was forced to desperately summon help from the outside to deal with half a battalion of its own men.

In a further blow to British superiority, the mighty white empire needed the help of a rising Asian state. Japan was a key part of the rescue coalition as Britain's then treaty ally. After the mutiny was suppressed, a Japanese journalist named Koji Tsukuda boasted of the new status accorded to Japan. Filling despised service economy niches in Singapore like prostitutes, craftsmen, small traders or barbers, their sailors and local volunteers had shown a proud and martial side of Japan:

> Up till now slighted both by the British and the native and regarded
> as contemptible in trade, it now devolved upon us to protect the
> feeble and pitiable British…. All races without exception, gave way
> to the Japanese on the footpath… we were in military possession
> of a Portion of the British territory – it is true only for a very brief
> period, but what is the significance to be attached to the fact that
> the flag of the Rising Sun was set up in the centre of Singapore?
> Alexandra barracks are in the heart of Singapore island, and
> Singapore is the heart of Nanyo.[6]

The 1915 Singapore mutiny emitted weak signals of a new balance of power being formed in the region. It was a dry-run for the coming Japanese invasion of Singapore. The myth of British invincibility was eroded as it took 48 hours to regain the initiative, a week to establish full control and nearly two months to round up and deal with all the mutineers. In Singapore, the British and allied forces of Russian, French and Japanese marines and volunteers ended up killing more than 50 mutineers and suspected rebels. Over 200 sepoys were court-martialled, with only one man acquitted and more than 47 given death sentences. Several rounds of executions were conducted in public including a badly botched mass shooting of mutineers propped up against the wall of Outram Prison.

British officials were not dismayed to serve up a version of rough-and-ready justice if it helped to bring the natives to heel. After all, up north in Kelantan, the Sultan's British advisor detected a sneering attitude that erupted in an uprising of Malays that had to be quickly put down. The planned, broader February 1915 uprising in India had also turned out to be a poorly planned operation that fetched a crushing British response. What followed were scores of executions or imprisonment of sepoy plotters and the bands of overseas insurgents in India.

After containing the threat in Singapore, the colonial authorities quickly convened a committee of inquiry to examine its causes. They did not like the results. The committee's final report was stored in the archives for the next half century. It was embargoed for release only in 1965, co-incidentally, the year of Singapore's full independence. The committee members conceded that political motives were at play and also recognised the impact on the mutineers of the call to arms by Indian revolutionaries. Publicly, however, the usual white-wash was generated to hide the incompetence, weakness and complacency of certain high-placed British officials as well as some among the junior officer class.

The formal imperial version of events bolstered British rule and authority over its possessions. Imperial self-confidence had to be shored up while enemies of the Empire and their propaganda had to be countered. Defenders of Empire had good reason to shape the narrative in their favour. The truth was that the British were struggling to defend their far-flung possessions in the throes of the first global war. As the historian Tim Harper puts it, there was a "crisis of imperial globalization" also known as imperial overstretch, which had helped to midwife the "Birth of an Asian Underground."[7]

The battle over the history of the mutiny raged years after it had receded from popular memory. In 1969, Sir Richard Winstedt, an English Orientalist and Malay scholar who served in Malaya between the two world wars, considered it: "the merest pustule in the world's up-heaval."[8] As the sun began to set on Empire, he could be counted on to back the imperial version. Winstedt was a former colonial administrator who personally broadcast British propaganda in the Malay language to Japanese-occupied Malaya during the Second World War. According to the pustule narrative, the events of 1915 were a slight blemish on the benevolent face of British imperialism. Mutiny? Emeute? Revolt? Riot? *Jihad*? A hybrid *Jihad*-Mutiny? A sideshow prelude to a new Indian War of Independence? The merest pustule. Keep calm and carry on. In stark contrast to Winstedt's stiff upper lipped downplaying of the event, the Japanese historian Sho Kuwajima's pioneering work on the Singapore Mutiny claimed that it was a turning point in the modern history of Asia.

My own account of the Singapore Mutiny tries to show that some-where between these positions lies the truth, on strata buried beneath the surface of facts – a web of official reports and enquiries, formal communiques and jingoistic or stringently censored newspaper reporting. Some pain-staking excavation was required to extract these elements of the mutiny's secret history and to trace its connections to the broader revolt against the British Empire. Archival records from the period have sadly been lost over time, whether during the Japanese Occupation, the end of Empire in Singapore or the violent partitioning of India. Tracts of history probably remain buried somewhere in the Ottoman archives.

The sepoys were not lettered men who kept diaries. Much of what is left to the present had to be mined from fragmentary service records, confessions and witness statements. This includes self-serving testimonies to escape capital punishment or a harsh sentence. History in general has been unkind to the ranks of sepoys who served under British rule. As the historian Nile Green observed:

> According to a popular Persian idiom, the anonymous masses of history are referred to as *siyahi-e-lashkar*, the "blackness of the Army". Nameless and forgotten… in comparison to the wealth of studies of the British officer and (to a lesser extent) foot soldier, the intellectual, emotional and spiritual world of the sepoy is lost in the anonymity of the lower ranks.[9]

Along with the lived world of the ordinary sepoy and their Indian officers who were often promoted from the ranks, I shed light on the bungling of the British military officer class. Their decisions, choices and conduct partly shaped the mood, attitude and outlook of their sepoy sub-alterns. Socially, most of the officers were at the level of the settlement's *tuan kechil* (small bosses), engaged in day-to-day operations protected by solar topi and the unequal laws and customs of Empire. The British and Indian officers of the 5th were at sixes and sevens and undermined each other badly as they involved themselves in regimental factionalism.

My narrative provides a window into the settlement's so-called *tuan besar* (big bosses). These were senior British officials who governed Singapore and formed its local elite. Although some were birds of passage, a good number struck roots. They contributed to the success of the colony and even laid the foundations for modern Singapore. They built port infrastructure, drafted laws, supervised schools and found cures for tropical diseases. Some even stoutly opposed the opium trade sanctioned by their own Empire. I also shed light on a historically neglected Singapore Governor, Sir Arthur Young, who spent an eventful nine years in that role.

Not to be overlooked are the perspectives of ordinary Chinese, Indian and Muslim residents of Singapore – the "small voice of history"[10] – in the words of an Indian historian and pioneer of the Subaltern Studies School. For instance, I share the story of a Singapore Chinese business-man who hid over a dozen British civilians in his home to protect them from mutineers. Never properly recognised, he was unjustly accused by colonial authorities of exaggerating the risks he faced. I also use part of an overlooked war diary of a Singapore Malay volunteer sergeant who helped to put down the mutiny. The climax of the mutiny – a public execution – is seen through the eyes of a six-year-old Chinese boy. He was one of the last living eyewitness to share his experiences of the event.

In telling the story of the Singapore Mutiny, I have carefully shaped a historical re-enactment of the broader revolt against the Raj, including its background and period atmosphere, while remaining faithful to the facts. A profusion of fascinating characters was responsible for igniting the uprising in India. I have tried to give equal time to celebrated revolutionary actors like Har Dayal, Veer Savarkar, Rash Behari Bose and Gurdit Singh as well as lesser known figures like Hussain Rahim, Nawab Khan or Harnam Singh Tundilat. I have also focussed on the men who pursued them across borders, like the imperial policeman and spy Inspector William C Hopkinson. I have done so because I believe that the pull of the past, including the perspective of "history told from below" and cries of the "small voice of history" demand to be heard and brought to light. Instead of dutifully consuming the standard top-down narrative, if we cannot appreciate what was, who was, or embrace a submerged history, we risk missing out on the possibilities for the future. We will also end up uncritically accepting the sketching of events that only appear over the waterline.

There is another reason to uncover the hidden history of events. Amid the rise and fall of Empires, and time's pitiless swallowing of countries and personalities that lose their relevance, the curves and spikes of history must be anticipated This is an increasingly difficult task in an era of chronic disruption and accelerating change. In a world of liquid borders hardened by security measures; of unequal flows of capital and labour; a world where global communications networks ignite more micro-mutinies than we can imagine. One where the proxies of global geopolitics all compete and clash for space and attention, including pan-Islamic *jihad* in search of a new caliphate, anti-Western rebellion, ethno-populist nationalism and right-wing nativism, the search for dignity and other markers of identity politics. These were all themes complicit in the growth of the Ghadar Party, the 1915 revolt in India and the spill-over Singapore mutiny, reverbating in our own time with modern avatars like the threat of violent extremism, of rival *jihad*s and the use of religion for political ends. Forces accelerated today by technology, pulsating on digital screens to test the unity and mettle of communities and nations.

To be sure, history doesn't repeat itself. And it may rhyme without reason. History is not a straight line or a rising crescendo, but a series of circular crises, big and small, that shamble in mysteriously recursive loops impenetrable to both natural and artificial intelligence. All unfolding under the disk of a sun that keeps spinning the same loop of pain, pleasure and the all too human search for relief, for respite and for reason.

PART ONE

[I]

TRIAL BY FIRING SQUAD

The end is always a good place to start. Even in the face of its own extinction the mind believes it will go on.

Under the light of Singapore's early evening sun, 16 men are being led out of His Majesty's Criminal Prison on Outram Road. A crowd of about 6,000 have gathered on Golf Hill opposite Pearl's Hill to watch the unfolding spectacle. Men, women and children representing all the races and faiths of Singapore – Europeans, Eurasians, Malays, Indians, Chinese and Christians, Buddhists, Muslims and freethinkers – about to participate in an ancient ritual of public justice. Gently sloping heights that had served as the sixth hole of the Sepoy Lines golf links now double up as a viewing gallery. The onlookers have an unobstructed view from a space looking out towards Outram Park, to be levelled and occupied in the near future by the Singapore General Hospital.

Among the spectators is a six-year-old boy named Chan Chon Hoe.[11] From his home in Pagoda Street, he had followed the military band of Volunteers that marched up New Bridge Road to Outram Road. Now Chon Hoe peeks out from between the legs and shoulders of the gathered crowd to catch a look at the prisoners. The prisoners are all former sepoys, soldiers of the 5th Native Light Infantry of the British Indian army. Shipped in to defend Singapore, they have now been charged with mutiny in the middle of the First World War. The prisoners' armed escort are an imposing squad from the Sikh Police Contingent policemen. The tall and burly Sikhs carry Lee Enfield .303 bolt-action rifles that resembled toys in their massive hands.

Heads bowed, the 16 mutineers are ordered to stand to attention by British Army Major E H Hawkins of the 4th Shropshire Light Infantry. They obey instinctively, surrounded by two companies of the 4th Shropshires and other British soldiers from the Singapore garrison. Like surplus

33

caddies, British non-commissioned officers and enlisted men hurriedly form three sides of a square with the prison wall. It has become a full-dress show. Colonial officials are sensitive to the spectacle of British power and its salutary effect on the natives. The difference between loyalty and treachery to King and Emperor must be made clear. Imperial officialdom uses the civilizing veneer of ceremony and procedure to demonstrate that the Empire's rule of law trumped the barbaric whims of a debauched Eastern potentate. Never mind the hasty court-martial or the macabre theatre that is about to be staged. This Empire had offered the world the Magna Carta. Its ruddy-faced representatives will now serve up an object lesson on the fate of those who ate their salt and then spat it back in their faces.

The prisoners and their escort of Sikh constables are a study in stark contrast. The hand-cuffed sepoy mutineers wear ill-fitting long *kurta* shirts, Indian dhotis or Malay sarongs. The Sikh lawmen, with their headquarters situated next door in Pearl's Hill, represent the force of order in these parts. The police sport striped blue and white *pagris* (turbans) and wear impassive faces behind groomed, raven-dark beards. Their perfectly pressed khaki uniforms are secured by shiny belt buckles while mirror-polished boots under neat puttees reflect glints of dying sunlight.

Recruited and drilled by their colonial masters, guards and prisoners alike belong to the so-called martial races of India. Both sets trace their origins to the widest reaches of Punjab, Rajputana and the North-west Frontier, well before its violent partitioning between Muslim and non-Muslim in 1947. Hardy specimens hand-picked to perform a lifetime of military labour. Trained to ensure that religion comes a distant second after loyalty to the British Raj. The Sikhs hail from the fertile west of Punjab, while the mutineers are mainly Muslim Rajputs known as Ranghars from small dusty towns in the then more backward eastern reaches of Punjab known today as Haryana. These were towns and villages where camels roamed and home of the sturdy black Murrah buffalo, with the nearest Sikh and Punjabi speakers further up north.

British orientalists and linguists understood these differences. They know that unlike the Ranghars, Sikhs did not wear a cone-shaped *kulla* hat under their tall *pagri*. The colonial social engineers of efficient power maintenance shaped and created the martial races and used the age-old caste and class system to their full advantage. Singapore's Chinese and Malays are largely ignorant of the shades of the sub-continent. These lesser subjects of His Majesty the King deride the darker South Indians as *kling*, derived from Kalinga, an ancient Indian kingdom, but derogatorily was said to be from the sound of the chains that hobbled them as convict labour. And they label Sikhs, Rajputs and Pathans collectively as

Bengalis, because they sailed from Calcutta port in Bengal to Malaya. Some are confused, having once seen the Ranghars, now bare-headed, wearing turbans with some even full whiskered like their Sikh guard.

While some spectators may struggle to discern between the regimented Indians and those in rags, the Sikh police know all the difference between faith and faithlessness. And they have no love lost for the mutineers who had tried to kill some of them in the Central Police Station and even wounded fellow constables. Outram Prison had also come under attack. Now the only remaining link of values between the Sikh police and the sepoy mutineers was a devotion to the code of *izzat*, or reputation and respect. A question of manly pride, of honour and of shame. *Izzat* made good soldiers. But if offended it made them vendetta-hunters seeking revenge at any cost. And *izzat* required them to die like men.

Major Hawkins reads out the court-martial sentences of the prisoners. The 16 prisoners receive sentences with varying lengths of imprisonment. As each verdict is announced, a mutineer is ordered to step forward. Four ex-sepoys of the Taiping-raised Malay States Guides receive the lightest punishment possible – below two years without hard labour. The remaining dozen from the 5th Light Infantry of the British Indian Army are slapped with far harsher penalties. Some face "transportation for 15 years", or hard labour in a penal colony. Eight of them stare at "transportation for life" in the dreaded Andaman Islands. The Andaman Islands Cellular Jail is the Indian Alcatraz. The Indians know it as *Kala Pani* (Black Water), for it lay across the forbidding waters of the Indian Ocean. Only the fit and those under forty were sent to the *Kala Pani*, overseen then by a vicious Irish warden familiar with all the dark secrets of living purgatory. This could mean being shackled like a donkey to a mill, circling in endless loops to grind oil. Or to sit in pitch dark for years with no face or voice apart from your own.

Fates confirmed, the bedraggled group of 16 are marched off back behind the grey prison walls by their police escort. The huge crowd massed behind the cordon of British soldiers has not come all the way just for this. This has merely whetted their appetite for the main show that is about to begin.

Spread on and below Golf Hill, 6,000 pairs of eyes follow the final steps of a smaller group of men emerging from the prison gates. A new scene in the theatre of public instruction unfolds. Unlike the 16, the five are handcuffed. And their escort this time are not the straight-backed Sikh police but white-suited British prison wardens who form a close guard. Affirming British prestige, only the superior race may dispense with ultimate justice. The wardens are in no mood to give any quarter, after one of their own was killed outside Outram Prison by the mutineers.

The execution will be carried out in full public view; a spectacle revived after almost 20 years of its prohibition in Singapore. The natives must be taught their manners, including little Chon Hoe. The condemned men are marched to their execution spots with military precision. The weathered and peeling execution wall faces a flat piece of ground on the western side of Outram Road, rising gently to become Golf Hill. An eerie silence holds as the five prisoners are marched in. Quite unusual for a large crowd who produce Singapore's constant market hubbub. All are captivated now by the sight before them.

Two of the five ragged prisoners had worn officer's uniforms in the British Indian Army. Dunde Khan is the senior of the pair of cashiered officers. Fat and fair-skinned with a beard and moustache once neatly trimmed, the ex-Viceroy Commissioned Officer (VCO) had once flashed the two-star epaulette of a *subedar* (captain) on his shoulder straps. Now ordered to march forward, his muscle memory completes a familiar drill. In step by his side is a lean, sharp-faced former *jemadar* (lieutenant) sporting a long, flowing beard named Chiste Khan. Garbed in rumpled and soiled civilian clothes, former Subedar Dunde Khan and ex-Jemadar Chiste Khan struggle to retain some soldierly bearing and dignity.

A few weeks earlier, the pair of Khans had been in a very different position. Both were native officers of the 5th Light Infantry garrisoned in Singapore. Dunde commanded B Company of No 1 Double Company and Chiste had D of No 2 Double Company. They had turned out with their battalion for a Monday morning inspection parade by Acting Brigadier-General Dudley Ridout, the General Officer Commanding (GOC) the Troops in the Straits Settlements. Ridout was conducting his farewell inspection of the regiment just before its redeployment to Hong Kong. The inspection coincided with the Chinese New Year holidays. The festivities had begun the day before. At the stroke of midnight, the settlement's Chinese population exploded in riotous celebration. Official hours for firing small bombs and crackers were midnight until 1 am and 5 to 6 am. The large Chinese community in carnival mood could hardly be expected to obey the rules.

In the fast evaporating cool of a humid tropical morning, the paraded sepoys were in no mood to celebrate. And they were eager to break a different set of rules. Many, especially those from the Ranghar half of the dual-race battalion, looked sullen and unhappy. A hard core was ready to explode, itching to do the unthinkable. The Pathans from the other half were in a better state, with several of their own up for the coming promotion test.

Physically, the pudgy-looking Ridout with his bristly toothbrush moustache did not inspire fear or respect. But looks are deceiving. Short and stout, Ridout's benign and inoffensive appearance was sharpened by cold, piercing blue eyes. He had tried to rally the men with a rousing speech. The Khans and their sepoys listened to his words. Or rather half-heard its translation into Hindustani by their regimental commander, Lieutenant-Colonel Edward Victor Martin. The perennially sleepy-looking Martin was an isolated figure, unpopular with his fellow British officers and judged by some as too sympathetic to the sepoys.

In the rising heat and humidity of the morning, Ridout's speech rehearsed a tired formula: "The empire is vast and the duties of guarding it are great"[12] – words meant for the British Tommy, not Jack Sepoy. Describing his burden of command as General Officer Commanding the Straits Settlements was the last thing the already troubled, confused and demoralized sepoys needed to hear. Later that day, Lance-Naik (Lance-Corporal) Najaf Khan wrote a letter to his brother in India lamenting:

> As this war is such that no one has returned out of those who have gone to the war. All died. And those who have enlisted will not live alive. Believe this. World has died. No one has escaped who has gone to the war. All have perished. And there is recruiting open, don't let any men enlist. As all are being taken to the war. All will be caused to be killed.[13]

With a battalion and their own minds in disarray, some of the sepoys developed their own conspiracy theories. With help perhaps from passing agents of influence. Their once-disciplined heads held many confusing ideas. Some noble, others dangerous and mixed with trivial feuds and simmering frustrations. They were being sent away from Singapore to fight and kill Turks – their fellow-Muslims. This contradicted the one true faith. Even worse, they speculated that their ship was to be sunk en-route to their next post. Their colonial masters expected to lose the war and they were surplus to requirements. Reflecting the Rajput Hindu origins of his Ranghar identity in a moment of great stress, Sepoy Shaikh Mohammed wrote to his family reflecting Hindu ideas of resurrection:

> It is with sighing, crying, grief and sorrow to tell you that the transfer of the regiment on the 20th February is now a settled fact. It will go to Hong Kong. But don't know this, whether it is going to the war. God knows what kinds of trouble we will have to confront. What is this war? It is resurrection. That who goes there, there is no hope of his returning. It is God's punishment. If God released us from this calamity we will take to have reborn. We are very much confused and shocked. All the regiment is in sorrow together.[14]

On their part, the pair of ex-officer Khans, now standing with their backs against the walls of Outram Prison, had done their own listening, thinking, and whispering. Quiet intriguing was soon followed by bold declarations and preaching. As Viceroy Commissioned Officers, men like the Khans were expected to know better than to encourage such seditious talk. They sat at the top of the pyramid of Indian military labour recruited to defend the British Empire. Raised from the ranks of the sepoys for good service, they were trained not to question why but to do or die.

Fat Dunde certainly didn't look the part of a recruiting station officer. But he appeared to have something to prove. Displaying a maverick streak, he wore non-regulation earrings, a Rajput custom to project warrior virility. Dunde also had unusual interests for a professional soldier and an officer at that. In Singapore he had taken personal music lessons from a musician from his village of Bajpur in Gurgaon. Dunde was fond of playing his newfound instrument and singing to his men, an officer doubling up as an entertainer from home. Located in the far East of then undivided Punjab, the district of Gurgaon was mid-way between Delhi and the sacred city of Mathura. It was not far from the place of legend, where the Hindu god Krishna was supposed to have sported with the cowherds' maidens on the banks of the river Yamuna. The people of Gurgaon were fond of song, poetry and the edible cannabis known as *bhang*. They were the original hippies of India.

In Singapore, Dunde also found other attractions. With Chiste, he enjoyed the company of a wealthy and sociable Singapore merchant named Kassim Ismail Mansoor. A Gujarati Muslim from Bombay, Kassim was a Walter Mittyish character who dabbled in sedition. The 65-year-old *jihadi* socialite opened his weekend bungalow in Pasir Panjang Road to the officers and their sepoys. Chiste was also a disciple of the enigmatic Nur Alam Sham. A mysterious Muslim preacher and Sufi Master (*pir*), he had a cult following among Indian and Malay Muslims in Singapore. Nur Alam Shah delivered sulphurous sermons at his mosque on Kampong Java Road, just down the road from the house where Singapore's first Prime Minister, Lee Kuan Yew, was born a few years later.

As the First World War turned into a brutal conflict of attrition, Nur Alam Shah had raised thorny questions for the sepoys to consider. To whom was loyalty owed? To which Kaiser and to which Emperor? Charismatic Chiste also had a way with words. He persuaded some of his men that the tide was turning against British rule. Largely illiterate and unschooled, the thoughts of the sepoys did not match the precision or logic of trained minds. This thinking was dangerously open-ended and tumbled through their heads like the fake news Lance-Naik Fateh Mohammed shared with his father on the day the mutiny broke out:

The war increases day by day. The Germans have become Mohammedans. Haji Mahmood William Kaiser and his daughter has married the heir to the Turkish throne, who is to succeed after the Sultan. Many of the German subjects and army have embraced Mohammedanism. Please God that the religion of the Germans (Mohammedanism) may be promoted or raised on high.[15]

All it took was a spark, which eventually ignited. An explosion of gunfire amid the noise and smoke of Chinese New Year firecrackers and bomblets. A cluster of little rebellions had erupted within the regiment. Soon the sepoys had the run of the island. Chaos. Confusion. And then the inevitable betrayal. Secret agents in their midst. The prisoners they sprung who went their own way. The rounding-up. Wounded and blood-ied after his capture, Chiste was heard reciting the Qur'an. Its familiar *su-rahs* both balm and support. The trials. The cover-up. Documents sealed away for half a century or more in dusty archives, eaten by termites or firebombed or misplaced.

Turn back now to the scene outside the Outram Road Criminal Pris-on in 1915. A moss-splotched grey wall and three lines of khaki-clad sol-diers forming a square on the green turf. A red, laterite road separates the spectators from the spectacle. The little six-year-old boy staring wide-eyed. The Khans with three others. About to face their earthly fate in a few moments. They are not being sent back across to the *Kala Pani*, the dreaded black sea they had crossed to reach Singapore, but to a blackness of another kind – *sakrat-ul-maut* – senselessness. And not before *jan-kandani* – the agonised sucking out of life.

One choice remains for the proud Ranghars – they must uphold the Rajput warrior tradition. Dunde Khan son of Khan Mohammed Khan, Chiste Khan son of Mussalam Khan, two *havildars* (sergeants) and a sepoy (private) next to them hold their heads up and look straight ahead. They see heavy wooden posts sticking out of the ground like dead men stand-ing. But their *izzat* of manly honour requires them to remain as steady and as erect as those poles.

Khaki-clad army officers scurry about in the square making final preparations. They are joined by a gaggle of civilian officials and ward-ers. The civilians are in pristine white cotton drill suits with matching so-lar pith helmets on pomaded heads. To the spectators atop Golf Hill, the harried officials down below resemble brown and white ants in frenzied activity. The bureaucrats of Empire dash around fussing right up to the moment the five condemned men are marched to their execution spots.

The firing squad is composed of 25 men from the Royal Garrison Artillery under the command of Second Lieutenant Frank Vyner. Wearing large khaki pith helmets, with their knobbly, white knees peeking out between pulled up socks and "Bombay bloomers" shorts, the firing squad resemble overgrown school boys. In fact, they are artillerymen who have exchanged their large-bore guns for rifles.

With little fanfare the doomed men are strapped to the five-foot timber stakes that throw long, ghostly shadows on the prison's high outer perimeter wall. Their naked brown ankles are secured firmly by cotton thongs. The final whispered murmurings of the large crowd are hushed. Major Hawkins steps forward. He reads out a statement in a firm and loud voice:

> These five men, Subedar Dunde Khan, Jemadar Chiste Khan, 1890 Havildar Rahmat Ali, 2311 Sepoy Hakim Ali and 2184 Havildar Abdul Ghani have been found guilty of stirring up and joining a mutiny and are sentenced to death by being shot to death[16]... All these men of the Indian Army have broken their oath as soldiers of His Majesty the King. Thus justice is done.[17]

Translations of Hawkins' promulgation are read out quickly in Malay, Chinese and Hindustani. For those about to die, the agony is prolonged. The translation is intended for the settlement's large Chinese population, who outnumbered the colonial elite by 50 to 1. They had to hear the message as a warning, particularly the triad and secret society members who were prone to challenge authority.

The formalities complete, the officer in charge of the execution party raises his sword. Second Lieutenant Vyner gives his first order: "Ready!"

"Load!"

The firing squad load their rifles, clips fit into grooves in the rifle breech and cartridges ready to slide down the clip when pressed into the magazine. Five men brace up. Their bodies taut. An instinctive reaction to the coming spit of lethal fire from ten paces. Otherwise they neither flinch or waver. Not outwardly at least. They have refused any blindfolds. Instead they look straight ahead, calm and dignified, at their executioners who look like the caricature of British imperialism – nasty, brutish and in shorts. The condemned men impress some in the crowd and not a few British officials with their stoic calm. Nor their stoic helplessness.

"Aim!"

The artillerymen squint into the rifle sights, remaining steady. The crowd leans forward.

"Fire!"

Two minutes after the condemned men are marched into the square it is all over. They have crumpled into heaps of rags, torn flesh, blood and bone. The smoke of rifle-fire drifts away like a grey spectre. Chinese prison convicts bobble into the square to untie and stretcher the dead bodies back into the prison, to be taken away and buried in unmarked plots lost to history.

At rush hour today, crowds surge in the Outram Park Mass Rapid Transit underground station linkway beneath the old walls of the prison demolished long ago. The execution wall facing Outram Road between Second Hospital Road and College Road has become part of the station extension project. The thunder and rumble of trains brings people from one part of the island to another, drowning out the cries of old ghosts who have not found their peace.

For the boy Chan Chon Hoe, one man's face – perhaps Chiste's – will remain fixed in his mind for the next 87 years of his life. He will tell of the mutineer who "had a strong, fierce face and shrugged off the soldiers as they tried to blindfold him."[18] Nicknamed Sam Kau (third dog in Cantonese) as he was his family's third son, Chon Hoe will marry three times, father 10 and sire 23 grandchildren. He will live until the opening years of the following century in his flat in Tiong Bahru. But the former Boy Scout and winner of the silver Defence Medal during the Second World War will also confess right at the end: "That soldier will remain in my mind forever, and I have tried to have as much dignity and honesty in my life as he had in those few seconds."[19]

The end is always a good place to start. Even in the face of its own extinction the mind believes it will go on.

DON'T MIND THE BLACK SMOKE, GOVERNOR

Singapore's mighty proconsul, His Excellency Captain Sir Arthur Henderson Young, Knight Commander of the Most Distinguished Order of St Michael and St George, was known to pace his office in Government House. Hunched forward, hands clasped behind him, the Governor would denounce in righteous terms some injustice or intrigue in the privacy of his office.

Publicly, he personified courtesy, restraint and good manners. His tastes were simple and he shunned the frills of office. A graduate of Britain's prestigious Sandhurst military academy, he had a genial, avuncular face and a drooping walrus moustache. The 60-year-old former army officer centre-parted his hair without fuss and his eyes, though weary, were not without life. Young had been described by contemporaries as a "typical English gentleman who took infinite pains in the carrying out of his duties."[20] This included his devotion to his tough and no-nonsense wife, Lady Evelyn Young, who kept a dog and a noisy cockatoo on the grounds of Government House.

Dutiful civil servant and devoted husband he was, but Young was certainly not English. The former Scotland rugby international barged shoulders with England's gentlemen playing a ruffian's game. Young had learned competitive but fair play on the proving fields of Rugby School. An enthusiastic sportsman in his youth, he had excelled in, besides rugby, cricket, lawn tennis and golf. These were all popular leisure sports in Singapore that determined the relative standing of the young male colonial elite. He had also generously sponsored the Arthur Young trophy for Singapore's football-loving Malay community.

Young gave vent to passion only on the playing field. Professionally, he spoke cautiously and weighed his words carefully in the finest tradition of the civil service. He had spent over a quarter of a century as a soldier and then as a colonial administrator in Cyprus. He learned to carefully manage his phrasing in discussions with the fiery Cypriots of the Mediterranean. In Malaya, during a casual discussion among friends speculating on possible candidates for the post of Governor, Young, then the front-runner as Chief Secretary, had drawn himself back and offered only one sentence: "Well, I should be inclined to back the field".[21] He certainly didn't let on that he had already secured the job. After all, Young knew how to keep secrets, open or otherwise.

Promoted from Chief Secretary of the Federated Malay States (FMS) to Governor in August 1911, Young carried a flowing title that required small print on a large calling card. He was now Governor and Commander in Chief of the Straits Settlements and their dependencies including Labuan, the Cocos-Keeling Islands and Christmas Island, His Majesty's High Commissioner for the Malay States and Brunei and British Agent for Sarawak and the State of North Borneo. Despite the cascade of designations as the King's foremost representative in these parts, one disturbing fact sat awkwardly among the flourish of titles. This was a sensitive matter to be addressed during Young's forthcoming annual Budget Speech in the Singapore Legislative Council Chamber. The Budget Speech in just over a month's time was just one of several issues requiring Young's attention on the morning of Tuesday, 26 August 1913.

From his perch on Government House, Young had a commanding view of the crown colony he administered as capital of the Straits Settlements. Both land and sea were visible from the seat of colonial government, with snatches of the town, the port and the busy shipping beyond in the Strait. Sitting resplendent on a hill, with its well-proportioned, neo-classical features set in a rolling landscape called the Domain, Government House was the finest example of colonial prestige architecture in the Far East at the time. Known to the locals in Malay as *Tuan Gubenor punya rumah* (Sir Governor's House) it projected confidence, power and propriety and stately self-assurance.

Young would no doubt have understood the importance of projecting balance, proportion and reason. There was enough madness and insanity in the humid and trying conditions of the Straits Settlements. Alcohol or drug abuse, syphilis, debts or mental or physical infirmities carried away its victims without pity. Just the previous Friday, a lunatic had sneaked into the Wesley Methodist Church on Fort Canning Road. In the vestry where the sacred books and liturgical items were stored, the vandal had made a bonfire of all the church's bibles and hymn books. Even the beautifully bound leather bible used in the pulpit had been charred to ashes. The arsonist was an unstable Chinese vagrant caught after some cat and mouse detective work. But the vagrant's act of sacrilege may well have

Sir Arthur Young

come across as a foreboding to the superstitious. And there was no shortage of superstitions in Singapore's melting pot of factions and faiths that the Governor had to manage with a steady hand.

Almost on cue, even before breakfast on this fine morning, Young received the tragic news. A pillar of the local community had crumbled. Mr Edward F H Edlin was found dead at 2.30 am in his residence on Syed Ali Road, today's Newton Road. A prominent and popular lawyer with the firm of Drew and Napier, Edlin was Young's junior by a decade at Rugby School. Edlin had been in Singapore for twenty years and was an institution. Everyone, including Young, knew him as Peter. President of the Golf Club, an enthusiastic member of amateur theatrics, Peter also dabbled in rubber stocks and had a share in a pharmacy. At university, Peter had survived a tetanus infection which killed 14 others in his group.

But something deadlier had been eating at Peter, something apparently incurable. He was known to self-medicate regularly and had a touch of hypochondria. A trip to England had not cured his condition. Now Peter was gone. He had ended his suffering violently, by severing a major vessel in his throat with a razor. He died less than a minute later. His wife, Bertha, found him dead in a pool of blood, a novel and Dutch-wife pillow by his side, his pince-nez still perched on his nose. Peter was staring lifelessly up at the mosquito netting three feet up. It was splattered with his blood. He seemed deeply troubled in his last days, frightening her with his dark mood. He left her to raise their eight children, with five in boarding school in England. Senseless. The Coroner's official verdict was "temporary insanity." Peter's young sister had been institutionalised before. But there were rumours of financial embarrassment, speculation on the rubber market that could bring down the good name of Drew and Napier. All casting a gloom on everyone. Could anything worse happen to Singapore's small and tightly-bound British community?

Life everywhere was precarious, brutal and uncertain – even for the small and privileged elite that ruled over the writhing mass of Oriental humanity and barbarity alike. Indeed, Young himself had to deal with a nagging growth on his right hand. He knew this would eventually require some looking into. The Governor could not attend Peter's funeral at Bidadari Cemetery later that day at 5.30 pm. It would naturally be full of mourners among the settlement's great and good who were grieving for the popular lawyer. Duty called him elsewhere. As a mark of respect, Young decided that he would send his private secretary to the funeral.

The Governor had two important functions that very afternoon. After presenting the King's honour to a member of the community, he was to attend the opening of a landmark dock facility at Keppel Harbour. The burying of the dead would have to make way for the honouring of the meritorious living and the christening of the latest addition to Singapore's vital trade infrastructure. The King's Dock was the second largest dry dock in the world. The suicide could not be allowed to cast a pall over a moment of celebration of quiet achievement. The British Empire in the Far East could justifiably take pride in its successes of industry and feats of engineering. However, not everything His Excellency represented was quite so clean or straightforward or placed the Empire and its proconsuls in the best light.

How to put it delicately?

A pastor in Singapore's Presbyterian Church, G M Reith had a few years earlier written a handbook on the Crown Colony of Singapore. In his little guide for the casual traveller, the man of God revealed: "Pepper, gambier, indigo, spices, liberian coffee, tapioca… with cocoanuts, pine-apples and other fruits are cultivated to some extent: the prosperity of Singapore does not, however, depend on these, but on the fact…"[22] If the good pastor was speaking out loud, it is easy to imagine the island's colonial officials holding their breath before releasing a deep sigh. Their superiors in London may have each arched an imperious eyebrow to display mild consternation. The pause holds, and then the exhale and concession instead of the confession. "…on the fact that it is the great entrepot for Eastern commerce, and an important coaling station."[23] Reith was polite enough not to mention a certain product or its farms in Singapore licensed by the government.

If nothing else, you could count on British courtesy and politesse to avoid the unmentionable. British officialdom had mastered the dark art of blowing smoke. Even blowing smoke about black smoke. Black smoke? Yes. Not clear enough? Best to hold one's nose and get on with it. Opium, the dried latex of the *Papaver somniferum* better known as the poppy. An ancient pain-relieving narcotic known locally in processed smokable form as *chandu*, its trade was captured by the British in a lucrative monopoly. Thus, the government had licensed and farmed out opium to local businessmen to generate government revenues. But it was all getting rather messy and out of control. And anti-opium sentiments were growing as visible signs of drug addiction spilled out into the streets or dropped dead in front of passengers pulled on rickshaws.

Young, being the proconsul of imperial power in British Malaya, was chief administrator of Britain's regional opium monopoly, though the role was certainly not acknowledged on his calling card or among his official titles. In 1908, Young's predecessor John Anderson had chaired the first Straits Settlements Commission to look into the opium question. The anguished and recently departed Mr Edlin had been an upstanding member of the select Commission. Unlike fellow Commission member

Bishop W F Oldham of the Methodist Church, Edlin had endorsed the Commission's conclusion that opium was relatively harmless to health and should not be prohibited. After all, it was an important source of revenue for the Straits Settlements. The Commission had also agreed that the Straits government should take over the manufacture and sale of opium.

The fact was that Singapore's colonial government sold opium wholesale to licensed retailers, levying license fees on opium shops and smoking lounges. With the import of prepared opium a government monopoly, a civil servant with the title of Superintendent of the Government Monopolies of the Straits Settlements had powers to prosecute any individuals who peddled opium or its derivatives. Only the government had the right to traffic wholesale in deleterious drugs. A government factory had been established in Telok Blangah, opposite the P&O Wharf. It was clearly marked out in government maps as a "Chandu factory", with a hill near the government plant named Opium Hill, or Bukit Chandu. Government-licensed shops and opium dens even had their own government designed packages – a triangular packet, letters in lucky red on a white background that read "Opium Monopoly", the use of red chosen by officialdom to attract the Chinese coolies. Yet, to protect Britain's working class from this scourge, the same coolies would be arrested for smoking opium in London or Liverpool.

But in Singapore, His Majesty's government produced and sold the "black smoke" of opium quite freely. From Government House (today's Istana), it was quite clear to Young that Singapore was distant from the mother country. And it was the only one of His Majesty's colonies where an immigrant population formed the majority, outnumbering natives. To the British, Singapore town smelt and felt more Chinese than any other Straits Settlement colony. Chinese coolies were the backbone of Singapore's prosperity. Port coolies toiled away in back-breaking tasks loading and unloading ships while rickshaw coolies dripped sweat in the unforgiving heat and humidity of Singapore. Scattered showers were a blessing until the red laterite roads became mud and the rickshaw coolies resembled bloodied soldiers in trench warfare.

Essential services would collapse without the coolie underclass who did the majority of menial tasks. Mostly bachelors who came to Malaya to eke out a tough living, opium was used to erase their pain and loneliness. And for comforts of the flesh, Singapore's most desperate red-light areas were next to the rickshaw tenements, between South Bridge Road and New Bridge Road. Gambling and alcohol also helped distract the coolie class from pitiless reality, and these balms offered the Government lucrative sources of taxable revenue. Young was not an amoral man without scruples. But he had a job to do. This was his seventh year in the Straits Settlements. He knew the score. Some realities had to be finessed.

Without the narcotic, and the tax and licensing revenues from the other three evils of wine, woman and cards, the colony might not be able to support itself as a Free Port, established thus by Sir Stamford Raffles with visionary foresight. The port city would also lack the necessary diversions for those in transit or those who serviced the transit traffic. So a clear connection existed between the white smoke of the passenger and cargo steamers and the black smoke of the *chandu* that sustained the crown colony's coolie class. Young would know better than most that the colony had to be self-supporting and a going concern, not a charity case. This was the fundamental problem of British imperial government in managing its colonial possessions. How to administer on a shoestring budget and find ways to collect revenue to ensure that His Majesty's Government remained in the black.

As Governor, Young had a clear but simple mandate from London – deliver peace, stability and prosperity. No source of possible revenue could be sniffed at or snubbed. But then there was the issue of wider British prestige. Global opinion was turning against opium. International meetings had been held in Shanghai in 1909 and just the year before to discuss how to eradicate this scourge. Anti-opium activists were taking up the cause globally. To make matters worse, angry young natives were raising their heads in British India to deplore the practice. These rebels, unlike the right proper Western Oriental Gentlemen, were getting ahead of themselves! But why not? After all opium was harvested in British India but consumed in China and by the Chinese coolies in Southeast Asia. Geographically, British colonies like Singapore and Hong Kong stood at the centre of this trade as major distributors and consumers. The British were handing out interest-free loans in India for opium production but not for any other agricultural products. Was this not another example of British hypocrisy posing as benevolence? The matter was coming to a head during Young's tenure as Governor.

Traveling on a steamer out of Japan, the American anti-opium activist Ellen La Motte, who had visited Singapore's opium dens, recounted her meeting with an articulate "young Hindu" Indian. The nationalist made an indignant speech to her along these lines:

> How can the British establish the opium trade in my country, even making it one of the departments of Indian Government? This is the worst example of what Britain is doing in its empire. It is because of this that India needs self-government. We must have a voice in the control of our own affairs, to protect ourselves from this evil![24]

The opium that drugged the masses into quiet obedience was also awakening the consciousness of nationalists and budding freedom fighters. The question posed by a Shanghai-based Indian revolutionary to his comrades is relevant: "If the opium-addicted Chinese can establish *panchayati raj* (a republic), why can't the Indians do so? We have to follow in the footsteps of China and other countries that had a revolution."[25] Scales were falling from Eastern eyes. The unquestioned supremacy of the British and their claims to moral superiority and fitness to lead was being eroded, slowly but surely. Britain's greatest imperial possession, India, was slowly beginning to shake off its slumber. The question was whether it chose to do so violently or by peaceful means.

With the new forces of communication, whether by steamship or wireless, the world was most certainly shrinking. Revolutionary ideas and agents of change were sailing the seven seas. La Motte's young Indian informant was a pioneering independence activist from Bengal, the hub of early Indian nationalism. Seeking refuge in Japan from British persecution for his opposition to the partition of Bengal, Taraknath Das made his way to the United States. He was the first Indian there to claim political refugee status, and also one of the key enablers of the global mutiny movement as we shall see. Young Asian revolutionaries and Westerners with a troubled conscience were making common cause. What struck La Motte on the ship was the young Indian's argument that without self-government his country was powerless to end the opium trade Britain had forced on India. Taraknath had even debated the Russian savant and novelist Leo Tolstoy on Britain's tyranny in India and the ethics of violence in the struggle for freedom. He told Tolstoy that British imperialism had peddled opium and liquor to make natives weak and dependent.

La Motte was entranced as the young Indian "produced his facts and figures, showing what this meant to his people – this gradual undermining of their moral fibre and economic efficiency – we grew more and more interested. That such conditions existed were to us unheard of, and unbelievable."[26] She could scarcely believe that in her day and age, with public opinion firmly opposed to the sale of habit-forming drugs, and with laws to limit such practices adopted by what she believed to be civilised governments, that in Asia opium trafficking was routinely a government monopoly. Even more shocking for the American was that it was done openly by Britain, which she considered "one of the greatest and most highly civilised nations of the world, a nation which we have always looked up to as being in the very forefront of advanced, progressive and humane ideals."[27] Of course, Young, chief representative of the country at the "forefront of advanced, progressive and humane ideals",[28] would beg to differ with Miss La Motte. And besides, he had more immediate concerns to defend. In mid-October, when he gave his annual Budget speech at the Legislative Council, he would have to offer facts and arguments, not defend ideals. Fortunately, the budget was more than balanced, based on the work done by his shy, quiet and meticulous Colonial Secretary, Richard James Wilkinson.

An indispensable administrator, Young's deputy was a multi-lingual scholar. The Colonial Secretary of the Straits Settlements spoke several European languages, the Chinese Hokkien dialect and even high, literary Malay. With his austere, skull-like features, deep-set eyes and furrowed brow, a slim and slight Wilkinson stood in some contrast to Young physically and intellectually. Lacking Wilkinson's sharp intellect, Young depended more on charismatic affability and on not rocking the boat. Although briefed by then of an unexpected budget surplus, Young was catching up with worrying figures showing that opium revenue was not only on the decline but precariously so.

Young's speech to the Legislative Council Chamber in Singapore in October would require him to once again defend the risible. He discussed the subject with eminent Straits-born Chinese businessmen who had bent his ear many times already about the effects of freely available opium. He faced pressure on two fronts. In the Legislative Council of the Federated Malay States in Kuala Lumpur, Young had to deal with Councillor Eu Tong Sen, a prominent merchant and philanthropist. And in the Legislative Council of Singapore, Councillor Tan Jiak Kim, another prominent businessman and philanthropist, made his disquiet known in private. However, in collegial fashion, Tan voted with the consensus as a member of the Opium Commission.

In Kuala Lumpur, Eu floated a simple plan to deal with the scourge – raise the price of opium beyond the reach of the Chinese coolie class. Young was not so enthusiastic. Coolies, after all, could switch to alternatives like cocaine or morphia, which represented a market opening for some wily Straits Chinese merchants. Were they being businessmen or philanthropists first? It was so clear to Young, who relied on his deputy Wilkinson and his team of brilliant Malayan civil servants to find the right formula. Their standard argument was that drastic measures to supress opium smoking would be counter-productive unless countries that manufactured morphia and cocaine took proper measures to control the production and export of these two drugs. Never mind that one of those countries producing "morphia" was their mother country Britain! But the brilliant British civil servants of Empire were quite used to find ways out of knotty moral issues. And more importantly, they needed to preserve the base of tax revenues from the sale of opium.

At noon, when the guns at Fort Canning fired the traditional time cannon for ship captains and citizens to set their clocks and watches, Young found himself in the surroundings of the Council Chamber of Singapore. It was not yet time for the Budget Speech. He had had the relatively pleasant duty of officiating at a ceremony to admit his old friend Mr John Rumney Nicholson, Chairman and Chief Engineer of the Singapore Harbour Board, as a Companion of the Most Distinguished Order of St Michael and St George. The Singapore Harbour Company, formed only the month before, was now running all of Singapore's port services. The efficiency of its operations was pivotal to the settlement's life-line of trade.

Nicholson was a distinguished, serious-looking man with light eyes set close together in continual concentration over a neat moustache. Known for getting things done, he managed the privately owned Tanjong Pagar Dock Company which had a monopoly over the port services of the Keppel Harbour. A versatile engineer also known to be a tough task-master, Nicholson had run the port efficiently for three years. However, the Tanjong Pagar Dock Company lacked the resources to expand in response to the growing demand for port services by transoceanic steamships. And the deep anchorage of Subang Bay in the Philippines was threatening to steal this valuable business. In the long run, a monopoly over efficient port services was far more valuable than the opium monopoly or the opprobrium attached to it.

A Cumberland man, Nicholson represented all the best values of the British, which helped the British Isles to global prominence. Both he and his wife were key members of the European community in the colony. His wife opened their pleasant home in Grange Road to newcomers. President of the Keppel Golf Club and a keen member of the Singapore Volunteer Corps, Nicholson always stood ready to lend a hand in times of trouble. Among the crooked timber of humanity and swaying palms of the tropics, he appeared to be a rare straight oak. Such quietly successful striving had to be honoured.

The ceremony was a brief but dignified formality. As the King's representative, Young took his seat in the Council Chamber. Nicholson approached him accompanied by Young's deputy, Wilkinson, and Tan Jiak Kim. Bespectacled, small in stature but wise-eyed and large-hearted with an abiding concern for the city's underclass, Tan was unofficial leader of the Singapore Chinese community and was the first from the large Hokkien community to be honoured by the British. He had received the Companion of the Order of St Michael and St George the previous year and proudly wore the medal fastened on his *changshan* tunic next to his Coronation medal, earned as a Straits representative at the coronation of the King in Westminster Abbey. He was familiar with imperial pomp and provided local flavour to what would otherwise be an all-European affair.

Young's Aide-de-Camp, Lieutenant Cecil Orme Olliver, carried Nicholson's award insignia on a velvet cushion. Olliver was watched by his prospective father-in-law, the General Officer Commanding of the Straits Settlements, Major-General Theodore Stephenson and Archdeacon Izard, who would oversee Edlin's funeral later in the day. Also present was the unofficial Singapore Arab community leader, Syed Mohamed Alsagoff, and others representing the great and good of Singapore's government and business circles. Looking at Nicholson, Young told him: "I am very glad that it has fallen to my lot to present to you this insignia."[29] There was a round of polite applause as the clubbish and close-knit elite slapped each other on the back. The 5-minute ceremony was over as Young shook hands with Nicholson.

Standing behind the formalities and stilted speeches was the simple, hard financial aspect. Earlier in the year, Nicholson had produced the best financial results for the company since government takeover. The harbour and the port facilities could make money as it prepared to deal with the growing trade and demand for Singapore as a perfectly placed stop-over for trans-oceanic trade. As the driving force behind the dry dock development, he supported the long-term development of Singapore's port, doing more with less to pay its way.

After lunchtime, the Governor and Lady Evelyn headed towards Keppel Harbour for the day's second big ceremony – the opening of King's Dock, which sat at the foot of Mount Faber across from Pulau Blakang Mati. The 879-foot King's Dock was the largest in the world after Gladstone Dock in Liverpool. To launch the all-European ceremony, the Youngs were led to a small shed built on the Dock's west wall, the location of today's Corals at Keppel Bay apartment blocks. The privileged invitees were about to witness a marvel of British engineering. If placed in barrels end to end the concrete used for the project would stretch across Singapore from east to west. The King's Dock could repair any of the world's sea-going ships except for the largest, the German passenger liner SS *Imperator*. The 906-foot German liner even dwarfed the *Titanic*, already by then sitting in its watery grave. But reflecting the can-do spirit behind the Empire's rise, Nicholson declared: "The *Imperator* is a few feet longer but were she to honour us with a visit, we would express our welcome by spoiling the beautiful symmetry of the north end of the dock by removing a few feet of concrete and thereby give a comfortable berth".[30]

Nicholson did not know it, but before too long a much smaller German imperial naval cruiser called the SMS *Emden* would give Singapore's sister settlement Penang up north much trouble, creating panic across Britain's merchant fleet. For now, he could revel in his success with friends in the community. He invited Young to press a button on a silver plate. Immediately, the whirring of engines was heard, water poured in a frothy burst through the massive culverts and the dock floor was soon flooded. This was a moment of great pride for the little crown colony. The ladies took their tea. The men visited the machine shops or the store to study charts displaying the type of ships the new dock could take for repair. And then it was all over. Another splendid show.

A few weeks later, *The Straits Times* leader page published a response to Young's budget speech. Singapore's newspaper of record noted that the "improvement of the port and the fullest recognition of its shipping interests are points upon which the prosperity of Singapore is absolutely dependent."[31] Prepared for the eventual loss of the colony's opium revenue, *The Straits Times* editorial made clear that in the long run, Singapore's true importance was its strategic location. This was where Singapore's future potential lay, and its relevance to the world as a key outpost of Empire. Opium could only go so far. Singapore had a destiny even bigger than just entrepot trade as a valuable piece of real estate.

Still, British India was the brightest and biggest jewel in that imperial Crown. India's viceroy Lord George Curzon had only recently declared that "As long as we rule India, we are the greatest power in the world. If we lose it, we shall drop straight away to a third-rate power."[32] In a moment of greater candour, an East India Company official admitted that "our system acts very much like a sponge, drawing up all the good things from the banks of the Ganges, and squeezing them down on the banks of the Thames."[33] As one of the smaller gems in that imperial crown, Singapore was a useful way-station for the colonial spongers. Black smoke could be replaced by the white smoke of steamers and the grey smoke of the big navy guns transforming Singapore into the Empire's most strategic garrison East of the Suez. Everything was going swimmingly well. Young had a handle on things for now at least.

But it takes so much effort to make everything look effortlessly in order. That is the magic of good government. Secrets had to be kept, amid the smoke and mirrors of defending double-standards between the imperial capital and its colonies. Young had to keep a tight hold on the purse-strings of a colony open for business to anyone ready to make a deal. But perhaps not quite anyone. Certainly not trouble-makers, those who could not decide whether they were idealists or businessmen, and mixed business with politics. And certainly not open to the agents of sedition who would feel the brunt of the "Brutish Empire". Dangerous individuals who threatened to expose its secrets and weaknesses. Conspirators and intriguers, who would rally the divided sects and faiths of the Empire under the banner of a brotherhood of revolt.

[III]

THE BRUTISH EMPIRE

From a little village in Britain's south coast of Cornwall, the imperial Eastern Telegraph Company operated 100,000 miles of transoceanic submarine cable by 1902. This so-called "All-Red Line" connected London to far-flung parts of the British Empire via electrical telegraph. Singapore was a connecting hub for a submarine cable stretching from Aden to Hong Kong. Prior to global telegraphy, a letter by post from London took 45 days to reach Singapore. Now a telegram was received in just a matter of hours, sped in electrical impulses through the submarine cables.

Journeys by steamship, faster trains and mass-produced automobiles revolutionised travel. Wireless telegraphy and transoceanic cables revolutionized war, business and politics. Travellers without passports and telegrams with breaking news shaped new forms of globalised consciousness across borders. Then as now, convergence existed alongside divergence. New modes of transport connected diaspora communities while rapidly developing communications technologies forged partisan identities or carved rifts between rulers and the ruled.

Fast becoming pan-Indian and then global across outposts of Empire, the Indian revolutionary movement was gathering force in an increasingly interconnected world. Started in Bengal but spreading to Punjab by 1907, on the fiftieth anniversary of the Indian Mutiny, the movement against British rule spanned violent revolutionaries as well as non-violent activists. Kick-started by Hindus but including Sikhs, Muslims, Buddhists and free-thinking anarchists, the loose independence network brought together disparate ideas. Men and women of different creeds and backgrounds shared the objective of armed overthrow of British rule in India.

To take just one odd pair of future revolutionaries – Har Dayal and Nawab Khan – born in 1884 to different faiths and backgrounds.

As a boy, Har Dayal loved books. Nawab Khan did not.

Har Dayal was an urbane Punjabi Hindu from Delhi while Nawab was a Rajput Muslim farm boy raised in the heart of Punjab. Both were sons of a subcontinent yoked together politically only by the lean, no-nonsense and exploitative efficiency of British imperialism – a rule both came to despise and collaborated to violently oppose. Their sharply contrasting upbringings played a part in the roles each eventually would play as revolutionaries against British rule.

Har Dayal, the youngest son of a Delhi district court officer who was a loyal servant of the British Raj, learned the history and the literary arts of Urdu, the courtly language of the Mughal Muslims, from his father. It proved a fertile combination for a high-caste Hindu of the *Kayastha* or writer's caste as he grew up in the shadow of Old Delhi's decaying Mughal era monuments in Cheera Khana. This was part of the Chandi Chowk (Moonlight Square) area designed by Mughal Emperor Shah Jahan's favourite daughter. Known today as Har Dayal Katra, Cheera Khana sits next to an Old Delhi landmark called *Paranthewali Gali* (Lane of Paranthe or Flatbread makers).

When Har Dayal was born, the area was known more for its silverware shops, but the waft of fragrant fried flatbread was already in the air with the first shops selling the staple delicacy. At nine, Har Dayal would have noticed the tonga horses getting their hooves stuck in the newly laid coal tar replacing the gravel on the main Chandi Chowk road. Har Dayal would have walked the road that stretched between the shade of neem and peepul trees or navigated the tight side-lanes connecting the crumbling, architectural splendours of the Mughal Dynasty.

Three hundred kilometres to the northwest, Nawab was exploring the vast, open fields of Ludhiana, the bread-basket of Punjab. Nawab spurned his village school's rote-learning. Instead, the boy picked up a rustic Punjabi dialect in his homely village of Halwara, just south of a branch of the River Sutlej that flowed towards the setting sun. As a Muslim Rajput of the Manj clan, Nawab was a descendant of Hindu Rajputs who had converted to Islam in the 14th century and settled in Ludhiana. He was destined go where the grain and water took him, to speak the colourful and direct dialect of farmers and sepoys who served abroad.

Har Dayal's mother-tongue was Punjabi, but he achieved a higher order of language and thought in several other languages. In cloistered study and focused on the life of the mind, he could never develop the physical vigour of the Rajput farm boy. But like Nawab, he too was destined to roam on behalf of a cause that would shake the foundations of British rule in India and its imperial possessions, including a little island called Singapore. The Hindu scholar and Muslim fortune-seeker nev-

Har Dayal

er saw each other in India. The pair only met as young men in their late-twenties in San Francisco, USA. The encounter of nomad and wandering scholar took place as the militant Ghadar movement began to find its shape. Nawab would fall almost immediately under the spell of the slight, bespectacled and silver-tongued Har Dayal.

Har Dayal did not know it then but he would play a key role as chief propagandist for the revolutionary Ghadar movement. Before that time of reckoning, other magic would also work their spells on both minds. Alternative routes beckoned before fate stamped its form in the complex and overlapping cross-currents of time.

Nawab yearned for adventure like most young men from small villages. But he also sought out direction and mentors. His was a restless spirit in need of approval. In 1901, aged 16, he left home to join his elder brother who was serving with the Hong Kong Regiment, a unit dominated by Punjabi Muslim sepoys. Stationed at their specially built barracks in the Tsim Sha Tsui area, today's Kowloon Park, the Regiment was known for its swagger and sharp-shooting.

In British Hong Kong, Nawab had his first taste of the British Empire's size and how imperial Indian practice filtered to its farthest reaches. In the exotic colony, he would have witnessed novelties like the sight of the 1st Chinese Infantry Regiment under British officers. On parade, the Chinese soldiers wore dark blue turbans just like Indian sepoys, but had nary a whisker on their faces.

Half a year after his arrival, Nawab's regiment was disbanded as the colonial government in London could not afford to maintain all these regiments. Nawab returned to India and enlisted next in the 8th Cavalry as a *sowar* (cavalryman) in Nowshera, east of Peshawar on the famous Grand Trunk Road. For a young man of his robust physical disposition and simple background, becoming a *risaldar* (cavalry officer) was a worthy achievement at the time. But it also required some dedication of service and fixity of purpose. These were qualities Nawab lacked.

As Nawab did mind-numbing drills in the military cantonment of Nowshera, Har Dayal enrolled in the University of Punjab in Lahore. This followed his preparatory studies under the guidance of earnest missionaries at St Stephen's College, Delhi. In an examination, he was given twelve questions and asked to answer six. He answered all twelve and invited the examiner to choose any of the six to mark. Already extremely well-read, Har Dayal had clear ideas of his own. Physically, he was ungainly but held his own intellectually. He believed in doing his own thinking, even as he benefited from encouraging mentors. The earnest and obliging Christian missionaries in St Stephen's offered him the example of belief in a higher cause and a sense of purpose.

At Lahore, the precocious Punjabi delighted in mental gymnastics. Har Dayal did not like being bested by anyone, and certainly not by a fellow Indian. Told that a Maharashtrian Brahmin was touring Punjab and demonstrating amazing feats of memory, Har Dayal apparently decided to go one better. Har Dayal was already known for reciting chunks of Shakespeare's plays after just one reading. He set up a chessboard, asked a fellow student to hold a bell, asked another two to choose separate passages from Sanskrit and Latin and prepared to solve a math problem. Then at one go, with only a slight side-effect of dizziness, he tackled the math problem, repeated the passages recited in Sanskrit and Latin by his fellow students, played chess with another and counted the number of times the bell rang.

A different bell was tolling for Nawab Khan. After languishing for two years in the isolated cantonment on the sandy plain east of the Kabul River, he quit service again and looked for another opportunity in the East. By 1906, he had enlisted in the Penang-based artillery section of the Malay States Guides. The British-officered Guides, formed in 1896, were composed mainly of Sikhs with Muslims from the Punjab. Headquartered in Taiping in Perak State, the Guides emerged from the nucleus of the Perak Armed Police, a sepoy force protecting the Federated Malay States (FMS) against civil riots between feuding Chinese secret societies. The Guides also performed garrison duties in the Straits Settlements.

The Guides were chocolate box soldiers during Sepoy Nawab Khan's time in service. His first recorded service highlight was the annual military parade on the occasion of the King's Birthday in 1906. A sideshow event compared to the bigger parade in Singapore, the Guides in Penang were lacklustre under their inexperienced Detachment Commander. Poorly drilled compared to their counterparts in Taiping, Perak, they scraped through their rites of loyalty to the King. Another highlight was the Duke and Duchess of Connaught's inspection visit to the Sepoy Lines in 1907 during their Far Eastern Tour. With no less than the King's brother His Royal Highness Prince Arthur inspecting in his Field Marshal's uniform, the Guides were paraded more effectively by their Punjabi-speaking Commanding Officer, Colonel R S F Walker.

Despite a highlight or two, life in Penang's Sepoy Lines lacked the dash of the Nowshera cavalry. By the following year, Nawab appeared to have had enough of service in the Straits Settlements. He resigned and returned to India. But this was not Nawab's final encounter with the Guides or his last visit to the Straits Settlements. The former sepoy was destined to return to Singapore and Penang on a special mission, to play his part in what the British named sedition, the Indians called a fight for freedom and, in his case, would turn out to be neither.

Har Dayal found himself flourishing in the meantime in Lahore's stimulating intellectual environment. He also participated in Lahore's vibrant political scene, carving out his outlook and belief in an environment where independent-minded Punjabis chafed against high handed British rule. In Lahore, Har Dayal met Lala Lajpat Rai, a major nationalist leader inspired by the Arya Samaj (Sanskrit for the Aryan Society) movement. The Arya Samaj was an orthodox Hindu reformist movement based on the teachings of Swami Vivekananda Dayanand Saraswati. Resisting Western influence, the movement sought to return Hinduism to the pristine word of the ancient Sanskrit scriptures known as the Vedas. Arya Samaj supporters believed in one God, rejected idol worship and spread its word through a network of missionaries in India and globally. The socio-religious movement had a major political impact on the Indian independence movement.

Two decades after the 1857 Indian Mutiny, Swami Dayanand called for India's political independence: "Say what you will, self-government is by far the best. A foreign government perfectly free from religious prejudices, impartial towards all the natives and foreigners – kind, beneficial and just though it may be – can never render the people perfectly happy."[34] A supporter of Indian unity and self-reliance, Dayanand was believed to be the first Indian to use the word *swaraj*, or self-government. He was the first to proclaim India for Indians. He also told his followers to reject the label "Hindu" imposed on them by the British and use their native term "Aryan" instead. Hence, the Arya Samaj or Aryan Society.

Har Dayal absorbed the nationalist idealism of Lajpat Rai and of Dayanand. In Lahore, Har Dayal became close friends with an Arya Samaj missionary named Bhai Parmanand. A lecturer at the Dayanand College at Lahore, Bhai Parmanand encouraged his students to think about how to achieve independence for India. Parmanand would crop up at significant junctures in Har Dayal's life over the next decade. Despite their differences, as we shall see later in the narrative, the pious Parmanand would be on hand to prop up a faltering Har Dayal at crucial moments. However, Har Dayal spurned his friend Parmanand's attitude towards religious belief. When Lajpat asked him to join the Arya Samaj, he replied that "we should not think in terms of religion. Our only religion is service of the motherland. We cannot owe allegiance to two gods at the same time… (e)ither be a reformer or a revolutionary. You cannot fill both roles together."[35]

Across Asia and even in the Middle East, budding nationalists and intellectuals were forming political study groups and secret societies to achieve national self-determination. It was part of the ferment of the times. Instead of the Hindu revivalists of the Arya Samaj, Har Dayal joined a secret society in 1905 run by the enigmatic "Sufi" Amba Prasad. Born in 1858 in Moradabad in the United Provinces (Uttar Pradesh), Amba was a fiercely independent mind who advocated Indian independence and Hindu-Muslim unity. A Hindu from a prominent Moradabad family, he came under the influence of a local Sufi mystic after the untimely death of his wife, earning his nickname "Sufi" Amba. Wiry, witty and strong-willed, he was born without a right hand. He joked that he lost the hand in his last life while fighting the British during the 1857 Mutiny and when he was reborn the following year, God forgot to add it.

As an Urdu-language newspaper editor, "Sufi" Amba was fluent in English, Hindi and Persian. He had a wicked turn of phrase and was completely fearless, having already been arrested twice for his "seditious" writings in the 1890s. The first time was soon after he penetrated the household of the British Resident in Srinagar. Serving as a cook, he published an exposé on the intrigues of the Resident that earned the ire of the British and forced them to recall their Resident. "Sufi" Amba would play a key role in the Indian independence movement in Punjab and then in Iran, and we shall meet him again. Har Dayal's links with men like Amba led a British Criminal Investigation Department agent to file a report on Har Dayal in 1904, noting that "a sense of revolt had taken deep root in his mind and even permeated strongly a select circle of his friends."[36]

Despite being monitored by the British police, Har Dayal secured a prestigious state scholarship to study in England. As the first Punjabi to win the award, the expectation was that he would return to government service after graduation. He could then prove useful to His Majesty's government in India as part of the elite Indian Civil Service where a token number of high-scoring Indian graduates were admitted to serve alongside British officials who governed India. Har Dayal was already cultivating a legend about himself among his cohort. At his scholarship interview, when asked by his British interviewer what he believed to be the key to "administrative success", Har Dayal replied: "*Divide et impera* – this much we have learned from you."[37] The 21-year-old was not failed despite his cheeky response on Britain's time-tested policy of Divide and Rule.

Har Dayal opted to study at the historic St John's College in Oxford University. In the quiet and pristine, hermetically sealed world of the dreaming spires, he charmed his fellow students and professors with his sharp mind and clarity of thought though he was among his own kind intellectually. He spoke English without a trace of an Indian accent and threw himself into the world of ideas and concepts.

He had left behind an already raucous and colourful India in uproar. The then Imperial Viceroy of India, Lord Curzon, had put in place measures designed apparently to repress the growing Indian spirit of independence. This included the partitioning of the politically powerful state of Bengal in 1905, the hub of growing nationalism, which became a major trigger issue for Indian nationalists. Japan's remarkable military victory over Russia had also showed Asians that European powers were not permanently superior. It was all part of the broader awakening that swept the wretched of the earth. In response to the partition of Bengal, Indian Hindu nationalists banded together to start a boycott of British goods known as the Swadeshi Movement which promoted local enterprise. The movement's message spread from Bengal to the rest of India. Har Dayal's protege and cousin by marriage, Gobind Behari Lal, would recall the ferment of the time:

> This was the year not only (of) the declaration of independence
> by India but also by Ireland; also the women's movement; also the
> socialist movement in England. They all came out about that time.
> And two great historic things… the war between Japan and Russia in
> 1904-05… when the Japanese licked the czar which was supposed to
> be the greatest monster in the world in those days… and before that
> in fact, was the tremendous resistance of the Boers to the British (in
> South Africa)… it was just a kind of shock wave, that the Almighties
> were not so Almighty. When these things happened, there were
> reverberations all over the world. And these reverberations were
> certainly part of the picture behind the rise of the Indian Liberation
> Movement in a direct sense [of] independence.[38]

For an Empire that ruled by dint of prestige and implicit power garbed in the rule of law and the glint of holstered weaponry, these were all worrying signs. Angry young men enraged by the partition of Bengal and the moderate response of older politicians were starting to take matters into their own hands. Influenced by Russian anarchists and nihilists, and Irish revolutionaries, they promoted the philosophy and politics of the bomb and acts of terror and assassination. Away from this tumult, Har Dayal encountered his own troubles. His physical voyage to England and initially rewarding intellectual journey in Oxford was eventually accompanied by a struggle to moor himself in an alien environment.

Har Dayal kept up with old friends from India like the Arya Samaj missionary Bhai Parmanand who was studying at King's College in London. But the support of old friends from home was not enough to stabilise him. Har Dayal experienced the traditional crisis of identity and the search for authenticity encountered by many before him and many since.

It did not help that he was separated not only from his family but his wife, Sundar Rani, whom he had married at 17. When he married her, she was an attractive woman with "an oval face, a slightly aquiline nose and a fair complexion."[39] At Oxford, Har Dayal was faithful to her. He lived simply, avoiding alcohol and tobacco and paying little heed to fashion, food or femmes fatale. He avoided the decadence or the high jinks of the Western Oriental Gentleman. Instead, he dropped his Anglophile pretensions picked up at missionary school in India and plunged into politics. He spent time with Indian nationalists in London, meeting the anarchist Alexander Kropotkin and the socialist playwright George Bernard Shaw.

In his first term at Oxford, Har Dayal was also introduced to the foremost Indian moderate politician of the time, Gopal Krishna Gokhale, a Marathi Chitpavan Brahmin from Bombay. The Marathi Chitpavan Brahmins had produced a clutch of Indian independence leaders of varying political shades. The meeting with Gokhale would help chart Har Dayal's future political direction towards revolutionary nationalism. Deeply influential at the time, the moderate Indian National Congress faction leader Gokhale mentored two men who would shape the future of independent India: Mohandas Karamchand Gandhi and Mohammed Jinnah. Destined to lead India's non-violent independence movement, Gandhi would become the Mahatma (the Great Souled). Gandhi called Gokhale his political guru while Jinnah aspired to become a Muslim version of Gokhale, and eventually went on to found the state of Pakistan.

The arch-moderate Gokhale invited Har Dayal to join his gradualist Servants of India Society. British rule in India depended on the ideas of men like Gokhale. His politics could help to sustain the majority of moderate public opinion. Gokhale's Society aimed to unify Indians through charitable and relief work and by opposing British rule through constitutional means. But the cocksure, young Punjabi coolly rebuffed the Marathi Brahmin: "One of the rules of your society is that every member should be loyal to the British Government. My conscience does not permit this."[40] Gokhale, twice Har Dayal's age, challenged the young firebrand's agenda for change and defended his own moderation: "Could you then suggest any other means of India's independence? I hold that by pushing on the path of evolution we can achieve our goal with the help of Britain...."[41]

The words "with the help of Britain" set Har Dayal off. Before Gokhale could explain his point, Har Dayal interrupted: "Yes, but then you can't enthuse any people for freedom."[42] Har Dayal was fixated on finding ways to rouse the slumbering masses from their apathy and to actively support the fight for independence.

After their confrontation, Har Dayal returned unexpectedly to Delhi.

He was no longer the same young man who had sailed away to England. He confided to his closest friends that he was no longer interested in joining government service, his family's dearest hope. He told them point-blank: "Our only duty is to the nation. There is nothing left in life".[43] But Har Dayal still had his loved ones. And he had another immediate act of rebellion to perform.

Against her family's wishes, he insisted on bringing his wife Sundar back with him to Oxford. The couple was in love. Har Dayal was ready to violate the ancient custom of purdah-zenana which forbade a wife from breaching the sanctity of her cloistered home to travel abroad. For orthodox Hindus, crossing the black ocean violated their sanctity. According to one version, Har Dayal disguised his wife as a man in a madcap escape. He smuggled her out of the house and onto the train to Bombay. They were chased all the way by the irate family members of Sundar, whose grandfather had been the Chief Minister of Patiala state. Sundar's Hindu cousin scuffled with Har Dayal's traveling companion, a Muslim classmate from Lahore. At the train station, Sundar's cousin roused a crowd with his cries, "Where are you taking her?"[44]

Passangers in Indian train-stations bored by the infinite wait for their train are always ready for a distraction. The crowd turned menacingly towards Har Dayal. Sundar cried out that she was his wife, and the mob turned back to the cousin who continued scuffling with Har Dayal's Muslim classmate. In the confusion, Har Dayal and Sundar got away and boarded the ship. Later, on parental instructions, his brother Kishan Dayal unsuccessfully tried to board the steamer to retrieve Sundar. Kishan was close to Har Dayal and was unlikely to have made a determined effort to rescue his sister-in-law. Safely on board, Har Dayal appeared on deck and waved at his angry in-laws and his family members. His livid father-in-law was heard to yell in colourful Punjabi, "That mad genius is going to ruin himself and my daughter's happiness. All this comes from reading the *Ramayana*. Sita was kidnapped. Never read that old book."[45]

This escape was a prelude to Har Dayal's bigger rebellions and sudden flights at short notice. As Sundar's cousin and Har Dayal's loyal accomplice Gobind Behari Lal described it: "That was Har Dayal's first deed of revolt – a revolt against his own community tradition."[46] A Delhi newspaper, covering the incident, contrived a memorable headline: "Wife Kidnapped by Husband."[47]

[IV]

DESIGNERS OF THE
SECOND GREAT MUTINY

Not far from the tomb of Karl Marx stands a house in London's Highgate. Once upon a time, the Victorian red-brick mansion was a refuge for Indian students called India House. Dubbed the "House of Secrets"[48] by the British press, the student hostel also gave young Indian political activists a space for their regular gatherings. Tram, underground and bus connections were all conveniently nearby along with three sprawling parks. The good transport connections were helpful not only for the students but for detectives from Scotland Yard who were starting to monitor the house. Fortunately for the Indian student radicals, London's lawmen were then still educating themselves about political crime and sedition. The undercover police monitoring number 65, Cromwell Avenue had yet to coordinate with the British Indian Secret Service.

Soon after his return to England, Har Dayal met with one of the students who lived in the India House hostel. It would prove a fateful encounter for both men. The student's name was Vinayak Damodar Savarkar. Just a year older than Har Dayal, he was already making waves in the struggle for Indian independence. His ideas of revolt went much further than Har Dayal's violation of ancient customs. And he had earned his nickname Veer (braveheart in Sanskrit) as a pre-teen, after leading his Hindu classmates against a group of Muslim boys who had confronted them for stoning the village mosque during sectarian riots.

Savarkar had arrived in London in July 1906 ostensibly to study Law. He was a Marathi Chitpavan Brahmin from the same clan as the arch-moderate Gokhale whom Har Dayal had rebuffed at Oxford. Savarkar had also sneered at Gokhale's moderation and embraced instead another Marathi Chitpavan clansman, the nationalist Bal Tilak. Dubbed by the British as "father of the Indian unrest", Tilak strenuously

Vinayak Damodar 'Veer' Savarkar

advocated self-rule and radical activism. He formed the *Garam Dal* or the Army of the Angry to oppose Gokhale's moderate approach in the Indian National Congress Party. Tilak endorsed Savarkar's scholarship in London under the sponsorship of fellow radical and India House founder, Shyamji Krishna Varma, the first Indian to secure an advanced degree at Oxford University. Varma also published the weekly *Indian Sociologist* newspaper which had politicised many students.

Growing up, Savarkar had heard his parents recite passages from the Sanskrit epics like the *Mahabharata* and the *Ramayana* as well as martial stories of the 17th century Marathi warrior-king Shivaji. These examples shaped his mind. At 14, after learning that the British had executed two of his nationalistic clansmen, Veer had made a solemn promise before the demon-slayer Goddess Durga that he would drive the British out of India. In Hindu myth, Durga could take the form of a fierce fighter and wreak terrible destruction. He also came to admire the pioneers of early 20th century revolutionary nationalism and political violence. The era's defining act was the assassination of the Russian Emperor Czar Alexander II in 1881 by the Russian revolutionaries of Narodnaya Volya (People's Will). Veer's forceful personality and ideas had a profound impact on Har Dayal's own outlook and development. One associate recalled that Savarkar's "charm was such that a mere shake-hand could convert men... as Har Dayal (and) not only convert but even bring out the best in them."[49]

Bespectacled and broad cheek-boned like Har Dayal, Savarkar was smaller in build and fairer, almost ivory-skinned, with more delicate looks compared to the slightly darker and stronger-jawed Har Dayal. Intellectually, Savarkar was also shaded differently from Har Dayal. He made up in strong, impassioned argument and conviction what he lacked in refinement and subtlety of thought. Savarkar was dubbed by one of his biographers as an "extremist patriot" connecting with Har Dayal's "fanatic intellect."[50] The first few meetings between the two firebrands produced both sparks and chemistry with one described as thunder and the other as lightning. But it was the storm of ideas and writing generated by Savarkar that would leave a deep mark on the revolutionary movement.

Still barely in his twenties, Savarkar had translated into Marathi the biography of the Italian revolutionary nationalist Giuseppe Mazzini. The era's Che Guevara, Mazzini was the most influential revolutionary in Europe. Fighting for Italian independence and unification in the mid-19th century, his mix of nationalist and republican ideas offered idealistic Indian freedom fighters a template for thought and action. Savarkar's translation became a cult text among young Indian nationalists, selling 1,000 copies a month. Mazzini's Young Italy secret society was also the model for Savarkar's own secret society called the Abhinav Bharat Society (Young India Society), which he ran with his elder brother, Ganesh. Savarkar was not merely a *pracharak* (propagandist) but a controller of the *praharak* (striker) cells as well. He would take care of the propaganda as well as the operational aspects of the propaganda of the deed. Har Dayal was sworn in as a member of the Abhinav Bharat, which became a secret terror and assassination unit. Savarkar told all prospective members, including Har Dayal, before they took the oath: "Understand what it implies. Become our member only if you have the courage to stand the dangers. Otherwise join the Militants or Moderates. They too are patriots at the lower stage of our struggle for freedom."[51]

With Veer Savarkar assuming the role of marginally senior mentor to Har Dayal, both men became fast friends. The relationship proved productive. Har Dayal completed what he considered a "Sketch of a Complete Political Movement for the Emancipation of India".[52] The work outlined a programme of action and an organisational structure for the Indian freedom movement. The plan would be executed in three phases. One, to develop national pride among Indians through study of their history and politics. Two, exposing the evils of British rule. Third, a violent struggle against British rule. This programme later became known as Hardayalism which formed the basis of the Ghadar party in the United States. Har Dayal's focus was on propaganda to cast himself as chief *pracharak* for the cause. But it was *pracharak* and *praharak* Savarkar who lectured weekly at India House on Italian freedom fighters like Mazzini and on Indian heroes of the 1857 Mutiny. Savarkar lobbed verbal bombs at his audience during his talks. A smitten young Englishman described Savarkar's effect on him in glowing terms. He said the activist had "the most sensitive face in the room and yet the most powerful" and the "intensity of faith and curious single-minded recklessness which were deeply attractive to me."[53]

The meetings were held in the dining room of the India House on Sundays. Indians sat around a long table with curious Englishmen with radical sensibilities leaning against walls. Spitting out his words convulsively, Savarkar told rapt listeners how Mazzini induced Italian soldiers to join secret cells against their repressive Austrian rulers. He connected events in Italy with the struggle for Indian independence. Not all were convinced. As Savarkar recalled it, Indians who heard his lectures always asked: "How can you compare Italy with Hindustan?" The skeptics in his audience would probe further:

> where are the necessary arms for us to fight? How can we face the rifles and guns of the British? Indian soldiers under the command

of the British are illiterate mercenaries and loyal to the British. They would never rebel against the British. They would never rebel against the English. Moreover, the Indian masses are disarmed. So how can we try an armed revolution in India? Your dream is a mirage. It will never become a reality.[54]

The Brahmin rebel in Savarkar identified with the Brahmin sepoy Mangal Pandey. The sepoy had fired the first shot of the 1857 Sepoy Revolt (known in Delhi as *Gadar i San Sattavan* or Revolt of '57) sparking a wider rebellion in India. Savarkar considered Pandey a martyr and the first real Indian nationalist. He answered the doubters firmly:

The arms being borne by Indian soldiers under the British command are our arms. True, our Indian soldiers are illiterate, but they too must have some desire to make our country independent. Spread the fire of movement for freedom among them and see how the same soldiers turn against the English with the same arms and ammunitions![55]

Savarkar would not waver in his belief. He resolved that the best way to advance his arguments was to rewrite the history of what happened in 1857. The story of the seminal event in India's history had so far only been told by British imperial historians, who had named it the Sepoy Mutiny of 1857. Surreptitiously researching the topic at London's India Office Library, Savarkar wrote his 470-page book in Marathi, the language of warriors. He entitled it *1857 Ka Swatantrya Sama* or *The Indian War of Independence 1857*. Completed just before the mutiny's 50th anniversary, the 24-year old radical wanted his book on the first sepoy revolt to inspire a second and more successful uprising against British rule. Savarkar questioned the standard account of the rebellion as a mere sepoy mutiny. He argued that it showed India's martial spirit as a modern revolutionary movement seeking freedom from colonialism. Recalling Mazzini, he focussed on the rebellion's formation of secret cells. In a nationalist drum-beat, he also called for Hindu-Muslim unity as "brothers by blood" against the common foe. Savarkar summoned Indians of all faiths to own their history and to shape their future. He declared:

The nation that has no consciousness of its past has no future. Equally true it is that a nation must develop its capacity not only of claiming a past but also of knowing how to use it for the furtherance of its future. The nation ought to be the master and not the slave of its own history... hatred against the Mahomedans was just and necessary in the times of Shivaji (warrior-king and founder of the Maratha Dynasty) but, such a feeling would be unjust and foolish if nursed now, simply because it was the dominant feeling of the Hindus then.[56]

Alarmed by the possibility of disturbances on the golden anniversary of the 1857 Mutiny, the British Indian government banned Savarkar's book. The British Director of Criminal Intelligence deemed it seditious literature and more harmful than cocaine, apparently oblivious to the irony that the Empire he served manufactured and sold opium to the Asian masses. However, copies were smuggled into India wrapped in the dust-covers of Charles Dickens novels. Fetching a high price in the black markets, the book became an ideological manual for Indian revolutionaries and nationalists. It would have a deep and formative effect on Har Dayal's thinking.

In May 1907, the nationalist leader Lajpat Rai, Har Dayal's mentor from Lahore, was arrested. There was serious unrest in the Punjab, coincidentally on the fiftieth anniversary of the Indian Mutiny. Ex-sepoys and farmers had been given land to farm in newly developed areas. But the British drafted new laws to re-appropriate the freshly farmed land, transforming free farmers to landless toiling peasants. These measures touched a raw nerve, True to form, the farmers fought back. The Punjab was paralyzed by rallies and protests through 1907. A protest leader named Ajit Singh emerged to lead the Punjabi agitation. With "Sufi" Amba Prasad, Ajit Singh led the nationalist Bharat Mata (Mother Goddess India) secret society, which also counted Har Dayal among its members. Har Dayal, anticipating looming conflict with the British, wrote to his brother Kishen:"(o)ur business is to prepare for that struggle quietly and rapidly and thus strike the blow when we are sure of success."[57] Har Dayal shared with Kishen his plan to turn the youth of India to a vision of radical change. He included trivial but touching details like producing little clay statuettes of nationalist leaders and traditional folk heroes of India. These were trifles dismissed by his hard-headed friend Savarkar who had bigger worries.

Meeting with Savarkar in India House, a young student militant from Bombay named P M Bapat proposed delivering an ultimatum to the British for the release of Lajpat Rai. When someone posed the question, "or else?" Bapat thundered: "If they do not do so, then I will make a suicide attack on the Prime Minister of Britain. It will be a glorious way for me to die."[58] Savarkar took a more strategic approach, replying: "There is no doubt that there will be thunder and lightning in the darkness of our present condition. But what of the deadlier darkness that will descend on our mission?"[59] With his fingers still stained from the picric acid of failed bomb making experiments, Savarkar continued: "It will be more profitable to disseminate this art of bomb-making through our different branches of the Abhinava Bharat and equip them with a weapon that is more effective."[60]

Bapat was ordered to Paris to locate Russian revolutionaries who could offer help in developing bomb technologies. Fleeced by fake revolutionaries on his first attempt, Bapat finally found some authentic anarchists and returned with a bomb manual. In the meantime, Har Dayal had to confront personal issues. He had an offer to return to India after graduation to manage public education in Kashmir, but had not been invited to join the prestigious, administrative elite of the Indian Civil Service. Har Dayal was not passed over because he could not measure up to the tasks intellectually, but as one of Har Dayal's confidantes explained: "He passed the I.C.S examination but due to physical shortcomings and inability to pass the horse-riding test, he could not join the service. His visit to England brought him face to face with the slavery of the Indians and inability to get a job further led to the development in him of an anti-government sentiment."[61]

Har Dayal decided to resign his scholarship at Oxford and dedicate himself full-time to agitating against the British. His nationalist friend Bhai Parmanand tried to talk him out of it: "Your final exams are so near, only a few months are left".[62] Parmanand failed at the attempt. Har Dayal reasoned: "If I spend the next year in working for an Oxford degree, it might prove to be so much time wasted, for I have not got to take service anywhere or to parade my academic diplomas... one year is so much precious time in a revolutionary's life, which is necessarily short and precarious."[63] It took a lot of bureaucratic to-ing and fro-ing before his resignation was accepted. No scholar had willingly abandoned the prestigious scholarship. After six months and thirty pieces of correspondence, the British India Office decided that it was not a resignation but "forfeiture". They had maintained the upper hand and moral high ground on the matter. Symbolism was nine-tenths of British rule. This suited Har Dayal. For him it was about the *tamasha*, the controversy and its value for simultaneous self-promotion and for publicizing the cause, not the self-satisfied verdict of one side.

By 1908, Har Dayal was back in India because his wife, Sundar, was pregnant. She was unhappy in Britain. Normally calm, she was driven to the edge of hysteria by the unfamiliar surroundings and Har Dayal's efforts to radicalise her. For Har Dayal, marriage and family would increasingly take a back-seat. Sundar could not measure up to his exacting standards of knowledge on history and politics or the stress of his efforts to transform her into a political missionary. Back home, Sundar had a dramatic, tearful, typically Punjabi family reunion with her parents who refused to reconcile with Har Dayal.

Har Dayal had become petulantly anti-British. He placed a sign outside his door warning Europeans and Christians they were not welcome and childishly refusing to send letters with British stamps. In an article during that period, he declared that although Indians had lost their country, "they should not part with their *izzat*, which is the most valuable asset of the nation, by salaming to Englishmen indiscriminately and standing before them like *khansama* [butlers, stewards]."[64] Writing on Indians in government service at the time, Har Dayal thundered that India would be better off if the Indian Civil Service had been reserved for Europeans and if the "ships which conveyed Indian noblemen to England in order that they might appear in the civil service examination had gone down to the bottom of the sea."[65] It makes for interesting reading in light of his own alleged failure to be selected for civil service, although his confidant and cousin-in-law Gobind Behari Lal maintained that even before leaving for England nationalism was Har Dayal's priority. He had told Gobind, "The hell with government service."[66]

But Har Dayal was not merely venting personal grievances. He was also developing a theory of self-reliance that would allow Indians to break free of a mentality of submission to British rule – in a word, disassociation. His political work continued to attract the attention of the authorities, especially after bomb attacks protesting the partition of Bengal. Har Dayal resolved to leave British India after concluding that "repressive laws and spies were making further work impossible within the country."[67] He may also have been tipped off about an impending arrest warrant. Despite strong, anti-British sentiments and his seditious writings, Har Dayal was permitted to go to France. Leaving India just a few days before his wife gave birth, Har Dayal would never see her again nor set eyes on his daughter, Shanti.

Har Dayal had embarked on something bigger than family – a mission for freedom, perceived as outright sedition by the imperial police. Ironically, the double-standards of British rule that angered radicals favoured Indian activists. England's Home Government applied far more liberal laws towards political radicalism than it did in India. In England, Indians were spared close surveillance and indignities of imperial policing. London detectives were restrained and did not infringe on basic civil liberties. English institutions would not surrender their jealously guarded freedom to the authorities over mere suspicions. The mother country England was a democracy after all.

From France, Har Dayal crossed over to England. Back in London, he found Savarkar effectively managing India House. The "House of Spies" was now a centre of Hindu revolutionary nationalism and covert paramilitary training, a base for the Abhinav Bharat secret society. Savarkar wanted to achieve in reality the sequel to the 1857 mutiny he had written about. Adding to his bomb-making experiments, he conducted secret firearms training. Savarkar also linked up with other international freedom fighters, including Irish nationalists.

Har Dayal felt out of the loop. Savarkar was firmly in charge and Har Dayal did not appear content to play second fiddle, least of all to a contemporary, even if he was a friend. Living on the barest subsistence, he appeared to have some sort of breakdown of his always delicate health. In 1909, Har Dayal made his way to Paris to recover among a clique of Indian radicals, including Madame Bhikaiji Cama, the Socialist and Indian freedom fighter. Two years earlier at a Socialist conference in Germany, Madame Cama had unveiled the first version of the Indian national flag coloured green, red and yellow. A Bombay Parsi, Cama proudly waved the tricolour of green for Muslims, red for Hindus and yellow for the Sikhs. With her support, Har Dayal started the Indian nationalist journal *Bande Mataram* (Praise to Thee Mother!), named after a popular Bengali poem. The banned poem eventually became part of the Indian national song.

In London, Savarkar was now being monitored closely. British intelligence had uncovered Savarkar's plot to use the cook at India House to smuggle Browning pistols to his elder brother, Ganesh, in India. Before the weapons were seized, Ganesh, who had single-handedly raised Savarkar and his other orphaned siblings, was arrested and charged. A livid Veer Savarkar plotted revenge when Ganesh was sent to the dreaded *Kala Pani* of the Andaman Islands for six years of penal servitude. At his secret London gun range, Savarkar trained a young, unsettled Indian Punjabi studying mechanical engineering in University College, London. Under Savarkar's tutelage, Madan Lal Dhingra committed the first act of Indian revolutionary violence overseas. In July 1909, Sir William Curzon Wyllie, a senior aide to India's secretary of state for India, was attending a welcome party for new Indian students in London. As he enquired about their well-being, Dhingra approached him with a smile and a gun. Five shots were fired at close range into Wyllie's face. The sixth bullet killed a Parsi doctor running to render aid.

At his trial, Dhingra adorned his bloody deed with an eloquent statement. Schooled by Savarkar, Dhingra maintained that his act was morally justified: "I do not want to say anything in defence of myself, but simply to prove the justice of my deed... Just as the Germans have no right to occupy your country, so you have no right to occupy mine."[68] Dhingra's

Madame Bhikaiji Cama with the
first version of the Indian national flag.

act was the definition of political terrorism – propaganda of the deed in substance and form. The future Mahatma Gandhi labeled Dhingra a coward. Gandhi believed in the peaceful approach of the Hindu God Rama, not the violence of the Goddess Durga embraced by Savarkar who would, many years later, be implicated in Gandhi's assassination.

As an early disciple of the moderate Gokhale, Gandhi claimed to feel only pity for the impressionable young Punjabi. He believed that Dhingra had been "egged on to do this act by ill-digested reading of worthless writings."[69] He also believed that the statement explaining the act was not his work. Gandhi took issue in particular with Dhingra's statement that it was "perfectly justifiable on our part to kill the Englishman who is polluting our sacred land."[70] Gandhi distinguished between combatants and innocent civilians. Dhingra's statement appeared to justify indiscriminate acts of terror to support militant anti-colonial resistance. For Gandhi, his was not a brave act, and he believed Dhingra was drunk on a "mad idea" like "wine or *bhang*."[71] A brave act for Gandhi was the ability to suffer "deeply and over a long period,"[72] as he would seek to practice as the Mahatma.

Avoiding the tougher personal experiments with truth Gandhi experienced, Dhingra lacked the patience to figure out how to peacefully throw off the mentality of subjugation. Dhingra was disowned by his father, the Chief Medical Officer in Amritsar, Punjab, for his act. But walking with a smile from the court's dock to the gallows, Dhingra appeared content. He was at peace with his own experiment with reality and that guaranteed a sort of immortality. His last words at the gallows were: "The only lesson required in India at present is to learn how to die, and the only way to teach it is by dying ourselves. Therefore, I die and glory in my martyrdom. My only prayer to God is that I may be re-born of the same mother and I may re-die in the same sacred cause till the cause is successful. *Bande Mataram*! (Mother, I bow to thee.)"[73]

The arch-imperialist Winston Churchill confided to a friend that Dhingra's act would be remembered for time immemorial. He admired Dhingra's statement as "the finest ever made in the name of patriotism."[74] Compared to moderates like Gokhale, Churchill saw Dhingra and Savarkar as worthy opponents. They were locked with the empire in a struggle of power and survival with only one winner.

The hawks of the Empire and the violent revolutionaries fed off each other in a deadly and escalatory dynamic. A few months after Dhingra's execution, another British official was assassinated in Savarkar's birthplace of Nasik. His assassin was a 17-year-old student. The murdered man, A M T Jackson, was a Sanskrit scholar and an administrator who was popular in his district. But Jackson had also overseen the trial of

74

Savarkar's brother Ganesh. And the murder weapon was part of the cache of Browning pistols smuggled into India by Savarkar through the cook at India House. It was a politically inept act with disastrous consequences. India House was closed down. The students lost their refuge. The Indian Secret Service in Simla now coordinated closely with Scotland Yard. With all fingers pointing at him, Savarkar ran to evade the long arm of the law.

By January 1910, Savarkar was in Paris with Har Dayal. All of Savarkar's brothers were now in custody. His emotions were flowing over like the River Seine which had reached record levels after heavy rainfall flooded the streets of Paris. Guilt-wracked about his freedom, he told Har Dayal that he could not be free while his brothers were rotting in prison. Har Dayal begged him to stay on in France, imploring, "No, you cannot go! You must not go! If you go, it will be end of everything! You are the soul of the organisation. If you are removed, the movement will lose its force!"[75] Har Dayal failed to persuade his friend. In March 1910, Savarkar decided to return to England. He would recall wistfully the outwardly calm but sad face of his "dearest friend"[76] Har Dayal at the Paris train station. That was the last time he would ever see his fellow revolutionary in person.

Savarkar was arrested at London's Victoria Station. Taken immediately into custody, he was shaken by the court ruling extraditing him to India. Savarkar was to be returned to his homeland under close guard. He would face trial under the harsher code of Imperial Indian law. Sailing back to India on a P&O liner in July 1910, Savarkar's ship stopped over at Marseilles. In the French port, the slight revolutionary squeezed through a toilet porthole, jumped ship and made for shore. Marseilles was special for Savarkar. His hero Mazzini had sought refuge in Marseilles and started the Young Italy organisation which inspired Savarkar's own secret society. One of Savarkar's trusted aides had been contacted earlier and along with Madame Cama was supposed to rescue him. But driving down from Paris, the pair had taken a long tea-break and quite simply lost track of the time. After an adrenalin-fuelled swim, Savarkar scrambled to the wharf and ran for 300 metres. There was hope for him and inspiration from Mazzini. He knew that even without friends, food or shelter, Mazzini had gone underground and had been successful in starting an uprising against Austria.

History was not about to repeat itself for Savarkar in Marseilles. Wet and bedraggled, wandering about looking for Madame Cama, Savarkar was apprehended by a pair of French policemen. The marine *gendarmes* spoke no English. They did not understand the Indian's repeated requests for amnesty. His British gaolers had launched a boat and yelled out to the French *gendarme*s that the Indian was a thief. After futile attempts at communication, he was returned to his English captors. Standing trial in India, Savarkar was described by the English Governor of Bombay as "one of the most dangerous men that India has produced."[77] Sentenced to 50 years imprisonment, Savarkar was transported to the *Kala Pani* to join his elder brother, Ganesh. The author of the Indian War of Independence was in chains. This loss hit Har Dayal hard. To him, it was the end of an era.

With close monitoring and tough policing, Har Dayal recognised that continuing the struggle in India would be futile. He knew that the fight for India's freedom had to be concentrated beyond its shores. Patriotic Indian students in North America and even Japan had to be enlisted for the cause. Writing in the weekly magazine *Bande Mataram*, Har Dayal reasoned: "We should now realise that even if the Government succeeds in checkmating us in India at every step, there is ample scope for work for several years among Indians living abroad."[78] Har Dayal took a leaf from the playbook of Savarkar who believed in recruiting support from a broad base overseas. Har Dayal was also trying to repair his own shattered morale; he had great difficulty in mustering the energy and purpose required to continue the work begun by Savarkar. Depressed by the cascade of setbacks, Har Dayal began a period of reflection and meditation that took him around the world. Meanwhile in prison, Savarkar began work, writing about Hindutva, the ideology which extolled the pride of being Hindu as the essence of Indian nationalism. He declared: "Muslims and Christians cannot be incorporated into Hindutva because their holy land is in far off Arabia or Palestine."[79]

[V]

PROMISE AND PERIL
ACROSS THE PACIFIC

After a decade of drifting, ex-sepoy Nawab Khan was still a rolling stone. The roaming Rajput had a tendency to wear out his welcome at each way-station. Standing at 177 cm (5 feet 10 in), the lean and fighting-fit Nawab weighed 67 kg (148 pounds).[80] With a quarrelsome streak, he was still being formed by his scrapes and was arrested in India in 1909 on a charge of rioting. With a reputation for vanity and boastfulness among associates and acquaintances, he sported a visible scar on the left side of his chin, and a prominent mole over his left eye which he may have considered more of a beauty spot. Wed by 1906 to a woman in India named Harmut, he seemed unwilling or unable to settle down. For the repressed Rajput, the call of adventure remained strong. And out in the New World, fortune beckoned this former brown warrior of the Raj.

America's gold rush had stripped its farms of labour. Many Chinese and Japanese left behind an Asia in tumult to find work and stability in North America. Opportunities soon opened up for Indian migrants. With unusually sparse monsoon rains in the Punjab from 1905 until 1910, its farmers had a stark choice – move or face mounting debts and possible starvation. Many migrated to Malaya or cities in China, Thailand and Burma. Others ventured even further. Hope for a better future brought them from Punjab, the land of five rivers, to North America. There had been glowing accounts from sepoys visiting Canada after the Queen's Diamond Jubilee Celebration in 1897 when colonial troops were paraded in imperial celebration.

Touring Canada, the Empire's trophy sepoys noted the fertile farming opportunities and a climate similar to the Punjab. A few pioneers left service soon after and migrated to British Columbia, part of the Confederation of British possessions in North America that had become the self-governing Dominion of Canada. As the sepoys turned farmers achieved prosperity, word soon spread about the riches of the Western seaboard states of North America. The fertile area quickly became a promised land for the hardy, independent Jat or farming caste of the Punjab, especially those from its populous parts. Mostly Sikhs or Punjabis, they relied on their status as British subjects to migrate to Canada.

Migration opened new doors of opportunity for these men beyond military service or retirement to the hemmed in life of a small farm in Punjab. Surplus Punjabi farm labour could aspire for more than the rank and pay of a *risaldar-major* (cavalry senior captain), the peak of achievement for landless and uneducated Punjabis. Success abroad could also boost incomes and family prestige at home, where the cost of marriages and even funerals could bankrupt the farmers with small land holdings and many sons. It also allowed some to escape embarrassment, financial or otherwise. Sohan Singh Bhakna, destined to become a leader of the Ghadar Party in the US, admitted that he left India because of a drinking habit. He confessed: "I had frittered our property [on alcohol], I had no choice but to head overseas."[81] And sons at a loose end who could not be integrated into the Punjab's messy and complex family land-holding ownership structures chose to migrate to find their fortunes.

Nawab Khan was one of those at a loose end. The Ranghar from Halwara left India for North America in December 1909. He arrived, aged 26, in the US following a three-month journey across the Pacific. Six months after landing, the ex-sepoy made his way to Vancouver, Canada, to search for direction and a living. Nawab's apprenticeship and political education in the West was about to begin.

Nawab encountered an enigmatic Gujarati businessman with a colourful past and supreme confidence who introduced himself as Hussain Rahim. Twenty years older than the Rajput, the 46-year-old Rahim became Nawab's first mentor and his guide to political activism. Wily, worldly and independent, the detail-oriented Rahim was a man who got things done. Always on the look-out for opportunities, his personal diary recorded his first impressions after arriving in Vancouver, British Columbia, on 4 January 1910.

Rahim had recoiled at the sight of the "ugly, rickety, weather beaten rows of sheds"[82] of the wharf which blocked the view beyond of a bustling and prosperous Vancouver city. The arrivals took a "dirty, miserable path"[83] away from their ship, the route skirting the depot of the Canadian Pacific Railway whose tracks were laid by Punjabi labour. After the grimy first impression, a picturesque expanse of railway sidings came into view. Rahim noted with approval the "palatial railway cars, the acme of comfort, beautifully illuminated by electricity."[84]

Hussain Rahim
aka Chagan Khairaj Varma

Visitors to Vancouver were greeted by these sharply contrasting visions, polluted and postcard pretty in turn – two sides of a coin that would both inspire and disappoint waves of migrants like Rahim, Nawab and the large contingent of Sikh hopefuls. As Rahim recalled, passing the boarding platform for passengers, the new arrivals walked uphill on a narrow and creaky wooden walkway. Care had to be taken to avoid slipping on the muddy road running parallel to it – a metaphor for the precarious road to prosperity. Treading purposefully, Rahim seized the opportunities that came his way. Some time after his arrival, he bought a large share in a real estate firm known as the Canada-India Supply and Trust Company. Appointed as its Managing Director, he took a ground floor office in Vancouver's Main Street. A vehicle for pooling and investing the earnings of Sikh immigrant labour, the company was a useful form of insurance for the Sikh and Punjabi immigrants. With shares in the company, the migrants had some insurance against quick deportation if they lost their jobs.

Rahim was a troubling mystery to fellow Indians and the Empire's secret police. Fond of wearing trilby hats, Rahim came across as a mix of East and West. In a photo portrait, his turban tied in the Gujarati style is matched with a suit jacket and an Edwardian wing-collared, white shirt. Powerfully built and sporting drooping whiskers with a short neck and hunched shoulders, he resembled a bull-dog always ready to pounce on some bone of contention. Described by a Vancouver business associate as "the man of round head, hot temper,"[85] he did not fit the usual boxes. He had been variously described as Sikh, Muslim and Hindu. In truth, he was none of the above. Delhi-born like Har Dayal, Rahim belonged to the Lohanas, a Bania (merchant) caste community from Porbandar in Gujarat, where the future Mahatma Gandhi was born about the same time as Rahim. Unlike Gandhi's caste, Rahim's merchant clan of Lohanas maintained a fluid identity. The Lohanas encompassed Hindus and Ismaili Muslims. They had carefully and quietly converted Sufi masters of the Nizari Ismaili sect. These were the original so-called Assassins of Islam, who had won over Hindu converts by mixing Islam with elements of Hindu tradition.

Rahim's real name was Chagan Khairaj Varma. Imperial secret police records suggest that he had come to Vancouver under false pretences, as a tourist enroute to Montreal after spending 15 years in Japan and Hawaii. This allowed him to evade the laws restricting immigration into Canada. Leaving behind a failed textile business in Kobe in Japan, he had apparently bolted to Hawaii with a large sum of money pilfered from his Bombay Parsi business partner. He arrived in Canada under the assumed name of Hussain Rahim, a Hindu posing as a Muslim.

Rahim's rumoured haul from Japan allegedly bought him the controlling stake in the Canada-India Supply and Trust Company. After a stint at a lumber mill, Nawab became Rahim's assistant in this immigrants' trust company. Rahim's decision to manage the savings of the Sikh workers was a pragmatic mix of business and politics. It was a blend that drove several other prominent nationalist and Ghadar leaders. For cash-clueless political agitators like Har Dayal the romance of revolutionary politics and persuasion was the driving force. However, self-made men like Rahim felt comfortable mixing radical politics with trade and business.

With the help of Nawab and other assistants, Rahim aggressively marketed his fund to the Sikh immigrant community; to men like Harnam Singh. Born in 1882 to a farmer in the village of Kotla Naudh Singh in the ancient Hoshiarpur district of Punjab, Harnam had studied in his little village school until the age of 13. Showing literary talent, he continued his studies informally under a village ascetic who taught him poems and other classics. He read books on Sikh history. However, poetry, history and a small land holding could not feed an extended family. Following the traditional route of advancement in Punjab, Harnam joined the army in 1902, aged 18. At 175 cm (5 feet 9 inches), Sepoy Harnam was a strapping and fair-complexioned young man with expressive eyes. He wrote and recited his poetry while training with the 25th Punjabi Regiment.

In the army, the literate sepoy was given mail duties and taught Urdu to fellow sepoys. One day, he came across in the mail a series of articles by a Punjabi Hindu philosopher named Swami Ram Tirath. The charismatic poet-monk had been a Professor of Mathematics in Lahore until his transformation into a globe-trotting Vedantist Hindu. Harnam avidly digested Ram Tirath's reflections on his experiences of lecturing and living in America. He found out to his surprise that an ordinary worker in the US earned as much in a day what a sepoy earned in a month; the American earned between 6 to 7 rupees a day (about US$2.50 at the time), compared to a sepoy's pay of 9 rupees per month. A seed had been planted in his mind.

Harnam was determined to move to the US. He wracked his brains to gather funds for the journey. Several sepoys from his unit had already migrated. A fellow villager who worked as a watchman in Singapore wrote to Harnam and shared his plan to migrate to America. Harman learned that the journey from Malaya cost as much as 300 rupees – almost 3-years pay. It seemed beyond his reach to gather such a sum. As more letters streamed in about friends' travel plans with invitations to join, Harnam felt a growing frustration. In February 1906, Sepoy Harnam turned out for the general parade at Rawalpindi Cantonment. As a post office orderly, Harnam had not done drills for more than a year. With a distracted mind and rusty muscle memory, his poor posture earned a humiliating rebuke from the inspecting captain. Sepoy Harnam snapped after the scolding. Collapsing on the rain-soaked ground, he soiled his uniform and rifle. Harnam had been a good soldier, topping an earlier promotion test. The outburst was unlike him. He told his stunned platoon *havildar* to clean the dirty rifle himself. Instead of throwing him in a military brig, his *subedar-major* (senior captain) fast-tracked his promotion to *lance-naik* (lance-corporal).

But Harman was determined to leave. He had completed his minimum service requirements. So, he jumped on the midnight train back to his village, and two months later, embarked on his journey East. His brother had secured a loan of 350 rupees from a village money-lender. Migration to America was still a novel and risky undertaking. To avoid obstructive family members, he left with two companions from his village in the dead of night. He recalled:

> All the three of us left our village on 11 May 1906 stealthily at night. We took the rail to Calcutta and took a British ship to Hong Kong. The third-class fare was rupees thirty-five which included "third class" food also. But most Indian travelers, afraid of being served food prohibited by religion, took their rations along. But we did not do so. We had no taboos and my views had undergone change in the last few years. I had been liberated of much superstition and religious cant.[86]

After a stopover in Hong Kong, Harnam sailed across the Pacific in June 1906. He landed in Vancouver, Canada, two weeks later with more than 50 other Punjabis. On average, one third of the arrivals were not let in. They could be labelled LPC (liable to becoming a public charge) for not being able to support themselves, or DCD (a carrier of dangerous contagious disease) and refused entry. Harnam's ship carried the largest single batch to date, raising the influx of Sikhs by 50 percent in Canada. The new arrivals wrote to their friends and relatives. The trickle became a flow and then a near flood – another 10,000 migrated in the next three years from the Punjab alone. Pull had combined with push. Less than a year after Harnam's departure, the Punjab was rocked by serious unrest. Protests started over the highly unpopular Punjab Canal Colonisation law and the government's poor handling of a major plague epidemic. Rousing chants of the song *Pagri Sambhal O Jatta, Pagri Sambhal O* (O Proud Peasant, Guard your Turban/Dignity) were heard across the region. Worn by men across India, not just the Sikhs, the turban symbolised their cultural dignity and self-respect. The song decried British affronts to the dignity of the rural warrior class of the Jat Punjabis and soon became the anthem and label for a pan-Punjab protest movement organised by the Sikh nationalist revolutionary Ajit Singh.

The Punjab protest movement came as a surprise to the British. Sikh steadfastness during the 1857 Indian Sepoy Mutiny had fixed perceptions of the community. Compared to restive Bengal, Punjab was seen as loyal and pliant. And the British wanted to keep it that way. The bulk of the Indian Army supporting their rule was drawn from the region.

Ajit Singh was among the first Sikhs since the 1857 Mutiny to openly oppose British rule. Working in clandestine fashion with the one-handed "Sufi" Amba Prasad and more openly with the prominent Punjabi nationalist Lala Lajpat Rai, he mobilised the farmers to oppose the new laws created by the Canal Colonisation Bill which harmed their interests. For the base of the Pagri Sambhal O Jatta movement, Ajit Singh selected the newly developed Lyallpur district in the Punjab. As he later explained, the "district had attracted people from all over Punjab and was especially populated by retired soldiers. I was of the view that these retired army personnel could facilitate a revolt in the army."[87]

Like Savarkar, Ajit saw the potential of rousing ex-sepoys to help start a mutiny against British rule. He reminded the military pensioners that all they got in return for loyal service were heavy taxes and a loss of independence. In April 1907, more than 200 Sikh sepoys joined a rally in Multan. Riots erupted in a number of towns with government property and infrastructure damaged and destroyed. European passers-by were beaten or humiliated. Sepoys refused orders to fire on protestors.

The British were seriously unnerved by this ominous turn of events that unfolded on the 50th anniversary of the 1857 Mutiny. The Lieutenant-Governor of Punjab sent a desperate message to Viceroy Lord Hardinge: "Punjab is on the brink of a rebellion being led by Ajit Singh and his party. Arrangements must be made to halt it."[88] What was especially worrying was the radicalisation of Punjabis who had formed the backbone of their army and who had stayed loyal during the 1857 Mutiny. It was time for some drastic measures. Ajit Singh was arrested with Lala Lajpat Rai who was found "guilty of tampering with the loyalty of the Punjab sepoy."[89] Both were deported to Mandalay Jail in Burma under emergency legislation. Orders were given for a firm crackdown on the protests. The situation was in hand, at least for the time being.

Given the volatile conditions in the Punjab, the exodus of Sikhs to Canada was no surprise. But just as new doors of opportunity opened up, barriers were raised. Frugal Punjabi peasantry who worked with far more hunger, efficiency and industry threatened the livelihood and self-image

Ajit Singh

of white Canadians. The Sikhs also stood out from other immigrants with their flowing beards and their *dastar*s (turbans). Across the border, in the US, Hindus who adopted Western ways were assimilated. Some were even allowed to take on citizenship. But for Sikhs, shedding symbols integral to their faith such as the turban and beard was not easy. White Americans and Canadians used to an easier pace of work and higher wages vented about a "tide of turbans"[90] and unclean Indians. It was a rerun of complaints about the "yellow peril"[91] of Japanese and Chinese. Race-baiting politicians in Canada and the West Coast of the US supported groups like the San Francisco-based Asiatic Exclusion League. The League relied on crude pamphlets likes "Meat vs Rice - American Manhood against Asiatic Coolieism"[92] which claimed that rice-eating Asians would drag down the standard of living of meat-eating whites. White mobs started anti-Asian riots in West Coast cities in Canada and the US. Efforts were made to extend a ban on immigration from East Asians to the South Asians. The white racists vented their feelings in a popular song heard in whisky saloons:

> For white man's land we fight.
> To Oriental grasp and greed
> We'll surrender, no, never.
> Our watchword be "God save the King,"
> White Canada forever.[93]

Amid the tumult, Harnam made his way from Canada across the border. His interest in connecting poetry and political advocacy determined his future trajectory, fating him to cross paths with Har Dayal, Nawab and others in the Ghadar movement. Harnam secured steady work at a lumber mill in Oregon's scenic Bridal Veil Falls on the Columbia River. He toiled at the mill located 30 miles downstream from the town of St Johns near Portland, Oregon. The area was in the midst of an economic boom, attracting a flood of labour. But the work was not easy. It required size, strength and stamina, which the Punjabi Jat peasants appeared to possess. A popular saying compared the typical Punjabi Jat to a bullock, stubbornly resilient compared to a bull, which had strength without resilience. One immigrant described what it was like to do one of the "lighter jobs" in logging:

> I was given one of the lighter jobs... I had to separate the smaller logs from the others in the channel, so that the circular chain saw would not get stuck. I worked continuously, carrying logs for more than an hour, till my body gave in due to fatigue. I fell down and

the log fell upon me and injured me. Working at the speed of the machine was not an easy task. My friends rescued me and virtually saved my life.[94]

On top of the back-breaking work, the migrant Indians had to deal with angry whites who resented the influx of Asians. In March 1910, Harnam's Punjabi compatriots at St Johns were brutally attacked by a mob of 300 white racists who robbed many of their life savings. The outnumbered labourers defended themselves with their fists. It was not a fair fight. Their attackers included the city's mayor, police chief and a newspaper reporter. It was not the first and would not be the last act of mob violence by ethno-nationalists.

The Punjabis and Sikhs were unhappy. Not only were they unequal subjects of the Empire, but they were accorded less protection than other Asians. Nominally British subjects like white Canadians, they lacked diplomatic representation. The British Consul in San Francisco refused to offer consular support. In contrast, Japan's diplomats had been far more zealous in protecting their countrymen than the English officials of the Indian government. The Chinese government had also taken action, ordering a boycott of Americans goods to protest the maltreatment of Chinese railway coolies in the US. Adding insult to injury, the British had supported measures to restrict Punjabi immigration. The Punjabis were caught between the hammer of repression at home and the anvil of increasing racism and exclusion in their new home. New rules under Canada's Asiatic Exclusion Act made it too costly for immigrants to bring over their families. Husbands were thus cruelly separated from wives and children. For those who had risked their lives as soldiers, all this was deeply resented. The observance of a code of *izzat* that made them loyal soldiers could push them to extremes to preserve their rights.

In response, the Sikh Temple executive committee in Vancouver decided that no member of its executive committee could wear a military uniform, insignia or medal. One former Sikh sepoy publicly burned his certificate of honorable discharge. These acts were harvested by activists and militants. Discrimination and racism drew Harnam and Nawab and hundreds of their compatriots towards radicalised politics. This was the ember of the Ghadar movement that was flickering to life. But it needed a personality who had fire in his belly to lead them.

In North America, several Indian groups had formed to look after the interests of Sikh and Punjabi labourers in Canada or those of students and workers in the United States. The Azad-e-Hind (Free India) Party in the US had about 5,000 members. The Sikhs had their Khalsa Diwan Society. However, the disparate groups were not pulling together.

Bhai Parmanand

Without a strong leader and agenda, the Indians were riven by the usual factionalism. What was urgently required to set minds alight and pull all in one direction was a leader who spoke in the language of the majority of rustic Punjabis. Har Dayal was a prime candidate. But he was still in limbo. He wandered around aimlessly, taking a long break in the Caribbean after knocking about in Algeria. Har Dayal had day dreamed about creating a new religion with Buddha at its center. The Buddha's warning against pointless metaphysics resonated with Har Dayal. He held that such worthless belief was India's curse. It took the intervention of fellow Punjabi nationalist, Bhai Parmanand, to bring Har Dayal back to reality. His old friend Parmanand knew his cast of mind. The Arya Samaj missionary was sailing around South America to better understand the plight of Indian labourers. He felt he had to prod Har Dayal to stop wandering and do something useful.

On his way to British Guyana, Parmanand learned that Har Dayal was sulking on the remote Caribbean island of Martinique. Stopping over, the Punjabi missionary found Har Dayal in ascetic crisis mode. But Har Dayal was happy to see a familiar face. Frog-marching Parmanand back to the ship, Har Dayal retrieved his friend's luggage and forced him to stay with him until the next ship arrived. The 4-week stay was not a comfortable time for Parmanand. Sleeping on the bare floor next to Har Dayal, he subsisted on his friend's diet of boiled grains and potatoes. Recoiling from the bland food, Parmanand added spices and salt and started working on Har Dayal. In a series of long and difficult exchanges, Parmanand persuaded Har Dayal to return to the real world of action and reaction. Still, Har Dayal shunned the thought of any further activism, telling Parmanand that his plan was to leave for the US to continue his work on Buddhism. He still hoped to find a new synthesis of the various faiths and to achieve some peace of mind. In the US, Har Dayal would not find interfaith harmony or inner peace, but war, anarchy, socialism and mutiny, with a bit of free love thrown in.

[VI]

PROBLEMS WITH OR
WITHOUT PASSPORTS

In his memoir, *The World of Yesterday*, the Austrian Jewish writer Stefan Zweig recalled travelling from Europe to India and on to America before 1914 "without a passport and without ever having seen one."[95] In Zweig's experience, travelers crossed borders "without questioning or being questioned, one did not have to fill out a single one of the many papers which are required today."[96] He regretted new frontiers "with their customs officers, police and militia, (which) have become wire barriers thanks to the pathological suspicion of everybody against everybody else."[97] Writing in the gloom of the Second World War, Zweig was indulging in nostalgia about a vanished past. The world before the Great War boasted a remarkable level of mobility and freedom of travel. It was also, of course, a white man's world where skin colour served as an unofficial passport. An Austrian Jew buffeted by the forces of Fascism, Zweig was experiencing what Indians and other Asians long endured in the form of racism, imperialism and surveillance.

In the summer of 1911, Nawab Khan stood at a border crossing between Canada and the United States. He faced US immigration officials stationed by special arrangement on the Canadian side of the border in British Columbia. To get across, Nawab had to meet admission procedures and assure officials that he was not an excludable alien. Land border inspection procedures between the US and Canada had been started three years earlier. In 1909, Canadian immigration inspectors in Vancouver warned US immigration officers of the threat of Indians crossing from British Columbia to the US to promote sedition against the British government. Officials in Washington DC were asked to deploy Secret Service officers in Seattle to investigate the Indians who crossed the border from Canada. Brown-skinned immigrants were subject to search with a rigorous examination of their documents and motives for crossing.

US immigration officials who had done their research on Nawab would have cause for concern. Nawab was by then fully initiated into the turbulent world of socialist political and militant union activism by his mentor in Canada, Hussain Rahim. Aside from running the Canada-India Supply and Trust Company servicing Sikh migrants, Rahim had become a card-carrying member of the Socialist Party of Canada. After Rahim made checks and queries on the loopholes and possibilities of immigration, the imperial secret police labelled him a dangerous adventurer. They closely watched him for his links to undesirable groups and individuals in India's nationalist movement.

One of these secret policemen appeared to nurse a particular grudge against the Indian revolutionaries. William Charles Hopkinson knew the Indian diaspora in North America well. Born in Delhi in 1880 to an English soldier father and Indian mother, Hopkinson joined the imperial police at 16. The Eurasian never really knew his own father – mutinying Afghan troops had killed him as he tried to protect the British envoy in Kabul. Hopkinson was left stranded and fatherless in his mother's arms in Lahore. He knew quite personally what mutinies and revolts could do. The former police inspector from Calcutta in Bengal had also worked for the police in the Punjab, gaining valuable experience in both hubs of unrest in India. He became an expert in thumbprint and measurement identification and could ferret out suspects under assumed identities.

Arriving in Vancouver in early 1908, Hopkinson took up a new job as a permanent translator in the city's immigration department. He met a recent British immigrant named Nellie, an auctioneer's daughter two years younger than him, and the couple was soon married. Hopkinson looked distinctive enough. Tall, with a slight stoop from his height, and with high cheekbones, round, slightly bulging eyes, a full lower lip on his obsessively clean-shaven face, he appeared both charming and menacing at the same time. A perfect combination for a spymaster; one with the right complex of motives for the savvy imperial intelligence to exploit for their own purposes. Denying his mixed parentage, he claimed pure English blood to further his career. On the Canadian immigration department application form, he blatantly lied about his place of birth, stating England instead of India. Ironically, he would spot just this sort of lapse to deport troublesome Indians.

Tasked to look into the problems posed by Indian immigration into Canada, Hopkinson drew double pay as immigration official and Dominion police officer on special duty at Vancouver. It is not entirely clear if he was sent to Canada by the India Office in London to investigate Indian revolutionary activity or if he cleverly carved a niche for himself to commoditise his special knowledge, experience and skills. Hopkinson

William Charles Hopkinson

spoke excellent Hindi, which was literally his mother tongue. Although his Punjabi was halting, he could pass off as a Sikh in disguise given the linguistic overlap. Using the name Narain Singh, he penetrated secret revolutionary meetings dressed as an uneducated Sikh worker. One of his assistants admitted that "he used to dress in a turban with a false beard and moustache and old clothes and go to the temple."[98] To complete his cover, he even maintained dwellings in a hovel in a poor part of town. At other times, he would pose as a white lumberman looking for Sikh workers. A trained stenographer, his wife Nellie typed up his secret reports on Indian revolutionaries.

Insecurity about his origins may have fired his zeal to police Indians with revolutionary aims. Hopkinson ran his own stable of double agents and spies in the Indian community, effectively operating as a one-man intelligence agency monitoring politically suspect Indians on the Pacific coast. Thus, he was a formidable presence in Indian immigration circles in North America, monitoring activities on both sides of the border.

Soon after his arrival, Hopkinson encountered the Bengali activist Taraknath Das, who the reader will recall had impressed the anti-opium activist Ellen La Motte with his points about British hypocrisy in the opium trade. Taraknath worked as an interpreter on loan at the US Department of Immigration office in Vancouver. Hopkinson considered Taraknath no mere workplace competition, but an agent of sedition. As a teenager in India, Taraknath had agitated against the partition of Bengal, widely seen as an attempt to kill its freedom movement. Taraknath belonged to the Anushilan Samiti (literally body-building society). The society's name was a calculated snub of the British who routinely derided Bengali males as a non-martial race. In India, along with other middle-class Bengalis, Taraknath trained in martial arts, sword-fighting and wrestling in an *akhara*, a gymnasium for martial training.

Taraknath was in fact a disciple of a charismatic, intense young nationalist named Jatindranath Mukherjee, better known as Bagha ("Tiger") Jatin after killing a Bengal tiger with nothing more than a Gurkha *kukri* (knife).[99] Idealistic young men like Taranknath rallied to Bagha Jatin after the British Viceroy announced the decision to partition Bengal along religious lines. Hopkinson, from his service in the Bengal police, would have known that Taraknath's mentor was the guiding light behind secret societies like Anushilan Samiti. Bagha Jatin led the most militant faction in the Anushilan Samiti, which became Bengal's oldest paramilitary unit, carrying out terror and assassination attacks against British interests. Collectively, the freedom fighting secret societies that formed under men like Bagha Jatin became known as the Jugantar or alternatively Yugantar Party. Yugantar referred to a new era or a transition to a new

Taraknath Das

epoch, pointing to a future of freedom without British rule. The Bengal-based liberation party offered a template for the freedom movement in Punjab and, later, the mutiny movement among Indians in America. Like Savarkar, Bagha Jatin encouraged mutinies among India's sepoys to topple the British, inspiring Ajit Singh in the Punjab. Under Bagha Jatin's guidance, the teenaged Taraknath spread the message of revolution and even tried to set up a revolutionary base in Southern India.

Taraknath found himself hounded by British criminal intelligence. Making a dash for it, he fled India on a livestock-carrying French ship. With little to eat, rough seas and among animals destined for the slaughterhouse, Taraknath was headed for Japan. The Japanese were then Asia's rising power. Young Indians transfixed by an Asian victory over a European power in the Russo-Japan War flocked to learn its secrets. But the 21-year old's attempt to receive military training was thwarted by the Anglo-Japan Treaty. British officials pressured the Japanese to eject him. Opaque Japanese customs and culture also made it hard for him to assimilate, although he was destined later to return to Japan and develop strong links with Japanese ultra-nationalists who promoted "Asia for the Asiatics."

Forced from Japan in 1906, Taraknath sailed for Seattle on the West Coast of the US as one of Bagha Jatin's emissaries. To survive, he did odd-jobs before arriving in San Francisco where he found menial work in the University of California in Berkeley. A kindly American professor found the young exile sitting in a corner engrossed in a book, engaged him in conversation, and admitted him for special studies in the chemistry department. It did not take long for Taraknath to become politically active among the Indians, starting the California Hindu Students Association with a dozen members. He went on to found the Indian Independence League, linking up Indian students and workers in the farms. But his political activities could not provide a steady income. To make ends meet, he secured a sought-after job as an interpreter for the US immigration across the border in Vancouver. During the day, he earned a living as a junior official helping to regulate Indian immigration. In the evening, Taraknath taught the Punjabi workers English and their rights as immigrants. He started a self-help Hindustan Association in Vancouver. From 1908-1910, Taraknath even published the bi-monthly *Free Hindustan* with the help of friendly socialists who let him use the Socialist Party press room. His English language newspaper targetted Punjabis who had served in the military, persuading them that loyalty to the British Raj was misplaced. His newspaper also reported on examples of Britain's poor treatment of Indians in the colonies.

The paper's strong anti-British tone caught the eye of the authorities.

The Canadian government was also troubled by the links between Socialists and radicalised immigrants. With encouragement from Hopkinson's secret reporting, the Canadians soon identified Taraknath as a key leader of "Hindu agitation." With his experience in Punjab and Bengal, Hopkinson was perfectly placed to trace the connections and perceive the potential risks for Empire. He put the heat on Taraknath, forcing him to leave the British Dominion of Canada. Before heading back across the border to the US to continue his work, Taraknath bitterly denounced Hopkinson as a British spy.

With Taraknath Das out of the way, Hopkinson turned to Hussain Rahim. The Gujarati was considered a little too friendly with trouble-makers like Taraknath. Hopkinson had been tracking Rahim since his arrival. He also kept a close tab on Nawab Khan as Rahim's aide. He wrote special reports on the Indian activists for the Canadian Deputy Interior Minister W W Cory, including profiles on Rahim and Nawab. In one report, both were accused of assisting members of the Industrial Workers of the World, a transnational, militant labour union popularly known as the Wobblies. Active in the US and Canada, the Wobblies challenged the basis of North American capitalism. The syndicalist organisation sought to empower the working class with direct action instead of appealing to the political authorities and engaging in negotiations. Led by their blunt, burly founding member Bill Haywood who never shied from a fight, the Wobblies were considered a dangerous nuisance. Fully exploiting the right to freedom of speech, Wobblies activists gave angry public speeches criticising capitalism and the entire established political order. Predictably, the established order hit back with tough policing and legal measures, including limits to the Wobblies' free speech. Rahim helped to bail out some of the Wobblies arrested for creating alleged street disturbances. Hopkinson's report noted that Nawab Khan was "closely associated with Rahim in his business and the recent bailing incident."[100]

Rahim's links to the Wobblies and the Socialist Party of Canada, of which he soon became the most senior non-white card-carrying member, and his support for Sikh immigration rights were red flags for the imperial authorities. The fear was that the Indians would be influenced by Socialist ideas and bring these dangerous concepts back home. As a socialist, Rahim did not identify as an Indian subject under the King. He was promoting the Indian worker as a free wage-labourer with demands equal to those of other wage-labourers everywhere. In his secret report, Hopkinson wrote to Cory of the danger posed by men like Rahim:

> The Hindus have up to the present never identified themselves with any particular Political party and the introduction by Rahim of the

socialist propaganda into this community, is, I consider a very serious matter, as the majority of these people are uneducated and ignorant and easily led like sheep by a man like Rahim.... [T]he question is what effect will all these Socialistic and Revolutionary teachings have on the people in India on the return of these men primed with Western methods of agitation and Political and Social equality.[101]

Socialism and labour activism threatened the foundations of British imperialism. The colonialist venture relied on extracting resources and exploiting labour at coolie prices with no rights to citizenship. Significantly, most of the Sikhs in North America were from the major military recruitment districts of India. Colonial officials were naturally concerned about the planting of troublesome thoughts in turbaned heads. Hard work and loyalty for a steady job on low pay was perhaps not the be-all and end-all, as Rahim told the Sikhs.

Being fluent in English, Rahim was not easily put off by the imperial police. Hopkinson resented Rahim's attitude and pulled him in for a special session. Rahim, however, did not flinch. He stared back at Hopkinson and spat out: "You drive us Hindus out of Canada and we will drive every white man out of Canada."[102] But Hopkinson was not about to let that rhetoric pass. Rahim's notebook was found and carefully examined. Hopkinson reported that it contained a newscutting about bomb making, which may have been planted, and names of Indian activists and revolutionaries. Hopkinson tried his best to deport Rahim after his arrest in October 1910. With legal help from the local Hindustani Association, Rahim challenged Hopkinson's effort. His lawyers argued that as "British subjects, we demand our inalienable rights to reside more freely in the British Empire and request immediate redress against high-handed, impolite and Empire-breaking actions of local authorities."[103]

Canadian courts ruled in favour of Rahim. His legal victory boosted his prestige and importance among Canada's Indians, including followers like Nawab Khan. Hopkinson wrote bitterly to the Deputy Interior Minister that the failure to deport Rahim from Canada "has so bolstered up his position in the Hindu community here as to make him a leader and a counsellor in respect to all matters concerning their community".[104] But Rahim also had a mean and competitive streak. He was ready to clash with anyone who threatened his own vision or interests. He went out of his way to radicalise Sikh immigrants who were more concerned about their own welfare instead of fighting for Indian independence.

It was not only Hopkinson who felt the sharp end of Rahim's wrath. He was not pleased to come across a mild and scholarly lawyer named Teja Singh who was active among the Sikh community in the mills and farms of the Pacific coast. Teja had been sought out by the Sikhs in their struggle to secure their rights as British subjects in Canada. He had helped a group of Sikhs when Canadian authorities tried to forcibly deport them to British Honduras. But Teja's real strength was in Sikh missionary work. The first turbaned Sikh to study at Cambridge University and Harvard University, he taught Sikh immigrants about their religion and returned them to the tenets of their faith.

Temperamentally, Teja avoided firebrands and confrontations. He opposed violence or direct action. His political instincts were moderate, although the ever-alert Hopkinson also monitored his activities closely and was convinced that he was subversive. In Vancouver, the tough and aggressive Rahim questioned Teja's moderate approach. He made life uncomfortable for the gentle missionary, running him down as an "illusionist", and an idealist who "resign their world in favour of Britishers, and turn to seek salvation."[105] Perhaps the real problem was that Teja was also the founder of the Guru Nanak Mining and Trust Company to pool and manage the investments of Sikh workers. This enterprise competed with Rahim's own trust company.

For a complex mix of business and ideology, the fiery Gujarati with a Muslim name took his fight against Teja into the sanctity of the Sikh *gurdwara* (temple). In 1911, Rahim became the first non-Sikh included in the temple committee of the local *gurdwara* in Vancouver. Still posing as a Muslim, Rahim started the United India League in support of Indian rights. Tellingly, he inaugurated it on the very same day that Teja Singh founded the Sikh religious and welfare organisation known as the Khalsa Diwan Society. Rahim made sure that he pressed the case for Sikhs far more forcefully than Teja. A few days after creating his League, Rashim wrote a long petition to the Canadian government asking for the repeal of restrictions on Indians. The petition highlighted the "fidelity and heroic loyalty" of the Sikhs in defending the British Empire and regretted that the status of Indians was "wholly differentiated from that of other Oriental immigrants."[106] In his reply, the Canadian Minister of Interior held the line laid out by the Viceroy of India Lord Hardinge, noting that "there is a very strong feeling among classes wielding considerable political influence in Canada against any relaxation of the restrictions."[107]

Rahim was building his base of subscribers to his fund in competition with the moderates. An assertive man under pressure from surveillance and the weight of several responsibilities, Rahim's temper and combative nature was not easy for anyone to handle. Nawab, for one, was also not quite as pliable or committed to him as some of Rahim's other young followers. Before long, their relationship began to deteriorate. To intimidate Nawab, Rahim encouraged another young Muslim from his retinue to file a lawsuit against him. Thus, Nawab lost his mentor and gained a powerful enemy. In desperation, he wrote to his elder brother who advised him to leave Canada for good. He, however, put to good use the skills picked up from his estranged mentor and talked his way across the border to the US.

After crossing over, Nawab sought out new friends with similar ideas. He found himself drifting towards another new mentor – a dapper, broad-shouldered Punjabi who introduced himself as Ghulam Hussain. Arriving in the US from France in August 1911, Ghulam's rich political experiences during his travels opened up a whole new world to Nawab. Unlike Nawab, Ghulam moved with mission and purpose. Just a year older than his new follower, Ghulam had joined the revolutionary leaders Ajit Singh and "Sufi" Amba Prasad in the Pagri Sambhal Jatta (Guard Your Turban/Dignity) movement in the Punjab. Not only did he have strong connections to the freedom movement in the Punjab and Bengal, he also had links to the anti-British, pan-Islamic movement in Turkey, which attracted Punjabi Muslims like Nawab.

The Punjabi revolutionary sported a Muslim name, just like Hussain Rahim. And like Nawab's first mentor, Ghulam Hussain was also not Muslim, but in reality a Hindu from the Punjab named Thakur Das Dhuri.[108] The subterfuge was encouraged since Hindus and Sikhs dominated the Indian freedom movement and it leaders sought more Indian Muslims to broaden their support base. Apart from appealing to Ottoman pan-Islamists, a Muslim alias could also throw the imperial police off the trail. In Ghulam's case, spies had meticulously tracked his movements for the Department of Criminal Intelligence in British India. The DCI suspected that Ghulam was helping to extend the Indian radical network to the Pacific Coast of North America.

As they forged bonds in their new surroundings, Nawab would have discovered his new mentor had an even more exciting background than Hussain Rahim. Ghulam had made his way back to the Punjab in 1905 after a quick visit to the US. Working in the Patiala accounts office, Ghulam assisted Ajit Singh and "Sufi" Amba Prasad in building the Pagri Sambhal Jatta movement against the unpopular, anti-farmer laws in 1907. When the British cracked down and deported Ajit to prison in Burma, "Sufi" Amba Prasad sought sanctuary in Nepal, while Ghulam had to lie low. Ajit was released after six months when the British caved under the pressure of strong public opinion in Punjab. But the imperial police were monitoring Ajit and Prasad closely. Both men were given little room to operate. To escape the stifling surveillance, the revolutionary pair of Sikh and Sufi soon slipped away to Karachi port.

Leaving Ghulam behind in the Punjab, they decided to make their

"Sufi" Amba Prasad

way to Iran, which offered a sanctuary to Indian revolutionaries. The Sikh and the Sufi were fluent Persian speakers and they did not require passports. From Karachi, Ajit and "Sufi" Amba hopped on a boat to Bushire (Bushehr), Iran's most important port and a centre of British trade and political influence. The leader of the Iranian Revolutionary Party welcomed the Indian revolutionaries, but as Bushire was a hub for British diplomats and spies, they did not stay around for long. "Sufi" Amba's deep knowledge of Sufism helped build allies in Iran, given the overlap between the theology of Shi'ism and the Sufism of Sunni Islam. The men forged links in the broad land of the so-called Islamicate culture beween the Nile and the Oxus rivers. Ajit and "Sufi" Amba also developed good ties with nomadic Turkic tribes in Shiraz known as the Qashqai. Proud warriors with an instinct for independence and an aversion to the British, they understood the Indians' need for freedom and gave them protection.

But the British were not about to give the Indian revolutionaries free reign in Persia. London's great fear was that Germany would unite Iran and Turkey and use bases in Afghanistan to threaten British India. Their fears materialised during the First World War when the Indians formed a government in exile in Kabul. "Sufi" Amba would heroically lead former sepoys and Indian revolutionaries against the British army in a series of skirmishes in Iran. But that was still in the future. More immediately, to track down the pair, the British Department of Criminal Intelligence cornered their associates. After evading the first round-up, Ghulam was ensnared in the dragnet. Securing bail, he promptly absconded and made his way to Shiraz, the capital of the province of Fars. Fars was part of the no man's land formed in 1907 after Iran was carved up by Britain and Russia. The British made sure to seize those parts that commanded the approaches to India. The birthplace of the great Persian poets like Hafiz, Shiraz inspired Ajit and "Sufi" Amba to start their revolutionary journal *Hayat*.

Ghulam arrived just in time in 1909 to warn the pair that the British secret police were hot on their trail. As British intelligence agents tightened the noose, Ajit fled Iran under the Persian Muslim name Mirza Hassan Khan. Thakur borrowed the trick and changed his to Ghulam Hussain, a name that stuck. The men made good their escape while "Sufi" Amba stayed and assimilated himself into Iranian society to lead Indian exiles in harassing actions against the British forces in the region.

The Indian revolutionary movement, like all radical groups, always featured a string of variable and fluid pairings and partnerships. From Iran, Ghulam made his way to Constantinople (Istanbul) where he discussed Indian affairs with the Turkish republican leadership. He accompanied Ajit to Paris to consult with Madame Cama and her coterie. In the summer of 1911, Madame Cama decided to send Ghulam to North America to help mobilise the Sikhs. As a Punjabi Hindu with a pan-Islamic veneer, Ghulam could prove useful to the radicals' cause in the US. As the Punjabis were settled in towns along the Columbia River in Oregon, Ghulam based himself upriver in St. Johns, not far from ex-sepoy and poet Harnam's mill in Bridal Veil. St Johns was a perfect starting perch, a growing commercial center surrounded by shops and restaurants.

Indian mill-workers had been brutally attacked in the area by men demanding a "white Canada". By the time Ghulam arrived a year later, Oregon was becoming increasingly pragmatic about the Indians in their midst. Welcome as useful labour, they were expected to leave after completing their jobs. Nawab was working in St Johns as a mill-hand when he came across Ghulam. Giving Nawab lessons in political and revolutionary work, Ghulam built on the basics of labour activism laid down by Hussain Rahim in Canada. So here was a Hindu educating a Muslim on anti-British, pan-Islamic causes, including support for the Ottoman Empire which was fighting a league of four Balkan states.

Ghulam would have taken some delight in pointing out to Nawab that the double-faced British supported Turkey's Christian enemies in the Balkans. As Turkish losses deepened, Ghulam instructed Nawab to join a mass meeting of Indian Muslims in Sacramento, California, in 1912. The young Rajput was appointed to a committee of four to tour the US and collect funds to support Turkey's fight against the Balkans League. A British Punjab police intelligence report noted that "the touring and speech-making on behalf of Turkey inclined (Nawab) to further political work."[109] As a practising Muslim, Nawab proved useful to Ghulam. He could draw Muslim support to the Hindu and Sikh dominated nationalist movement in North America. Nawab got into the game of political organisation, granting him status and recognition as a community political leader.

In Astoria, Oregon, Nawab formed a regular gathering of Sikhs, Hindus and Muslims ostensibly to promote mutual understanding and bridge differences. The weekly meetings featured readings from newspapers on breaking developments and discussions. Tucked snugly between river and hills, Astoria was a multi-ethnic town also known as the "Helsinki of the West" because of its large population of Finns. A number of these Finns were radicals who supported the Wobblies of the Industrial Workers of the World that had so troubled Hopkinson in Vancouver. Known for its relative tolerance and support for working class causes, Astoria attracted close to a hundred Indians. Most were employed at the Hume Lumber Mill and lived nearby in a row of bunkhouses on the waterfront which became known as "Hindu Alley". For Americans then, all Indians – never mind their religion – were Hindus. Identities were in flux, with nation, state, religion and empire in a plastic phase of definition.

Mentored by two Hindus posing as Muslims, Nawab's process of political education and radicalism was now about to be completed by Har Dayal, an anarchist and narcissist with Buddhist leanings posturing as a nationalist revolutionary. The polyglot Punjabi radical thrilled his listeners with turns of phrase like *safed patang ki kali tang* (the black tail of a white kite) to mock Indians who sought British favour. A British Punjab police intelligence report concluded that "Nawab Khan's seduction from honest work to the trade of a revolutionary leader is similar to many others in America who fell under the influence of Har Dayal."[110]

So, Astoria, the small town perched on the mouth of a river opening out into the Pacific Ocean, offered a launch-pad for the revolt embraced by both Har Dayal and Nawab Khan. One was a rebel looking for a cause, and the other a cause searching for rebels.

[VII]

A CAUSE IN SEARCH
OF REBELS

After sunny Martinique with its turquoise sea, swaying palms and pristine sand, Har Dayal resigned himself to the cold and grimy hubbub of a New York winter. By February 1911, he had made his way to Cambridge, Massachusetts, with permission to use the Harvard University library for his research on Buddhism. In a break from the book-stacks, Har Dayal met with the Sikh missionary Teja Singh who was completing his Masters degree in English Literature at Harvard. The mild-mannered Teja told Har Dayal that the Punjabis desperately needed a leader to articulate their concerns and secure demands for equality and decent treatment. Teja's outlook still reflected the moderate stance which had created his rift with Hussain Rahim in Vancouver.

Har Dayal heard Teja's earnest pitch but was not immediately convinced about helping the Sikhs in North America. The radical narcissist was still healing from events in Europe. His view of Sikh immigrants in America was that they were "simple oriental peasants." In a 1911 article, he had sketched them out in stereotype – "timid, shabby and ignorant rustic that landed at San Francisco or Seattle in search of a livelihood."[111] In classic Orientalist fashion, he admitted he admired their ability to get things done by "silent resolve rather than by tall talk and empty bluff."[112] While deeply committed to the idea of Indian independence, Har Dayal still lacked operational focus in advancing the cause. He could not yet see that the "simple oriental peasants" could be the tip of the spear for the revolt against the Raj.

Har Dayal was also selfishly reluctant to sacrifice his personal quest for spiritual enlightenment. Seeking out a warmer clime, he hopped over the West Coast to reach Hawaii. Dragging along a trunk of books, he found sanctuary in a cave on Waikiki beach. Surrounded by volumes of Karl Marx and Eastern Philosophy, he read and meditated to the roar of the Pacific Ocean, indulging in long discussions on Buddhism with Japanese fishermen. Once again, it took the untiring Bhai Parmanand, who appeared like a genie, to remind him of his obligations to the cause. With great reluctance, Har Dayal left his paradise of books on the beach.

Crossing over to Berkeley, California, in April 1911, Har Dayal wrote copiously on American culture. He was dabbling and searching, his magpie mind experimenting and observing every new trend with wonder. Bhai Parmanand lived in nearby San Francisco, enrolled in a pharmacy college, and happily made introductions for Har Dayal as he kept a worried eye on his brilliant but unfocussed friend. Bhai Parmanand tried to free Har Dayal from his usual delusions and to get him to do some real work. He arranged for Har Dayal to deliver lectures on Hindu philosophy, going so far as to rent a hall with the help of a local benefactor. At one of these lectures, Fremont Older, editor of the *San Francisco Bulletin* heard him speak and was entranced. Articles soon appeared in the local media, which gave Har Dayal visibility and social prominence. The seal of American approval and publicity would prove invaluable to Har Dayal as he gained a platform and extended his networks as a leader in the Indian community on the West Coast.

Through influential friends in the media, Har Dayal plunged into the intellectual, leftist, Irish nationalist and anarchist circles of the Bay Area of San Francisco. Writing breathlessly about America, Har Dayal called it a "mighty alchemist, wonderful magician of the modern age, lodestar of all and everybody whom the overburdened mother earth has rejected."[113] Har Dayal rhapsodised that America was "perhaps the only country in the world from which a solitary wandering Hindu can send a message of hope and encouragement to his countrymen."[114] A regular at lecture circuits and social soirees, he even inspired a character named "Dayal Har" in a 1913 novel, *The Little Lady of the Big House*, the last work of Jack London, the author of *The Call of the Wild*.

With his fame and social standing, Har Dayal was sought out by his fellow Indians. The gentle missionary Teja Singh was approached by the Sikhs in Stockton, California, for an introduction. Teja connected Har Dayal to Jowala Singh, a prosperous potato farmer from nearby San Joaquin Valley. Heavy-set and broad-nosed with a mole on his right cheek, the 46-year-old had left Amritsar in 1905. He had worked his way through Shanghai as a policeman, followed by Panama and then Mexico before migrating to San Francisco in 1908. A former *granthi* (priest) in a Sikh cavalry regiment, the now wealthy farmer was about to set up the first Sikh temple in the US. In January 1912, Har Dayal persuaded Jowala to sponsor Indian students at the University of California in Berkeley. Har Dayal felt that their training and exposure could help the independence movement. Six scholars were selected out of a field of 600 by a committee that included Taraknath Das and Teja. One of them was Gobind Behari Lal, cousin of Har Dayal's wife, who became an admiring disciple of his Punjabi kinsman.

For Punjabi labour toiling in the mills and farms across the Pacific seaboard states, the scholarships were of little relevance. They had come to make a living and hopefully achieve prosperity, while the students sought credentials for professional success. But both groups were being socialised into new mindsets by their exposure to the ways of the West. Bhai Parmanand observed that the Punjabi immigrant labourer, after staying a few years in the United States, was able to dismiss the thought of unequal status of India from their minds and "they too began to regard themselves like the rest of mankind, with self respect and dignity."[115]

As a former professor in India, Parmanand was impressed that students in America did not "pay any special deference to their professors" and that in his college the "attendants are paid the same salary as that which professors start with."[116] But racial discrimination, anti-Asian prejudice and other barriers remained in place. Frustrations were building among the Sikhs who faced the brunt of racism because they looked obviously different. Labour leaders began to take matters into their own hand. Men who had experienced or witnessed the traumatic riots at St Johns, Oregon, fought back by organising themselves. Starting the log rolling was a 29-year-old Punjabi Hindu mill manager from St Johns named Kanshi Ram. With typical Punjabi industry, he worked his way up from labourer to labour contractor before managing a mill. In the Punjab, he had been a disciple of "Sufi" Amba Prasad, whose Bharat Mata secret society Har Dayal had joined long ago and whom Ghulam Hussain also knew well. Kanshi had fled India after police harassment over his links to "Sufi" Amba. A member of the Arya Samaj like Bhai Parmanand, Kanshi ticked all the boxes for leading the Indians in North America except one. He was not a Sikh like his rank and file workers.

Fortunately for Kanshi, his close friend and associate Sohan Singh Bhakha was what Har Dayal would call a "rustic" Sikh, and one with a following. The Sikh lumberman lived two miles away in Linton in Washington State. He kicked his habit of heavy drinking after leaving Amritsar and was saving his pay to retain the family farm in the Punjab. Sohan earned enough respect to take a leadership role among the Sikh immigrant workers. Serving as their *granthi*, he read from the Sikh scriptures every Sunday at the local *gurdwara*. Sohan preferred to get things done with Kanshi; he trusted a man who had worked with his hands. Both disliked the young, educated *babus*[117] who they suspected were using the independence movement as a ruse to cheat naive immigrants.

Kanshi Ram

In March 1912, Sohan and Kanshi mobilised the Punjabi workers in Portland to form the Hindustani Association of America. But neither had a gift for rousing the masses with words. For this, they needed help from a young, educated *babu*, as much as they hated to admit it. The same month, a letter to the editor of a Lahore-based newspaper, *The Panjabee*, called for a volunteer to sail to Canada to mobilise all Indians and "take a lead here for India."[118] Someone who could articulate their mounting grievances – a leader with a strong voice who could appeal to the Punjabis in their language. Someone like Har Dayal, Ajit Singh or even Bhai Parmanand. But Ajit was stuck in Europe. Parmanand's membership of the purist Hindu missionary Arya Samaj was a problem as it considered Sikhs as misguided Hindus. Parmanand was descended from the line of the Sikh martyr Bhai Mati Das, sawn in half on the orders of the Mughal Emperor Aurangzeb. But even his ancestor's faith and fate at the hands of a Muslim emperor of India could not overcome his purist Hindu associations. Bhai Parmanand had to decline the offer.

As for Har Dayal, he had just secured a job lecturing on Indian philosophy and Sanskrit at Stanford University in Palo Alto. He had agreed to work for a very small honorarium at the brand-new liberal arts college. Living like a hermit, he survived on earnings from his writing and remittances from his brother in India. He took a studio apartment on Kipling Street near the clattering tracks of the Southern Pacific railroad. Har Dayal slept on the floor, condescended to have a single chair for guests, and maintained a diet of milk and bread. In such austerity, Har Dayal voraciously imbibed his reading and spouted a rich vein of radical ideas. He questioned all the sacred cows of India quite literally. This included its beloved *Bhagavad Gita*, which he considered a compendium of metaphysical jargon and contradictory theories that was too antiquated for India.

That summer, Har Dayal had the luxury of debating whether to write on the 19th century labour movement, the feminist movement, the basics of anarchism, the elements of sociology, or education and anarchism. Trying his best to get the novelty-seeking intellectual to focus, Bhai Parmanand complained that "Har Dayal never occupied a middle position; he was always going from one extreme to another. Almost immediately from communism he had passed to anarchism."[119] His other long-time friend, the Stanford professor Van Wyck Brooks, claimed to see through the charade of his academic perch. Brooks believed Har Dayal was the archetypal "revolutionist" as described by the arch-anarchist Mikhail Bakunin – one who "has no interests, no affairs, no feelings, no attachments of his own, no property, not even a name".[120] He was convinced that Har Dayal was teaching philosophy but "mainly to conceal his real life-work as an organizer of Indian rebellion."[121]

Somehow, the diamond in the rough had to be used to good effect for the cause. Har Dayal's intelligence, charisma and gift for public speaking were far too useful to the Indian nationalist cause to be wasted on academic dabbling or spiritual pursuits. Ghulam Hussain and Bhai Parmanand continued their individual efforts to get Har Dayal back on track. Har Dayal declined a request by Madam Cama, his old revolutionary comrade in Paris, to work with Ghulam. But Ghulam was persistent. He wrote Har Dayal a stream of letters. Har Dayal's talents could be put to use mobilising immigrant workers in the West Coast. He would find ready ears among hard-working Sikh labourers at the fringes of Empire, as Teja Singh had told him at Harvard University. But the egotistic genius had yet to develop a passion for the broader cause of the Punjabi labourers in North America and to connect it with his own scheme. Maddeningly for Parmanand and Ghulam, Har Dayal pursued his other interests, considered not only revolutionary for the time but an unnecessary distraction.

The Stanford don from India openly supported the concept of open marriage. Apparently under his influence, one of his Swiss students, Frieda Hauswirth, contracted an open marriage with an American medical student. All this created quite a scandal in the tight-knit academic community. One can imagine the wild rumours of a *ménage à trois* gone wrong. The open marriage did not last. Hauswirth returned home and Har Dayal started to write the Swiss blonde impassioned letters from Stanford.

> I wander about the streets sad and weary, thinking of all that has been, the room where you typed my essays on Hindu philosophy, the 127 C house where we would sometimes stand talking in the street, till midnight, the room in Miss Mills' house where Dr Jordan (the University President) was present at the party and you in your glory, the walks by the creek – do you remember? I think of all those days and my heart is sick unto death.[122]

After their teacher-student fling, Hauswirth no longer reciprocated his ardour. She responded instead with the psychological insight gifted to younger women courted by older men: "You have literary talent. You have oratorical talent. But, my dear friend, all this will be useless if you don't develop steadiness, the capacity of taking pains and pursuing an aim confidently."[123]

Har Dayal was not one to admit to his weaknesses. Compensating for his failed romance, he began to throw himself energetically into advocacy work in the summer of 1912. He widened his network among anarchists, Wobblies, revolutionaries, socialists and socialites. But trouble was also brewing for him. He persisted in chasing each and every radical idea he came across. Har Dayal's self-appointed discipline master Bhai Parmanand warned him to keep his anarchist views to himself and to refrain from any talk of free love with females in his class.

Har Dayal ignored his friend's sensible advice. Predictably, Stanford University prepared to eject him from his teaching post. His radical ideas on marriage and the affair with the Swiss blonde had done him no favours. Even the sympathetic Stanford President could not help him. Stubbornly, Har Dayal refused to disown his ideas and was finally forced to resign in September 1912. Thumbing his nose at Stanford, he gave an interview to a San Francisco newspaper endorsing the free-love marriage contract between another former student and the daughter of a noted author. Dubbing him a "Savant sponsor for free love", the article quoted Har Dayal praising the "courage and wisdom" of his former student for "defying custom and conventionality by entering into this so called 'free love' contract before marrying". He also denounced the "entire fabric of slavery and hypocrisy that is called the 'marriage system.'"[124]

This attack on liberal, bourgeois and middle-class values was too much, even for broad-minded California. Stripped of his university post, Har Dayal adopted the style of a freelance preacher and recruiter for a cause. But he wasn't sure what that cause was. He relied on the force of his ideas and personality on a public speaking circuit, subsisting on the barest diet of milk and buttered bread. Wearing a simple, brown-tweed suit, he stuck his folded-up speeches into the jacket's front pocket instead of a kerchief like the dapper Ghulam.

Ghulam had taken a curious Nawab to hear one of Har Dayal's lectures in San Francisco in December 1912. The subject was the "Non-Existence of God". The theme was not so important. He explained his approach in a letter to his friend Van Wyck Brooks: "You must not think that I attach much importance to public lectures. A lecture is only a kind of drum to bring people together. The real work begins with the slow interpenetration of personalities."[125] Now as he beat of his drum, a slow interpenetration of revolutionary personalities was about to take place. The farm boy from the Punjab was about to meet the city boy from Delhi in the far away earthquake-prone city.

After the talk, Ghulam ushered Nawab to the front of the hall to meet Har Dayal. Parmanand was engaged in deep conversation with Har Dayal as Nawab approached. It was a slightly awkward first meeting. After pleasantries, Har Dayal explained to Nawab (at least in his telling) that he chose the theme of atheism "to create a breach among Christians."[126] Nawab tried clumsily to ingratiate himself with a condescending offer: "Would you permit some of us to present a new suit to you? Frankly your tattered clothes do not look good on you."[127] Examining Nawab Khan's fine suit from behind his steel-rimmed glasses, Har Dayal replied, "You are most kind, but until the poor brethren in my country gets proper clothes, I have to dress like them. You too should live more simply."[128] Har Dayal was perfectly conscious of the value of dressing badly – a useful political statement instead of a mere fashion statement. His friend Van Wyck Brooks provided an insight into Har Dayal's mode of operation:

> Har Dayal's nationalist propaganda, – which he soon ceased to conceal after I knew him, – was rather a strain when one perceived that every breath he drew and every hand-shake had an ulterior purpose. He sent propaganda chocolates to the children of his friends, bestowing on them propaganda kisses, because he thought the friends might serve his cause....[129]

As Nawab engaged Har Dayal in awkward conversation, Ghulam seized the opportunity to invite Har Dayal to visit Portland. He wanted him to speak to the Indian mill workers at the local Hindustani Association started by Sohan and Kanshi Ram. Har Dayal agreed to go up to Portland on Christmas Day 1912. A thrilled Ghulam quickly spread the news among the Indians in the area. Word of Har Dayal's visit caused a stir. Har Dayal was a political and social celebrity and his pending arrival was a major event for the community. Downriver from Portland in Bridal Veil, the poet and ex-sepoy Harnam Singh eagerly awaited Har Dayal's arrival along with his fellow workers. It had been a harsh winter with heavy snowfall closing the mills for a month. The men were restless and bored. Anticipation built slowly in the long, cold winter days leading up to 25 December 1912.

And then Har Dayal simply failed to show up. Having made calculations between the value of engaging the rustic workers and students, he accepted a clashing invitation to have dinner with the Indian undergraduates in Berkeley. There was disappointment among the mill workers and labourers. An embarrassed Ghulam assured them that Har Dayal had merely postponed the visit. Harnam and the others slowly dispersed to their hutches. They watched the snow melt. They were still waiting for Har Dayal to appear when the mills reopened and they returned to work. Har Dayal still could not see that taking up the cause of the workers was the backbone of any revolution. He had to decide soon, because events were catching up with him. It would take nothing less than a bomb to blow away his indecision.

[VIII]

THE PHILOSOPHER
OF THE BOMB

If it was a Christmas present, it arrived two days early in the late morning sunshine. Its contents and mode of delivery were not typical of the season of giving. Gramophone needles, nails, and screws were tightly packed among explosives in the home-made bomb. The package of terror was lobbed at the *howdah* (carriage) strapped to a caparisoned elephant named Moti. It was aimed squarely at the Englishman perched stiffly on the ceremonial pachyderm.

Lord Charles Hardinge, Viceroy and Governor-General of India, ruled the sprawling patchwork of states and territories known as Hindustan. Some parts were harder to manage than others. Bengal and the Punjab come immediately to mind. The Punjab was still simmering after the 1907 unrest. Now Bengal was restive again over the decision to relocate India's capital from Calcutta to Delhi. Smacking of imperial high-handedness, Hardinge's *saavari* (procession) was meant to commemorate the move. Rumours circulated that 100,000 Bengalis would be forcibly resettled in Delhi. The radicals in the Bengal hub of India's revolutionary movement decided to send the Viceroy a message. The plot was hatched just north of Calcutta by a group belonging to the Yugantar Party, the underground Bengali revolutionary movement. The cell leader in charge was a heavy-set, ordinary-looking 25-year-old named Rash Behari Bose. Rejected several times by the British Indian army, he worked as a senior clerk in the Forestry Department of Dehra Dun. A British Indian criminal intelligence bureau report would later describe him with a mix of lurid fascination and respect:

> Born 1878; height 5' 8"; stout build; sallow complexion; broad forehead; large and somewhat protruding eyes; a marked cleft on the chin; said to be uniformly cheerful but to be quick tempered; speaks

slowly; has a benevolent expression; one finger of right hand badly injured which still shows a scar and some crookedness: is said to have a scar on right foot, said to have been caused by the bursting of a soda water bottle.[130]

The unprepossessing Rash Behari appeared an unlikely terror mastermind. But appearances can be deceiving for he was a master of disguise, cool, cunning and a careful planner. According to the intelligence report, Rash Behari was "known to have adopted many disguises" and that it was "probable that his appearance and facial expression change greatly with the shaving of his head, beard and moustache."[131]

The day before the procession, Rash Behari had brought along his 16-year-old "wife" in a *tonga* (carriage) to recce the site of the bomb attack. The Bengal group was conducting a joint operation with a Delhi secret society and one of the Delhi-based plotters recalled the excitement generated by Hardinge's procession: "Great preparations were made for the Viceroy's *saavari*. Seats were arranged in the middle of Chandi Chowk and tickets ranged from Rs. 50 to 300 in the black market."[132] But the crowd was about to witness something quite different than they had imagined. While his slim, young "wife" may have attracted some sly glances, Rash Behari drew little attention to himself among the excited onlookers. The "wife" picked to throw the bomb was, in reality, a 16-year-old boy named Basant Biswas. He had practised throwing for months. Other members of the cell stood nearby in backup positions.

Lord Hardinge himself was just beginning to enjoy the ride with his wife, Lady Winifred Hardinge. The *howdah* supported by a sturdy elephant rocked gently through the route lined by three English regiments, Gurkhas and other uniformed personnel. At least 2,500 plain-clothes officers mingled among the throng. Crowds cheered wildly as the leading elephant approached Moti Bazaar in Chandi Chowk. Moti, the elephant carrying Lord Hardinge, soon approached a three-storey building in Katra Dhulia which housed the Punjab National Bank on its ground floor and residences on its upper floors.

Impassively overlooking the scene was the iconic Northbrook clock-tower. It was exactly fifteen minutes to noon. Sitting on its clock-hands, roosting pigeons had stopped time in its tracks. And then in a flash the hands were free to turn, as pigeons and people scattered at the sound of a deafening blast. Moti the elephant froze. Lord Hardinge felt like someone had struck him hard on his back and then poured boiling water over him. He noticed his helmet lying below on the road. He checked on his wife, Winifred, also his first cousin. She appeared unhurt. He inspected the *howdah*, streaked with the tell-tale yellow powder of picric acid ex-

Rash Behari Bose

plosive. With British understatement, Lord Hardinge informed his wife: "I am afraid that was a bomb."[133]

The Chief of Police retrieved the Viceroy's helmet and returned it on the edge of a lance, requesting further instructions. Carry on, ordered the still-stunned Viceroy with a stiff lip that may well have trembled. In the crowd a young boy lay dead, while some soldiers inspected the dents in their shrapnel pocked helmets. There was a burst of cheering as the procession continued. Then Lady Hardinge noticed that something was missing. The sun was beating down on her as the parasol carrier who took the brunt of the explosion lay mangled and entangled in the *howdah*'s ropes. "There are dead men behind,"[134] said Lady Hardinge. Her husband now felt faint from a loss of blood from wounds in his back and shoulder peppered by nails and screws. Moti stood frozen in fear and would not kneel. Hardinge's powerfully built Aide-de-Camp stacked up boxes next to the *howdah* and carried the Viceroy down to receive medical attention.

In the confusion, Rash Behari and his gang slipped away through the crowds, via passageways, stairs or jumping over flat roofs. Rash Behari hopped on a train back to Dehra Dun. The clerk-cum-terrorist was soon back at his desk as if nothing had happened. A few months later, when a now fully recovered Viceroy visited the Forestry Department, Rash Behari took charge of the official reception. Welcoming Hardinge, Rash Behari expressed aloud his relief that the Viceroy had survived the perfidious assassination attempt. In his memoirs many years later, the Viceroy would marvel at Bose's unruffled demeanour.

The Viceroy had lived. But Rash Behari's cell had penetrated the thick security cordon guarding him. This in itself was a victory. It took several years for British criminal intelligence to round up the rest of the cell. Rash Behari remained at large, helped that his home was in the French enclave of Chandernagore near Calcutta. The British Indian police had not anticipated that a group consisting of educated and pious Hindus from Bengal could carry out such an audacious act of political violence. With only rudimentary political intelligence on the Hindu Bengali secret societies, the police were just about getting their head around the concept of terror and the propaganda of the deed. The Director of Criminal Intelligence in India, Sir Charles Cleveland, predicted trouble from another group abroad when he wrote: "The Sikh or Punjabi immigrant in Canada or America sometimes writes as if the extermination of the English in India were the desire of his heart."[135] Eluding the police dragnet, the slippery and cunning Rash Behari Bose would become a key leader in the Ghadar rebellion in India of 1915, connecting the Bengal movement with the returning Punjabis from North America in less than

Lord Charles Hardinge

a year. The act of terror he orchestrated helped to galvanise the flagging freedom movement. Significantly, it linked the terror movement in Bengal with Punjabi radicals in Delhi.

Har Dayal received news of the bomb attack as he dined with Indian students in Berkeley. It was Christmas Day and Har Dayal had stood up the Indian mill workers in Oregon, snubbing Ghulam's invitation. As he spread the news, the students started to dance, chanting *Bande Mataram*, the new watchword of Indian patriotism. Har Dayal rose to the occasion, his heart bursting with pride that the attack took place on his doorstep at home. Addressing the students, he ended his remarks with a quote from the Urdu poet Mir: "*Pagri Apni Sambhaliyeago! Aur basti nahin, yeh Dilli hai!*"[136] (Watch your turban! This is not any town. This is Delhi!), lyrics adapted earlier by the Pagri Sambhal Jatta movement in the Punjab. Focussed and energized after the dinner, Har Dayal immediately wrote a tribute to the bomb-thrower. He mailed the circular to his radical friends in Paris for publication, calling it the Yugantar (New Era) Circular in a tribute to the Bengali secret society behind the attack. Har Dayal rhapsodized about his own awakening as he wrote bombastically on the significance of the Delhi blast:

Hail, All Hail! Bomb of December 21, 1912! Harbinger of hope and courage, dear re-awakener of slumbering souls, thou hast come just in time, not a moment too soon. Thou wast indeed overdue... We don't know where this great deliverer came from. He came like a blessing to oft-repeated sighs and yearnings. He awakened us from our sleep – he flashed a dazzling light before our drooping eye-lids...[137]

For Har Dayal, the bomb opened up a new phase in the struggle: "This bomb of December 1912 opens up a new epoch in the history of the Revolutionary movement in India. Mark well our words. It is our resurrection. Henceforth the Revolutionary movement will don its armour anew and march from victory to victory. The lull is past."[138] He justified the attack as a fight for freedom against tyranny and one which cracked the spell of power:

...and whether it hits or misses, a bomb is a blessing of all such occasions. Where tyranny issues her proclamation, freedom must also do the same. No bomb at an "imperial' or "royal" procession is inopportune. It breaks the spell, it is antidote to the hypnotism of power, which paralyzes the people. It is the voice of millions speaking in a tongue that all can understand... Lo! the bomb has spoken. Let the young men and women of Hindustan answer![139]

The Christmas dinner in Berkeley and Har Dayal's philosophy of the bomb as "concentrated moral dynamite"[140] came to the attention of alarmed and embarrassed British secret police. Almost immediately, a request was made for a report on Indian seditious activities in San Francisco. To assist London, Canada despatched their special agent William Hopkinson to look into matters. Hopkinson would have welcomed the assignment and the change of scene. His near-fanatical monitoring of potential agitators in Canada had ironically ended up stirring distrust and provoking the sentiments that he was deployed to monitor. He confessed to his superior, the Canadian Deputy Interior Minister, that some of the Indians would have nothing to do with him. With his sources of information drying up, it was thought better to deploy elsewhere for the time being. Preparing for his next assignment, Hopkinson said goodbye to his toddler daughter and his heavily pregnant wife Nellie.

It was not Hopkinson's first mission across the border. He had crossed the previous autumn to check on Taraknath Das who was now in Seattle operating his anti-British newspaper *Free Hindustan*. The Bengali Taraknath had proved particularly troublesome after leaving Vancouver. He trained for a while at a military academy in Vermont. To disrupt his training, British criminal intelligence shared their suspicions with the Vermont academy that he had an interest in bomb-making. Taraknath was expelled from the school but remained set on remaining in the US. Getting wind of Taraknath's bid to secure US citizenship, Hopkinson warned that the Bengali could cause even bigger problems if he was allowed to return to India as an American citizen.

In San Francisco, Hopkinson called on the British Consul-General Andrew Carnegie Ross. He approached the British Consulate with some concern. On his previous visit, Ross had questioned his credentials. But now in the wake of the Hardinge assassination attempt, Ross helpfully listed for Hopkinson all the Indian students at Berkeley willing to inform on Har Dayal. He pointed him to a 21-year-old Tamil Catholic student named Henry Pandion. Ironically, the Tamil held one of the scholarships started by Har Dayal and funded by Jowala Singh. When he met Pandion, Hopkinson learnt that Har Dayal had bragged of his connection to the assassination attempt on Viceroy Hardinge. Hopkinson also met with a US Justice Department official who offered a register of all the mail to and from India handled by the Berkeley post office.

Hopkinson wasted no time in tailing Har Dayal to gather incriminating evidence. Apart from collecting leads from his informants, he also attended Har Dayal's lectures. Hopkinson was looking for a way to persuade the US to deport the revolutionary. He did not have to wait long. In January 1913, Hopkinson attended a talk organised by the Russian

Revolutionary Society in San Francisco's Jefferson Square Hall. Har Dayal spoke on the revolutionary labour movement in France. He noted that the revolutionary movement in the US was only in its infancy compared to France. He justified the use of explosives to carry out political assassinations to remove despots. However, he stopped short of endorsing bombing by anarchists. Hopkinson waited for Har Dayal to make a lapse – one he could pounce on to get him deported.

He did not have to wait long. A senior immigration official at San Francisco's Angel Island detention centre told him that the smoking gun was to secure evidence that Har Dayal was a known "revolutionist" or "anarchist" within three years of his landing in the US. After US President William McKinley's assassination by a declared anarchist in 1901, New York's highest court had ruled that the mere act of identifying oneself as an anarchist before an audience was a breach of the peace. For special agent Hopkinson, the key part of Har Dayal's long and wide-ranging statement was a throwaway remark. Har Dayal admitted to his audience that he would not have been allowed into the US had he declared his true affiliations as an anarchist. After recording his comments, Hopkinson's secret report to the Canadian Ministry of Interior concluded:

> Of all the Indian agitators who have visited the States and of all those whom I have a knowledge, I am led to believe that Har Dayal is the most dangerous. It is unfortunate that he should be located at Berkeley among the Indian students attending the University of California, as a man of his knowledge and influence and declared Anarchistic tendencies, is bound to wield a great influence on the young boys at the university.[141]

Hopkinson was building a case for deporting Har Dayal in any way he could. As it played out, it was not the "young boys" or students that would pose a grave threat. It would be the Punjab peasants found in mills and farms. They had come to North America to build their lives. Thwarted by racist rules and regulations from settling down, a force was growing among them. Har Dayal had declined Ghulam's Christmas Day invitation to Portland but changed his mind after the Delhi bomb. He agreed to address the members of the Hindustan Association of the Pacific Coast led by Sohan Singh Bhakna and Kanshi Ram. To sound the alarm on the threat posed by Har Dayal, Hopkinson jumped on a ship from New York to London. He was going to report in person on his findings on Har Dayal and the "seditionists" in North America. He was racing against the clock to get Dayal deported before his three years of residency were up. The Sikhs, swamis, students and spies all had their work cut out for them.

PART TWO

[IX]

THE HOUSE ON THE HILL

The once thriving lumber-mill station of Bridal Veil in Oregon is a ghost-town today. The remaining structures from its heyday are its cemetery and post-office. The cemetery closed long ago, but the town's name saved the post-office from extinction. Would-be brides from across the US still route their wedding invitation cards through Bridal Veil for its symbolic postmark. In its glory days, sawing, not stamping, made Bridal Veil famous. The town's rough mill was perched on Larch Mountain, just above the finishing mill. A-mile-and-a-half long log flume or slide would transport the felled timber down the hill to kilns in town. Loggers and mill-men on Larch Mountain were known to slide down the flume to catch the Saturday noon train into Portland.

At 5 pm on 25 March 1913, former sepoy-poet Harnam Singh was working at his sawmill machine in the Bridal Veil Falls Lumbering Company. The office telephone rang. Picking up the phone, he heard Kanshi Ram's voice. Kanshi told Harnam that both Har Dayal and Parmanand had just arrived in St Johns. It had been a three-month wait. Instructed to take the 6 o'clock train from Bridal Veil to St Johns, Harnam rushed from the lumber-mill to get to the train station. If he was in the rough mill, he could have enjoyed a joy-ride down the flume. Wherever he was, that phone-call would start a perilous roller-coaster for the Sikh immigrant.

Harnam arrived in St Johns by 9 pm. Heading directly to Kanshi's rented house, he was ushered towards Har Dayal and Parmanand. Ghulam and several others were also present. It was the third anniversary of the anti-Hindu riots in St Johns, and almost a year since the Hindustan Association of America was founded in that same house in Portland. Kanshi's home was used as a revolutionary salon for mill-workers and labourers as a branch of the Azad-e-Hind (Free India) Party. Through Ghulam, Kanshi provided the men access to revolutionary literature and

121

pamphlets like *Bande Mataram* sent from Madame Cama in Paris.

The men held discussions late into the night. Harnam recalled hearing Har Dayal's proposal to begin preparations in the US for an insurrection in India. Har Dayal called it a Ghadar, a mutiny or rebellion. A *Ghadar* newspaper should be printed in the US to spread anti-British propaganda among the Indians. The Azad-e-Hind Party should become the Ghadar Party. There was disagreement about the name of the party. One member opposed calling the movement a mutiny as it was actually a war of independence. Har Dayal scoffed at the nationalist pedants so clearly influenced by the 1857 label of his old friend Veer Savarkar. Har Dayal thought he understood his audience better. The Sikhs had been loyal to the British during the mutiny of 1857. The Sikhs and non-Sikhs would now unite under the banner of the new Ghadar – Mutiny.

But Parmanand opposed starting a mutiny at that time. He considered armed violence premature. He wanted funds to bring students from India to study in the US. He reasoned that armed with an education, these students could return to India to fight for freedom. However, most of the workers felt that students would be ineffective. The focus should be on raising funds for Indian labour, building revolutionary consciousness among the migrant workers and mobilising them for an armed overthrow of British rule in India. The final goal would be to establish a "United States of India."

Parmanand had accompanied Har Dayal to Oregon but was already homesick. Now the shoe was on the other foot. Har Dayal, who had a different conception of family from Parmanand, tried to dissuade his friend from returning to India. But, the next morning, Parmanand left for New York to make the journey home. Armed with his pharmacy degree, he would carry on the struggle in India. He would become the link between the Ghadar revolutionaries in America and the Bengali Yugantar, including the notorious Rash Behari Bose and Bagha Jatin. As his friend's train left the station, Har Dayal's revolutionary proposal was adopted. The Ghadar Party was born. Over the next few months, it would bring under its umbrella the broad network of Indian associations in North America.

Har Dayal's first stop after the historic meeting in St Johns was the town of Bridal Veil. Assembled by Harnam, twenty men gathered to hear him speak. After his talk, the workers signed up as members of the new Ghadar Party at voluntary subscription rates. The Bridal Veil branch was the first to be formed, with Harnam elected Secretary and establishing the template of branch organisation led by a Treasurer and Secretary. The next stop was Linton in Washington State at Sohan Singh Bhakna's residence where 100 men gathered. Kanshi Ram was elected secretary and Ghulam, treasurer. The party snowballed in support and subscriptions. The name "Har Dayal" spread among the immigrants. Even small groups of workers reached out to have him speak. The organiser of one such group was a precocious young Sikh named Kartar Singh Sarabha.

Orphaned as a child, Kartar was raised by his *dadaji* or paternal grandfather. He was too young to grow a full beard when he came to America in 1912 to study chemistry at the University of California in Berkeley. But at 16, he felt old enough to take on work as a farm labourer in Yolo near Sacramento, California. Kartar had felt the brunt of racism in the US as soon as he had arrived in the immigration queue, and his yearning for freedom and dignity grew. He was moved to mobilise his fellow Yolo workers after hearing Har Dayal's powerful oratory one Sunday.

> (A) good number of farm workers gathered in a field. They sat down all around us. There was no formality. They sat quietly and I said a few things. Then Har Dayal talked about the position of the Indian people and abroad, the need for independence... he finished and there was no applause or another visible response from the listeners.[142]

The silence stretched on but "a few minutes of silence and quiet was broken when one or two men came forward awkwardly, saluted Har Dayal with reverence and placed a few dollars before him, as they used to do when offering their contributions in a temple."[143] Within half an hour, a few hundred dollars in cash and cheques had been collected. Har Dayal declined the money, saying that it should be handled by a committee in a transparent and accountable manner. This sat well with the farm workers and fruit pickers. They had been warned about the glib and over-educated *babu* who used the nationalist cause to take their money. Some of the labourers-turned-revolutionaries said approvingly:

> We have been giving money to other babus, educated Indians, who say that they are doing work for the country.... They never give us any idea of what happens to the money they take. Lalaji (Har Dayal) let us manage the funds ourselves. That is our work now.[144]

Soon, the Ghadar Party was ready to go national. On 2 June 1913, Har Dayal headed for Astoria accompanied by Ghulam, Kanshi and Sohan. The men were received by Nawab Khan and the members of the local Hindustan Association. To draw a good crowd, Nawab had rented a pair of electric tram cars and a two other vehicles for the occasion. The cars were emblazoned with placards reading "India" and "Freedom". As he pulled in, Har Dayal was greeted with chants of *"Bande Mataram!"* Har

Kartar Singh Sarabha

Dayal ostentatiously declined Nawab's offer of a garland. After a meal at the nearby Hindu Hotel, the lecture took place in the Finnish Socialist Hall in Astoria's Uniontown. Nawab took notes of Har Dayal's speech:

> You have come to America and seen with your own eyes the prosperity of this country. What is the cause of this prosperity? Why nothing more than this, that America is ruled by its own people. In India, on the other hand, the people have no voice in the administration of the country. The British are mindful only of their own personal interests. As an agricultural country India is infinitely richer than any other country in the world, and yet we see famine ravaging our country.[145]

Har Dayal knew his audience. The students and men were from a farming background and warmed to his theme. He urged them to join hands, stop their petty religious quarrels and turn towards the salvation of India. After his fundraising pitch, Har Dayal proposed that the local branches should be amalgamated into a general association known as The Hindi Association of the Pacific Coast – the Ghadar Party's official umbrella organisation. The headquarters would be in San Francisco, in a house named Yugantar Ashram (New Era Retreat) which paid tribute to the movement in Bengal that carried out the attack on Lord Hardinge and was waging a low-intensity insurgency against the British.

Har Dayal revealed his plans to his listeners. A press machine would be installed in the Yugantar Ashram and a newspaper would be started as soon as possible. It would be despatched free of charge to India and the Indian diaspora to expose the tyranny of British rule in India. Members were asked to make a list of friends and relatives to be added to its subscription list. Heads from the various branches were also elected to the larger association. Sohan Singh Bhakna became the first President since he represented the majority Indian immigrant group in the US. Kanshi Ram became overall Treasurer and Har Dayal was elected General Secretary, making him in effect the Association's global spokesman.

As Nawab's organisation was folded into the broader Association, he began to feel the first stirrings of doubt and resentment. He noticed that cheque books and letterheads stamped "The Hindi Association of the Pacific Coast" were kept concealed nearby. Nawab concluded that Har Dayal was only pretending to consult but had come already prepared with a scheme of action. So even as its first seeds were planted, the movement was already infected by aspects that would imperil its future. Two days later at another lecture in Astoria, Nawab heard Har Dayal's exchange with an American in the audience. Responding to his queries, Har Dayal said that India had a population of 300 million locals with 125,000 "Englishmen."[146] When the American speculated that the small number of "Englishmen" could be stoned out of the country, Har Dayal agreed it was possible. He added that Indians gradually were becoming conscious of their powers. Such remarks were calculated to rouse his listeners.

The belief that stirring words could substitute for careful preparations became a fatal theme for the Ghadar movement. It created a habit of mind that did not help the long-term prospects of the cause. Har Dayal believed in the power of language to arouse rebellion and challenge British power. A clutch of Indian nationalist publications was being churned out worldwide. In Calcutta, the Bengali revolutionaries had published the banned underground journal *The Jugantar*. In London, the India House founder Krishnavarma Shyamji had issued the *Indian Sociologist* newspaper while in Paris, Madame Cama continued to produce the *Bande Mataram*. In Persia, "Sufi" Amba Prasad ran the *Hayat*. Taraknath Das had put out the *Free Hindustan* newspaper in Vancouver and Seattle and Virendranath Chattopadhyaya was moving his publication *Talwar* from London to Berlin. Har Dayal believed these efforts could be merged in a new publication to incite revolt against the British Raj.

San Francisco became the headquarters of Ghadar not only because it offered the convenience of a major port city. Har Dayal lived there and a good number of Indians also worked in California. It was also the political and economic capital of the West Coast with major newspaper coverage. Crucially, San Francisco had become a hub for revolutionaries from Ireland, China, Russia and elsewhere. The Ghadar's message of mutiny would be broadcast from a global revolutionary capital.

Ghadar Central, or the Yugantar Ashram, was located in a dull and drab two storey wooden house on a hill – 436, Hill Street to be precise. Har Dayal had located the premises at the top of a hill in the city's Mission District with Twin Peaks to the north. Har Dayal and the rest of the Ghadar Central staff would live and work in the house which had a backyard with a garden, large shady trees, a small pool, grass and pretty flower beds. It did not look like a fort. It was an ideal place for a philosopher like Har Dayal to combine revolutionary work with a retreat for meditation. Separately, a garage was also rented nearby at 1324, Valencia Street. It was fitted out as a printing press with the necessary electrically-operated lithographic machines to print texts in three languages: Urdu, Hindi and Gurmukhi for Muslims, Hindus and Sikhs respectively at the rate of 1,100 sheets an hour.

Several months went by and it appeared that Har Dayal's promise to his kinsman Gobind Behari Lal to start a "straight fighting newspaper"[147] might be all talk. Subscriptions worth US$2,000 had been paid. Harnam's friends shared their fears that Har Dayal might have taken their money and run like the other scamming *babu* revolutionaries. Some wrote to Har Dayal directly, asking him why he was sitting on his hands. The backyard in the house on the hill may have gotten a little too comfortable for Har Dayal. Or he might have been distracted by his busy social life in San Francisco. He cited illness and told the men to call Ajit Singh from Europe to help. But Har Dayal's speeches had struck a chord and instead of spurning him, some members of the Hindi Association of the Pacific Coast funded his medical treatment. The charismatic, young Sikh from Yolo, Kartar Singh Sarabha, came down to assist Har Dayal. The ambitious teenager had plans to learn to fly an airplane but, for the time being, had to be content with operating a printing machine.

The men living in the House on the Hill were the chosen few. Subscriptions were collected from across the western states for membership in the Ghadar Party. But only a handful of men were allowed to join the inner circle of the Yugantar Ashram. Members had to observe an arcane web of seventeen rules. Based on the model of Veer Savarkar's Abhinav Bharat Society, divulging its secrets meant death. With his team assembled and assistants keen to do anything to help, Har Dayal finally published the *Ghadar*. The newspaper's objectives were set out by Har Dayal in his signature editorial in its inaugural issue dated 1 November 1913.

What is our name? Ghadar! (Mutiny!)
What is our work? Ghadar!
Where will the Ghadar break out? In India!
When? In a few years.
Why? Because the people can no longer bear the oppression and tyranny practised under English rule and are ready to fight and die for freedom. It is the duty of every Indian to make preparations for this rising....[148]

Declaring the paper's name *Ghadar* as a mutiny or revolt, Har Dayal announced: "Our name and work are identical."[149] Of the Ghadar headquarters, he wrote: "This is not an Ashram but a fort from which a cannonade on the English raj will be started. This is not a newspaper, but a cannon, which will spare no tyrant."[150] He had thrown down the gauntlet. In another article from the first issue, Har Dayal exclaimed: "My heroes! O, Lions! O, Brave men! *Hosh sambhalo* (wake up)! How long will you continue to sleep?... Come! Brave men!... I am calling you. Preserve the honour of (your) forefathers. Prove yourself worthy sons of Singhs, Khans and Rajputs... Rise! Gird up your loins. Rise!!"[151]

With such incendiary rhetoric, Ghulam was worried that Har Dayal might be killed or kidnapped by the British or their proxies. It was agreed that Har Dayal needed a bodyguard. The first to volunteer was the ex-sepoy poet Harnam Singh. Early in the morning of 1 November 1913, just after the first issue of *Ghadar* had gone to press, Harnam arrived in San Francisco from Bridal Veil. He approached the gate of the House on the Hill with its pots of flowering plants on its front slope. Knocking on the gate, Harnam waited patiently. After some time, Harnam saw "a handsome young man of about 18 who had not sprouted a beard or moustache so far."[152] It was Kartar Singh Sarabha, who had been nursing Har Dayal to health and productivity. Harnam knew of Kartar by reputation and when he learnt his identity, the pair of Sikhs hugged. He went inside the house and greeted Har Dayal, who was reclined in bed, with the now standard revolutionary cry of *Bande Mataram*.

After introductions, Harnam was led to the lithographic press in Valencia Street. It looked like a cannon. He learnt that a "white American"[153] had been employed at 50 cents an hour to operate the machine and was teaching Kartar how to use it. The teenaged Sikh who did Gurmukhi translations, quickly figured out how to operate the press. Harnam helped out with the printing when he was not required to escort Har Dayal on his trips. Eventually, Harnam found a Sikh to replace the American at half the rate. The Sikh would later end up betraying the cause by turning "approver" or informer, but not before helping to print thousands of *Ghadar* propaganda sheets which were given out free of charge. A Punjab police report described the worldwide circulation of the newspaper:

> The circulation of the Ghadr newspaper rapidly extended and very large numbers were posted weekly to India from San Francisco, Vancouver and other centres. Copies were also sent to Manilla, Japan, Hong Kong, Shanghai, South and East Africa, and, in fact, to every place where Indians were known to be residing.[154]

The papers were recycled and forwarded in a chain:

> Indians to whom copies of the paper were sent were asked not to destroy them, but to send them on to friends in India after reading them in order to help on the good work; and within a few weeks it was found that copies were being received in India from Nairobi, Johannesburg, Singapore, Bangkok, Shanghai, Hong Kong, Tientsin and Moji (Japan).[155]

Each issue contained eight pages with some regular items. Instalments from Savarkar's book *The Indian War of Independence 1857* were printed on one page of each edition. Another regular item was *Angrezi Raj Ka Kacha Chitta* or A Balance Sheet of British Rule which listed Britain's exploitation of Indian resources with brute statistics and numbers to undermine the notion of benevolent rule. To appeal to the oral culture of the illiterate Sikh peasants, poems with stirring refrains were reproduced:

No pundits or mullahs do we need,
No prayers or litanies we need recite
These will only scuttle our boat
Draw the sword; 'tis Time to fight.[156]

The poems aroused strong passions among its readers to instil a spirit of revolt and to prepare for the coming armed overthrow of the British.

The time to draw the sword has come,
the time to wage war has come
the time to begin a revolt has come
Let us jump into battle

Quickly prepare for mutiny,
Destroy every trace of iron rule
Negotiations have ended in smoke
Take up sword and shield in your hands
Fight for the country – *maro firangee ko* (kill the whites)[157]

The *Ghadar*'s masthead identified it as "The Enemy of the English Race". In the first editorial, Har Dayal also made clear that the movement was making friends with England's enemies:

Recently, Von Bernhardi, a German officer, has, after travelling in Ireland published an article which has caused a great sensation throughout the Fatherland. He has shown that were Germany to go to war with England the Irish would side with the Germans in order to secure their independence. Indians also should now prepare for a rising. The tyrannical English are about to be hard-pressed from every side.[158]

The German officer mentioned by Har Dayal was the military strategist General Friedrich von Bernhardi. His book, *Germany and the Next War* had just been published in 1911, two years after the British writer Norman Angell argued that great power conflict was obsolete in *The Great Illusion*. Bernardi had no illusions about globalisation or economic integration. He saw war as inevitable and necessary and even outlined Germany's interest in supporting political Islam against the British Empire:

> England so far, in accordance with the principle of *divide et impera* has attempted to play off the Mohammedan against the Hindu population. But now that a pronounced revolutionary and nationalist tendency shows among the latter, the danger is imminent that pan-Islamism, thoroughly roused, should unite with the revolutionary elements of Bengal. The co-operation of these elements might create a very grave danger, capable of shaking the foundations of England's high position in the world.[159]

Bernhardi was a hardcore realist who advocated a policy of aggression. Although officially retired, he remained active and visited San Francisco in May 1913 to address 300 Germans in a meeting arranged by German Consul Franz von Bopp. He told his audience, "Law is a makeshift; force is the real weapon for strong nations."[160] The German Consul was to become extremely active in reaching out to Irish revolutionaries and Indian nationalists in San Francisco. Hinting at some possible understanding with the Germans, Har Dayal wrote in the second issue of *Ghadar* in mid-November 1913: "The Germans have great sympathy with our movements for liberty, because they and ourselves have a common enemy (the English). In the future, Germany can draw assistance from us and they can render us great assistance also."[161]

This became a running theme in the *Ghadar*, suggesting that in the event of a war, a certain sequence of events could be expected. First, the British would leave India and other colonial possessions to return to the battlefields of Europe. Second, this would be the best opportunity to strike and mutiny. Third, the Germans would supply guns and money to destroy the British. Repeated often enough it took on the appearance of an assurance. But rhetoric is not reality. In reality, the Germans had a different objective and motives. their military attaché in Washington, Captain Franz von Papen, would later reveal: "We did not go so far as to suppose that there was any hope of India achieving her independence through our assistance, but if there was any chance of fomenting local disorders, we felt it might limit the number of Indian troops who could be sent to France and other theatres of war."[162]

For the men of the Ghadar movement, the gap between the expectations they were creating and the gravities of reality would have consequences. On New Year's Eve on 1913, and literally on the eve of the coming World War, the Ghadar Party's Hindi Association of the Pacific Coast held a meeting in Sacramento. Representatives from different branches from Oregon, Washington and other parts of California were in attendance. Delegates from the Philippines and Brazil were seen mingling. Notably, the German Consul in San Francisco Franz von Bopp was invited as a special guest. He was seated on the platform with Har Dayal and other leaders of the Association and the Ghadar party. The men on stage included Kartar Singh. Hanging in the background of the stage were pictures of revolutionary martyrs like Mazzini, William Tell, Lenin, Sun Yat Sen and various heroes of Indian history. For one participant, it felt like "a silent introduction to the lessons of sacrifice."[163]

Har Dayal declared boldly that "Germany was preparing to go to war with England, and that it was time to get ready to go to India for the coming revolution."[164] He read out a passage from Bernhardi's *Germany and the Next War*. Har Dayal claimed that Muslims were now joining the revolution and urged Hindu-Muslim unity. In earlier issues of the *Ghadar*, Har Dayal claimed increased Muslim participation in the movement. In truth, their numbers were small. Nawab Khan was one of the few prominent members of the movement whose name matched his faith. By now, the mentally restless Nawab had already grown disenchanted with Har Dayal. He blamed Har Dayal for breaking a promise to support a young Muslim student on the scholarship scheme started with the Stockton farmer Jowala Singh. Having denounced Har Dayal and Jowala Singh at an earlier meeting, Nawab urged other Muslims to do the same, but won little support.

Publicly, Har Dayal kept up appearances of interfaith unity. For now, he was happy also to advance the German agenda for stoking revolution through a pan-Islamic lens. This would help draw Turkey towards the German cause. Technology was also enlisted. As Har Dayal spoke, slides were flashed on a screen with a "magic lantern" Bioscope slide. One picture featured an Indian Muslim woman in South Africa being punished for supporting the Indian nationalist cause. Har Dayal told his audience that it was their duty to return to the motherland and overthrow the British once they were busy fighting in Europe. A Sikh victory cry was heard in the hall. The young and bright-eyed Kartar Singh began to sing:

Chalo, Chaliey, desh nun yuddha karan,
Eho akhiri bachan, te farman ho gai.
(Come on, let's go, let us go and fight the battle for our freedom;
Why waste time, the final order is issued, let's go.)[165]

The hall chorused in unison. All vowed to march in step for the uprising. But there were also men among them who marched to their own beat. Nawab Khan watched the scene and, as usual, felt strangely divided.

[X]

THE SIKH COLUMBUS

Self-made and self-taught individuals possess re-markably similar traits. With his strong personality and stubborn streak, Gurdit Singh was always meant to achieve something if he put his mind to it. Ghadar revolutionary and later Pulitzer Prize winner Gobind Be-hari Lal compared the Malayan Sikh businessman-activist's venture to that of Christopher Columbus: "a dramatic voyage, under the leadership of the Sikh Columbus, marked a revolutionary change in the mentality of the common people of India, of the Punjabis (in particular)."[166]

His beginnings were humble. Born in 1859 in the village of Sarhali near the Sikh holy city of Amritsar, Gurdit Singh was one of five chil-dren. His family were Majhi or heartland Sikhs of the Punjab. The Pun-jabi language forged out of the Majha heartland dialect featured witty, homespun, rough and ready phrases. The Majhis had a reputation of being fearsome warriors in battle. Their Majha region was the cradle of the powerful Sikh Empire founded by Maharaja Ranjit Singh. After the Sepoy Mutiny of 1857, the British felt it was best to co-opt the war-like group and rebuilt the sepoy army on a base of Majhi manhood. Gurdit's grandfather joined the pioneer batch of the reformed sepoy army. His son Hukum Singh, Gurdit's father, preferred farming. But after the severe drought of 1870 took away his livelihood, Hukum Singh found himself at a loose end.

His fortunes turned when a British colonial adventurer named Captain T C S Speedy arrived one day in Sarhali. A swashbuckling Victorian-era explorer, Captain Speedy had recently resigned as police superintendent at Penang. During his service in the Straits Settlements port city, Speedy had witnessed thousands of Chinese immigrants, mainly Hokkien and Cantonese, arriving from China. The immigrants used Penang as a base to head inland into Larut in Perak where the valuable commodity of tin was found in abundance. In Larut, the aspiring tin-miners were protected by masonic type triads. The Cantonese found protection under the wing of the Ghee Hin while the Hai San looked after the Hokkien.

When open warfare erupted between the clans, the *Menteri Besar* (Chief Minister) of Perak had a problem on his hands. The feuding triads took sides in royal family politics as they squabbled over new found riches. There was havoc as the feuding Chinese secret societies fought for control of Perak's lucrative tin mines. The Malay Chief Minister himself had sided first with the richer Hokkien Hai San clan but later switched allegiance. Now he was losing control of the situation. His own ineffective Malay forces were breaking up and aligning either with the skirmishing Ghee Hin or Hai Sin clans.

It was time to assemble a neutral force and the Chief Minister reached out to Speedy in Penang. A veteran of the 1857 Indian Mutiny, Speedy knew the Punjab and its martial races well. As a former Lieutenant in the 10th Punjabi Regiment of the British Indian army, he could quite easily raise and lead a special force from Punjab to restore order in Perak. Standing nearly 2 metres tall with rugged good looks, Speedy set up base in Lahore. In the land of the five rivers, he looked for men of a certain physical stature like himself, men whose mere presence could send a message of resolve and help set things straight. Moreover, armed with Krupp rifles and the warrior code of the Khalsa (of the pure and observant Sikhs), they could help subdue the riotous Chinese.

Speedy visited rustic villages like Sirhali to recruit men, enticing them with an enlistment bounty and beguiling with his dominating presence and heroic stories. The fittest were persuaded by Speedy to lay down farm tools for a rifle and leave their families to defend an unfamiliar land across the seas. Gurdit Singh's father, Hukum Singh, was among those reeled in and selected by Speedy to join his hand-picked force. With a few Punjabi Muslims and Pathans thrown in for good measure, Speedy's 200-strong force quickly returned to Perak. Led by the colourful and dashing adventurer, they crushed the Chinese clans and re-established control over the area. Under the command of their giant white *sahib*, the men of the Punjab had stamped their mark as guardians and enforcers in the Far East.

After Speedy's unit dispersed following its initial success, several members of the force, including Hukum, later joined a paramilitary unit known as the Perak Armed Police. They were joined by new arrivals with years of previous military experience. The physically imposing presence of the Sikhs, topped by towering turbans and thick beards, helped maintain the peace. Even the unit's Punjabi Muslims donned turbans with beards to match the Sikhs in uniform. Touring Malaya, a lady travel writer described a single Sikh "driving four or five Chinamen in front of him, having knotted their pigtails together for reins."[167] The Perak Armed Police were also described in lyrical prose as "splendid looking men with long moustaches and whiskers"[168] who wore "large blue turbans, scarlet coats, and white trousers" and "to all intents and purposes soldiers, drilled and disciplined as such."[169] The men were:

> devoted to the accumulation of money, and very many of them being betrothed to little girls in India, save nearly all their pay in order to buy land and settle there. When off duty they wear turbans and robes nearly as white as snow, and look both classical and colossal. They get on admirably with the Malays, but look down on the Chinese, who are much afraid of them.[170]

As one of these "classical and colossal" men, Gurdit's father, Hukam Singh, spent several years in the Perak police saving up his money, making rare trips back to see his family. In the Punjab, Gurdit was proving to be a headstrong boy. At six, he ran away from his village school in the *gurdwara* after arguing with his *giani*. The priest was the only man in the village who offered lessons in basic literacy. At 11, Gurdit felt ashamed that he could not write a letter to his father in Malaya. Determined to find a way on his own, he found an alphabet primer and taught himself how to read and write.

Gurdit toiled as a farmer until he was 18. Then, inspired by his father and his comrades, he decided to join the British Indian army. However, Gurdit failed his physical at the regimental recruiting station in Ambala, the recruiting officer finding him too slightly built. In the following years, Hukam concluded that his sons would have a better life in Malaya. His eldest son, Pahlu, had agreed to join him in Perak. Gurdit was by then 25 years old and married, but with little formal education or experience. His first wife was barren. He too had little to lose. He took a second wife who travelled East with him to join his father and elder brother.

In the Malay States, Sikhs who failed the grade as policemen and soldiers sought out jobs as bullock-cart drivers, watchmen, money-lenders or tin- or iron-ore workers. Gurdit, who lacked the brawn to don a uniform, or desire to do menial work, had the brain of an entrepreneur. He threw himself into a variety of commercial interests. Picking up Malay and Hokkien Chinese and learning Malayan business practices, he worked with a Chinese pork dealer and learnt how to import cattle from India. He started a dairy to supply milk to the Malay States Guides, formed out of the Perak Armed Police. He also sourced labour from India for the Malayan railway, bought rubber plantations and made real-estate deals.

Gurdit Singh

Gurdit became a regular visitor to the law courts of the Straits Settlements of Penang and Singapore. With his many business interests, he learnt how to litigate in civil cases to protect his enterprises. After his brother Pahlu was charged in a murder case, Gurdit used his business litigation skills to defend him. The case went all the way to the Privy Council, which decided in his brother's favour. Thrifty, cunning, entrepreneurial and hard-working, Gurdit was making good money and soon became an influential member of the Malayan Sikh community. He roved between Kuala Lumpur, Singapore, Taiping in Perak, Serendah in Selangor and the Punjab. He knew a number of British officials and could be counted on to give fellow Sikh businessmen advice as long as they were not in direct competition with his own trade. He became known by the title, "Kapten de Bengal" – as a leading businessman from the Indian community.

In Singapore, "Kapten de Bengal" would have been quite comfortable walking into Veer Singh's popular tandoor restaurant in Anson Road, or striding into the *gurdwara* in Queen Street. He would have been a familiar sight in the homes of fellow Punjabis in Serendah, Selangor, or in the port of Penang. In Perak, he would not been out of place in the Malay States Guides' *gurdwara* in Taiping. In the nearby Ipoh *gurdwara* he could listen to preachers like the temple's *granthi* (custodian of the holy book) Tara Singh, who had been converted to revolutionary thought by a roving Sikh preacher named Bhagwan Singh Jakh.

Bhagwan hailed from Viring, near Gurdit's own home village, a tiny hamlet of 150 souls known for its primary school, liquor store and little else. A fiery orator, Bhagwan descended from a line of Hindu Brahmin priests. He was the only one of nine siblings to live into adulthood. An exponent of traditional *pehlwani* wrestling, Bhagwan had completed a three-year programme in Sikh devotional hymns in just one year. A member of the 1907 Pagri Sambhal Jatt Movement led by Ajit Singh, Bhagwan was brilliant but opinionated, and more political than religious. The 29-year-old had no problem shaving and cutting his hair to evade detection by British secret agents. He spent a productive few months in Perak spreading views considered highly seditious by the British. In a personal letter written many years later, Bhagwan confessed his part in stirring up sleepy Ipoh and taking the credit for starting disaffection among the Malay States Guides:

> I carried on the best I could the message of revolutionary India to Malay Straits, Singapore... and spent nearly two months in Malay Straits, particularly in Ipoh where our famed regiment Malay Straits Guides was then stationed....[171] With a little effort I converted Sant

Tara Singh Granthi and through him many soldiers including several *subhadars*. They were so inflamed by what little imparted to them, of what little I knew at the time of India's pathos, her tragedy and her state of slumber, of the humiliating indifference of her people to their economic, social, cultural and intellectual status under foreign imperialism.[172]

Bhagwan ignited a chain of thoughts in the men that he could barely control – relevant when understanding the mindset that could lead to mutiny:

How six-footers with a yard-long chest, the majesty of manhood, stood erect and at attention to an emaciated little Englishman, saluting him with such gusto – it was too corroding to the self-respect of our own manliness. They became powder kegs ready to explode. Discovering the danger of any immediate action, knowing the natural Sikh temperament, I realised the prematureness of the situation and thought it best to leave this aspect of the "sleeping giants" alone a while longer, until the masses were readier.[173]

Bhagwan, with the orator's gift and knowledge of the scriptures, impressed the mostly illiterate Sikhs. Converging from different parts of the state to worship at the *gurdwara* on Sundays, the Sikhs exchanged gossip and employment opportunities and heard the views of men passing through. Over *langgar* (free kitchen) meals they would have the opportunity to press Bhagwan Singh further to expound his views. By 1910, Bhagwan Singh had set his sights on North America. Stopping over in Hong Kong, a key transit point for Punjabi migrants to North America, he preached in its recently opened *gurdwara*. Impressing the temple management, he was offered a job as *granthi* in Hong Kong.

Gurdit in the meantime earned his keep as a businessman while developing a social conscience. Preachers like Tara Singh and Bhagwan Singh shaped his thinking and widened the businessman's outlook. Beyond his everyday business transactions, he was introduced to new ideas of freedom and what the secret agents of empire would consider seditious thinking. Visiting an English planter's rubber estate in Malaya, Gurdit investigated the living quarters of the rubber-tappers, men from Madras (Chennai) in South India. He was shocked to discover that the accommodation was worse than that of the planter's horses. Confronting the colonial planter, Gurdit asked why the beasts rested in clean stables while the Indians lived in cramped squalor. Unfazed, the planter offered a matter-of-fact explanation:

Bhagwan Singh Jakh

a horse would bring him Rs 1500 whereas a coolie not more than Rs 40 or Rs 50. I also learnt on enquiry that the horse cost him Rs 4 per day for its fodder and upkeep while a coolie was made to live and keep fit on one anna and six pais a day. So, one horse cost as much as 42 human beings. This was my first-hand knowledge of the European estimate of the value of labour of an Indian as compared with that of a lower animal.[174]

But Gurdit soon learned that Indians were complicit in the prevailing system of slavery. In Penang, he saw what he called the "traffic in Indian blood" as newly arrived South Indian coolies were locked in cells. The buyers and sellers of the coolies and the coolies themselves were all Madrasis. Posing as a buyer, Gurdit entered the cells and spoke to the coolies. He discovered that the Tamil brokers had licenses from the British government. They had plied the coolies with tempting but false promises and brought them over as "human chattels." This caused Gurdit to reflect on the broader situation of Indians:

> The Indians had to go to the British Dominions as coolies in any number to sow for others to reap. But they had no claim to be treated as human beings and when their multiplication led to their domicile in those places they came to be felt as regular thorns on their sides. The most ugly manifestations of this feeling have proved the utter hollowness of the equality-cult of the Western democracies. Colour-prejudice is almost a disease with them.[175]

In 1913, as his ideas on racial equality and the hypocrisy of the British Empire took shape, Gurdit was already twice widowed. He had a six-year-old son named Balwant and a web of business interests to mind. In December, Gurdit set off on a trip that would change his life forever. His business partner Mool Singh had cheated Gurdit and fled to Hong Kong with $1,200. This was not a small sum in those days, and Gurdit was not going to let it go. With little Balwant in tow, Gurdit went after Mool and his money.

Arriving in Hong Kong, Gurdit headed for the Central Sikh Temple in which, through his contacts and influence, he set up an office. The temple was a waiting-room, community centre, place of refuge, free kitchen, hostel, place of worship and revolutionary school for Sikhs biding their time as they waited to make their way across the Pacific. Gurdit learnt from these stranded Sikhs some startling facts which he took to heart. His head interpreted the same facts as a possible business opportunity.

By 1908, Canada had passed two regulations known as "orders-in-council". Mindful about not openly excluding subjects of the British Empire in India, the orders established that, apart from existing residents, no Indian immigrants would be allowed to land unless they fulfilled two conditions. First, they would have to arrive after an unbroken voyage from an Indian port. Second, they had to carry at least $200. This was a sneaky dressing up of a racist immigration restriction. No steamship company had a direct route from India to Canada. The minimum financial requirement of $200 was also prohibitive – the sum could buy a good, three-to-four course meal every day for an entire year in a good restaurant in Vancouver. These restrictions had put the Hong Kong Sikhs in limbo, some for as long as two years, even as new arrivals added to their numbers.

In the Hong Kong *gurdwara*, the fiery *granthi* Bhagwan Singh was accused of fomenting sedition with revolutionary sermons to the huddled Sikh masses. Copies of the *Ghadar* newspaper were already circulating in Hong Kong. Bhagwan had support from the temple committee, but the *gurdwara* President Lal Singh faithfully served the British Hong Kong Police. Lal spied on Bhagwan, leading to his arrests in 1911 and the year later. Forced out of Hong Kong six months before Gurdit's arrival, Bhagwan was given a rousing send-off by his supporters. He slipped into Vancouver on the SS *Empress of Russia*. Assuming a false identity, he talked his way past the ever-vigilant inspector Hopkinson.

Bhagwan wasted no time starting his fiery preaching in the Vancouver *gurdwara*. He exhorted the Sikhs to greet each other with the nationalist slogan of *Bande Mataram* instead of the traditional Sikh greeting of *Sat Sri Akal* (True is the name of God). A Hopkinson informant named Bela Singh who had travelled on the SS *Empress of Russia* with Bhagwan revealed his real identity to the secret policeman. Playing his usual game, Hopkinson tried to recruit Bhagwan as a spy. When he failed, he had Bhagwan arrested and deported from Vancouver. Hussain Rahim of the India Independence League and his Sikh supporters did their best to challenge the deportation order, but Hopkinson won the round. Bhagwan was frog-marched back to the steamer he had arrived in just three months earlier. Roughed up and pushed up the gangway, the wrestler-preacher bit a policeman's hand and took a piece off another's ear. Beaten into submission, he was trussed up, loaded on board and locked in a cabin.

The congregation in Hong Kong leant of Bhagwan's deportation through the fifth issue of the *Ghadar* newspaper. The issue identified the informers who had betrayed Bhagwan, declaring that their lives were forfeit. An excitable Munsha Singh Dukhi, nick-named Abdullah for briefly converting to Islam, contributed an enraged poem about Bhagwan's deportation entitled '*Zulum! Zulum! Gore Shahi Zulum!*' (Tyranny! Tyranny!

White Man's Tyranny!). In December 1913, Hussain Rahim presided at a special assembly in the Vancouver *gurdwara* and asked for a volunteer to do away with the informers. Munsha read out his poem, asserting that a nation that let its traitors live would not survive.

The following month, Gurdit found himself standing before Bhagwan's restless congregation in the Hong Kong *gurdwara*. The Sikhs were there to mark the birthday of the faith's tenth and last Guru, Gobind Singh, who had shaped the Sikhs' warrior ethos. Addressing the gathering, Gurdit recalled his experience during a recent trip to India. He described his recent pilgrimage to Hazur Sahib, the holy place where Guru Gobind Singh was mortally wounded. In Hyderabad, enroute to the holy site, a group of men from the warrior-race of Marathas had mocked Gurdit. They told him scornfully that the Sikhs had sold the Indians out to the British during the 1857 Mutiny. Taken aback, Gurdit explained that it was not the Sikhs as a race but individual princes and rulers who assisted the British but he was shooed away. Reflecting on his experience, it dawned on him that Sikhs were invariably seen as the "sword-arm" of British India. Their martial identity was bound up with loyalty to the British Raj.

As he confronted difficult questions about his own Sikh and national identity, Gurdit felt he had to do something to help set things right. He had to prove that men of his race and faith were the right kind of patriots. Gurdit told the congregation that "the British government does not take us to be men, so we have to become men first before we can do something."[176] A few men from the congregation approached Gurdit after his speech. They wanted his help to migrate to Canada. Their charismatic former preacher Bhagwan Singh had been thrown out of Vancouver. But a recent arrival from Vancouver named Behari Varma was making the rounds in Hong Kong sharing his plans to charter a steamship. The young Hindu's idea was to sail with a boat-load of migrants to Canada and mount a challenge of its racist and exclusionary immigration laws. Despite impressing the Sikhs with his wide range of contacts in Canada, Behari Varma seemed young and uncertain about how to do business in Hong Kong and the Far East. The stranded Sikhs of Hong Kong saw the seasoned Gurdit as the man of the moment. They believed they had found the man who could transform their sense of frustration into direction and purpose. Affected by their plight and earnest entreaties, Gurdit made a solemn promise to help them. He was prepared to hire a ship to undertake the risky journey to Canada.

Returning to Singapore by February 1914, Gurdit immediately got in touch with a Chinese friend who was an assistant manager in the Straits Steamship Company. He was introduced to a shipping agent who showed him two ageing vessels in the dockyard. Although relatively cheap hires, both were barely fit to cross the Pacific. Despite Gurdit's repeated efforts, he had little luck in finding a vessel that was cheap, burned coal economically and ocean-worthy. Returning to Hong Kong, he continued his search among shipping companies in the British territory. It was Gurdit's resourceful assistant, Daljit Singh, who found a British firm prepared to lease a ship for HK$9,000. But when the firm backed out at the last moment, Gurdit suspected the hand of the imperial secret police. The barriers thrown in his way suggested a pattern.

Gurdit turned finally to a German shipping agent in Hong Kong who offered him a 24-year-old, Japanese-owned steamship. Built in Glasgow and measuring 100 by 12.5 metres (329 by 41 feet), the steamer was registered as the SS *Komagata Maru*. Although it had first-class cabins for sixteen passengers, it was built for steerage, accommodating 600 second-class passengers on its four open-plan compartments on the spar deck. The ship did not have a system for desalinating sea-water, but it had electrical lighting and lavatories with running water. It would cost HK$11,000 to hire, including its Japanese Captain Yamamoto and 45-member Japanese crew. There was also no wireless telegraphy but it would just have to do.

Gurdit was prepared to put in HK$150,000 into the venture. It could be considered sunk costs as the start of his own shipping line. Business and revolutionary philanthropy would be combined in what he called a "test voyage". It was indeed a trial of strength and a trial of Canadian immigration law. As Gurdit put it:

> The proposed voyage would be a test of the sincerity of the
> Government of Canada in framing the rules. If we complied with
> all the provisions of the law regulating the immigration of foreigners
> into Canada, it was up to the government to permit us to land and
> prove itself to be just and fair. My scheme was to arrange for four
> ships, two to ply in the Canada Calcutta line and two in the Bombay
> Brazil line.[177]

On 24 March 1914, he signed a charter for the ship under the auspices of the Guru Nanak Steamship Company which he had formed care of the *gurdwara* office. His assistant Daljit priced tickets at HK$240. This was more than double the price of the third-class fare on a Canadian Pacific steamer from Hong Kong to Vancouver. But this was the price of the risk he assumed on behalf of Indian passengers. Excitement built as the Sikhs in limbo learnt that there was finally an escape to America.

Lal Singh, the vigilant President of the Hong Kong *gurdwara*, soon got wind of this scheme. The loyal policeman of the British Raj had already done away with the troublesome preacher Bhagwan Singh. Now was the time to get rid of Gurdit who had become another problem right under his nose in the *gurdwara*. The day after Gurdit signed the ship charter, the British Hong Kong police raided his office in the *gurdwara*, arrested him and seized his papers. Fortunately for Gurdit, the magistrate decided that the police had no case and ordered his release. But the police attention had done the work perhaps intended all along by scaring away many passengers.

A week later, Daljit was still collecting passengers with no clear indication if the ship would be allowed to sail. Gurdit was not disheartened and continued to press on. He was conferring with Daljit and some of his close associates when he heard his name being called out. He turned and saw a familiar Englishman sitting in a rickshaw. It was Claude Severn, former District Magistrate in Selangor who had developed respect for Gurdit from his time in Malaya. He was now Colonial Secretary in Hong Kong, and Acting Governor.

Recognising Severn, who would have been fully aware of his arrest and release, Gurdit quipped: "I did not know you were holding such a big position now, otherwise I would have come to see you earlier."[178] They made small talk on the street for about 15 minutes before Severn invited Gurdit to meet him in his office the next day. Gurdit kept the appointment bearing gifts worth about $500. This earned him a gentle rebuke by Severn: "You are my friend and you are perfectly aware that I never accept nor have I any desire for any present; how dare you bring these presents to my presence?"[179]

Chastened, Gurdit replied that he had spent time in India recently and had become used to the practice of gift-giving. Severn was savvy enough to maintain a warm and friendly demeanour as Gurdit made his apologies. The Oxford-educated Englishman and the self-taught Sikh engaged in conversation in Malay for the next hour and a half in the Cantonese-speaking city. Gurdit asked him point-blank why the ship could not sail for Vancouver. Seven replied that he had asked the Canadian government in Ottawa if they had any view on the ship sailing. They had not replied after nearly a week. Severn prolonged the conversation, creating the opportunity to gain intelligence on Gurdit's scheme. Finally, he gave the good news: "You are… at liberty to embark, but can you kindly let me know your object in making this voyage to Canada?"[180]

Gurdit gave a long, winding and conflicted reply. He began by saying that his object was to promote the material well being of his country as "the enslaved people of India are in the throes of a fierce economic, and political struggle."[181] But he concluded with the claim that his "object is purely commercial and economic and is in no way political."[182] Severn then asked Gurdit what he would do if he was not allowed to land in Vancouver. Gurdit's answer was that the ship would proceed to Brazil. According to Gurdit, Severn promised to write to the Canadian and Indian governments to allow him to land. He assured Gurdit that it was the latter's duty to help.

Severn was not necessarily being altruistic. In true bureaucratic fashion, he may have just decided to kick the ball down to the next bureaucrat. Shiosaki Yokichi, owner and engineer of the *Komagata Maru*, believed that the Sikh police and Indian sepoys in Hong Kong were a key factor. The Hong Kong colonial government did not want a riot or mutiny on their hands in Hong Kong. At the same time, Severn took the precaution of writing to Gurdit's lawyers. As a British official he had to work within the bounds of the law. He was also familiar with Gurdit's litigious nature and self-amassed legal skills. He stated clearly that permission to leave Hong Kong did not mean permission to land in Canada. But Gurdit had heard what he wanted to hear.

With leave to sail, Gurdit went straight to the *gurdwara* to share the good news. Prayers were said and the *Komagata Maru* was renamed the *Guru Nanak Jahaz* (Guru Nanak's ship) after the first Guru of Sikhism although the ship would remain better known by its original name. They would set sail the very next day on 4 April 1914. But they first had to welcome on board the ship's most important passenger. The Sikh holy book, the Guru Granth Sahib, is accorded the same respect as the ten human Gurus of the Sikh faith. The last Guru, Gobind Singh, declared that after him the holy book would be the eternal Guru to guide the Sikhs. In a *gurdwara*, the book is put to its own bed in a room every night. No Sikh turns his or her back on the book. The granthi who reads from it waves a *chauri* – a yak-tailed whisk – over it to keep it cool like a living dignitary. Each morning, it is carried to its own place on an elaborate platform called the *Manji Sahib* to avoid placing it on the defiled ground.

Under the bemused eyes of the Japanese crew, Gurdit had transformed the steamer's 186-sq-m (2000-sq-ft) forecastle into a prayer area or *diwan* hall. In what was the first floating *gurdwara* in world history, Gurdit even built a *Manji Sahib* with a richly draped canopy for the holy book. Its first passengers – 175 Sikhs, Muslims and Hindu – were led to believe by Gurdit that they had rights equal to other British subjects in its white-ruled Dominions. That they would be treated equally, and that they had the right to go where they chose in the Empire. No such laws actually protected them. Instead, as they sailed into the inky night and towards legally uncharted waters, all they truly had were their sacred hymns and poems to hold them together.

A day after the *Komagata Maru* set sail, the Colonial Secretary of Hong

Kong, Claude Severn, received a reply to the queries he had sent to the Canadian government. Ottawa had decided to prohibit entry by the *Komagata Maru* as it did not fulfil the conditions of its orders-in-council. But by then, it was too late. The ship was already pulling into Shanghai, its first stopover.

Anchored in the Huangpu River, the steamer waited while Gurdit Singh collected more fares from new passengers. He had to pay the ship owners another instalment to embark on the next part of its journey. Copies of the revolutionary *Ghadar* newspaper were brought on board. Daljit Singh assured the passengers that they would be allowed to disembark at Vancouver. Getting wind of the purpose of its journey, an American journalist with Shanghai's *China Press* climbed the gangway to the ship. He found Gurdit Singh napping and woke him up for an interview. Daljit served as translator. The "gray whiskered, kindly eyed patriarch" was apparently happy to talk to him through a "voluble interpreter."[183] Gurdit told him: "If we are admitted, we will know that the Canadian government is just. If we are deported we will sue the government and if we cannot obtain redress we will go back and take up the matter with the Indian Government." The reporter asked the obvious question: "And what then?"[184]

"I cannot answer,"[185] replied Gurdit as his companions clustered around him broke into laughter, some more nervous than others. They were making things up on the fly – characteristic of the Ghadar movement, now on a wave and a prayer.

[XI]

CHANGING GUARD
IN SINGAPORE

As the *Komagata Maru* with its Indian immigrants prepared to sail to Canada, another ship filled with Indian soldiers had departed Calcutta for Singapore. The latter movement of troops was a mere part of the massive management of logistics and manpower involved in the running of the British Empire. It was a strain on the resources of the British Isles. Well before the outbreak of war, the British lacked military labour for its far-flung colonies. There were far too many pieces of pink on the world map, coloured by British cartographers to magnify their island-nation's power. Recruitment in British India offered the War Office a way out. With a population five times bigger than Britain's, India provided the military muscle for its imperial garrisons overseas.

Sepoy battalions from India were regularly rotated to settlements across the Empire by troop-ships, roads and railways. The chain movements were done on a strict timetable. In March 1914, with marching orders in hand, the officers of the 5th Light Infantry made preparations to leave the Nowgong depot in Central India. They were rostered to replace the 3rd Brahmans infantry regiment who would soon complete a three-year posting in Singapore. The transfer was to be done before end of the "trooping season" in April, while weather in India and conditions on the sea-routes were still tolerable.

The 5th's move to the capital of the Straits Settlements would begin with a thousand-kilometre overland journey on 24 March. Wearing khaki uniforms and a distinctive, canary-yellow fringe facing on their *pagri* (turban) wrapped around cone-shaped *kulla* hats, the sepoys travelled east by train from Nowgong military cantonment to the port city of Calcutta. Cantonments in India were spread far and wide with Nowgong considered a favourable posting, better than the depots in Dinapore or Calcutta. The hardy sepoys were used to packing up and being on the move. But this was the first overseas deployment for the men filing into the Royal Indian Mail Steamer (RIMS) *Dufferin*.

The 5th belonged to the Jhansi Brigade commanded by Major-General C V F Townshend. In their inspection report two months before their departure, Townshend found the regiment "smart" in turn-out, "quite satisfactory" in drill and manoeuvres and "fit for service."[186] The regiment had been recruited from the region around Delhi and from districts of Eastern Punjab like Rohtak, Gurgaon, Karnal and Hissar in today's Haryana province. The battalion's common language was Hindustani and, to the untrained eye, these soldiers looked to be of one class, an all-Muslim regiment from the Eastern Punjab. In reality, the 5th was largely composed of two "classes", the Ranghars and the Pathans. In a confidential memorandum, the 5th's former Commanding Officer in 1902 shed light on his recruitment principles:

> The main objection to a class regiment being that it is difficult to ascertain what is going on under the surface, I decided on Rajputs (Ranghars) and Pathans… these classes being, as I ascertained on various recruiting and other visits to villages in the district, on somewhat antagonistic terms... I found no difficulty, during the 7 years I commanded it, in finding out what was going on.[187]

By raising class-based units with separate identities, the British played the races off each another. These methods were inspired by the Divide and Rule tactics employed after the 1857 Mutiny. The Pushtun, originally from the border zone with Afghanistan, called themselves Hindustani Pushtun. The Ranghars were Muslims of Rajput descent, proud warriors of Rajasthan. An Indian Army handbook described the Ranghars thus: "they are a turbulent body of men and do not bear the best of characters in their districts."[188] The handbook's authors complained that they had been over-recruited and now "good recruits up to infantry standard are not so easy to be procured". In contrast, it reported that the Pathans of Rohtak district were of "good quality and fair physique"[189] and that the 5th had a "very good connection in the district."[190] The 5th's British officers found the Ranghars to be more soldierly and "fine fighting stock".[191] The handbook's authors were eerily prescient about the two groups.

The sepoys of the 5th knew their regiment as *Jansen-ki-Paltan* or Johnson's Band of Brothers, named after one of the regiment's early commanders. A personal relationship between commander and sepoy was supposed to hold together the bonds of loyalty. The Colonel-sahib's birthday was considered more important than the King's birthday. According to imperial belief, the officer-*sahib* was *mam-bap* or mother-and-father combined, doling out both care and discipline to his sepoy. Properly fed, clothed, led, armed and disciplined, the sepoys would remain loyal and perform for their officer-sahib. But by 1914, Captain Jeremiah Johnson of *Jansen-ki-Palten* fame was long-gone. Lieutenant-Colonel Edward Victor Martin was the 5th's newly minted Commanding Officer.

Martin had joined the 5th at the end of 1911 as a Major and its second-in-command. He began his military career as a young cavalry officer back in 1887, but the 51-year old had never seen active service. And Martin's previous commander did not think much of him. His damning assessment was: "Lt Col Martin, who was transferred from the 17th Infantry about a year before he succeeded to the command of the 5th is from my small knowledge of him a sleepy, easy-going officer."[192] According to the doctrine of leadership in the Indian Army, the British officer-sahib had to project a balance of qualities in order to effectively lead his sepoys. In the words of a military historian explaining the supposed differences between the British sahib and sepoy of Indian stock: "Indians who were intelligent and educated were defined as cowards, whilst those defined as brave were uneducated and backward… (therefore)… only British gentlemen combined both the intelligence and courage necessary for a man to become an officer."[193]

Martin was disliked by some of his fellow British officers. They believed he was too soft and that the sepoys needed a harder crack of the whip. He had been posted away from the 5th for a few months because of an adverse report and his Battalion Commanding Officer's doubts about his fitness to command. However, his Brigade Commander, General C V F Townshend, backed Martin, passed him during a 2-month probation he personally supervised and had him posted back to assume duties as the 5th's Commanding Officer. Townshend wrote of Martin in his confidential report in early 1914: "He was severely tested in command of a mixed brigade in presence of Army and Divisional Commanders. A hard working, energetic, reliable officer; fit for promotion and in all respects fit to command a battalion."[194] Cerebral and courageous and popular with his men, Townshend was also known to be narcissistic and stubborn. He would later be responsible for one of the British Indian Army's worst debacles during the First World War, when thousands of sepoys were killed by the Ottoman Turkish Army at the siege of Kut after Townshend underestimated his enemy's strength and his own weakness.

The troop-ship carrying the 5th set sail on 30 March. Accompanied on the journey eastwards by his wife and daughter, Martin and his officer-sahibs were bringing out this batch of sepoys across the Indian Ocean for the first time. Among the British officers on deck were the 5th's second-in-command, Major C S Stooks, his wife, and Stooks' brother-in-law, the battalion adjutant Lieutenant Wyndham G Strover. Accompanied by his wife and toddler, Strover was considered "active" and "energetic" with "lots of tact and and a particularly nice disposition" as well as "a very good Adjutant"[195] by his former Commanding Officer.

The other officers on board included the Australian Captain Lionel Plomer Ball, "a lithe, active officer" considered "not intellectual but a good regimental officer", Captain William Draper Hall, "popular with his brother officers" and "an active intelligent officer" who was "good at games and fond of sport", and Captain Perceval Boyce, "well-educated and intelligent" but who was "over-wrought, nervous and depressed" when over-worked. With them was the young Lieutenant Harold Seymour Elliott who was "particularly well mannered" and believed to have "the makings of an excellent officer."[196] The next newest officer was the Medical Officer, Lieutenant R V Morrison, who joined the battalion just two days prior to their departure from Nowgong.

A good number of sepoys had declined to make the trip and had quit or asked to remain in the regimental depot in India. The sepoys would serve out a three- or four-year posting in the new station. They had to adapt to unfamiliar surroundings, a different diet and uncertainty about their next stop. Ominously, the regiment had brought along its baggage, physical and otherwise, including its petty jealousies, rivalries and vendettas. Despite his predecessor's high opinion of Strover, Martin considered his 26-year-old adjutant a dangerously well-connected social climber. The youngest son of a Colonel who had been the Commissioner of Lower Burma, Strover was indeed ambitious. He had a tense relationship with Colonel Martin. The older man suspected that his subordinate was using his connections to get his brother-in-law, Major Stooks, to assume command of the 5th.

As the ship sailed, the men dispersed to their tasks or the holds. Many would have suffered sea-sickness as the ship pitched. A thin organisational veneer masked the barracks politics and battalion intrigues already festering under the surface. All told, Martin commanded a dozen British King's Commissioned Officers, 16 Indian Viceroy Commissioned officers (VCO) and 809 non-commissioned officers and sepoys. In terms of formation, everything was nicely and neatly set out with administrative precision. The 5th was cleanly split down the middle between the Ranghar right wing and a Pathan left-wing of four companies each.

However, there was a more troubling sort of division in the ranks of the Indian VCOs, a subordinate type of commissioned officer promoted from the ranks of the Non-Commissioned Officers. The scheme gave the more senior and capable sepoys a route of advancement. However, the VCOs had no authority over white British soldiers with the most junior

Adjutant W G Strover
with Indian Orderly Officers, 1922.

white private not required to salute them. A newly commissioned British 2nd Lieutenant out-ranked the Subedar-Major, the most senior rank, followed by the mid-level Subedar and finally the entry-level VCO known as a Jemadar. The key native appointment of Subedar-Major was carefully rotated between the Ranghars and Pathans.

The 5th's current Subedar-Major was a Ranghar from Gurgaon named Khan Mohammed Khan. The seasoned and heavy-set Subedar-Major was Lieutenant-Colonel Martin's right-hand man in managing the sepoys. He performed the role of Native Battalion Adjutant and Regimental Sergeant-Major, advising on their welfare, customs, religion, discipline and recruitment. To be effective, the Subedar-Major had to command the full respect of all the VCOs and the personnel of the battalion's Ranghar right-wing and Pathan left-wing. While the Pathans were generally under control, he could barely keep his own Ranghar officers together. The men sailing on the *Dufferin* knew all about the the trouble among the Ranghar VCOs carried over from their previous depots in Dinapore and Calcutta.

One clique of VCOs on-board was led by Subedar-Major Khan Mohammed Khan and his friend the A Company Commander Subedar Wahid Ali Khan, a big man with a large round face and a red henna-dyed beard. Forming the other clique was the fateful trio of the portly B Company Commander Subedar Dunde Khan from Gurgaon, the wiry D Company Deputy Commander Jemadar Chiste Khan from Rohtak and the fit and active B Company Deputy Commander Jemadar Abdul Ali Khan of the battalion scouts. Bad blood between the Subedar-Major Khan Mohammed Khan and Dunde ran deep. In a depot in India, the Subedar-Major had reported Dunde to Martin's predecessor for three separate breaches: The loss of a rifle bolt, missing jewellery and a mishap on the rifle range. Dunde was almost sacked from the 5th. A few months before their departure on the *Dufferin*, big, red bearded Wahid Ali Khan had a bad quarrel with the sharp-faced Chiste. These differences were not easily forgotten even as the troop-ship steamed towards the lights of Singapore in the early morning hours of April 5.

The *Dufferin* approached Singapore from the west via the narrow channel of the Malacca Straits, navigating between the Malay Peninsula on the port side and Sumatra on the starboard side. Lines of fishing stakes stretched out to the sea from Malay coastal villages nestled among coconut palms. Battened-sail Chinese junks of various shapes and sizes floated by among Malay *prahu*s with their double hulls and triangular sails. After a 6-day voyage across the Indian Ocean, the island of Singapore must have emerged like a dreamland to many of the sea-sick sepoys. Daubed in various shades of peaceful green and covered with low, undulating hills above plantations and mangrove-lined coast, the island looked picturesque and serene.

Passing the Sultan Shoal lighthouse, the *Dufferin* slowed its engines and prepared to cut power like other steam-ships making the final harbour approach. A harbour pilot's launch would guide the troopship through the muddy shallows, offering the sepoys a better view of the posts they would help to guard in the months ahead. On the left, Pasir Panjang Fort and the Labrador Battery were visible to those on ship-deck. Across and rising up on the right was the island of Blakang Mati ("Behind Death" in Malay) with Mount Siloso and other strongly fortified hills manned by the Royal Garrison Artillery. Known much later as Sentosa ("Tranquility" in Malay), Blakang Mati provided a natural breakwater for the mainland's docks and wharves.

Next to Blakang Mati, a smaller island name Brani (meaning "Brave" in Malay) came into view. Pulau Brani was the base of the Royal Engineers, with a fort and an Ordnance Depot. Tall, industrial chimney stacks peered out of the island's tin-smelting plant. Brani was also the original home of sea gypsies, the *orang laut*. Their descendants lived in a small village, Telok Saga, built on piles over the sea. Telok Saga's boys and men made a living by rowing out in their tiny canoes to dive for coins flung out by passengers on passing steam-ships.

The *Dufferin*'s crew and passengers could now see the city of Singapore. It curved before their vision in a crescent for over 5 kilometres before ending in a faint smudge of palm groves. The waterfront displayed an impressive skyline formed by Government buildings, shipping offices, shops, banks and hostels that matched the diversity of vessels that dotted Singapore's busy waters. Prominent landmarks were the lighthouse above the green slopes of Fort Canning, the clock-tower of the Victoria Memorial Hall and the spire of St Andrew's Cathedral rising from a spread of foliage. Government House sat in its isolated splendour on a verdant hill.

The coin divers from Telok Saga would ply their trade near the dock. Like many other travellers approaching the harbour, the men of the 5th may have seen the famous Wak Melan. Sitting in his canoe with a dark *cheerot* between his lips and a paddle in hand, he would call out for coins. If a coin was thrown from the deck of the *Dufferin*, he would spot it in a flash. As it touched the water and sank, he would reverse his *cheerot* to keep the lit end in his mouth and dive into the murky depths. As he resurfaced with the coin in hand, he magically reversed the cheerot and signalled his success with a puff of smoke. It was a good show put on by Wak Melan for Singapore's new arrivals till the day he was ripped in half by a shark twenty years later.

As the 7,500-tonne *Dufferin* drew alongside the P&O Wharf, a band played as part of the military reception. Teams of Chinese harbour coolies dashed to opposite sides of the vessel to snatch up its hawsers and secure them to the bollards on the quay. With gang-planks secured, the battalion – including its usual complement of 100 "followers", the non-combatant servants and support staff for the officers and sepoys – could proceed to disembark. Some of the "followers" were sent ahead to spruce up Alexandra Barracks, which the 5th Light Infantry would take over from the 3rd Brahmans.

The men of the 3rd Brahmans were not sorry to leave. They had had their own share of problems in Singapore. The barracks were set in a hilly area, just off the midpoint of Alexandra Road. Surrounding the barracks was thick jungle with snakes, rats and lots of insects. The milk supplied to their barracks from a licensed supplier was found to be adulterated. And good food in Singapore was not cheap. The 3rd Brahmans also had a few trouble makers. One of their sepoys, Amanat Ali, was known as the "Bad Man of the Brahmans" locally.[197] Teaching himself English, he had forged a fellow sepoy's signature to withdraw his life savings from the local bank. He was later arrested after spending time in the home of a dancing girl. As she took a post-coital bath, he had robbed her of all her money and jewellery.

As the 3rd Brahmans packed up, the Singapore courts were still taking evidence for a brutal murder of one of its members. Sepoy Rampadareth Massil, who was over 183 cm (6 ft) tall and powerfully built, was found lifeless on a pathway between the barracks and a nearby Malay village. His skull and right arm were broken, with three deep gashes on the right side of his face from a parang. Massil was last seen alive by a fellow sepoy near a hut with a young Javanese woman while her husband was out working at a nearby rubber factory. It appeared to be a crime of passion; the enraged husband had been accused of ambushing Massil with several accomplices.

At 4 pm the day after the arrival of the 5th, the 3rd Brahmans marched out of Alexandra Barracks. They were led by the band of the 5th. It was a one-hour march from the Barracks to the P&O Wharf where they would board the *Dufferin* for Calcutta via Rangoon. Almost as soon as they left the Barracks, the heavens opened up and poured torrential rain on the parade. However, according to an observer, the "men's spirits were by no means damped by the drenching they received and they responded with ringing cheers to the salutations of the many friends who saw them off."[198] They appeared relieved to be quitting Singapore and handing over their duties to the men of the 5th.

As the Commanding Officer, Lieutenant-Colonel Martin, and his British commanders found their billets in the Barracks, one officer was

Map of Alexandra area

noticeably absent. Through his father's connections, the ambitious Lieu-tenant Wyndham Strover had spent his first week in Singapore living comfortably in the salubrious Tanglin residence of Lieutenant-Colonel Ridout, Commanding Officer of the Royal Engineers, the island's most senior Colonel. Strover even paid a call on Government House. The Governor and other notables would have entirely ignored the "turbulent body of Ranghars" that had joined the garrison but could have hardly missed this charming young officer making the social rounds.

[XII]

TANGLIN HIGH SOCIETY

His Excellency Sir Arthur Young and Lady Evelyn Young were expected to arrive, just after tiffin time on 15 April 1914, for a wedding at the newly constructed St George's Garrison Church at Tanglin Barracks. The Governor and Commander-in-Chief did not ordinarily attend marriage ceremonies. However, Young was obliged to witness this particular exchange of vows. His deputy Aide-de-Camp was marrying the daughter of the General Officer Commanding (GOC) of the Troops in the Straits Settlements.

The GOC, Major-General Theodore Stephenson, was nearing the end of a 4-year posting in Singapore. His daughter and son-in-law had announced their engagement the previous October. The 24-year-old Lieutenant Cecil Orme Olliver and 23-year-old Philippa Stephenson's wedding was eagerly anticipated by the socialites of the Straits Settlements. Boasting 300 select guests, the wedding was the closest the island-colony would get to a high-society event. *The Malaya Tribune*'s front-page report the day after gushed that it was one of the "most brilliant functions in the history of Singapore."[199]

The Sultans of Johor, Kelantan, and Perak and the Raju Muda of Perak were travelling all the way down for the occasion. For the Youngs, it was a much shorter and leisurely drive from Government House to Tanglin. Young had a soft spot for the Wolseley, a solid and dependable British-made car. To get to the church on time, the Governor's limousine would first have to make its way down a lane gently sloping through the sprawling parklands that surrounded the stately residence. Known as the Domain, the lush and manicured gardens were carefully crafted to resemble a placid English landscape. Crossing the threshold of the massive iron gates of Government House, the limousine swung past the Abrams Horse Depository and Veterinary, which was beginning to sell cars as well as its

156

staple of horses. The next landmark at the bottom of Cavanagh Road was the always handy Yong Lee Seng grocers. Next was Koek's Bazaar, with its still new red brick and white frontage. The market was normally packed with cooks and servants in the cool of the morning hours.

Leaving the Bazaar behind, the limousine would have ducked quickly under the railway bridge near Emerald Hill. Cars and pedestrians normally stopped at the clacking sound of the Federated Malay States train crossing via Cuppage Road. The Chinese considered it bad luck to cross as the Bukit Timah Station-bound train clattered overhead. This appeared logical as the Tai Shan Ting cemetery – a final resting place for the Teochew Chinese community – loomed into view on the limousine's left. Superstitions endure and when the cemetery was redeveloped into the landmark Ngee Ann City building, it was designed like a traditional tomb. Lion statues and joss stick icons were added to placate dead souls of the past – a past still occupied by Young and his wife as they approached their destination.

After passing the cemetery and overtaking rickshaws and horse-drawn gharries, the Youngs would enjoy the smoothest part of their drive. It was a straight run along the tree-shaded Orchard Road towards the largely European residences, whose inhabitants led a pampered life in a series of bubbles between bungalow, office, racecourse, Cricket Club and Raffles Hotel. In the prestigious Tanglin district, the European elite of Singapore felt safe and sound near the military barracks housing British infantry officers, soldiers and their families. As the Youngs passed the Post Office followed by the main gate of the Botanical Gardens, Tanglin Barracks came into view on high ground. Trundling up the hill, their limousine passed the garrison golf links facing the modest-looking Officers' Mess and Quarters. A minute later, the Governor and his wife were safely delivered to the church and received a warm welcome by the officers of the King's Own Yorkshire Light Infantry (KOYLI) battalion.

The St George's Garrison Church building sported a red brick and white louvre façade and rounded arches resting on concrete foundations. The place of worship showed no extravagance of architecture but was constructed with the hot and humid weather in mind. Gaps in the brickwork allowed air and sunlight to enter the barn-like structure next to the barracks parade ground. With twenty feet between church-floor and eaves, the structure was low and compact, functional and modest. But it was also solid and dependable, like a good colonial official. The great and good of Singapore were assembling in the new church, with the first guests arriving soon after 3.30 pm. Most, visiting it for the first time, were impressed by the beautiful stained-glass windows above the chancel. The sanctuary had been lovingly decorated by the KOYLI garrison wives with flowers and palms plucked from the Botanical Gardens nearby.

Among those waiting for the ceremony to begin was 35-year-old Roland Braddell. Bespectacled, smooth shaven with a prominent aquiline nose and a sharp penetrating gaze, he was at the peak of a brilliant legal career in Singapore. Grandson of Thomas Braddell, the first Attorney General of the Straits Settlements, and son of Thomas de Multon Lee Braddell, the Chief Justice of the Federated Malay States, he would take an important part in the legal proceedings that followed the Singapore Mutiny. But for now, he would have had ample time to recall his own wedding to Dulcie Sylvia, an amateur theatrical actress. It had been a bit of a disaster. His frock coat had not fit. And he had been positioned under a large arrangement of flowers. Every now and then he would feel an insect from the massive bouquet falling down his back.

But reveries are always cut short by handshakes and introductions. The guest-list was a who's who of Singapore, a ruling and business elite whose names would stick as prominent street names in the Singapore of the the future: Adam, Anthony, Braddell, Cuscaden, Elias, Everitt, Jiak Kim, Liang Seah, Ridout, Still and Tong Sen.

The men in uniform could not be missed in the garrison church as they returned smart salutes. Standing out among the island's clutch of Colonels was Lieutenant-Colonel Charles William Brownlow. Commanding the Royal Garrison Artillery on Pulau Blakang Mati for the past year and a half, the tough and no-nonsense 52-year-old was a seasoned veteran of Britain's small but deadly frontier wars. He had spent most of his career on the dangerous and restive Northwest Frontier of India. In service since 1880, he was known as a man who kept his head when things got hot and preferred action to desk-work. Brownlow would play a key role in mustering a relief force against the Sepoy Mutiny before presiding over the court-martials. With the groom Lieutenant Olliver by his side during the mutiny, some would even credit him with saving the day with decisive action. But we are getting ahead of the story.

Look next to Brownlow and see Lieutenant-Colonel Dudley Ridout, a shrewd and ambitious 47-year old officer of the Royal Engineers, with his wife, Maud, and their 8-year-old son, Dudley Gethin. Ridout had been commissioned as an officer at about the same time as Brownlow. While Brownlow was in the thick of frontier action, Ridout had served behind the lines in wartime intelligence during the Boer War. They were a study in contrasts – a hard charger and a chess-player, an artilleryman and an engineer. Arriving in Singapore just a little before Brownlow, Ridout was working against the clock to get his next promotion to full Colonel within three years or be forced to retire. The Colonel's quota in the Royal Engineers was quite full, but Ridout was a quiet achiever determined to

Dudley H Ridout

progress despite the odds.

As a future GOC of the Troops in the Straits Settlements, Ridout would inspect the final sending off parade of the 5th. Ironically, on that very same evening of the mutiny, the cerebral officer would find himself promoted ahead of Brownlow. But that was still in the future; one he had little inkling of at the society wedding. Also present was the newly arrived Commanding Officer of the 5th Light Infantry, Lieutenant-Colonel Edward Victor Martin. For Martin, his wife and daughter Kathleen, the wedding was a perfect opportunity to get to know the notables of Singapore. There was much socialising to do. Mrs Brownlow, like Lady Young, Mrs Stephenson, Mrs Ridout and Mrs Braddell were all enthusiastic members of the Garrison Ladies Rifle Club. But Mrs Martin never joined the club. Like Martin's previous commanding officer, Ridout did not think much of Martin, who he felt had an unfortunate personality. This may be credited to the wily Battalion Adjutant Lieutenant Strover who, in his first week in Singapore, had ample time to clue Ridout in on Martin's failings, while enjoying Mrs Ridout's hospitality.

As a gentle breeze swayed the palm fronds outside the church, the guard-of-honour of KOYLI officers stood ramrod straight. The 24-year-old bridegroom faced the altar decked with white flowers. Next to him stood his best man, Lieutenant D McGregor Black, Stephenson's Aide-de-Camp. As ADCs to the Governor and the General Officer Commanding, Olliver and Black were popular young figures. Olliver was an artilleryman, a decent cricketer, and had impeccable family connections. Keen on golf, lawn tennis and billiard, the Sandhurst-trained Black was a broad-shouldered and handsome infantry officer with a trimmed moustache and a soldierly bearing, looking like a young general in the making.

At exactly five minutes after four o'clock, guests heard a neat click of the honour guard's rifle butts near the church porch. From the western end of the church, the regiment's string band started playing Lohengrin's *Wedding March*. General Stephenson entered the church building with his smiling daughter perched on his right arm. Described as a "charming-looking bride" by the admiring correspondent of the *Singapore Free Press and Mercantile Advertiser*, her outfit matched the occasion: "She wore a lovely gown... of ivory satin duchesse, a draped tunic of old Limerick lace, with a spray of orange blossom... a much valued possession of the Orme family."[200] Carrying a rich bouquet of white tiger lilies, the bride proudly sported her sparkling diamond pendant, a present from her fiancé. Dudley Ridout junior looked "courtly"[201] in a white satin costume. The boy, destined to be a General in the next World War, now commanded the bride's magnificent train of ivory duchesse satin. Draped with lace flounces, the fabric was over half a century old, worn over three generations of weddings in her family. For his trouble, little Dudley received a watch from Lieutenant Cecil Olliver as a keepsake. It was certainly meant to mark a happy time, not a portent of the troubled time that lay ahead.

The Governor's ever reliable right-hand man, R J Wilkinson, sitting next to his wife, watched the bridal procession as it made it way to the chancel. Just a fortnight ago, the 57- year-old colonial official had called on the Japanese Consul in Singapore. He informed the diplomat that the government would be deporting 37 Japanese pimps who had been operating in Singapore and the Straits Settlements. A sensational exposé published two years earlier, *The White Slave Market*, had created the impression of Singapore as Asia's hub for illicit sex, prostitution and sex trafficking. The carefully choreographed purity of the wedding ceremony was in stark contrast to the seamy issues Wilkinson managed in administering Singapore. These open secrets included the two large, regulated brothel areas of Malay Street Quarter and Smith Street Quarter, and the secrets of Sheikh Madrasa Lane with its unregulated brothel of child prostitutes.

As the bride draped in pure, vestal ivory-white reached the steps, voices were joined in the familiar sacred hymn, "The Voice that Breathed o'er Eden" which sang of a "primal marriage blessing" and the "pure espousal of Christian man and maid." After the General gave his daughter to the Lieutenant, Singapore's Bishop Reverend Charles James Ferguson-Davie began his address. Sensitive to Singapore's reputation as a den of vice, the Bishop's took the opportunity to deflect criticisms that marriage in Asia was contracted far more casually than the solemn vows made at home in England. His point made, he pronounced a benediction on the couple. The bride and bridegroom approached the vestry to sign the register, witnessed by Lieutenant-Colonel Arthur George Marrable, the voluble and sentimental 50-year old Commanding Officer of the 1st Battalion of the KOYLI.

As the marriage was formalised, the band played the delicate looping strains of the romantic *Traumerei*. The paperwork over, the bridal procession proceeded to the nave, passing through the traditional "arch of steel", a roof of raised sabres of the guard of honour. And as Mendelssohn's *Wedding March* echoed throughout the church, they exited towards the sunlit porch across from the parade square. After the slow-motion pomp of the official ceremonies, the couple took a quick drive down Middlesex Road (now Sherwood Road) to the Officers' Mess, which has become Singapore Foreign Ministry, where the reception would be held. In the predictable daze of all newlyweds, the Ollivers posed for their picture under a stunning floral bell of blossoms with the gorgeous fuchsia pink of honolulu creepers. Soldiers from the bridegroom's regiment lined the way to the Mess.

After the official photos, the couple quickly took up their position in the waiting-room in the Mess to greet their guests. British, Europeans, Chinese and Malays freely mingled, but apart from servers and bearers, not a single Indian had been invited. The reception guests included Mr J C Harper, in his spare time a Lance-Corporal in the locally raised Singapore Volunteer Corps, Dr Edward Denis Whittle, a 32-year-old surgeon in the Colonial Medical Service, along with his wife. Also mingling was 2nd Lieutenant J H Love-Montgomerie of the Malay States Volunteer Rifles. Newly arrived 5th Light Infantry officers Captain Perceval Boyce and Lieutenant Harold Seymour Elliott had an opportunity to make new friends in the reception.

Captain Perceval Boyce and Lieutenant Elliott would be the first to fall in the coming mutiny. Dr Whittle would be gunned down in a street in town while Love-Montgomerie would be shot just down the road while manning the camp guard-house. Harper would also be killed down the road. But death was furthest from the minds of the Major-General and Mrs Stephenson as they took a commanding position at the top of the main Mess stairs to receive the wedding party. The GOC's uniform was covered in decorations from many old battles. *The Straits Times* correspondent noticed Mrs Stephenson wearing a homely smile as she greeted guests in her saxe-blue gown of Liberty silk crepe and a hat of crinoline straw. The talented water-colourist had gifted her new son-in-law several of her paintings for the wedding and now held a bouquet of pale blue flowers which he had presented to her in turn.

Everything was in good order. The day's final event, the cake cutting ceremony, was held in the Mess billiard room. Guests ringed the couple who stood in the middle of the room decorated to resemble a winter garden. As Mrs Olliver stood poised with her husband's sabre in hand, the KOYLI's Commanding Officer, Colonel Marrable, took centre-stage. Marrable was in high spirits. He was due for eight-months home leave the next morning. Like the veteran Brownlow, Marrable had fought in a number of Queen Victoria's "Little Wars" in Burma, the Northwestern Frontier, the Khyber and in the Boer War. He had a chestful of medals and appeared to speak from the heart as he rose to toast the couple.

Never before had the "antique ruin" of the Tanglin Officers Mess seen such a "connubial ceremonial", began the long-winded Marrable.[202] The bride who married a soldier was also the daughter of their General, a trite observation which produced polite applause. In some stations, the GOC was a personality of great power whose commands had tremblingly to be obeyed. In Singapore, the military had realised their good fortune in their good general who was at heart the youngest soldier in the garrison. Eliciting laughter, he ploughed on. Although an old and experienced campaigner, Marrable noted approvingly that the General had participated in their pastimes and pleasures. Referring to the bride's mother, he said that everyone knew her for her "social sway" founded on "loving kindness."[203]

Conscious of his mawkish talk, Marrable quickly moved on to more manly concerns. As an English officer and gentlemen, he was expected to maintain a stiff upper lip and restrain his emotions. A rugby star in his younger days, he decided to talk about British manhood and their great sporting spirit. He noted that the bride's husband was a good gunner, a capable cricketer and a straight sportsman. He added that the whole social community of Singapore appreciated the constant courtesy and tact with which Olliver discharged his delicate duties as ADC to the Governor, and his considerable power of administration and organisation. This was the standard language of officers' confidential reports with which he tried to spice up his speech along with some fatuous humour.

Marrable wondered aloud whether military success would prove of equal service in matrimonial matters. Warming to this theme, he declared that "a woman is meant to be loved, not to be understood"[204] and asserted that Cupid had been busy recently "among the jaded inhabitants of this enervated island".[205] He drew polite laughter as he noted that one of the God of Love's most successful campaigns had resulted in the happy union before them. Begging to be pardoned for the inadequate speech he made, he finally made his toast to the health of the couple. The toast produced a burst of cheering and music as the wedding party celebrated the end of Colonel Marrable's rambling speech. The bride gratefully cut into the cake with her husband's sword and distributed the slices.

Sent off with further cheers, the couple departed for their one-week honeymoon in a cottage in Changi. The Ollivers would make their home in a bungalow on Pulau Blakang Mati, near the barracks of the settlement's Artillery. It was a happy occasion, with dark clouds of fate looming in the distance. The driver of the bridal car to Changi would be the first officer in the battalion to die on the Western Front. The best man would also die after leading his men in a suicidal charge against the Ottomans at Gallipolli.

The bridegroom Olliver stayed behind in relatively safe and secure Singapore – until the mutiny at least - to serve under Brownlow. The Ollivers' fairy-tale military wedding at Tanglin lasted 11 years. The Lieutenant gave the General another grand-daughter, before jumping ship and marrying a Major's daughter. Still everyone agreed it had been a "brilliant military wedding"[206] that April of 1914 before the world went to war and the mutiny of the 5th hit Singapore. Much like Europe's perfect summer before the guns of August changed the world.

[XIII]

THE RIGHT TO ENTER

The tensions of love and war were also felt on the Pacific Coast on other side of the world. Har Dayal was especially delighted to receive a letter from his old Swiss flame, Frieda Hauswirth. Since leaving the US and after her divorce, Hauswirth had decided to carry the torch for India (though not for Har Dayal) with plans for a solidarity visit. The Swiss blonde was proving that she was not just another lightweight flirt melting into anonymity in Europe. She would marry another Indian nationalist, meet the Mahatma Gandhi, paint his portrait and write astutely about the Indian leader. Hauswirth, "with whom both Taraknath Das and Har Dayal had some sort of a relationship during their Stanford days,"[207] added strain to the relationship between Har Dayal the Punjabi and Taraknath the Bengali, the best-networked Indians in North America at the time. Taraknath Das had warned Hauswirth against visiting India at the time. He had also warned Har Dayal not to try and recruit her for the global mutiny.

Taraknath should also have advised Har Dayal to keep his mouth shut. In a careless interview to a US-based Indian newspaper, Har Dayal had blurted out that the assassination of a previous US president, William McKinley, was an example "to prove that in civilised countries the assassin's dagger is used as an essential weapon of advancement."[208] So, the British had the case for deportation fall into their laps. Upon receiving the British intelligence report, the US Immigration Department issued an arrest warrant for Har Dayal on charges of being a member of excluded classes, an anarchist or advocating the overthrow of the United States government by force. Hopkinson finally had his man. The Eurasian policeman was confident that his nemesis would be swiftly deported.

But the anarchist philosopher slipped the policeman's eager grasp. The British were 24 hours too late. The arrest warrant was issued a day after Har Dayal had completed three years of his US residency, which gave him legal protection. But he was seized for good measure on 24 March, coincidentally the day of Gurdit Singh's arrest in Hong Kong. Just before his own arrest, Har Dayal told Indians in San Francisco that if he was forced to leave the US, he would go to Germany to prepare for the coming mutiny.

Once in custody, Har Dayal arranged for a telegram to be sent to friends in high places including the former Governor of Oregon. Har Dayal complained that immigration officials had "blundered and acted in a high-handed manner in arresting me after expiration of three years from entry."[209] This set into motion a whole lobby of support for Har Dayal, including Oregon notables, the Friends of Russian Freedom, the French League of the Rights of Man and England's liberals. This motley lobby condemned his illegal detention. Garbled news of the arrest even reached Savarkar in his cell in faraway Andamans.

Amid the excitement of his arrest, Har Dayal received a letter from Frieda Hauswirth asking for advice. Still-smitten, he saw her message as a love-letter and replied passionately:

Oh, Frieda, my mind is a welter of joy and surprise. To have found you again – the very thought bewilders me. But sure it is true – it is the same Frieda, sure she is, the same dear friend of those unforgettable Palo Alto days, which mark a turning point in my life.... I have often through in this year: "When I lecture in Europe, I may meet Frieda at a meeting in Switzerland, and then I shall go up to her and say, "Holloa Frieda, *comment ca va*? In such reverie I have found solace.[210]

Amid his reveries, Har Dayal was interrogated and then released on bail. His attorney had learnt that the US government was not so keen after all to deport him but could possibly be persuaded to offer him asylum. However, he warned Har Dayal: "You can never trust the government; they might decide to extradite you on some pretext or another, so if you wish to go, go."[211] Heeding his warning, Har Dayal handed over operations of the *Ghadar* to Ram Chandra, a 31-year-old newspaperman from Punjab who had joined the Yugantar Ashram in January after sojourns in Japan followed by Seattle. Chandra was a "sturdy, handsome, light-skinned 'Pathan looking' Brahman scholar and fiery nationalist, who wore his native dress - baggy pajamas, long kurta, turban with an Afridi style '*kulla*', peaked cap in the centre of the turban.... (H)e was ruddy, vivacious, compared with the anaemic looking Delhiwallas."[212] A staunch Hindu unlike the secular Har Dayal, Chandra revered Swami Ram Tirath, whose articles had inspired Harnam Singh to seek his fortune in the United States.

With the *Ghadar* newspaper in Ram Chandra's hands by early April, Har Dayal made secret plans to find refuge in Switzerland and seek out Frieda Hauswirth. His letter promised her that "we'll pick up the thread again."[213] She was not quite as keen on him. After receiving his letter, Hauswirth told her friend and future husband, Sarangadhar Das: "This letter disappointed me deeply at the time because instead of the expected advice and suggestions concerning India, for which ALONE I had reopened connections, nothing but a personal outpouring came, BARELY ONE WORD touching upon my problem of work in India...."[214] Frustrated by his advances, Hauswirth confided: "Where the problem of sex HINDERS my work, I say as I said to Har Dayal: DAMN SEX."[215]

While Har Dayal weaved between tangled personal, philosophical and political commitments in San Francisco, across the Pacific in Shanghai, Gurdit sorted out the *Komagata Maru*'s various passenger, payment and fuel issues. Picking up an additional 100 passengers on the Huangpu in Shanghai, the ship steamed towards Moji, a coal and timber station on the island of Kyushu in Japan, where 85 Sikhs from Manila embarked. The *Komagata Maru* was fast becoming a migration caravan to test the laws of Empire.

It was a journey of discovery and heady adventure for many of those on-board. Copies of the *Ghadar* were read aloud with revolutionary poems from the *Ghadar di Gunj*. Japan also proved an eye-opening and even eye-popping experience, especially for those straight out of little Punjabi villages. Some curious passengers frequented Moji's red-light district, picking up infections that kept the ship's young Rajput doctor busy all the way to Vancouver. Gurdit Singh was hosted by the *Komagata Maru*'s shipping line agent and his Japanese friends at a hotel in Shimonoseki, just opposite Moji across the Kanmon Straits. In an atmospheric dinner featuring speeches, geisha girls, obligatory sake and the local speciality *fugu* (puffer-fish), Gurdit's intoxicated hosts swore that if India woke up to claim its freedom, Japan was ready to help. Together, India, Japan and China would form an Asia strong enough to defeat Europe. Encouraged, Gurdit told his hosts that a mutiny of 10,000 Indian sepoys would push back the British if they continued to block the passage of the *Komagata Maru*.

After the beer talk, wine, women and songs, the steamer's next stop was Yokohama where the passenger manifest climbed to 376. There, the *Komagata Maru* passengers from Hong Kong saw a familiar face with an older-looking companion. It was Bhagwan Singh, the fiery orator who had moved from Perak to Hong Kong and then Vancouver. Deported to

Hong Kong from Canada in handcuffs after the violent ear-biting scuffle with the police, he had jumped ship in Yokohama. Bhagwan had been living in Yokohama for the past 5 months plotting his next move. His host was Abdul Hafiz Mohammed Barkatullah, a 54-year-old Muslim scholar, pan-Islamist writer and roving revolutionary from India's Bhopal state. Barkatullah had been Professor of Hindustani in Tokyo University since 1909 and was editing the weekly *Islamic Fraternity*. A political as well as religiously pious Muslim, he had performed the first three conversions to Islam in Japan, of his Japanese assistant, his wife and her father.

The British despised Barkatullah. He was a troublemaker connecting three movements, the Pan-Islamist, Asians for Asiatics, and Indian seditionists. All three movements shared a common aim – to free Asia and Turkey from European domination. Barkatullah reconciled the Pan-Islamic and the Pan-Asian movements with the Indian nationalist struggle. He was among the earliest nationalists to support Hindu-Muslim unity against British rule in India. Close to Krishnavarma Shyamji, the founder of India House in London, and Madame Cama in Paris, Barkatullah had also hosted Ram Chandra and Gobind Behari Lal in Yokohama.

Bhagwan spent a productive few months discussing strategies with the Muslim scholar revolutionary who thought long and hard about the geopolitical reach of Islam. In a March 1912 article in *Islamic Fraternity*, Barkatullah praised the Emperor Wilhelm of Germany as the one man "who holds the peace of the world as well as the war in the hollow of his hand."[216] Predicting a pending major war in Europe, he wrote that "it is the duty of the Muslims to be united, to stand by the Khalif; with their life and property, and to side with Germany."[217] After the British banned his weekly from India that October, Barkatullah started writing rabid anti-British pamphlets. In June 1913, his screed, *The Sword is the Last Resort*, predicted a war between England and Germany and declared that "Indians should make preparations for an armed rising."[218] Enough was enough and the British swung into action. Citing the Anglo-Japanese Accord, the British Ambassador in Tokyo pressured the Japanese government to remove Barkatullah from him academic post.

Stripped of his tenure, Barkatullah walked up the gangway of the *Komagata Maru* with Bhagwan. Handing out the latest copies of the *Ghadar*, they reached out to the congregation of Sikhs, Hindus and Muslims on the floating *gurdwara*. Bhagwan delivered one of his classic fiery sermons, but privately, he looked Gurdit straight in the eye and told him that the ship would not be allowed to land in Canada. Bhagwan had a certain authority of experience in the matter after his own ejection. But Gurdit felt otherwise and was prepared to make a leap of faith across the ocean. The imperial police believed he was literally taking his passengers for a ride, fully aware of the restrictions but attracted to profit. His motives were indeed mixed, blending business with revolution – he had raised money from the passengers and had a reputation as the leader of a cause. Why should he back down?

The *Komagata Maru* set sail on the 2 May 1914 for Victoria Harbour in British Columbia without Bhagwan Singh and Barkatullah. They had boarded another ship bound for San Francisco via Honolulu. The Canadian government received an alert on the ship's departure from British diplomats in Japan. Two days later, Malcolm Reid, Hopkinson's superior in the Vancouver Immigration Department, sent out a wireless message to check on the steamer's location. He failed to get a fix on the *Komagata Maru* which had no wireless.

On board the ship which chugged silently towards Canada, Gurdit confined himself to his own stuffy, first-class cabin, where he prepared food for his son in a private kitchen. He spent most of his time conferring with his personal secretary, Daljit, and half a dozen men. The other passengers were spread out in the open on their bedding across 533 wooden benches, cooking on portable coal stoves. As the *Komagata Maru* neared Vancouver on 23 May, Barkatullah and Bhagwan landed in Honolulu and took the next vessel to San Francisco. As soon as they arrived, the Sikh and the Muslim met with the Bengali revolutionary Taraknath Das. He had been writing about Bhagwan and his deportation in Hussain Rahim's *Hindustanee*. Thus, the Punjabi-Bengali revolutionary connection was renewed in San Francisco as the duo proceeded to the Yugantar Ashram to meet Ram Chandra, Har Dayal's successor in the *Ghadar*.

The Hindu, Sikh and Muslim trio would now do the work of one man, Har Dayal, to drum up support for the global mutiny movement. Gobind Behari Lal recalled the almost accidental formation of a Hindu-Muslim-Sikh united front in the Ghadar Party: "The Pandit, as Ram Chandran came to be known, was the "Brahman" chief, Barkatullah the Moslem chief, Bhagwan Singh the Sikh chief: such became the triumvirate, with the Pandit in the centre.... The Big Three, practically, became The Governing Body of The Gadar."[219] The Mutiny Movement seemed to evolve organically without a clear guiding hand as he explains:

> All this did not happen in any formal fashion; it was just the inevitable consequence of two circumstances: (1) Har Dayal had left a vacuum which no one person could fill and (2) the "public" understood and supported such an arrangement. The "public" of course, were the Indian community, especially the manual workers in fields, orchards, factories, and the small Indian shopkeepers in Stockton, Sacramento and such towns in the Pacific Coast.[220]

The Indian community learnt of the *Komagata Maru*'s plight through the *Ghadar* newspaper. After 49 days on the high seas, the steamer approached the shores of British Columbia. The populist local Member of Parliament H H Stevens who was violently opposed to Asian immigration rallied his "white Canada forever" political base. As the so-called "ship of sedition" neared the port, the Premier of British Columbia, Sir Richard McBride, established a red line. He promised *The Times* of London that the "Orientals" would not be allowed to land on Canadian soil.

But the Indian community in Canada were already preparing to fight back. Learning from contacts in Yokohama of the ship's pending arrival, the indomitable Hussain Rahim led the charge. He formed a Shore Committee to facilitate the landing of the passengers from the *Komagata Maru*. His close associates from the Socialist Party of Canada were enlisted to the cause. Joseph Edward Bird, a lawyer and party member, spotted an oversight in the Canadian order-in-council that had prohibited the landing of the immigrants – a port in British Columbia had been accidentally omitted from the order. This meant that the ship could berth in Port Alberni which sat at the finger-tip of Alberni inlet that poked deep inside Vancouver Island. But there was no wireless on-board the *Komagata Maru* to convey this crucial piece of information.

Rahim and Rajah Singh, his tall and imposing Secretary at the United India League, decided to make a dash for the ship. At Port Alberni, they found a 12-m (40-ft) motor launch. Their plan was to go to a bay sheltered from the powerful Pacific Ocean, scan the horizon and then intercept the *Komagata Maru*. In the meantime, Hopkinson and his boss Malcolm Reid had got wind of the Shore Committee's mission. Reid personally reported the breaking development to the populist MP Stevens and ordered a customs inspector to find and sabotage Rahim's motor launch. But Rahim and Rajah powered up the launch in the nick of time. The pair reached a secluded area on the ocean-tossed southwestern coast of Vancouver Island, battling the waves for hours, looking out for the *Komagata Maru*. Exhausted and drained, they finally retreated to calmer waters at the entrance of the Alberni inlet – just as the *Komagata Maru* sailed past behind them towards Victoria Harbour on the southern tip of Vancouver Island.

In their own race against time, Reid and Hopkinson jumped on a boat from the mainland to reach the ferry port city of Nanaimo, about 80 kilometres from Port Alberni. En-route, they received word that the *Komagata Maru* had pulled into the William Head Quarantine Station near Victoria. The pair of immigration officers rented a Ford and made a 120-kilometre, 7-hour drive through the night to find the *Komagata Maru* already snug at anchor, beautifully framed by the mountain peaks and alpine forests on the American side of the border.

The *Komagata Maru* had dropped anchor in Burrard Inlet on 23 May. Its final destination was Vancouver City, opposite its mooring on the mainland. At dawn, the passengers on deck saw the city stretch out before them. Behind them, on Vancouver's northern shore, a wooden Catholic church and frame houses with mountains in the background made a postcard-pretty scene. The Indians who sailed across the Pacific surveyed reservation land belonging to the Squamish Indian tribe. Gurdit had made it, or so he thought. His meticulous secretary, Daljit, had completed all the necessary paperwork as the ship was fumigated and the passengers vaccinated before the next stop on the mainland port. Everyone was dressed in their best suits with their bags packed, ready to disembark. News reporters who boarded the *Komagata Maru* were surprised to find a clean ship and orderly people. They had been told that they would face an oriental horde of savages. The *Victoria Times* correspondent noted that most of the men on board had served in the British Indian army. He noted approvingly that the majority knew some English and "some of them converse in it remarkably well." He described the passengers as "a handsome lot... superior to the class of Hindus which have already come into the province... stand very erect and move with an alert action... their suits are well-pressed... their turbans are spotlessly clean."[221]

Gurdit had a few hours to enjoy the air and the scenery and savour his success when he heard the chug of a launch. Clambering on board were Inspectors Reid and Hopkinson, tired and bleary eyed from their long drive. Just one glance at the tall, dark and unhandsome Hopkinson and Gurdit would have recalled Bhagwan's description of the half-breed policeman. Reid was next to him, paler, moustached and stiff – unyielding in manner and appearance. These two officials were far more junior in rank and pay compared to the men Gurdit had dealt with in the Malay States and Claude Severn in Hong Kong. But they were the authority he would have to manage on the ground – and they represented an inflexible immigration policy – one supported by politicians who sought to appease supporters who blamed all new arrivals for Vancouver's tight job market and economic slump. Gurdit did not make small talk. Addressing Hopkinson directly, he said: "What is done with this shipload of my people will determine whether we shall have peace in all parts of the British Empire."[222]

The ship's captain was given the green light to move to the other side of the Burrard Inlet, closer to Vancouver City. As they steamed towards their final destination, the passengers could be forgiven for believing that law and justice was on their side and that they were going ashore. And then a kilometre before their promised landing, the ship dropped anchor

*Gurdit Singh (in white turban) with his son, Balwant,
on the deck of the* Komagata Maru *on the morning
of its arrival in Vancouver.*

once more. Those on board now had a clear view of the immigration building at the bottom of Burrard Street, and the welcome figures of turbaned Sikhs waving at them from land. They were agonizingly close to their goal. Then a former sepoy on shore started signalling the *Komagata Maru* with semaphore. But he was chased off by the Vancouver Police who were working hand in glove with Reid and Hopkinson.

Reid and Hopkinson refused Gurdit permission to land. Despite his protestations that he was a merchant, not an immigrant, they insisted that he would have to undergo all the immigration formalities imposed on the other passengers. Hopkinson claimed that Gurdit tried to bribe him for a fast-track landing. Charter fees had to be settled with the ship's agent in less than three weeks to avoid being forced back to Hong Kong. The immigration inspectors intended to make him miss the deadline by stretching out the passengers' medical examinations. What would normally take an hour was extended to several weeks. The Vancouver immigration officials were going to drag their feet on each and every procedure to run out the clock on the passengers of the *Komagata Maru*.

Hussain Rahim and his Shore Committee joined in the battle of wits. The wily Gujarati had to work fast to raise the necessary funds for Gurdit to settle the charter. After the ship's owners agreed to extend the deadline, Rahim chaired an urgent fundraising meeting organised by the United India League in co-ordination with the Khalsa Diwan Society at the Dominion Hall in downtown Vancouver. Hopkinson made it a point to attend and report on the proceedings.

Some 500 Indians attended and Rahim managed to pull in another 120 sympathizers from the Socialist Party of Canada. Rahim rallied the men as he spoke of a return to the spirit of the 1857 Mutiny, the possibility of self-rule for India, the warrior spirit of the Sikhs and the injustice of Canada's exclusion laws against Indians. Rahim's lawyer and friend Joseph Edward Bird also spoke.

A card-carrying Socialist, Bird compared the struggles of the Indians to his own Irish forefathers who had emigrated to Canada because of poverty and oppression. "Now gentlemen, they are coming out here and knocking politely at the door of Canada and asking for the privilege of coming in and of coming in lawfully,"[223] he thundered. Bird told the audience that the Indians were "physically their superiors and mentally their equals"[224] and that there was more than enough farming land to go around for everyone. He detailed the unfair measures taken by the Dominion government to keep the Indians out.

The audience stomped their feet in loud agreement when Bird called the Immigration Department "the most autocratic of our institutions" and quipped that when they "talk about socialist and anarchists, there is no set of anarchists in Canada like the Immigration Officials who defy all law and order..."[225]

After more rousing speeches, the audience came forward with cold, hard cash. A pile of Canadian currency grew on the table in front of Rahim and the speakers. Sikhs have a tradition of putting contributions to the *gurdwara* fund in a receptacle in front of the Sikh holy book. But now these sums far outstripped the usual token amounts. Hundred-dollar bills were donated and one contributor even put down the grand sum of $2,000. By the end of the meeting, $5,000 had been raised with pledges of more than ten times that amount backed by property deeds. The contest of wills between Reid and Hopkinson on one hand and Gurdit on the other was now joined by Rahim's Shore Committee.

The situation became critical as the passengers began running out of food and water. They had become prisoners on a floating jail with no certainty of what lay ahead. When Rahim sent out a boat with food supplies, the Immigration Department insisted on taking over the shipment. Paying a visit to the ship soon after, Hopkinson felt a mood of increasing uneasiness. An unpopular Immigration Department guard had been forced by some passengers to walk the plank a week earlier. Unruly as some of them were towards Canadians in uniform, the passengers still retained the highest respect for Gurdit who maintained solidarity and unity of purpose with daily evening meetings in the ship's *gurdwara*.

One side believed their cause was just while the other believed they were breaking the law. Whatever the rights of wrongs of the issue, the plight of the ship was reverberating beyond Vancouver. In mid-June, a special Ghadar meeting was held in Portland, Oregon. A band was hired to lead a procession of members to draw attention to the event. The Indians discussed the *Komagata Maru* issue, and the participants swore to join the coming mutiny and to expel the British from India.

Despite the increasingly grim mood on board, the passengers showed no sign of backing down. But when the harbourmaster ordered the Japanese captain to move the ship a few hundred metres up the Burrard Inlet to make way for two Japanese destroyers, he agreed to comply. Reid hoped that the Japanese war-ships could be used to intimidate the Indians under the terms of the Anglo-Japan accord. However, as soon as the passengers heard of the move, they rushed to the engine room with makeshift weapons. The captain backed down. Hopkinson reasoned with the passengers for an hour, but they stood firm. Then the harbourmaster agreed to leave the errant steamer in its berth, stranded in no man's sea. In *The Vancouver Sun*, a would-be poet named Franck Vosper published a taunting lyric declaring victory:

O Gurdit Singh! O Gurdit Singh!
Why did you to this country bringh
A crowd of Hindus 'neath your wing
Against our laws, O Gurdit Singh?

O Gurdit Singh! O Gurdit Singh
Your ship at anchor there will swingh
And turn to junk or anything
Before you land, O Gurdit Singh![226]

It seemed to be a victory for the agents of the British Empire, but one which would prove Pyrrhic.

[XIV]

THE GOVERNOR
TAKES A BREAK

In Singapore, Sir Arthur Young was owed a holiday after three years of hectic activity. It had been a non-stop round of meetings, consultations, inspections, commemorations, parades, weddings and funerals. The title of Excellency was a burden with a few privileges and many heavy responsibilities, not just in Singapore but across the swathe of territories he had to cover. The Governor and his wife were only due for home leave just before Christmas 1914. However, as they felt the strain, Singapore's First Couple decided to bring this forward by half a year. They would now sail for England in the early evening of Tuesday, 16 June. In hindsight, the timing could not have been worse. Less than a fortnight later, the heir to the Austro-Hungarian Empire would be shot in the throat by a Bosnian Serb assassin. The bullet in the Balkans produced a cascade of events that sent Europe spiralling into a World War. The Youngs would still be on the high seas during the assassination and on leave in early August when Britain declared war on Germany.

Rather inconveniently, the Youngs were sailing home on a German mail steamer, the SS *Prinz Ludwig*. The steamer was managed by a major German shipping line, North German Lloyd. Young may not have minded that the *Prinz Ludwig* was sufficiently well provisioned, comfortable and specially ventilated for voyages in hot tropical climates. Even the German Crown Prince and his wife had used it for their passage east just a few years earlier. The British Governor and his wife would be berthed in the same plush saloon used by the German royals. The old-timers of Singapore, who respected Young for his patriotism and lack of swank, knew exactly why Young spurned a British-flagged ship from the good old P&O Line.

As is nearly always the case with travelling couples, his wife had objected. Lady Evelyn's problems with the premier British shipping line started many years earlier. News of her quarrel with the P&O had even reached Britain's House of Commons. While her husband was still Colonial Secretary in the Federated Malay States, Lady Evelyn tried to bring her favourite dog on one of her voyages. She was refused point-blank by the worthies of the P&O. The rules could not be bent even for the wife of the Colonial Secretary. So, henceforth at her urging, her husband agreed to sail on German steamers where their dog would be comfortably kept with them. The experience of Teutonic comfort and efficiency sold the Youngs on German ships. They were so impressed and grateful that they had even hosted dinner in January for naval officers from the visiting SMS *Gneisenau*, an armoured cruiser of the German Imperial Navy's formidable East Asia Squadron based in Tsingtao in Northern China. The Squadron included the light cruiser SMS *Emden* whose daring raids would haunt the Straits Settlements in just a few short weeks.

The *Prinz Ludwig* sat now in the West Wharf of Keppel Harbour. Standing ready at Johnston's Pier opposite the city's commercial district was a Government launch to ferry the couple to the ship. The Youngs' departure on holiday would invariably become another Singapore event with full press coverage, a send-off parade and many well-wishers – precisely what the Youngs needed a respite from. With a shaded pavilion covering its approach, the T-shaped covered pier had been prettied up for the occasion. The fanfare and protocol helped to mask the state of the dilapidated pier which was not altogether clean and heavily barnacled. Receiving a stream of important visits in the past, the sixty-year-old structure had seen better days. It was no longer the best introduction for first-time visitors to Singapore, or convenient for ladies in flowing dresses.

The Governor allowed himself a little holiday dash for his departure outfit, exchanging his workaday solar topee for a white Panama to match his light-blue serge suit. This was not too different from the suit worn by John Jacob Astor, the richest passenger on the doomed *Titanic* two years earlier. But Young was not an overly superstitious man who paid attention to grim sartorial forebodings.

Hoisting the regimental colours to salute the Governor, a guard-of-honour composed of 150 sepoys from the Pathan left-wing of the 5th Light Infantry. Marched from Alexandra Barracks to Johnston Pier, the sepoys were under the fervently loyalist Subedar Suleiman Khan, Commander of "G" Company in Captain Draper Hall's No. 4 Double Company. True to form, the aspiring battalion adjutant Lieutenant W G Strover seized the opportunity to register his presence. He had tagged along, ostensibly to ensure that the native *subedar* knew his business, but no doubt to profile himself once again.

Crowds began to gather in the streets with curious onlookers streaming in from Fullerton Square opposite the pier. The 5th's guard-of-honour took up its position. At the head of the column were 50 bandsmen, the bass drummers with full-frontal tiger-skins over their uniforms, a tradition which British military bands borrowed from old African drummers. The 5th had only been in Singapore for a few weeks but were already making their mark in the sport-obsessed settlement. The month after their arrival, the sepoys' hockey team trounced the favoured Singapore Cricket Club 7-0 on its home ground on the Padang. Their sepoy predecessors had never managed such a score-line. The team was praised for its pace and athleticism, in particular a quick and fit Ranghar Lance Naik named Feroze Khan.

The pier was now packed. Army officers in full uniform rubbed epauleted shoulders with civil servants and prominent worthies. The *tuan besar*, wearing white drill *tutup* suits tailored in High Street, emerged from colonial-style buildings opposite the waterfront on Collyer Quay and Johnston's Pier. Perched on their pomaded heads were solar *topees* made by Heath's of Bond Street, London, and sold by the Robinson and Company department store in nearby Raffles Place.

Thirty leading Chinese businessmen headed by Hokkien merchant Tan Jiak Kim had arrived early, along with a group of diplomats. Prominent among the latter was the German Consul-General Herr K Feindel, also Acting Consul-General for the Ottoman Empire. The newly arrived General Officer Commanding (GOC) of the Troops of the Straits Settlements Major-General Raymond Reade, the Bishop of Singapore Ferguson-Davie, Colonial Secretary R J Wilkinson and the expected government retinue could all be seen mingling. Among the military top brass were the usual clutch of Colonels: Lieutenant-Colonel Dudley Ridout of the Royal Engineers, Lieutenant-Colonel Brownlow of the Royal Garrison Artillery and the 5th's Commanding Officer, Lieutenant Colonel Edward Martin. The new GOC Reade, the 53-year-old grandson of an Anglo-Irish Earl, did not mind Martin at all and had a far higher opinion of him than Ridout.

The Governor and Lady Evelyn arrived at the pier at 4 pm sharp. Lady Evelyn stepped out gracefully from the official car carrying a bouquet of carefully selected orchids. Young's appearance was a signal for the 5th's guard-of-honour to stand to attention and present arms. As he approached the pier steps, the band played *God Save the King*, and the military men offered smart salutes. Young halted at the steps, holding his white Panama hat. It was an ordinary moment of a couple going on home leave made significant and rousing by the music, the crowds, the pomp and ceremony.

After the last bars of the anthem, Young and General Reade inspected the guard-of-honour. Passing the regimental colours of the 5th Light Infantry, Young doffed his hat in a salute. *The Malaya Tribune* correspondent noticed Young's "keen interest in the sepoys, who were standing as as straight as young pine trees, in a line which was remarkable for its regularity."[227] Searching for a word to describe the sepoys of the 5th "with that conspicuous touch of bright yellow on their turban", *The Straits Times* correspondent present decided they were "stalwart".[228] Judging by their turn-out, Young would have agreed that the recently arrived battalion of sepoys were reliable and true to their salt. But he was only inspecting the better-adjusted wing of Pathans, not the internally divided Ranghars whose native officers continued to feud and bicker.

In reality, the Indians, whether sepoy or the locals, did not really preoccupy the Governor. The real concern was the 220,000-strong Chinese community which accounted for three-quarters of Singapore's total population. It was the Chinese who tended to riot and cause all sorts of trouble if not held in check or managed carefully. The prominent merchant Tan Jiak Kim now stood before Young. Next to him were ranged the notables of Singapore's Chinese community including his eldest son Tan Soo Bin. Once Lady Young caught up with her husband and took her place, Tan began with a short encomium. He unrolled a three-foot-long silk banner with decorations embroidering an already flowery speech. The merchant lauded Young for his support for the Chinese community, while astutely adding praise for Lady Young. In reply, Young told the crowd that without the loyalty of the Chinese the colony would be a "vastly different place to what it is."[229]

Young had exercised political control over the large Chinese population by maintaining good relations with the leading Chinese who now stood before him. He had won their support through pro-business measures, financial benefits and the occasional award. And although it would be gauche to say so openly, the sepoys of the 5th standing smartly near Young were part of his tool-box should the majority Chinese population make trouble.

The Chinese in Singapore and Malaya were all from south of the Yangtze but divided by five major dialect groups. In 1888, the Verandah Riots showed how easily roused the Chinese community could be over what the British considered mere municipal issues. When the Municipal authorities tried to clear Chinatown's verandahs of goods and stalls to allow for foot passage, the quarter rose in riots for three days. With the decline of the Manchus and the rise of Chinese nationalism, the Chinese required more careful monitoring especially over their growing factionalism. Radical political views had even infected some of the leading Chinese accompanying Tan Jiak Kim. One of them, a great-grandson of the storied "Kapitan Singapore" Tan Tock Seng, had joined the well-wishers for the send-off. Tan Boo Liat was a zealous member of the underground Tong Meng Hui (Chinese Revolutionary Alliance), founded by Dr Sun Yat Sen. After plotting several failed uprisings from their Singapore headquarters, a villa located off Balestier Road, Sun Yat Sen and the Tong Meng Hui finally overthrew the Qing dynasty in the October 1911 revolution. Dr Sun returned to Singapore two months later to celebrate the revolution and thank his supporters. Mission accomplished, the Chinese revolutionary leader stayed in Tan Boo Liat's house, Golden Bell, today's Danish Seamen's Church.

Young knew to keep his friends close, but he kept potential enemies of stability even closer. Safe and secure Singapore provided comfort, connections and convenience of location, strengths that also helped the work of intriguers, agents and revolutionaries. China had been thrown into chaos after Dr Sun Yat Sen's revolution ended 2000 years of imperial rule. The tumult soon spread to the Federated Malay States, leading to the Towchang Riots, a serious incident in Kuala Lumpur which occurred under Young's watch.

In Kuala Lumpur, following celebrations of the first Chinese Republic in January 1912, Dr Sun's revolutionary anti-Manchu nationalists got ahead of themselves. Dr Sun was a Hakka who surrounded himself with Cantonese. During Chinese New Year celebrations in 1912, the Cantonese went around lopping off the pig-tails of the largely Hokkien pro-Manchu faction. Wearing the trademark Manchu queue, known in Hokkien as the *towchang*, signalled support for the Qing Dynasty which mandated these plaited pigtails. It did not help that some of the Chinese policemen wore queues while others did not.

The mass brawls among various clans continued for a fortnight, reaching a climax on 22 February. About 1,000 anti-Manchu Nationalists carrying their blue-and white flag charged the Central Police Station in Kuala Lumpur's Sultan Street.[230] The police opened fire on the charging mob, killing or wounding about ten men. After the dust and bodies were cleared, a standard official inquiry was held and the committee's completed report was forwarded to Young. But Edward Brockman, then Chief Secretary of the Federated Malay States and Young's deputy in Malaya, furiously opposed the report's conclusions.

In trademark fashion, Young mulled over the whole matter cautiously. He refused to be rushed into judgement on the causes of the riots. A different personality may have have acted faster given the simmering political tensions. But Young knew that sloppy narrative could be used by the pen-pushers in London to ascribe praise or blame to his administration. Working with trusted Chinese leaders, Young established that it was not Chinese nationalism or political differences that caused the riot, but merely a brawl between different dialect groups. Neatly put, it was not a political but a law-and-order issue. The Governor drove home the point in his own carefully crafted and belated memorandum to London's Colonial Office. He claimed that the clan disputes were isolated to trouble-making elements, that the majority of Chinese showed good sense under strong government and praised leading Chinese for help rendered to resolve the issue.

It would not be convenient for him to play up the role of the revolutionary nationalists, especially since key members, including the lead revolutionary Dr Sun Yat Sen, had been active in both Singapore and Penang – so active in fact that Dr Sun had been banned from entering Singapore for five years from 1900 until 1905. Supported by worthies like Tan Boo Liat, the Towchang Riots in Kuala Lumpur could easily be traced in part to the forces supporting Dr Sun. That the police force was poorly prepared and that he and his colleagues had not properly gauged foreign political influence on the Chinese community were other points Young thought better of highlighting.

Wiser after the fact and behind the scenes, Young worked quietly to strengthen laws and immigration procedures to deport Chinese political activists and nationalists. He worked off a discreet and cautious playbook. Young was not the sort to dwell on outlier possibilities. If Singapore could easily harbour revolutionaries who ended imperial rule in China, it did not follow that it would host a network agitating against British rule in India. Or that the sepoys presented for his inspection could become the instrument of an uprising.

In essence, Young was a man who knew how to assure his political masters that he could hold the fort. He discharged his task with the right combination of tact, firmness, courtesy and reasonableness. He prized common-sense, humility and cultivating good human relations. Now as he prepared to take temporary leave of his castle and keep, responsibility for the Straits Settlements would lie with his deputy R J Wilkinson.

Sir Arthur and Lady now walked down the pier's gangway and boarded the government launch. The guns on Fort Canning boomed out a farewell salute. The launch took them across the noticeably choppy waters to under the shadow of the *Prinz Ludwig* where the ship's band played a fanfare of trumpets as soon as they boarded the vessel. Three cheers echoed from the wharf as the massive ship flying the red, white and black flag of Germany was pulled out by two tugs to the open sea. Homeward bound, Young doffed his Panama hat once more to acknowledge the loud cheers.

The Friday after the Governor's departure, regular readers who opened *The Straits Times* with their morning tea were greeted by an indignant letter to the editor. The anonymous writer signing off as "Britisher" demanded to know why the "Governor of a British Colony" chose to travel by a "foreign mail boat" from a port like Singapore. Noting that the *Prince Ludwig*'s shipping line belonged to "a foreign government" which subsidized its operations, "Britisher" reminded all readers:

> we must remember that Britishers must stand or fall together for the glory of God and Empire and our tendency of late seems to be in the direction of too much individuality. Britain still rules the waves and if she wishes to continue to do so, she must not forget her mercantile navy.[231]

As if to nullify this accusation, *The Straits Times*' editorial page claimed that Young was "universally respected for those great qualities of caution and stability which go so far towards the making of a successful Governor."[232]

With the Youngs still at sea, news also reached Singapore by telegram of the *Komagata Maru*'s detention in Vancouver. *The Straits Times* published an editorial on the *Komagata Maru* affair, fervently upholding white might:

> We must never let ourselves fall into the error of thinking that there is any comparison between the white invasions of India, Malaya or even China, and the brown or yellow invasions of Canada, Australia or South Africa. The white never displaces labour or lowers standards of living... he creates a demand for labour and raises the standards of living....[233]

The newspaper of record went on to remind its readers that:

> (i)t would be an almost incalculable boon to the masses in China if thousands of whites and millions of capital poured into that country to stimulate and direct the energies of the people by giving them modern scientific guidance... we would have to risk the loss of India, if it came to be a question between preserving our white standards and giving Indians unlimited, unrestricted rights of settlement everywhere within the Empire.[234]

The great and good of the colony of Singapore had a clear-eyed view of the White Man's burden. They had to guide the natives and keep them in their place. But men like Gurdit and his radicalised passengers on the *Komagata Maru* would not go gently into the coming night as the lights began to go out in Europe.

[XV]

DECLARATIONS OF WAR

In July 1914, a series of momentous diplomatic moves played out in Europe's polished corridors of raw power. The killing of the heir presumptive to the Austrian-Hungarian throne by Serbian nationalists was not just a Balkans storm. The 28 June assassination produced a chain reaction that exposed the impossibly complex tangle of regional alliances that towed the world towards war. On one side backing Serbia was the Triple Entente of Russia with Britain and France. On the other side stood the Triple Alliance of Germany, the Austro-Hungarian Empire and Italy. The system of alliances served as a safeguard against a European war through this delicately poised balance of power. That was the theory at least. But a beautiful theory was about to be raped by a brutal gang of facts.

The miasma of secret diplomacy can be as lethal as the fog of war. Envoys and generals from each side guessed and second-guessed each other. They tried to nudge their own monarchs in the direction they believed to be the right one. The militarists feared that any delay in the inflexible time-table of massive army mobilisation would give the other an advantage in calling up men and equipment. Not everyone was as keen on war as the vengeance-seeking Austrians or the German Kaiser in one of his angry moods.

The Kaiser's own Chancellor Theobald von Bethmann-Hollweg feared the consequences of "rolling the iron dice" on the path to war. In reality, the fumbling pre-war diplomacy resembled less an "iron dice" than a massive Rubik's Cube. The puzzle's six scrambled sides were being fiddled simultaneously by dozens of gloved hands. The efforts to reconcile clashing agendas were knocking it closer to the edge of the negotiating table and into the fire. The series of potential chain-reactions to a single declaration of war was as follows:

if Austria declared war on Serbia, then Russia would declare war on Austria; if Russia went to war with Austria, then Germany would go to war with Russia; if Germany fought Russia, then France would fight Germany; and if France was attacked by Germany, via Belgium, then Britain would attack Germany. In the space of one week, every "if" became a when.[235]

On 5 July 1914, the German Kaiser Wilhelm II was at his New Palace in Potsdam. He was preparing for his annual summer cruise the following day but had one last bit of diplomacy to attend to before setting off. He was to host the Austrian Ambassador to lunch at noon. Over their meal, he read a series of messages the Ambassador had brought personally from his Emperor. After perusing the letters, the Kaiser looked up and made a promise that he would live to regret. He told the Austrian diplomat that as a loyal ally his Empire had Germany's full support.

The German Kaiser offered his imperial promise to the Austrians without thinking through the consequences. Incredibly, the impetuous and mercurial Kaiser was giving the Austrians a blank cheque to punish the Serbs for spilling royal blood. With backing from Germany's Supreme War Lord, the Austrians became mulish and unyielding. The decaying Austro-Hungarian empire wanted to go down in glorious combat, even if it meant taking down the rest of Europe. Kaiser Wilhelm II also fatally misjudged the positions of his Russian and English cousins in the opposing Triple Entente. Instead of rallying behind the cause of blue blood over the killing of a fellow royal, the Tsar supported Serbia and championed his Slavic red blood ties. In his gamble of committing support for the Austrians, the Kaiser had also wrongly assumed that his English cousin would stay out of the fight. On the side-lines of the European family affair, the Japanese, Ottoman Turks and others watched events unfold with a mix of fascination and alarm.

Across the Atlantic in the United States, few were paying much attention to the growing geopolitical storm known as the July Crisis as it thundered into the First World War. On the day the Kaiser made his promise to the Austrian Ambassador, a bomb went off in the California ranch owned by potato farmer and revolutionary Jowala Singh. The ex-sepoy poet and Ghadar revolutionary Harnam Singh had been following the instructions in the bomb manual procured from Russian revolutionaries in London, which Taraknath had delivered to California. Now as the smoke cleared, Harnam Singh looked down at the bloody stump of his left arm. The careless experiment left him with a new nickname – Tundilat or The Armless Lord.

Anchored off the Canadian shoreline, passengers on the *Komagata*

Maru wondered if they too had made a bad mistake as they experienced their own July crisis. A health department official visiting their ship submitted a damning report to Vancouver's immigration department: "I found a large accumulation of ashes and garbage on the upper deck. The toilets were exceedingly filthy and required flushing… (b)elow deck the accommodation is crowded; the floors are filthy, and the (passengers), some of them sick are expectorating over the floors."[236] The official's recommendation was to land the passengers in a quarantine station so that the ship could undergo a thorough fumigation, a good scrubbing of its woodwork and lime washing of its bunks. Reid and Hopkinson studied the report and filed it away without further action.

On 6 July, the German Kaiser embarked on his annual summer cruise. The Germans wavered between aggression and caution while the other powers tried to figure out if they should mobilise their armies fully or partially. As the Kaiser's royal yacht set out from Kiel port on the Baltic Sea, over on the eastern edge of the Pacific Ocean, Gurdit received bad news. After several legal challenges, the Court of Appeal of British Columbia had taken a stand. The court unanimously decided that it had no authority to interfere with the immigration department's decisions on the fate of the ship. As Europe found itself sleepwalking with eyes wide open towards war, the trapped passengers of the *Komagata Maru* had run out of options. On 10 July, they sent a plaintive letter in authentic Indian English voice detailing their plight to the *Daily News-Advertiser* in Vancouver: "Yesterday we asked Mr Reid to supply us with water and food. He replied he was thinking the matter, on this we requested him, 'How long will take for consideration?' and what would be the use of that when [we] are going to starve."[237] The letter continued:

> We set example before him, stating that if you are kept in this wretched condition for a day, you will of course come to know 'What the real hunger.' These are the words we spoke to Mr Reid and added, that it he will not arrange very soon, we shall be compelled to take boats to get ashore when starving. But there is a proverb 'Might is right'. Who hears us in our such a condition?[238]

The pleas fell on deaf ears. By 17 July, the necessary customs and immigration papers for deportation had been prepared. Water was pumped on the ship. The men on board were told that they had to leave or be removed by force. But after a two-month tug-of-war that left them tired, hungry and frustrated, the passengers were in no mood to cooperate. That same evening, four Sikhs crossed the border to the US and then back into Canada a few hours later. They told immigration officials they were going to see a friend.

The first of the four to return, Mewa Singh, was found carrying a revolver and hundreds of rounds of ammunition. He had been in Canada since 1906, worked in lumber-mills and had been brought into the circle of activist Sikhs in Vancouver. His three companions, including the Vancouver temple priest Balwant Singh, were all arrested on the US side of the border carrying automatic pistols and ammunition. Interrogated, they admitted to meeting with Taraknath Das and the wrestler-priest Bhagwan Singh. The Ghadar network was caught red-handed in the act of attempting to provide arms to the passengers on the *Komagata Maru*. Now, Reid believed that they had the right to up the ante and get the vessel out by force.

On Saturday, 18 July, the passengers took control of the ship. It was a passengers' mutiny to prevent the Japanese captain from sailing away. The same day, a harbour tug called the *Sea Lion* was deployed. Loaded on to the tug was 30-day send-off supply of food for the steamer's passengers. On standby were 125 police officers and an additional 35 immigration officers sworn in as special constables boarded the tug. Reid intended to storm the steamer, subdue the passengers, dump the supply of food on them and then pull it with its troublesome and rebellious load out to sea. Hopkinson was Reid's subordinate. But he had another chain of command to follow as a British Indian government operative serving an imperial intelligence network. The Viceroy of India had already warned the Canadians against using excessive force. He did not want them to make martyrs of the Punjabis and inflame opinion among Sikhs in India. Hopkinson sensed that a raid under cover of dark could be risky and produce a backlash. But his warnings were ignored. The gung-ho 31-year-old Vancouver police chief, Malcolm McLennan, thought that their overwhelming superiority and the cover of night would win the day.

The next evening, the tug approached the vessel riding at anchor. Past midnight, Hopkinson made one last effort to speak to the passengers when the tug came alongside the steamer. He called out for Gurdit but was rebuffed. A searchlight passed over the faces of the passengers. The men on the steamer leaned over, shouting and brandishing clubs, bamboo poles, stoking irons, axes, swords and other weapons. One passenger yelled out Hopkinson's name and told him in Punjabi: "This ship is going to stay here. She is not going to move. If you start a fight (we) will show you how to fight. If you make fast we will jump into your boat and you fight you and take chances. (We) are not afraid."[239]

The steamer had its share of trained fighting men. The ex-sepoys were primed for combat. The Vancouver police on the tugboat were likewise ready for action. The tug-boat gunned towards its target. A Canadian policeman hurled a grappling hook towards the *Komagata Maru* and caught its rail. The rope between the two ships became a tense link. After failing to dislodge the hook, one of the passengers produced an axe and started to chop at the rope. McLennan started up a water hose on the tug and aimed a stream of cold sea water at the axe-wielding passenger and those around him. The drenched men fell back. A few rallied and held their ground.

And then it began. The passengers of the *Komagata Maru* hurled lumps of coal, scrap metal and other hard objects down at the men in the tug-boat. Gurdit and his young son Balwant could hear the shouts, screams, crashes and thuds. Only parts of the fight were visible from the port-hole of their cabin where they had been kept for their own safety by the passengers. The Canadian police and special constables on the tugboat ducked out of the way of the flying projectiles. Those who were slow to take cover suffered head or facial injuries. One detective fell overboard and had to be fished out. The panicked men on the tug crowded to one side to get away from the fusillade causing the small vessel to list danger-ously. At the last minute, someone with presence of mind had shouted out: "Keep to the left or we shall sink."[240]

The Vancouver Police Chief Malcolm McLennan continued to man the hose, braving the rainstorm of projectiles. A former Sikh sepoy fired several warning shots but McLennan ordered his men to hold their fire. It was getting far too dangerous for the listing *Sea Lion*. Another yelled "Get her away!" and a constable cut the rope to free the battle-damaged tug. After fifteen intense minutes, the battle was all over. The *Sea Lion* retreated while Gurdit and his lions of the sea exchanged looks of wonder mixed with relief.

After the surprise reversal, the Canadians decided that it was time to call in the big guns, quite literally. On 21 July, a Canadian naval battle cruiser, the HMCS *Rainbow*, sailed and anchored alongside the *Komaga-ta Maru*. The war-ship was old and tired, but it bristled with a dozen heavy-calibre weapons and machine-guns. It would not threaten another battleship but the passenger steamer was certainly no match for it. Watch-ing from the upper floor offices of his friend and lawyer Edward Bird, Hussain Rahim said aloud in exasperation: "It is a big joke". The ship's guns were pointed at the steamer. "They could sink her with two shots" exclaimed Rahim.[241] Below them, thousands of spectators thronged the waterfront in anticipation of a one-sided naval battle in the harbour. On the *Komagata Maru*, a pair of musicians with a seven-stringed *sarangi* and a drum tried to raise spirits with a battle song. It was no longer a fair fight. Even the *Sea Lion* had returned, this time with a platoon of soldiers with fixed bayonets.

The Komagata Maru *with the* Rainbow.

The Komagata Maru *with the* Sea Lion.

Rahim agreed to discuss the situation with the passengers and boarded the steamer on 22 July. Wearing a trilby among the turbans, the stout chairman of the Shore Committee climbed aboard. Reid had given him an hour to persuade them to agree, but after several extra hours of negotiations, it was agreed that the ship would leave Vancouver for Yokohama before returning to Hong Kong. Rahim had the Shore Committee wire a message to the Ghadar Party in San Francisco:

> Fearless passengers repulsed first midnight attack, and were ready to face Marines today but settlement effected by Hindoo Committee to avoid bloodshed. Immigration will provision ship tomorrow for return voyage. People laughed bringing Cruiser against unarmed passengers. This inhumane treatment to be known all over. Ship may sail tomorrow.[242]

The Ghadar Party did not even wait for the steamer to set sail. The day before Rahim boarded for talks with the passengers, Ghadar Party President Sohan Singh Bhakna sailed for Yokohama from San Francisco. He wanted to intercept the *Komagata Maru* in Japan and arm it with 200 automatic pistols and 2,000 rounds of ammunition which the resourceful Bhagwan Singh had somehow found in the U.S.

On 23 July, the *Komagata Maru* pulled away from Vancouver and steamed out into the open sea. Some of its passengers leaned over its side. They were no longer holding coal-bricks or scrap-wood. Instead they wielded their shoes. With white foam cresting against the vessel's sides, they shook their footwear angrily in the direction of the *Sea Lion*. Hopkinson willed himself to believe that the gesture was a parting insult meant for Malcolm Reid, but Hopkinson would not escape the consequences of his own actions so easily. With their badges and uniforms and their apparent control over the immigrants' right to enter, Reid and Hopkinson represented the public face of oppression for the Indians. Hopkinson also had to manage a troubled group of Indian spies who were hunted by supporters of the so-called Shore Committee.

Three days later, on Sunday, 26 July, the Ghadar Party held a fundraising meeting in Oxnard in California. Now living in Oxnard, Nawab Khan came to hear Bhagwan Singh and Mohammed Barkatulla speak at the event drawing Sikhs, Hindus and Muslims. With Har Dayal's departure, the triumvirate of Hindu, Muslim and Sikh leading the party had done their best to heal the divisions. Nawab Khan had agreed to rejoin the party. After the loss of his Tokyo teaching post, Barkatullah had received funds from the Ottomans and the Emir of Afghanistan.

The *Komagata Maru*'s plight was in everyone's mind. It had featured at a special meeting in the previous month in Portland, Oregon, but the Ghadar Party network had no shortage of contentious issues to raise. The Sikh and Muslim speakers tailored emotional appeals to their audience. Bhagwan fired up the Sikhs by reminding them that the British had wantonly destroyed the walls of the sacred Rikabganj *gurdwara* in Delhi where a Sikh guru had been martyred. They had also taken control of Khalsa College, a seat of sacred learning. He implored his audience to contribute funds so that weapons could be bought for the coming uprising. Barkatullah told the Muslims in the audience that all Christians were enemies of Islam, but that the British were Islam's greatest foe. They should join hands, take up arms and drive the British from India.

Barkatullah pulled Nawab aside at the meeting, but Nawab had no idea then that he was talking to the Prime Minister of the future Kabul-based provisional Indian government-in-exile. In confidence, Barkatullah shared some startling predictions with his fellow Muslim. He told Nawab that Britain would be compelled to join the coming European war. Rebellions would break out in Egypt, Ireland, South Africa and elsewhere. Barkatullah assured Nawab that the timing was just right to go to India, seduce the sepoys and start the mutiny there against the British. Barkatullah even envisioned an alliance between the Asian powers of India, China and Turkey.

The Kaiser's yacht returned to its home port of Kiel in the Baltics the following day. Amid rising tensions and fearing capture by a British Royal Navy patrol, the Kaiser had cut short his summer cruise. Events were moving at breakneck speed. The morning after his arrival home he read an urgent telegram from London. His Ambassador in London warned of Britain's veiled threat to join the war against Germany. The last straw was a message from the Russian Tsar. The excitable, conspiratorial and impulsive Kaiser suspected some deception against him.

In apparent white heat, the Kaiser had scribbled out his furious reaction on the margins of the Tsar's message: "From the dilemma raised by our fidelity to the venerable old Emperor of Austria we are brought into a situation which offers England the desired pretext for annihilating us under the hypocritical cloak of justice... we squirm isolated in the net...."[243] Resolved to activate Islam and India's Muslims to take the crown jewel of Britain's colonies, the Kaiser was acting under the influence of men like General Bernhardi whom Har Dayal had quoted so approvingly: "our consuls... must fire the whole Mohammedan world to fierce rebellion against this hated, lying, conscienceless nation of shopkeepers, for if we are to be bled to death, England shall at least lose India."[244]

For the brash and petulant Kaiser, the war was between cousins and hereditary monarchs fighting for their honour and reputation. He was not about to back down and lose his honour. He began by declaring war on the Russian Empire on 1 August. The world was about to be plunged into fire. The Kaiser rolled the iron dice, bumped the scrambled Rubik's Cube off the table and watched as dominoes began to fall. On 4 August 1914, after Germany declared war on France, Britain in turn declared war on Germany.

The *Komagata Maru* was then at the halfway mark of its return journey to Yokohama. In San Francisco, the Ghadar Party immediately organised a rally. The audience were told to leave for India to fight the British. A list of volunteers was drawn up with more than 200 names taken. The 4 August issue of *Ghadar* published "The Trumpet of War" with a call to arms: "O, warriors, the time you have been awaiting has come. The bugle of war has sounded. The War between England and Germany has started. Now is the time for India. If you set up a mutiny now, England will come to an end. On the one side Germany will smite them and the other side you."[245]

In Singapore, the Adjutant of the 5th Light Infantry, Lieutenant W G Strover recorded tersely in the battalion confidential diary on 5 August: "9.40 AM Received news of Declaration of War with Germany."[246] The collapse of global markets was already being felt throughout the Straits Settlements. A flurry of telegrams and rushed instructions were received in Singapore's commercial offices and merchant houses along Collyer Quay. The messages were in this vein: suspend all purchases, get rid of stocks quickly at the best possible prices and approach all transactions with extreme caution. Firms stopped extending credit and transferred goods to British ships. The price of daily necessities jumped from between 20 to 400 percent. A tin of condensed milk almost doubled in price while a *picul* of rice – 60 kg or as much as a man could carry on a shoulder pole – was up by 20 percent. Rubber estates began hoarding the staple and prices threatened to escalate further. Sugar prices rose by 30 percent. A cup of coffee or tea with milk now cost twice as much and cigarette prices rose four-fold overnight. Singapore was not a cheap place. Now it was even more costly, putting further strain on the poorly paid sepoys who bought necessities out of their personal funds.

The garrison in Singapore had already been ordered to take up a precautionary period of mobilisation earlier on 30 July. From Alexandra Barracks, the sepoys of the 5th were sent to posts in Pulau Brani and Pulau Blakang Mati as well as to guard sea-side stations like Tanjong Katong. The phoney part of the war had begun. Late in the evening of 3 August, a unit of the 5th commanded by Pathan Subedar Sharuf-ud-din were manning their post in Tanjong Katong. Three unidentified boats headed towards the post, sailing over part of the submarine telegraph cable connecting Aden to Hong Kong. After the boats refused to stop or identify themselves, the sepoys were instructed to fire warning shots. A few days earlier, a police launch had been sent out to disperse sampans in the area. But the sepoys were not the only ones to see some action. From Singapore's all-white barracks at Tanglin, the KOYLI were despatched to their mobilisation stations including Keppel Harbour, the waterworks and cable depot. On 7 August, 21 soldiers from the KOYLI battalion were sent to Tanjong Pagar wharf to detain a group of 33 German reservists preparing to embark on a Dutch vessel to join the Imperial German Army.

At Alexandra Barracks, the men of the 5th Light Infantry had been observing their *roza* (fast) for the holy month of Ramadan since mid-July. Breaking fast cost a lot more with the rise in prices. The men were used to eating lots of spiced meat and drinking milk in India. Paid in rupees and living on a dollar standard in Singapore, they could barely afford milk and meat. The men also normally did light duties during the fasting month. But the 5th's Adjutant Lieutenant Strover had other ideas. Singapore, after all, was now on a war footing. Mobilisation orders should also put the Indian Muslim sepoys on a stepped-up operational tempo, like the white soldiers of the KOYLI who could be shipped out to Europe at any time.

Strover strongly hinted to his Commanding Officer, Lieutenant Colonel Martin, that the Muslims should break fast and perform regular duties. At Strover's insistence, the question was put to the Indian officers and the regimental *maulvi* (religious teacher), Faiz Ali Hassain. The sepoys told their English commanders what they thought they wanted to hear. But one of the Pathan sepoys, Fazal-ul-Raman, from No. 4 Double Company, opposed any breaking of fast. He told Strover that the *maulvi* "was interfering"[247] with their religion. Despite his lowly rank, Fazal-ul-Rahman had a strong following among the men.

An alarmed Subedar-Major Khan Mohammed Khan warned Martin and Strover that Fazal was "much too religious"[248] and that his ideas might cause problems among the men. Fazal was discharged and allowed to leave by December 1914. The hasty dismissal suggested he had struck a raw chord among some of the men. This was a weak but clear signal of early disaffection. His departure did not restore faith in the regimental *maulvi*, and the 5th's ranking Indian officer, the Subedar-Major.

So, holy month or not, on 26 August, Subedar Wahid Ali Khan, Jemadar Chiste Khan and 98 sepoys from "D" company of No. 2 Double Company under Captain Ball were sent off to the island of Pulau Brani to help man mobilisation stations. They relieved the KOYLI troops who were sent back to the mainland. The two senior Indian officers did not get along at all. The Pathan Jemadar Aziz-ud-din of F Company recalled that when the war broke out, he proposed to Lieutenant Strover that British officers should also wear a khaki *pagri* (turban) instead of western headgear to demonstrate unity. When the issue was discussed in the orderly room, Khan Mohammed Khan and Wahid Ali Khan agreed to it. However, Chiste, Dunde, Abdul Ali Khan and Mohammed Yunus Khan, the other Indian officers, vetoed it.

Separately, the Malay States Guides regiment in Taiping were quickly despatched to Singapore to bolster its defences. Leaving behind a skeleton staff, the Sikh-dominated Guides arrived in Singapore a week after the declaration of war. Setting up headquarters in the Rumah Miskin area of Balestier Road, the Guides consisted of three companies of infantrymen and a battery of three mountain guns from Nawab Khan's old section. The Guides' Muslim sepoys would be expected to also guard critical installations during the holy month.

Encouraged by his Subedar-Major Fatteh Singh and other enthusiastic Indian officers, Guides Commanding Officer (CO) Lieutenant-Colonel Charles Henry Brownlow Lees dashed off a message to the GOC Major-General Reade. Lees' letter affirmed that the sepoys of the Malay States Guides were keen to volunteer for service overseas. The 43-year-old Sandhurst trained officer had been assured by Fatteh Singh of their readiness to serve, but the Sikh Subedar-Major had overlooked the murmurings of discontent about an overseas deployment. The Guides had not signed up for this and the sepoys' contract had stated: "I will serve anywhere in the Federated Malay States, but in case of war between Great Britain and any other power, I will serve, if required, in the Straits Settlements."[249] The men of the Guides were quite comfortable in Taiping where they owned many of the coffee shops, most of the bullock cart transport business and also lent money. Keen on proving their loyalty, Fatteh Singh had overstated their readiness to serve outside the Straits Settlements. Fortunately for Lees, the matter however was not tested immediately as the War Office in London replied that they were not required at the time.

In the meantime, with the outbreak of war, the Ghadar movement finally launched its long-threatened insurgency from California. Sohan Singh Bhakna had arrived in Yokohama with the consignment of automatic pistols and ammunition, waiting for the *Komagata Maru* to arrive. Sohan was still on the high seas when war broke out. Few expected the war to start so soon. It put everything on an accelerated time-table. There was a rush to action. A day later, Nawab Khan attended a meeting in Fresno with, by some accounts, about 500 Indians while others counted up to 5,000. The Ghadar Party's Big Three – the pan-Islamist Barkatullah, the Sikh Bhagwan Singh and the Hindu Ram Chandra – told the Indians to leave for India at once. Ram Chandra addressed the gathering with fighting words:

> The ghosts of our ancestors are branding us as shameless progeny… these ghosts will never know rest until we cut down every Englishman. Our Motherland is summoning us to come and free her from the clutches of these tyrants. If you claim to be sons of India deposit your belongings with the Yugantar Ashram and be ready to board the ship for India. Let each of my countrymen, who is prepared to undertake the work, come to the hotel and give me his name. We shall see that you are supplied with arms on arrival in India.[250]

More than half the audience, mostly Sikhs, agreed to join the Indian insurgency immediately. On 11 August, a group estimated by some in the thousands turned up in Sacramento to hear the Big Three. The teenager Kartar Singh Sarabha, still churning out Gurmukhi translations at the *Ghadar* press, attended the meeting. Straining at the bit he wanted to take the first steamer back to India. His fellow revolutionary Prithvi Singh Azad recalled discussions over methods to defeat the British in India. This included the purchase of weapons, manufacture of bombs and entering barracks to seduce the sepoys. Prithvi had been a regular visitor to Jowala's farm and practised bomb making with Harnam Singh. In fact, he was present when the bomb blew off Harnam's arm. Standing at 170 cm (5 feet 7 inches), Prithvi had a strong build, a long nose and small eyes. His right arm was tattooed and he was not someone to be tampered with easily. He was no coward. But it dawned on the 22-year-old Prithvi that the men lacked a clear operational revolutionary programme. Instead the general view taken was "*jiwen da lagge, tiwen la laiyey*" (Let's take whatever action seems right and suitable).[251]

With a new wooden arm after his failed bomb-making experiment, Harnam Singh Tundilat had earned wisdom the hard way. He knew that the mutiny movement of the Ghadar was not prepared for an insurgency. But the issue was whether to take advantage of the fact that the British Empire was now bogged down in war. The leaders in the movement had different ideas on how to proceed. Sohan Singh Bhakna tossed and turned for two nights on the best course of action. The war was an opportunity to strike, but were they ready? Like Harnam, he concluded that whatever the condition of readiness, it was necessary to take advantage of the opportunity; there was no alternative. Having finally made up his mind, the founding President of the Ghadar Party sent instructions to

San Francisco: "All of you should reach India as early as possible, reach out to those forces which the British Government was to utilise for its benefit so as to convert them to the cause of liberation of the country."[252]

Prithvi would reflect later that wishful thinking ruled the roost – "We were ready to believe in the success of our mission... (b)lind faith is a powerful force."[253] Taraknath Das had decided to distance himself from an enterprise that was developing on the momentum of emotion. Har Dayal, now safe in neutral Geneva not far from his flame Hauswirth's hometown, had also surfaced doubts in a letter to his old friend Wyck Van Brooks. But for better or worse, the insurgency had begun. Over the next month, mobilisation calls were made across the West Coast in towns and villages where Indians worked or studied. They were all told to raise the banner of revolt in India, board ships and return to India via Asian ports including Hong, Kong, Shanghai and Singapore. Passion and improvisation ruled the day. It was the revolutionary version of a shotgun wedding. An oft-recited poem among the revolutionaries was "The lions will march forward, only jackals will stay behind."[254] Few noticed the vultures circling overhead.

[XVI]

INSURGENTS AND RAIDERS

Inspector Hopkinson had helped to chase away Gurdit Singh and the *Komagata Maru* from Canada. But the secret policeman had little time to savour his victory. He had sent a cable warning his superiors of serious consequences if British troops were taken out of India. The Indian sepoys in the barracks could not be fully trusted. Now, as he tracked a pattern of departures at the end of August, Hopkinson was kept busy compiling reports of Indian revolutionaries leaving San Francisco and Vancouver in regular batches. The British authorities were put on alert. A black list was compiled to arrest hundreds upon their return to India. No ship with more than 200 Indians on board would be allowed to land. In a note circulated by an officer of the Department of Criminal Intelligence the warning was made clear:

Prima facie, every Indian returning from America or Canada, whether labourer, artisan or student, must be regarded with the greatest suspicion as a probable active revolutionary, or at any rate a sympathizer with the revolutionary party. Similarly, those returning from the Far East, other than government servants and other persons vouched for by the Hong Kong and Shanghai authorities, must be regarded in the same light.[255]

Among the first Ghadar revolutionaries to leave for the US was Kartar Singh Sarabha. The teenaged insurgent boarded the SS *Nippon Maru* bound for India via Colombo. The one-armed Harnam Singh Tundilat also boarded a steamer for India via Colombo. Right under Hopkinson's nose, the SS *Mexico Maru* left Victoria Harbour for Hong Kong followed by the SS *Canada Maru*, which departed Vancouver with a number of Ghadrites. The Indians preferred the cheaper but reliable Japanese vessels, which also avoided British shipping lanes and possible detection.

The exodus of revolutionaries was public knowledge by the second week of August. *The Portland Telegram* of Oregon in its 7 August 1914 issue headlined its report from Astoria: "Hindus go home to fight in revolution". The newspaper breathlessly reported that:

> Every train and boat for the south carries large numbers of Hindus from this city, and if the exodus keeps up much longer Astoria will be entirely deserted by East Indians… majority of Hindus employed at Hammond Mills have gone… the men are returning to India by way of San Francisco… a vessel had been chartered to aid in a revolution which is expected to break out in India as a result of England being occupied in the general European war.[256]

The *Komagata Maru* pulled into Yokohama on 16 August. The passengers learnt a week late that the war had started. Sohan Singh Bhakna arrived in Japan just ahead of Gurdit. He was waiting at the port as Gurdit's ship pulled in. Sohan boarded with his load of smuggled weapons and ammunition as well as the latest issues of the *Ghadar*. The contraband was hidden with the help of a sympathetic Japanese crew-member. Bundled in sheets, the weapons were placed in a water tank. From Yokohama, the steamer sailed to Kobe. The British now refused permission for it to return to Hong Kong. While its final destination was being decided, Gurdit enjoyed the hospitality of revolution-friendly Sindhi merchants who garlanded him and paraded him around town on a rickshaw.

In San Francisco, Nawab Khan was at the Yugantar Ashram when he bumped into fellow Ghadrite and Astoria lumber-mill workmate Kesar Singh. Before he knew it, he found himself being ushered aboard the Pacific mail steamer SS *Korea* later that day. Kesar Singh was one of the leaders of returning revolutionaries on the ship. Kesar was packed and all ready to go while Nawab barely had time to gather his belongings. When he protested that he had no money on him for the voyage, Kesar berated him: "What need have you of money, you are going to lay down your life?"[257]

Like many others, Nawab Khan the Ranghar rolling-stone was now being swept along. Rajput honour could have made it hard for the ex-sepoy to decline. On board, he found himself alongside Jowala Singh, the prosperous potato farmer from Stockton. For the time being at least, they put aside earlier differences over the issue of scholarships and Sikh-Muslim rivalry. Jowala Singh came along with Jagat Ram, a Punjabi Hindu who was on the permanent staff of the *Ghadar* press in San Francisco. He too had taken part in the bomb-making experiments in Jowala Singh's farm with Harnam Singh Tundilat. The Hindu Jagat and Sikh Jowala on one hand and the quarrelsome Nawab on the other had little love between them, but they would have to put up with each other during the voyage.

As the SS *Korea* prepared to lift anchor, the Ghadar Party Big Three of Ram Chanda, Bhagwan and Barkatullah boarded the ship. Like all good admirals, they were not going to sail but came to give the men their orders. Nawab took note of their pre-departure instructions:

> Your duty is clear. Go to India and stir up rebellion in every corner of the country. Rob the wealthy and show mercy to the poor. In this way you will win universal sympathy. Arms will be provided for you on your arrival in India. Failing this you must ransack the police station for rifles. Obey without hesitation the commands of your leaders.[258]

With planned stopovers in Yokohama, Kobe, Nagasaki and Manila before arriving in Hong Kong, the SS *Korea* would turn out to be a key Ghadar vessel. The men had become pinballs with different itineraries on the shipping routes that had become roads to revolution. Some of the men would break journey along the way and reunite later in Hong Kong. Jagat Ram planned to stop at Yokohama, head for Tokyo to procure arms and then divert them to Manila before rejoining Nawab and Jowala Singh in Hong Kong. From Hong Kong, the men on the SS *Korea* would take another Japanese steamer, the *Tosha Maru* headed for Calcutta through Singapore and Penang.

*Jatha*s (squads) were formed to distribute the forces quickly after their arrival. They could be activated at the right time and avoid clustering for easy capture. Nawab was asked to lead one of these squads. Prithvi Singh Azad, who was on the SS *Korea* with Nawab Khan, had doubts about the strangers around them. The tough and muscled Prithvi worried when he noticed that every decision was made openly and collectively amid suspected informants. Some of these spies reported to Hopkinson and the imperial intelligence network. The now not so secret plan was to land the revolutionaries in ports across India and then make their way to the Punjab. The returning insurgents would split up into their assigned *jatha*s and get to work persuading sepoys in the barracks to mutiny and join the uprising against the British. Enroute to the insurrection in India, the men of the mutiny movement would do what they could to stir up revolt among sepoy garrisons in various Asian ports of call.

To support the rising, Ghadar's operational headquarters would be established in the Sikh holy city of Amritsar. Jagat Ram told the revolutionaries on the SS *Korea* that if they wanted to get in touch, they could so through Har Dayal's old friend Bhai Parmanand at his pharmacy in Lahore. The vanguard of returning Punjabi insurgents arrived quickly in India. Kartar Singh Sarabha landed in Calcutta where he connected with Taraknath Das's mentor Jatin Bagha, the tiger-killer and founder of the revolutionary Bengali Yugantar underground movement. Bagha gave him a letter of introduction to Rash Behari Bose, leader of the branch of the Yugantar Party that had lobbed the bomb at the Viceroy that sparked Har Dayal's re-awakening and the Ghadar's launch almost two years earlier.

Based on the plans reported on by Hopkinson and the assorted intelligence networks, the British Indian government quickly passed two laws. The "Foreigners Ordinance" on 29 August restricted the return of expatriate Indians to India. The government could arrest these returnees as illegal foreigners. A week later, a follow-up law called the Ingress into India Ordinance gave legal cover for the police to detain returnees and confine them to their villages. These laws applied to India, but not Hong Kong, Shanghai, Manila, Singapore, Penang and Rangoon. These stop-over ports, with a significant community of Indian sepoys, constables, workers and traders, were lotus-pads for Indians seeking a passage to North America. Now they worked the other way with a returning influx of revolutionaries.

On 16 September, the *Komagata Maru* dropped anchor at the outer ports limits of Singapore en route to Calcutta. Gurdit tried to land to collect some of his belongings. He would have made out the familiar silhouette of the island as the ship anchored five kilometres out in the Strait of Singapore. That was the closest he would ever get to Singapore or the Malay States. Predictably, he was refused permission to disembark despite having had long residency in Singapore. No British controlled port outside India would take the ship of sedition. Like Gurdit's old acquaintance Claude Severn in Hong Kong, Sir Arthur Young wanted nothing to do with the ship. The Governor had returned from his truncated home leave, rushing back to Singapore by mail ship on 6 September, and proceeded directly to Government House from the wharf. He had enough to worry about and catch up on than deal with a former resident with apparent seditious tendencies. After three days of fruitless waiting, the Japanese Captain of the *Komagata Maru* had enough. He decided to lift anchor and sail for its final port of call in India.

The *Komagata Maru* and assorted Japanese steamers carrying returning insurgents were not the only ships troubling the British. With the raging war in Europe expanding to Asian waters, the British Admiralty faced the menace of German marauders. As the Japanese steamer inched up the Straits of Malacca towards the Bay of Bengal and Calcutta, the British navy was on high alert. Overseeing British naval interests was Vice Admiral Martyn Jerram. A bulky, broad-faced man in his mid-fifties, Jerram was viewed as a colourless but generally dependable naval officer of average ability. He was responsible for securing shipping routes that sustained the bulk of global trade. Less than a month after the war's outbreak, Jerram moved his headquarters from the China Station in Hong Kong to Singapore to better manage the British and allied trade routes. Jerram had a difficult task. He had to secure waters that London also wanted as far as possible left open to shipping.

In Singapore, Jerram set up base at the top of Fort Canning Hill, overlooking the harbour. From there, he was connected by a signal station to the British transoceanic telegraph cable network known as the All-Red Line. He also had recourse to the base radio station with its towering mast for wireless communications, but in practice the radio signals were constantly disrupted by the island's monsoon rains and frequent thunderstorms. His vast area of operation stretched east of Ceylon, encompassing the Indian Ocean, the Bay of Bengal, the Straits of Malacca, the South and East China Seas, and all the way down to New Zealand.

Jerram's scourge was the German light cruiser known as the SMS *Emden*. The cruiser was part of the East Asia Squadron commanded by the formidable Vice Admiral Maximilian von Graf Spee, who stationed his fleet in the German enclave of Tsingtao in China. In that glorious summer before the war, Graf Spee hosted his visiting counterpart, Vice Admiral Jerram, to a series of generous meals where British and German naval officers swore eternal friendship. Among the German officers was the SMS *Emden*'s Kaptain Karl von Müller.

A quiet 40-year-old with steely blue eyes, Müller, the son of a Prussian infantry officer, knew how to carry himself and commanded instant respect. He impressed Von Graf Spree and was given his first full command a year before the war. He had an experienced crew on board the *Emden*, including his exuberant 33-year-old second-in-command, Kapitan Leutenant (Captain Lieutenant) Helmuth von Mücke and the heavyweight Leutenant Julius Lauterbach. The barrel-chested Lauterbach also served as Prize Officer of the *Emden*, commanding the raiding crews that took over the operations of captured ships. The 39-year-old had sailed all around the region as a merchant navy captain and knew each and every port. Round, jolly and loud, he was a foil to his quiet, thoughtful and slightly built Captain Müller whom he had known since their time as naval cadets.

Captain Müller and his officers knew that the *Emden*'s 10.4 cm (4.1-inch) guns were no match in theory for the 15.2 cm (6 inch) armaments of a number of British cruisers. The SMS *Emden* could not even produce

Martyn Jerram (left)
Karl von Müller

its own freshwater. Instead of oil, it relied on coal supplied by its accompanying coal tender auxiliary ship, the *Markommania*. When war broke out, Vice Admiral Graf von Spee gave Müller the widest possible latitude to conduct operations across waters controlled by Admiral Jerram's forces. The SMS *Emden's* first point of entry was the Indian Ocean. Müller would use his ship as a commerce raider in a trade war on the high seas to disrupt and suffocate the Allies supplies of soldiers and provisions.

The *Emden* was one of a number of raiders which supplemented the German U-Boats that operated under the waves. The raiders laid mines and boarded and requisitioned ships as auxiliary raiders or coalers or sunk them after taking their load. The value of a single raider was that it generated fear and uncertainty and tied up fleets dedicated to sinking it. Five weeks after leaving its port in Tsingtao, the *Emden* turned up on 15 September at the mouth of the Hooghly River near Calcutta. From the lips of this 260-km long distributary of the Ganges, the *Emden* embarked on its virgin rampage, sinking five Allied steamers.

As the *Komagata Maru* inched its way towards India, the *Emden* was wreaking havoc on maritime trade routes. The successful sea guerrilla Müller wielded the *Emden* with apparent ease to raid or sink British commercial shipping. He also became adept at capturing allied ships as coal tenders, off-loading part of his crew led by Lauterbach to captain the seized ships which collected coal to fuel the *Emden* at pre-arranged spots. As Prize Officer, Lauterbach's key responsibility was not only to operate the captured ships but gather more information on further quarry. The big, hale and hearty German knew most of the merchant navy captains. Over beers and small-talk, Lauterbach would charm them into surrendering their log-books and newspapers, which provided fresh intelligence for the Germans on ship movements and evading the British dragnet. Skilled at playing mind-games, Lauterbach would later use this asset against his sepoy guards as their prisoner-of-war in Singapore.

Captain Müller also understood well the value of psychological operations in war. He was scrupulous in avoiding civilian casualties if he could help it. But he also believed that attacks on British India could unsettle the Indian subjects of the Raj. It would also puncture the myth of British prestige and invincibility and make them less willing to fight for their colonial master. For Indian revolutionaries, the vulnerability of British India to seaborne attacks proved that Brittania would not always rule the waves or the sub-continent.

After sinking a sixth ship in the Bay of Bengal, the stealthy *Emden* crept in the dark towards the South Indian coastline on 22 September. The German crew were surprised to find Madras (Chennai) port ablaze with light with few war-time security precautions. With their targets con-

Julius Lauterbach

veniently lit up, the *Emden* rained 125 explosive shells on the harbour area over half an hour. Only one small harbour gun returned fire to little effect. The German raider easily outstripped three British cruisers that gave chase. The brazen shelling of India's third biggest port and the spectacular destruction of its shore-line oil tanks created panic in the city with residents stampeding out. The rampage had a ripple effect, panicking traders and merchantmen from visiting India's biggest port in Calcutta. Indeed, for years after the incident, the word *emden* was used to frighten mischievous children into good behaviour and still denotes swaggering behaviour in dialects of South India.

Jerram struggled to outwit the wily German captain. He had not anticipated the embarrassing attack on Madras. He spared no effort to trap the troublesome raider, sending two of his ships to Direction Island in the Cocos-Keeling islands, southwest of Sumatra to ambush it. The island, a major hub with a towering radio mast, was where a number of transoceanic cables of the All-Red Line converged. Jerram expected the Germans to attack the hub and disrupt telecommunication – after all, this is what Britain had done to Germany's submarine cables at the start of the war. But Müller had other ideas for now. He was not content with raiding or sinking commercial shipping. What he wanted to do was to sink a proper allied naval cruiser, a British or French naval ship, in a local port.

Sometime in late September, the *Emden* and the *Komagata Maru* passed each other in the usually storm-tossed waters of the Bay of Bengal. The German and Japanese vessels would have exchanged signals with a lamp in Morse code. In that way, the two vessels that played a part in the coming Singapore mutiny, could well have given each other a mid-ocean wink of connivance.

On 26 September, the *Komagata Maru* entered the Hooghly River off Calcutta, near the spot where the *Emden* had terrorised British shipping less than two weeks earlier. The required inspections and searches were carried out respectfully and tactfully, but the British imperial police failed to find the stash of weapons. The decision was made to send the passengers back to Punjab by train. The ship would dock 27 kilometres upstream from Calcutta at the town of Budge Budge, on the other side of the Hooghly River from the train-station connecting to the Punjab. Citing security concerns, the British arranged for a special train to avoid going through crowded central Calcutta. Suspecting a plot, Gurdit Singh insisted that he had to visit Calcutta for personal business. After protracted negotiations, the passengers reluctantly agreed to disembark under the gaze of a platoon of policemen from the Punjab.

The last two dozen passengers left the ship with Gurdit Singh. He delicately lofted over his head its most important passenger, the Sikh holy book. Gurdit insisted that the *Guru Granth Sahib* had to be lodged at the *gurdwara* in Howrah near Calcutta. This would be done after a religious procession. Making the holy book travel on a train would be sacrilege. The logic did not seem very clear as the same holy book had travelled thousands of kilometres over the seas. Some of the passengers, sensing trouble, were peeling away by then. Eventually, only 250 passengers, mostly from Gurdit's region of the war-like Majha, remained with their leader. As they marched towards Calcutta, Gurdit and others took turns to carry the *Guru Granth Sahib* over their heads.

The Sikhs of the Punjab police kept a respectful distance. But also heading their way was a determined force of 150 white British soldiers of the Royal Fusiliers. And several kilometres away from Budge Budge, a smaller force from the Calcutta police prepared to block the procession. The Calcutta police led by Superintendent J H Eastwood were far less respectful than the Sikhs of the Punjab police. The aggressive Royal Fusiliers now formed up behind the police. Backed up by the force of arms, the Governor's deputy, William Duke, told Gurdit quite curtly that he could not go to the Howrah *gurdwara*. He simply had to turn around, return to Budge Budge and take the train to the Punjab.

It was now a contest of wills. The British had to make clear who was in charge. Given little choice in the matter by the overwhelming force of police and soldiers, the passengers trudged back towards Budge Budge. Gurdit passed the holy book to a fellow passenger and rode a bicycle purchased from a passing village-boy. Gurdit's young son Balwant was likely perched behind the crossbar. The sun had been beating down on the procession all day. When some of the *Komagata Maru* men tried to slip off into an alley to buy water, they found themselves kicked back into place by the brutal Calcutta police. Some of Gurdit's men were carrying the concealed hand-guns Sohan Singh Bhakna had supplied them in Yokohama. It was a wonder that none of them had exploded at the provocations under the hot sun. However, it was a matter of time after all they had endured since Vancouver.

As the sun set, the procession finally approached the Budge Budge train station. The Governor's deputy, William Duke, had come by motor-car and was waiting for them by the train. The police halted the group at a level crossing. No one was sure whether they should be brought back to the ship or immediately onto the train. The tired passengers collapsed on a grass plot just west of the railway line. Darkness quickly covered them. Gurdit was summoned to speak to one of the officials but told them to come to him instead. The wrangling continued until Superintendent Eastwood lunged at the group. As he tried to pull Gurdit out, all hell broke loose. The passengers of the *Komagata Maru* who had fought on the sea off Vancouver were now engaged on land on their own soil.

Amid the flurry of limbs and shoving of bodies, shots were fired on both sides. The enraged Sikhs charged the police. Gurdit's procession pulled bamboo sticks from nearby huts and began attacking constables. Eastwood was shot in the back. Several other British policemen were wounded. One police constable received several blows to the head, exposing part of his brain. Some in Gurdit's group were shot where they stood including a Sikh who received six shots at close range but somehow survived. In the confusion and alarm, young Balwant was separated from his father. Then the Fusiliers took up position and were given the order to fire at will. With a small group returning fire, the passengers of the *Komagata Maru* took cover in a ditch behind a grassy plot before quietly peeling away in the darkness. The only woman still remaining from the *Komagata Maru* was Kishen Kaur. She and her husband managed to keep their family, including a five-year-old son and a baby girl, together amid screams, moans and cries for help as bullets whistled over their heads.

When the smoke cleared and morning came, eighteen of the passengers had been killed, along with two Bengali passers-by, a Punjabi constable and a European volunteer. Superintendent Eastwood was in critical condition in hospital. Gurdit had taken cover in a nearby pool, submerging most of his head for several hours. He slipped away disguised as a Bengali and boarded a train for a city on the Bay of Bengal before finding his way to Central India. His son Balwant was found alive, protected by some Sikh passengers from the ship who were promptly arrested and jailed in Calcutta.

Meanwhile in Vancouver, the Sikh community was torn by a series of vendetta killings between Hopkinson's circle of informants and the *Komagata Maru* Shore Committee's revolutionary supporters. It all came to a head on 21 October at the Vancouver courthouse. Mewa Singh had been tormented after his arrest on the US-Canadian border on suspicion of smuggling weapons to the *Komagata Maru*. Hopkinson had pressured him to make a statement incriminating his Ghadar Party friends, including the wrestler-preacher Bhagwan Singh. Suspected to have been turned and used as Hopkinson's informant, Mewa found himself shunned by the Vancouver Sikh community.

For Mewa Singh, the situation had become intolerable. An outcaste among his own people with no *izzat*, he believed that killing Hopkinson and achieving martyrdom would redeem him in the eyes of his community. The 34-year-old knew exactly where to find his handler in the Vancouver courthouse. Suspecting scant danger from an informant he confidently controlled, Hopkinson stood with his hands in his pockets outside the entrance to a witness room. Approaching Hopkinson, Mewa casually pulled out a revolver and fired several shots point blank at his tormentor. Hopkinson sank to his knees, holding on to Mewa's thigh as he slid down and crumpled to the floor. After firing repeatedly, the Sikh clubbed Hopkinson with the gun. He was exorcising the demons Hopkinson planted in his head. Overpowered by court employees, Mewa Singh said matter of factly, "I shoot... I go to station."[259]

The deed was done. Hopkinson lay dead at his feet. Mewa had purged himself of his demons and avenged the honour of his community. He was ready to die. Hopkinson was accorded a lavish public funeral with thousands in attendance, including his widow Nellie and his two young daughters. Ironically, a monument to the *Komagata Maru* now stands on a prominent point along the route of Hopkinson's funeral procession. His killer Mewa Singh was tried and promptly hanged, with the Sikh's own funeral procession numbering only in the hundreds. But even after the passage of a century, the memory of Mewa Singh's martyrdom is still marked by Vancouver Sikhs with an annual procession, with his picture hung up in the *gurdwara*. Hopkinson's grave has sunk into obscurity. History remembers assassins and martyrs who died for a cause, not the secret policemen who trailed them so diligently to help keep the order of the status quo.

PART THREE

[XVII]

SEDITIOUS SHIPS AND
THE POUNCE ON PENANG

The morning after the Budge Budge outrage, the 1st battalion of the KOYLI sailed from Singapore on the troop transport *Carnarvonshire*. Leaving the island on 27 September was the entire Tanglin garrison of 887 English soldiers, 25 spouses and 44 children. With the British troops enroute home, the sepoys of the 5th and the Guides now assumed responsibility for the defence of Singapore.

On its way out, the *Carnarvonshire* passed Pulau Brani where Captain Ball, Subedar Wahid Ali Khan and Jemadar Chiste Khan were now stationed with No. 2 Double Company of the 5th Light Infantry. Taking advantage of the relative isolation of the little island near Keppel Harbour, Chiste Khan gave lectures on the progress of the war to the men of his D Company as well as C Company. He tried to wean them away from his old enemy, the red-bearded Wahid Ali Khan. Sub-Assistant Surgeon Robert Bell, the 5th's half-Indian, half-English medical officer witnessed on more than one occasion Chiste using a stick to trace maps on the ground. Chiste sketched out the theatre of war to half a platoon of sepoys and told them: "Belgium is taken, France is taken, Japan has left her friendship with England. The Germans will invade England."[260]

Bell noticed that the Chiste had more influence on the men than his immediate superior, Wahid Ali Khan. But he walked away and did not report Chiste immediately to Ball. Colour-Havildar Rahmat Khan had also heard Chiste speak to the men about the war. Under Chiste's influence, the sepoys began to ask themselves: "Why should we fight for England and be killed in Europe when we are only paid a coolie's wage and our wives and children will be left to starve on 2 or 3 rupees per month?"[261] Chiste was spreading ideas right out of the *Ghadar*. Some of the sepoys were soon infected and believed that Britain was losing the war in Europe. They were not alone in feeling uncertain about Britain's prospects.

The *Carnarvonshire* managed to clear the narrow Straits of Malacca, but the battalion's passage home was delayed by reports that the *Emden* was prowling the area. When the *Carnarvonshire* passed Colombo on 4 October, the transport's local *lascar* crew jumped ship. News of the *Emden*'s exploits had rattled the Southeast Asian *lascar* sailors and they deserted as a group. Without warning, they jumped into the sea and swam for shore. The KOYLI regimental police launched lifeboats to retrieve their crew, but the *lascars* were fast swimmers, outpacing the oarsmen and dispersing on land. Mustered in their place were sailors from assorted ships who had been stranded in Colombo after surviving earlier sinkings by the *Emden*.

As the *Carnarvonshire* rebuilt its crew, the SS *Korea* arrived in Manila after a stop-over in Nagasaki. Nawab Khan re-connected with Jagat Ram in the capital of the Philippines. He would have welcomed the appearance of Dost Muhammad Khan, a fellow Ranghar from his home-town of Halwara. Dost organised a meeting of local Ghadar Party sympathisers in his house chaired by their leader, Hafiz Abdulla, a Punjabi Muslim from Ludhiana. In Manila, Jagat and Nawab found a thriving hub of revolutionaries including a determined 24-year-old woman named Gulab Kaur. Part of Hafiz Abdulla's circle, the young Sikh woman had come to Manila with her husband, Mann Singh. The couple had been saving up to migrate to the US for a better life but had found themselves drawn to the revolutionary party in Manila. While Mann flirted with Ghadar ideas, Gulab was drawn deeper into the movement. They heard Jagat Ram exhort at the meeting in Dost's house:

> For sometime past we have been sending you the Ghadr newspaper in order to prepare you for the mutiny and now the time for mutiny has arrived. England is engaged in life and death struggle with Germany. With her attention thus occupied we can, without difficulty, drive the English out of India. Don't let this opportunity slip by you for you will never get another such for centuries. Join us now and be ready to kill or to be killed on arrival in India.[262]

The SS *Korea*'s arrival in Manila now forced the couple to choose between love or mutiny. Gulab proved the more committed half to the cause. Mann decided to continue to the US while his Sikh wife joined Hafiz Abdulla, Nawab Khan and the other revolutionaries on the *Korea*.

Enroute to their next stop in Hong Kong, the revolutionaries held daily meetings discussing the cause of mutiny on the SS *Korea*. There were readings of revolutionary poems from the *Ghadar-di-Gunj* collection. Learning that the passengers would be thoroughly searched in Hong Kong before being allowed to continue their journey, Nawab and Jowala screened the passengers. They looked for weapons and seditious litera-ture. As the ship approached Hong Kong harbour, copies of the *Ghadar*, the *Ghadar-di-Gunj* or cypher writing were thrown overboard.

Pulling into Hong Kong in early October, Nawab found himself on once-familiar territory. He had, however, little time to reminisce about his previous service with the Hong Kong Regiment. As a leader now in the central managing committee of revolutionaries, he got down to work almost immediately. The SS *Korea* arrived at the same time as four other ships loaded with returning revolutionaries from various ports of call. It was an assembly of returning insurgents who now spread out from the harbour area. With a trio of English-speaking Sikhs, Nawab paid a visit to the German Consul at Canton, seeking his help in the coming mutiny.

The German Consul was not new to this game. He had also received Vietnamese rebels seeking help to overthrow the French in Indochina. The Consul offered lip service, inciting them to start the revolution with-out delay. For the Germans, even badly planned and botched mutinies could have nuisance value in diverting enemy resources away from the front-line in Europe.

Nawab and his shipmates tried to influence the Sikh and Muslim se-poys of the 26th Punjabi Infantry regiment. The 26th had been stationed in Hong Kong since the 1911 Chinese Revolution. Nawab and his com-rades had some luck with the enlisted sepoys, but their Indian officers held fast, discouraging any revolutionary ideas and promptly reporting the growing dissent in the ranks. Undeterred, Nawab accompanied the Sikh Ghadarites to the Hong Kong *gurdwara* where Gurdit Singh had started his political odyssey six months earlier. Angry speeches and tur-bulent words resonated in the temple over eight days of Ghadar Party propagandizing. The staunch Muslim Nawab was among those who ad-dressed the congregation, along with his companion Kesar Singh who had pulled him onboard the SS *Korea* in San Francisco at the very last minute.

The Hong Kong authorities had become alert to the rising danger. A monthly newspaper, the *Bharat Ka Nagra* (Drum of India), addressed to two Indian officers of the 26th Punjabi regiment, was seized. The cov-ering letter had incited the pair: "Read this newspaper carefully and see what it has come, cease betraying your country and prepare yourself to die for it. Exhort your brave sepoys to fight for the nation. Instead of Subedars and Jamadars, you will be made Captains and Colonels. Come, brave men, consider and think well, and throw off the chains of slav-ery."[263] Sikh sepoys moved to mutiny were identified, with quick adjust-ments made in the barrack lines to isolate the troublemakers.

If they had sought to avoid arrest by discarding incriminating evidence, Nawab and his associates now risked arrest with their suspicious behaviour and seditious preaching. This group soon found themselves negotiating with the Hong Kong Police Superintendent for permission to leave. Despite the rabble-rousing, they were allowed to board the *Tosha Maru* for Calcutta via Singapore and Penang. The potato farmer revolutionary Jowala Singh decided to sail on the *Mashima Maru*. Both vessels were scheduled to make stopovers in Singapore and Penang. Half of the 300 passengers with Nawab Khan on the *Tosha Maru* were returning revolutionaries, including the female Ghadrite Gulab Kaur. She had begun to give inspiring speeches on liberty for India.

Although passions were fired, some of the more sceptical revolutionaries were beginning to worry about logistics. Suspecting that the promised German supply of arms and ammunition would not materialise in India, they discussed a Plan B. It was agreed that they would attack police stations or loot government treasuries to purchase weapons. These Indian Robin Hoods from America agreed to distribute a portion of their loot money to the poor to win support for the revolution. Leftover cash would be dedicated to the families of Ghadar Party martyrs or scholarships in America for Indian students.

Nawab discussed with his shipmates other plans for action once they secured their weapons. They would target post offices, railway lines and bridges and telegraphic communications. Prisons would be attacked with inmates freed and asked to join the revolution. Sepoys would be won over to the ideas of mutiny and any European or government official who opposed them would be murdered. This was a full-scale insurgency of guerrilla tactics mixed with wishful thinking. Missing was any element of hard thinking on tactics, organisational resilience and effective networking on the ground. And short of attacking police stations or looting treasuries or stealing into regimental armouries, everything hinged on a supply of weapons that the Germans were supposed to provide.

The *Tosha Maru* and *Mashima Maru* arrived in Singapore about the same time in mid-October. Nawab went off immediately to find his old comrades in the Malay States Guides. It is possible that he also met men of the 5th, who mingled with the Guides at Gujarati businessman Kassim Ismail Manoor's home in Pasir Panjang and in the mosques or *gurdwara*. The sepoys he met in Singapore asked Nawab why so many Indians from the US were returning home at the same time. His answer was unequivocal: they were returning to start a mutiny.[264] He encouraged the sepoys to defy their orders and take up arms against their officers. While his habitual braggadocio caused some of the sepoys to laugh at him as he tried to "seduce the troops,"[265] others from the Guides, and perhaps from the 5th too, were intrigued – sufficiently intrigued to board the docked *Tosha*

Maru to meet with the returning revolutionaries and hear from them first hand. Jagat Ram had also found time to speak to the sepoys in Singapore. He was an experienced propagandist who had handled the mail in the Yugantar Ashram in San Francisco. Another revolutionary named Sher Singh Veinpoin, who had sailed from Victoria on the *Canada Maru* to join the *Tosha Maru* in Hong Kong, also went ashore in Singapore. The son of a former Sikh Subedar stationed in Singapore, Veinpoin gave a speech on revolution to a group that may well have included sepoys of the 5th and the Guides.

As the *Tosha Maru* sailed to Penang, news of the massacre at Budge Budge began filtering through. Soon enough, the outrage against apparently unarmed Sikhs spread through the network of Sikh *gurdwaras* across Asian port cities including Singapore, Penang, Rangoon and Hong Kong. In the sanctity of the Singapore and Penang temples, the Sikhs shared copies of the *Ghadar* and revolutionary poems of the *Ghadar-i-Gunj*. News of the *Komagata Maru*'s fate reached the passengers on *Tosha Maru* after it arrived in Penang. The *Mashima Maru* pulled in soon after.

The ships were held in port as the *Emden* continued its rampage, sinking several merchant vessels in the Indian Ocean. Rumours were flying around in an atmosphere of heightened alarm in the British community. Nawab even heard accounts of a rising in India. The pair of ships, the *Emden* and the *Komagata Maru*, which had silently glided past each other somewhere in the Indian Ocean, produced very different reactions. While the *Emden*'s rampage had sown fear and confusion, the violent climax of the *Komagata Maru*'s voyage in Budge Budge had stirred deep anger. Both reactions were milked by the revolutionaries. With the *Tosha Maru* and *Mashima Maru* detained in Penang, Jagat Ram, Kesar Singh, Nawab and their fellow revolutionaries met and came up with a plan. They would approach the company of Guides sepoys in Penang to start a mutiny.[266]

Divided in four groups, the men of the *Tosha Maru* and *Mashima Maru* scouted Penang for gun-maker's shops and police stations which they could loot for weapons. Some visited the Penang *gurdwara* where the preacher welcomed them and where Kesar Singh even managed to fire off a quick sermon. But the authorities got wind of the potential subversion and the revolutionaries were barred from fraternising with the local Sikhs. It was all a bit of a shambles. The day after Jagat Ram led a deputation to meet the Resident Councillor of Penang, the pair of ships were ordered to leave with their troublesome passengers, even with the *Emden* still prowling the area. A mutiny was averted in Penang, but the revolutionaries had left behind some seditious ideas.[267]

The *Mishima Maru* headed for Colombo while the *Tosha Maru* steamed towards Rangoon in British Burma. Rangoon counted about 50,000

Muslims, many of whom were Gujaratis. Nawab and his band tried to tamper with its garrison of sepoys. They also tried to lecture at the *gurd-wara* but were stopped by an alert Indian officer. Likewise, Nawab failed to procure arms from a Pathan arms-dealer. The Ghadar propaganda did not spark a mutiny in Rangoon, but some in the local Muslim community and roving Ghadar agents did not give up. For all their efforts, they were rewarded when the Muslim sepoys of the 130th Baluchis posted to Rangoon the following month refused to go on active service against the Ottoman Army.

The *Tosha Maru* finally docked in Calcutta on 29 October with its 175 Indian passengers including Nawab Khan. The authorities in Calcutta, recognising the passengers to be "distinctly anti British and ripe for mischief"[268] exercised their new legal powers. They searched all the passengers thoroughly and questioned them to sort out the harmless from the revolutionaries. A suitcase was found containing four revolvers, two automatic pistols and hundreds of rounds of ammunition. Nawab Khan and Jagat Ram escaped the initial screening. Potato farmer Jowala Singh and the cell-leader Kesar Singh did not. With Bhai Parmanand as a common point of contact, those who eluded the dragnet made their way to the Punjab to regroup. In a cable to India, the British Consul in San Francisco warned of the role played by Bhai Parmanand: "We are not afraid of Hardayal; he speaks out his thought. We are most afraid of Bhai Paramananda (Parmanand) because he says nothing and one can never know what he is at".[269]

As the *Tosha Maru* was being searched for weapons and seditious literature, Young and Jerram received reports in Singapore of a devastating allied loss. There had been a major attack in Penang harbour. A month after the *Emden*'s brazen night-time attack on Madras port, and with most of the allied fleet still hunting it down, the raider's nerveless Captain Müller had done it again. Like a cobra, the *Emden* had silently pounced on Penang's Georgetown harbour, the Straits Settlements' second major port. Jerram had failed to draw lessons from the Madras embarrassment. In Penang, the buoys to the harbour channels as well as the harbour itself were lit up at night, while its two major lighthouses shone brightly. To be fair to the Vice Admiral, the British priority was commerce over security and the lights were to facilitate night-time shipping. There were, however, some basic lapses including sloppy monitoring of local shipping and little to no co-ordination between allied ships patrolling the area. Several allied ships, including French and Russian destroyers, were berthed in Penang but wireless communication between them was patchy. There was also no proper monitoring or early-warning system in place. Müller exploited these lapses to the fullest.

The *Emden* had crept into the lion's den with its jaws wide open, but Jerram and his military professionals were slack about analyzing the intelligence they received. They had failed to connect some basic dots that had given them an advantage over Müller. The German captain did not know that two of the *Emden*'s coal tender ships had been seized off Western Sumatra with their German crew. This was a clear signal to authorities in Penang that the raider was close by. Instead of doubling down on port security, in a show of confidence, the captured German crew were marched through the streets of Penang. Local newspapers also publicised the *Emden*'s signature subterfuge of raising a dummy funnel for a four-funnel silhouette to confuse look-outs. As the *Emden* sneaked into the harbour, Müller ordered the extra funnel raised. He had no idea that this ruse was already known, but the lookouts in Penang did not put three and one together when the fake funnel was hoisted.

A Penang harbour launch chugged by as close as 20 metres to the German ship, but complacently allowed it to sail right into the warship anchorage. In his memoir, the jovial but sly Leutenant Lauterbach recorded his impressions of Penang as they approached: "A spacious placid bay rimmed with green jungle-clad shores, a flat-topped green mountain, and at its foot, sprawling down to the shore, the fascinating city of Penang, with white houses, green palms, and gray, dirty piers and docks. It was all as peaceful and still as Garden of Eden. Penang was not yet awake."[270] The snake slithered among the sleepers in the garden. The *Emden* hoisted its colours just before the attack. Its first target was the 3,050-ton Russian light cruiser *Zhemtchug*. The *Zhemtchug*'s commander, Captain Ivan Cherkasov, was on shore leave with a lady friend. Most of his crew were asleep. According to a few reports, some were cavorting with Japanese prostitutes rowed in from Penang's red-light district.

With the *Emden* now deep in the harbour area, the Russian warship was struck by the first German torpedo launched into the dark waters. Wounded, the Russian ship retaliated with a dozen shells without effect. French warships nearby were alerted but inexplicably none attacked the brazen *Emden*. The second German torpedo was fatal, smashing into the bridge of the Russian ship and hitting its magazine. There was a tremendous explosion as fire rocketed into the air and the ship broke in half, disappearing under the swell in a huge, yellow cloud of smoke. Captain Cherkasov rushed from his bed in the Eastern and Oriental Hotel to the sea-front balcony to be greeted by a ship captain's worst nightmare. He rushed down to find a way to get to the harbour, far too late to go down with his ship. Confused voices echoed around him in many tongues.

"*Apa salah?*" (What's wrong)

"What is it?... Is the *Emden* come at last? Where is she?... Who is firing?..."[271]

Two hundred Russian sailors were hauled ashore, burnt, naked or half-dressed and many in shock. Eighty-nine dead and broken men were submerged or floating in the water with eyewitness claims of the lifeless forms of Japanese women of the night bobbing close by. The German warship was not done as it moved beyond the harbour reaches. It found the French destroyer the *Mousquet* in its sights and calmly took it down. Gallantly, Muller picked up the survivors from the sinking French ship. Another French ship gave chase, but the German raider made good its escape by disappearing into a sudden tropical rain squall. Near the equator, the weather can be both friend and enemy to contending navies.

Breaking out of the cordon, the *Emden* next made for the Cocos-Keeling Islands in the Indian Ocean. It would refuel through a coal ship, the *Exford*, that had evaded capture off West Sumatra. The *Emden* next set its sights on Britain's transoceanic telegraph cable hub located on tiny Direction Island in the Cocos-Keelings. Operated by the Eastern Telegraph Company based in Singapore, the cable station joined Africa, India and Australia and also boasted a tall radio mast for wireless. Destroying these targets could disrupt Britain's world-wide, imperial chain of communications on the All-Red Line. It would also send a message to Jerram, who anticipated an eventual attack by the *Emden* on Britain's critical infrastructure on Direction Island. As part of the cable wars between the two sides, Jerram's sailors had destroyed the German station in Micronesia earlier in the war, leaving the Germans with only a single cable that ran through British waters. And that cable was silently tapped and monitored by British intelligence.

After its refuelling rendezvous with the *Emden*, the coaling ship *Exford* was handed over to Leutenant Lauterbach. Müller instructed him to keep the ship safe as the Germans' last remaining coal tender. On 9 November, the *Emden* steamed towards Direction Island, adding its dummy fourth funnel and posing as the British ship HMS *Yarmouth*. It dropped a 50-strong landing party led by Kapitan Leutenant von Mücke who promptly went to work sabotaging the radio mast and cutting cables – but the wire they cut was a dummy one.

The *Emden*'s luck had also run out. The Direction Island's alert British station manager had observed that the fourth funnel did not emit smoke and quickly sounded the alarm. His wireless operators alerted a nearby flotilla, which despatched the Australian HMAS *Sydney*. The Australian battleship outstripped the German raider in armour, guns and speed. In a futile bid to escape, the *Emden* ran straight into the *Sydney*, and was outgunned and disabled after a brutal and bloody sea-battle. The *Emden* ended up impaled on a coral reef with dozens of crew members killed or wounded. For Jerram, the destruction of the notorious *Emden* was less a victory than a relief, which redeemed his command's failures especially in Madras and Penang.

For the *Emden*'s dispersed crew, the story was not over. Evading detection, Mucke and his landing party stole a schooner from Direction Island and made an epic 11,000-kilometre, 6-month escape via sea and land to Germany. Captain Muller was captured and brought to England. While captaining the converted collier *Exford*, Leutenant Lauterbach was intercepted by a British warship soon after Muller's capture. Taken prisoner with his crew, Lauterbach was brought down to Singapore to spend the rest of the war at Tanglin Barracks detention camp. But the wily old salt had other plans. Plotting an escape, he was reunited in Singapore with the resourceful businessman August Diehn who, like Lauterbach, hailed from the northern German city of Rostock. The tall blond managed the Singapore offices of the German-owned trading company of Behn & Meyer and was believed to have covertly supplied the *Emden*.

In its epic voyage of almost 50,000 kilometres, the *Emden* and its crew had destroyed two allied naval vessels, sunk 16 British merchant ships, plundered many others and even shelled two British-controlled ports. The German raider caused millions of pounds in damage and undermined British political interests. In recognition of their gallantry, the German government would permit the surviving men and families to attach the suffix Emden to their names as an inherited title in perpetuity.

[XVIII]

SEDUCING THE SEPOYS

In the ever-shifting fog of war, exploits and disasters are quickly overtaken by new events. The *Emden*'s spectacular sortie in Penang harbour was outdone a day later by the Ottoman Turkish Navy. On 29 October 1914, a fleet of Ottoman warships carried out a raid against Russian-controlled ports in the Black Sea. Posturing as a neutral state, the Turks had in reality signed a secret military alliance with the Germans. A German Admiral on loan had led the fleet into battle. Turkey's deception was exposed during the Black Sea raid when their navy sank a Russian warship.

At the time the world's only truly independent Muslim state and empire, Turkey had now openly joined the Germans. The wavering Ottoman Sultan Mehmed V had been forced to choose sides by his pro-German Minister of War, Enver Pasha. A former military attaché in Berlin, Enver was a prominent leader of the 1908 Young Turk Revolution that sought to modernise and strengthen the decaying Ottoman Empire. The 33-year-old War Minister had quietly schemed with Berlin to get his country to join their fight.

The Turks brought a new geopolitical dimension to the war. From his experience fighting the Turkish-Italian Wars, Enver Pasha had learnt about the power of mobilising *jihad* propaganda. Ottoman Turkish troops battled the Italians in Libya from 1911 to 1912. After being pronounced a holy war, the cost of the war was financed by sympathetic Muslims worldwide. Indian officers and sepoys of British Indian regiments, including the 5th Light Infantry, subscribed to religious charities supporting Turkey against Italy. It was not only the first state-sponsored holy war in modern times. It was also the very first to feature aerial bombardment by the Italians, while the Turks held the distinction of being the first to down a military aircraft with rifle-fire.

With the outbreak of the First World War, Enver Pasha had harboured serious reservations about the Ottoman Empire declaring *jihad* as a war ally of Christian Germany. Before the Black Sea raid, on 22 October, he told Kaiser Wilhelm II that proclaiming a *jihad* would not be a wise move for either side. He made a counter-offer – he would persuade the Sultan-Caliph to call on all Muslims under British, French and Russian rule to rise up in revolt. But this was not good enough for Germany. Pasha's Chief of General Staff conveniently happened to be a German General, who promptly received orders to get the Turkish War Minister to change his mind.

German strategists, including Kaiser Wilhelm II, had long fantasized about capitalising on an Ottoman call to *jihad* against the British. In 1898, the Kaiser visited the Damascus tomb of the pan-Muslim hero Saladin and declared himself friend of all Muslims. Saladin had defeated the crusading armies and recaptured Jerusalem and there was some irony in the Kaiser's statement since the Christian armies included German crusaders. Enver Pasha understood this contradiction. But perfectly conscious of history, Germany had used the formidable expertise of its Orientalists, Arabists and Islamic studies professors to construct a "*Jihad* Made in Germany"[272] to be issued by the Turks as their allies in the Muslim world. For the German generals, the idea was to get the Ottomans to stir up the Muslim subjects of Britain, France and Russia. This would distract their enemies and divert their resources as they battled *jihad*s and Muslim sepoy mutinies in their territories. Every British soldier diverted to fight the Turks or deal with a mutiny was one less soldier on the Western front against Germany.

A fortnight after the Black Sea raid, on 11 November, Sultan Mehmed V declared *jihad* against the Allied Triple Entente of Britain, Russia and France whose Muslim subjects, in theory, owed him both political and religious allegiance. As Caliph, the Sultan was the successor to the Prophet Muhammed. Waving a pan-Islamic banner, he declared that "Russia, England, and France never for a moment ceased harbouring ill-will against our Caliphate, to which millions of Moslems, suffering under the tyranny of foreign dominations, are religiously and wholeheartedly devoted..."[273] The Caliph-Sultan issued instructions to his own troops in the same breath: "throw yourselves against the enemy as lions, bearing in mind that the very existence of our empire, and of 300 million Moslems whom I have summoned by sacred Fetva to a supreme struggle, depend on your victory."[274] As a civil servant who served at the pleasure of the Sultan, the *Sheikh-ul-Islam*, the Ottoman Empire's highest religious authority, quickly supported the call to *jihad* with a legitimating fatwa or legal opinion:

Of those who go to the *Jihad* for the sake of happiness and salvation of the believers in God's victory... the lot of those who remain alive is felicity, while the rank of those who depart to the next world is martyrdom. In accordance with God's beautiful promise, those who sacrifice their lives to give life to the truth will have honour in this world, and their latter end is paradise.[275]

Meanwhile, in the Straits Settlements, Governor Arthur Young's administration was doing its best to deal with the damage done by the *Emden*'s exploits. Young also had to deal with the tangle over the *Komagata Maru*, concluding that "though the ship had no communication with the land, yet it left a bad effect."[276] He had to manage Penang's Indian Muslim community and end seditious talk amongst the rattled population. With the Straits Settlements under martial law, the authorities clamped down on loose lips that could demoralise the population. On the eve of the Sultan's declaration of the *jihad*, a hapless Tamil Muslim named Mahomed Ibrahim found himself seized and placed before the Second Magistrate of the Penang Court. He faced the following charge: "That you on or about November 8 or 9 did use words, to wit, by telling Govindasamy, Velayanadan, Mutu and others that the Germans were bombarding Singapore and were about to occupy Penang and take over the Government, thereby intentionally causing false alarm in the Settlement of Penang."[277]

The Muslim civilian faced a court martial for spreading rumours. Two 5th Light Infantry officers were seconded from Singapore to lead the case in Penang: the regiment's new second-in-command, Major William L Cotton, and Double Company Commander Captain Perceval Boyce. Cotton had only just joined the battalion at the end of September in Singapore. He barely had time to settle in or get to know his men before being despatched to Penang. Embarrassingly, it was soon discovered that the alleged "false alarmist" Mahomed Ibrahim had no obvious political agenda. He was no shadowy agent of influence but instead merely carried a grudge against the monopoly of *toddy* farmers. Ibrahim had spread rumours that if shops stocking palm liquor paid the *toddy* farmers or renewed their rental contracts they would have to pay double, first under the British, and a second time once the Germans occupied Penang by January 1915. The court martial was aimed at deterring further rumour-mongering.

On Pulau Brani, Lance-Naik Maksud heard Chiste tell the sepoys that the *Emden* had not been sunk; the British were spreading false news. Capturing the mood of rising panic, a Sikh gunner in the British garrison in China wrote to a relative stationed in France on 3 December 1914:

The English have suffered severely. Nothing is put into the news, but we know a good deal from day to day. The German ship *Emden* has sunk forty English ships near this land, and is sinking all the seventy English ships of war. She has not been much damaged although she gets little help. The English have eight kings helping them, the Germans three. We hear that our king has been taken prisoner. Germany said that if she were paid a *lakh* of rupees by five o'clock on the first of the month, she would release the king. The money was paid, but Germany refuses to let him go. I have written only a little, but there is much more for you to think of.[278]

Sensing the opportunity, the wrestler-preacher and Ghadar leader Bhagwan Singh, who had preached to the Guides in Taiping, issued a leaflet in Urdu called *Ailan i Jung* (Declaration of War) to be circulated among the sepoys:

Your brothers in arms have been sent to the war in Europe. What sort of astuteness is this that in battle the whitemen remain behind and in order to have them killed, place the Indians in front... Rise and kill these Firangi tyrants... the mutiny has commenced... In this rising Hindus and Muhammedans both take part because, over both equally tyranny has been practised and both of their rights and dues in the country are equal. For this reason dear Hindus and Muhammedans, join and destroy this Raj and make your own king.[279]

One hundred and sixty kilometres north of Penang, a wealthy Sikh community leader named Jagat Singh was doing what he could to hamper the British war effort from the Unfederated Malay State of Perlis and during trips to Penang. An influencer in the North Indian community, Jagat was known as the "Doctor", with the skill to treat animals as well as humans. He had learnt his medicine as a surgical assistant or dresser in an Indian cavalry regiment. After his discharge, he had made his way to Perlis while it was still under Siamese control and started various businesses. By the time of its hand-over to British advisers, Dr Jagat had earned the ruler's trust sufficiently to run the Perlis jail, the Perlis Sanitary Board and its public works department.[280] Like Gurdit Singh, Dr Jagat was well known among the Sikhs of Malaya and the network of *gurdwaras* in the Malay States and Straits Settlements.

A committed Ghadar Party sympathizer, the charismatic and competent Dr Jagat had developed a large circle and he offered interest-free loans to friends in need. His house was a regular meeting point for the community where he often held court. The ground floor served as a dispensary and office, while he had installed a small temple for common use upstairs. Punjabi Muslims, Sikhs from Perlis and other parts of Malaya – including the sepoys of the Guides – found a welcome sanctuary in Dr Jagat's home.

Raushan Din, a Punjabi Muslim who worked with Dr Jagat at the Sanitary Board, was a regular visitor who often heard the doctor speak of the war. Dr Jagat told Raushan that the Germans had taken Belgium and shared news of the imminent capture of Paris. According to him, Penang would soon be taken. After the *Emden*'s daring raid, he declared jubilant-ly: "You see with all the vigilance of the English the *Emden* could enter Penang."[281] He predicted that Sikhs and Germans would work together and win freedom for India. As chief warden, Dr Jagat had influence over the Sikh wardens in the Perlis jail. He translated English articles on the war into Malay for the Malay wardens. Another Punjabi Muslim, Syed Omar, Veterinary Inspector for the Perlis Government, also heard Dr Jagat speak of the *Komagata Maru* outrage at Budge Budge.

Down south in Singapore, the Guides' CO, Lieutenant-Colonel Lees, had barred his sepoys from using the Queen Street *gurdwara*. However, his precautions were insufficient. The Guides' Sikh officers let visiting Sikhs, possibly those in Dr Jagat's circle, including roving Ghadarite members, use the camp *gurdwara*. Places of worship became hotbeds of sedition against the British. Disaffection also brewed among Muslim sepoys. Men from the all-Muslim 5th Light Infantry and a few Muslim sepoys from the Guides began attending the Kampong Java Mosque in Singapore. Away from prying ears at the regimental mosque, the sepoys came under the spell of the Kampong Java Mosque's resident preacher, Nur Alam Shah. A Sufi *pir* or holy man, the 50-year-old was an enigmatic and fiery pres-ence believed to be a member of the Ghadar Party. There is no available evidence suggesting that Dr Jagat and Nur Alam corresponded or worked together but they certainly promoted similar ideas.

Sporting a trimmed, grey beard, Nur Alam Shah attracted *murid*s or disciples from the assorted Muslims in Singapore including Punjabis, Pa-thans, Malays and Tamils. The Punjabis called him *baji*, the Malays called him *habit* and the Gujaratis called him *shahsahib*. The *pir* preached the less-er *jihad* of action in the field and the greater *jihad* for the soul. Nur Alam attracted the 5th's Chiste Khan and Havildar Imtiaz Ali as his disciples. From the Guides, Jemadar Shah Zaman became the *pir*'s faithful follower. Nur Alam Shah's anti-British sermons quickly attracted a following in the mosque. The British were worried enough to send a secret agent from India to monitor him. The agent recorded that he had told the Indian officers and the sepoys: "You should resist being sent to the war, and you should fight and seize the city. The British Raj will come to an end in

March or April. They will be expelled from Singapore."[282] He also told the sepoys that German warships would come to their assistance and all Singapore Muslims would help them. The myth of the German warship was likely fired by the exploits of the *Emden*. It made a deep impression on his faithful followers like Chiste Khan and Imtiaz Ali.

Along with their mosque mentor, the sepoys of the 5th as well as some Guides found another local patron who dabbled in ideas of mutiny, revolt and sedition. Born in 1850, Kassim Ismail Mansoor hailed from a suburb of Surat, a city in Western Gujarat facing the Arabian Sea that was famous for its textiles. Mansoor was part of a Muslim cotton-trading community known alternatively as the Mansooris or Pinjaras which also claimed some connection to the Rajputs. This may or may not have helped him build a link to the Rajput Ranghars of the 5th. The Pinjaras were, according to their imperial handlers, a class known for business enterprise, thrift, loyalty and freedom from fanaticism, but Mansoor was not content to conform to easy labels of the British Orientalists. Instead, he indulged in the fantasies of frustrated sepoys as well as his own.

In his one-horse-drawn gharry, Mansoor often visited the quarter-guard hut or guardhouse of Alexandra Barracks, located where Hyderabad Road meets Alexandra Road today. Wearing a long and loose Shantung silk coat, with the headgear of a Bombay merchant, the white-bearded Mansoor was hard to miss. Just past the quarter-guard hut were the sepoys' brick barracks with the Indian officers' quarters located further up on the ridge. Mansoor did not venture as far as the bungalows of the British officers or their mess which overlooked the Parade Ground.

Atop the hill stood the bungalow (7 Royal Road) of the 5th's Commanding Officer, Lieutenant-Colonel Martin. Despite his dominating position, Martin struggled to establish his authority over the battalion. He lacked command presence, had petty quarrels with his brother officers and had the rank but not the respect he wanted, masking deeper interpersonal differences and resentment at his promotion. In October 1914, Martin rebuked Captain William D Hall, the Officer's Mess President, for "tactless persistency" and "aggressive spirit."[283] Hall had goaded Martin, insisting on framing for display in the Mess a thank you letter from officers of a visiting French naval ship for the regiment's hospitality. Martin had been embarrassed by mention of his wife and daughter in the French letter, especially after hearing some of the officers "chaffing"[284] about it. He protectively, if prudishly, pocketed the missive which described his daughter as *charmante et gracieux* ("charming and gracious").[285] When Hall asked Martin if he should in the future send all Mess letters for him to keep, Martin lost his temper: "If you make any more such remarks I will put you under arrest and report the matter to the General Officer

Captain William Draper Hall on his wedding day in 1922.

Commanding."[286] The GOC would of course not be terribly amused to have the CO of one of his battalions complain about a petty quarrel of this nature.

The 5th's newly minted second-in-command, Major William Cotton, whose house literally guarded the approach to Martin's, found himself in the middle of it all. He was the buffer between his CO and the irate British company commanders – Captains Hall, Ball and Lieutenant Strover and Elliott – who had formed a clique against their Commanding Officer. When not distracted by managing these little intrigues, Colonel Martin and Major Cotton could have used their time to scan the vista south-west of their commanding bungalows. They would have made out a spacious rubber estate plantation and Mansoor's weekend bungalows where he consorted with the sepoys of the 5th and the Guides.

Mansoor led the life of a wealthy Asian trader in Singapore. With a house in Telok Ayer Street in Chinatown occupied by his brother Ali, Mansoor also kept a shop in Singapore's business district. He had a wife in India and another in Rangoon. One of his sons ran a textile business in Rangoon, among a larger community of Gujarati settlers. In his bungalows on Pasir Panjang Road at the foot of Kent Ridge, Mansoor allowed the men of the 5th and the Guides to take breaks from the numbing routine of barrack life. Playing *jihadi*-socialite, Mansoor even invited a Malay Police Sergeant-Major home to meet the 5th's Indian officers and to break bread with them.

The British officers of the 5th had their own little diversions. Singapore was not nearly as exciting as Hong Kong or Canton, but there were movies in the Alhambra, Harima and Casino while seedy attractions were on offer in the Malay Street brothel district. For the virtuous, there were balls in the hotels, horse riding, sports of all kinds, and amateur theatre. Captain Hall, apart from his Mess President duties, was also a keen sportsman and actor. Born in Poona, India, the son of a railway bridge builder, Hall coached the 5th's sepoy hockey team well enough for them to regularly thrash the Singapore Cricket Club side on the Padang. Hall also enjoyed amateur theatrics with Lieutenant Strover. On 26 November, they acted in the play, *Packing Up*, at the Victoria Theatre. Included in the cast was the pretty, young Marjorie Michie. She was newly married to Belfield Morel Woolcombe, an older, fellow New Zealander who worked as an engineer for the Eastern Extension Telegraph Company.

As Singapore's European society found time for theatrical diversions and sport, the war on the Western Front settled into brutal and often static trench warfare. Bombardments and machine guns produced industrial-scale slaughter. The sepoys heard stories of the terrible carnage at the Western Front. A new front had also opened in East Africa with the arrival of a British Indian Expeditionary Force. Fresh troops had to replace the casualties put through the merciless meat grinder, including in new fronts against the Ottoman Turks in the Middle East. On 27 November, the Straits Settlements' military commander Major General Reade telegraphed the War Office in London that the Malay States Guides were more suitable for service against the Ottomans in Egypt because the 5th was "very Mahometan."[287]

Some British officers noticed a distinct difference in the 5th's behaviour since Turkey joined the fray. At Mount Faber signal station, Lieutenant R J Farrar supervised guards from the Malay Company of the Singapore Volunteers. Several signallers and infantrymen from the 5th were posted to his station. Before Turkey joined the war, the 5th's sepoys would visit him every evening after he received his newspaper to ask him to read the news. One of his Javanese signallers spoke Hindustani and served as Farrar's translator. He observed that the 5th's sepoys stopped visiting and talking to him after the declaration of war with Turkey. Their demeanour was no longer friendly. Instead, they kept to themselves and he heard them instead talk throughout the night, repeating the words "Roum" (Rome or the English) and "Stamboul" (Istanbul).

Young was quite prepared to release the 5th. However, unlike Reade, he had doubts about leaving the Malay Peninsula to the Guides. He thought they were not altogether to be relied upon. It emerged later that one of the Guides' officers, Captain Reginald Schomberg, heard talk among his men of a plan to kill the officers, march on Tanglin, free the German prisoners and loot Singapore. Worryingly, at the end of November, the Guides CO Lieutenant-Colonel Lees received an anonymous letter from a sepoy in the Punjabi Muslim No. 3 Double Company under the command of Captain Seymour Beaumont and Subedar Elim Din when stationed on Pulau Blakang Mati. The letter warned that some Indian officers had told the sepoys to refuse service abroad. The informant named two Muslim officers and a Sikh NCO. One of the officers, Jemadar Shah Zaman, was a follower of Nur Alam Shah at Kampong Java Mosque. He had told his men that "If the Sahib (i.e. Lees) tells me to go I will hand over my sword."[288]

All this was not entirely convenient for Lees. Based on assurances from his Subedar-Major Fatteh Singh that the Guides were loyal and willing to serve anywhere, Lees had earlier persuaded Reade to send a cable offering the service of the Guides on any front. Now Lees confronted Zaman and told him what he heard. Lees noticed that Zaman "was plainly staggered and unnerved and for quite an appreciable time could say nothing."[289] Recovering his composure, he told Lees that "you will have to prove that" before reminding him of his family's long service to the Raj. Quickly regaining his confidence, he added with bravado: "*Sahib* if I refuse to go on service you may cut my throat with my own sword."[290] Lees dismissed him and warned his Double Company Commander Captain Beaumont to watch him.

On Wednesday, 2 December, the War Office ordered the Guides to support operations in East Africa against the Germans. Two days later, the Guides' 28-year-old Adjutant Lieutenant Guy Fisher Turner told the men after morning parade that they had been ordered to the East African front. He felt that there "was certainly no enthusiasm, but there was nothing else."[291] Half an hour later, as he sat with Lees in the Mess, Subedar Elim Din came in with a worried look on his face. His company of Punjabi Muslims including his Jemadar Shan Zaman were especially disaffected. Elim had previously complained of the treatment of the sepoys, their paltry allowances for family and other issues. He told Lees flatly that his men had refused to go on service.

Soon afterwards, two Sikh company commanders burst into the mess with similarly bad news for Lees. In an emergency meeting, all the Indian officers were now summoned and asked to bring the men around. But the sepoys had been seized by rumours of a killing machine in the trenches which could slaughter anyone within a 10 miles radius. Lees struggled to explain whether the men feared combat or had been turned by German agents or through Ghadar propaganda and the incident at Budge Budge. A Sikh Jemadar, Samund Singh, whom he trusted completely, told him that the men had been turned by tales in the bazaar.

The Indian officers returned later to the Mess, where all the British officers were now gathered with their CO. They told Lees that the men definitely refused to go on service. A devastated Lees climbed into his car and drove down to the Brigade office to convey the news to Reade. Lees blamed the entire affair on Elim Din for turning the men on Pulau Blakang Mati. He told Reade quite unconvincingly that Elim Din, who coveted the Sikh *subedar*-major's post, was a mere shoemaker by caste and had only been promoted to *subedar* at the insistence of a British lady whom he had taught how to shoot. He added that Elim Din was a strong character who controlled his Punjabi Muslims "by terror"[292] and worked closely with his Jemadar Shah Zaman. Lees suspected that German and Turkish agents had got to these men, although he did not mention Nur Alam Shah or Kassim Ismail Mansoor by name.

Struggling then with a bout of poor health, the last thing Reade needed to hear at the time was news that the Guides had refused to fight in "German East Africa". Going a step further and spelling out their position in a collective memorandum, the Guides pointed out that they were only required to serve by contract in the Malay Peninsula and the Straits

Settlements. Technically this was true. But the mutinous memorandum also reflected dark sentiments, making special mention of the *Komagata Maru*. In his report to Ridout, Lees called the substance of the collective memorandum one of "concentrated sedition."[293] Indeed, it dripped with sarcasm and the venom of insubordination that revolutionaries like Dr Jagat Singh, Nur Alam Shah and Kassim Ismail Mansoor would have encouraged:

> As the memory of our brethren who have been shot in the *Komagata Maru* case have troubled and grieved us, some of us have lost dear brothers and other blood-relations, and we can never forget the kindness of the Indian Government (British) for shooting and slaughtering those dead who lost their living in India, in the hopes of earning money and gaining a better living in America, from which country they were expelled, and were not allowed to land and returned. But the Indian Government again taking the poor dead as seditious people, did not allow them to land at their own home even. When we have no right to walk freely on our own land then what do you want from us in other countries? As we are butchered in our own country we cannot expect better treatment from other countries, therefore we strongly tell you that we will not go to other countries to fight except on the terms mentioned in our agreement sheets.[294]

The memorandum was not an outright act of mutiny by the Guides, but it was an eerie foreshadowing of what would take place with the 5th not on paper, but in reality. The following morning on 5 December, Lees and his officers were summoned by Reade who told them icily: "Well gentlemen, your Colonel says you have been let down by your Indian Officers. I consider I have been let down by you."[295]

As the Guides' officers received their dressing down from General Reade, Chiste Khan and his company were returning to Alexandra Barracks from Pulau Brani. Colour Havildar Rahmat Khan and one of his loyalist sepoys Bopha Khan noticed Chiste speaking to sepoys in meetings after dark. The sessions lasted from 7 pm until 1 am outside Havildar Abdul Ghani's quarters behind today's 3A Hyderabad Road. Rahmat heard Chiste say that in a short time Germany would overrun England.

The Guides' refusal to serve had an impact on the men of the 5th, creating a domino effect. The 5th's Medical Officer, Lieutenant R V Morrison, who oversaw the physical and mental health of the men, noticed their demeanour take a turn for the worse because of the Guides' attitude. Even if not directly insubordinate, they were showing less respect than usual to their British officers. But the penny had not dropped for the British commanders.

On 7 December, Lees made another trip to Government House to see Young and Reade. Struggling to retrieve his unit's honour, Lees assured the Governor that the Guides were not refusing to serve because of seditious motives. Reade shared with Young that Martin had also assured him of his absolute conviction of the loyalty of the 5th. However, although Reade had confidence in Martin, he could not be absolutely sure himself. As for Young, he had already made up his mind about Reade after the debacle of the Guides' refusal to serve. The previous day, he had quietly sent a telegraph to the Secretary of State in the Colonial Office in London that Reade "could be spared to serve elsewhere"[296] once the Guides left Singapore. The men in charge of the island's security were at loggerheads and neglected to work together.

The clearest sign of bureaucratic log-jam amid clashing egos was when officials put issues on record in writing without ensuring they were addressed in reality. Right after their meeting at Government House, Reade sent a note to Young to put on record that German prisoners in Tanglin Camp may have tampered with their sepoy guards. He also assured him airily that steps were being taken to contain the damage. Reade had learned from Lees that the Guides sepoys guarding the Germans had conversed with them in Malay and were being indoctrinated by the enemy. Young instructed Reade to request the British Government in India to loan a secret service agent to investigate the situation. Before the Guides left Singapore on 8th December, the two regiments were kept apart to avoid infecting each other. Martin even pre-arranged with Lees to move his men out first before the 5th took over the Guides' posts on Pulau Blakang Mati. He did not want any contact between the men or the possibility of a shoot-out between the two groups of sepoys.[297] Everyone focussed on the chess-pieces in front of them, not the sequence of moves that would follow. Nothing was done by the Governor or the GOC to ensure that sepoys from other battalions like the 5th were kept away from the Germans.

Despite the jittery mood, some of the more optimistic among the officers even tried to swim against the tide of disaffection in the Guides. The Commanding Officer of the Guides' mountain artillery detachment, Captain Moira Francis Allan Maclean, admitted to Lees that his men were not keen on service when he read them the notice of their East Africa deployment. But he talked often to his men and over time felt sufficiently confident they could be brought around and agree to serve. Born in Texas, US, Maclean had moved to England as a boy. Debonair and dashing, the young officer opted to join the Indian Army and climbed the ranks. Keen to go to war, the 30-year-old encouraged his sepoys to stay loyal despite the mutinous murmurings in his unit. As the main body of Guides infantry prepared to leave Singapore, Maclean and his 98-strong unit of Muslim and Sikh gunners were allowed to stay behind with the 5th in Alexandra Barracks.

On 8 December at 7.30 pm, the Guides' infantry left by special train from Tank Road in Singapore to return to Taiping. In their carriages, the sepoys cheered loudly while their British officers sat in a reserved compartment holding their heads down. At Ipoh Station, a throng of local Sikhs cheered the returning Guides as heroes. Dr Jagat Singh and his sympathizers were very likely among the welcoming party. Their over-eager Subedar-Major Fatteh Singh resigned in shame after his return, but Young quietly arranged a post for him in the Perak State Supreme Court. Thereafter, he left to join an Indian unit in France and fought with distinction.

Upon the return of the Guides to Taiping, Dr Jagat Singh and several other men, including the Sikhs and Punjabi Muslims like Raushan Din and Syed Omar, met at the doctor's house in Perlis. Jagat Singh asked the men to donate money to a subscription for "turning the English out of India and for the establishing of a republic in India."[298] Mahinda Singh, who was present at the meeting, claimed that Jagat started the fund to help purchase arms, support a rising of Sikh sepoys in the Punjab and to urge the Guides to mutiny. After the meeting, two of the attendees, the *granthi*s of the Penang and Singapore *gurdwara*s, sailed for India on a Ghadar-linked political mission. The pair were arrested upon landing in Calcutta, where the police had already stepped up the scrutiny of all returning emigrants.

The wheels of the intended rising in Punjab had yet to come off but were spinning without direction. It was compromised – riddled with spies and informers reporting to an alert Department of Criminal Intelligence (DCI). Inspector Hopkinson was no more, but the DCI had a stable of motivated and committed agents and handlers unravelling the Ghadar conspiracy. The stuttering, low-level insurgency was floundering by the time the teenaged Ghadarite Kartar Singh Sarabha connected with Rash Behari Bose in the holy city of Varanasi. Bose had taken refuge in the city to elude the British dragnet after his failed assassination attempt on Hardinge. To locate Bose, Kartar had to negotiate the confusing and twisting streets of the Bengali quarter in Varanasi.[299] From his hide-out, the fat Bengali master of disguise instructed the young Sikh revolutionary to prepare for a rising in Punjab as he made the necessary arrangements. The former chemistry student at the University of Berkeley did as much as he could to bolster the movement, collecting arms, funds and setting up committees. Pedalling around furiously from village to village to spread the word, Kartar was a bundle of zeal and energy.

Captain Moira Francis Allan Maclean
among off-duty sepoys of the Guides Battery.

Other returning revolutionaries wandered about, committing minor raids and robberies and assassination. In the middle of November, the wheels of the enterprise started to come off. Rash Behari Bose was checking his bombs one night when one of the explosives went off, badly injuring his left hand. Out of action for the time being, he was forced to lie low while he recovered over the next two months. Jagat Ram, who had sailed with Nawab and spoke so stirringly in Manila, was arrested in Peshawar just before December. Nawab Khan led his own group but had no plan and lacked the necessary leadership qualities or tactical knowledge to effectively guide insurgency actions. From his home in Halwara he got together a rabble that marauded in nearby provinces. Nawab suggested a raid on treasuries to support the stumbling insurgency, but Kartar warned against it. He claimed that Bhai Parmanand believed that treasuries were far too dangerous to target. Kartar had the habit of using the older man's name to make up for his youth and sound more convincing when he wanted to win over sceptical comrades. Instead of robbing treasuries, Kartar told Nawab and his gang that a sepoy had promised Parmanand the keys to a cantonment arsenal in Mian Mir, Lahore. They agreed to target the arsenal and lead an uprising from there. However, that plan soon fell apart when some of the insurgents got cold feet, showing that the group lacked leadership and cohesion.

Their next scheme was to target another cantonment arsenal in Ferozepur, south of Lahore. The plan faltered after the Ghadar co-founder and labour contractor Kanshi Ram visited the nearby village of Ferozeshah with a group of insurgents. As they drew up in a convoy of horse-drawn *tonga*, local police and officials disparaged the men as "American Sikhs" and treated them roughly. Instead of calmly managing the situation, a member of Kanshi's group lost his head after a constable slapped his companion. In retaliation, he shot and killed a senior Indian police officer and a civilian official who happened to be nearby. After the murders, Kanshi and several others were chased down, arrested, sentenced and hung as common criminals. The resolute police action demoralised the insurgents and quite a few more decided to slink away back to their villages.

Stumbling around without any real impact as his revolving gang dwindled away, Nawab Khan was nabbed by the police on 19 December. To avoid conviction and imprisonment, he soon turned informant for the Punjab Police and Department of Criminal Intelligence. He squealed wholesale on his former comrades. Promising to provide information on the sly in exchange for a pardon, Nawab was about to do great harm to his former comrades as he spilled their secrets to save his own skin.

The British appeared to be gaining the upper hand. In Singapore a week earlier, Young and Reade had received the good news that Admiral Graf Spee's formidable East Asia squadron had been completely destroyed at the Battle of Falklands. This was a welcome development after the *Emden*'s raids and the debacle of the Guides' refusal to serve. It made it less likely that enemy forces could bomb or raid Singapore. The feared German battlecruisers *Scharnhorst* and *Gneisenau* had also both been sunk. On 14 December, on the back of the naval victory, Reade wrote to the War Office recommending that the 5th could be withdrawn for service elsewhere. The next day, he telegraphed the War Office proposing his own reassignment along with that of Lieutenant-Colonel Brownlow, the seasoned CO of the Royal Garrison Artillery. It was also recommended that Lieutenant-Colonel Ridout of the Royal Engineers replace Reade as General Officer Commanding the Troops. The field campaigner Brownlow had lost out to the staff officer Ridout in the bureaucratic manoeuvring. The proposed personnel changes were troubling. This would be the third change of GOC in less than a year.

Sentiments also swung wildly according to the fortunes of war. A few months earlier, the British merchant marine had lived in fear of the solo raider, *Emden*. And just a few months before the *Emden* was unleashed, the officers of the visiting *Gneisenau* had been warmly hosted to dinner by the Youngs who toasted their health. Now Governor Young and Admiral Jerram could raise a sardonic toast to his nemesis Admiral Graf Spee, his two sons and the young Germans who had become fish food at the bottom of the South Atlantic Ocean.

One German seaman who resolutely refused to be fed to fishes, now found himself in a fish-bowl of sorts. In the Tanglin German prisoners camp, the *Emden*'s former Prize Officer Julius Lauterbach was stuck behind barbed wire fences with an electrified outer perimeter and sentry boxes guarded by sepoys at every 50 metres or so. Lauterbach and survivors from *Emden*'s other prize crews and the coaling ship *Markomannia*, mingled with close to 300 German civilians from the Straits Settlements, all of whom had been interned by end November. Lauterbach, however, was granted his own private three-room bungalow just behind the general prisoners' barracks. He found himself excused from daily roll call or lights out at 10 pm and was quietly feted by his captors for the feats of the *Emden*. He was even allowed go into town to tailor a new suit for himself. Lauterbach secured for himself these privileges and freedom of movement from the Prison Camp Commandant, Major William Cotton who was concurrently second-in-command of the 5th. Lauterbach turned on his charm and won over the no-nonsense Mrs Cotton whom he considered an "angel."[300] Even General Reade had visited him and said: "I hope that you and our men will behave. We all think very highly of you and your men of the *Emden*."[301] Lauterbach would repay these favours by turning the sepoy guards of the 5th against their commanders.

Now the earlier bureaucratic jousting and confusion at the top was coming back to haunt the British. Reade had made a promise of sorts to Young that only white troops would guard the German prisoners after the Guides were found to be consorting with the Germans. But it was 50 sepoys of the 5th who were put on guard duty with a disaffected Jemadar Abdul Ali Khan in charge. It was a poor choice. A sepoy from the guard detachment, Ismail Khan, would fire the first shot that started the Singapore Mutiny. The guard detachment also included the Ranghar Imtiaz Ali, a "magnificent looking, tall, black bearded sepoy".[302] Considered "loyal and pain-staking"[303] in carrying out his duties, he had been recommended for promotion to officer rank a year earlier by the 5th's previous CO.

Martin also supported Imtiaz Ali's promotion to replace a Pathan officer who had fallen sick and died in December. But Cotton and Strover had their doubts. Hall, who commanded the Pathan double company, felt it would destabilise the regimental balance to promote a Rajput in place of a Pathan. The Rajputs already had their full quote of nine native officers. With his promotion blocked on three earlier occasions in favour of more junior Pathans, Imtiaz Ali had reason to be sour as Lauterbach courted him in his internment bungalow in Tanglin. Imtiaz became Lauterbach's key target on whom he focussed his energies of subterfuge. Lauterbach confessed later:

> Every day, I conversed with the Indian non-commissioned officers who had been entrusted with the immediate surveillance of the prisoners. "Sergeant" as I always called him, was the senior non-com and as such, had the run of the stockade at all hours. As the weeks went on he came more and more frequently to my bungalow at night, usually with a subordinate or two. We would chat for hours.[304]

Lauterbach had been adept in playing mind games with the Captains of captured merchant navy ships to elicit information on other targets. The senior German businessman August Diehn, who acted as the Turkish Consul in Singapore, played the game too. With no rules on fraternization, the German internees made sport of their Indian wardens, who took pleasure in expressing solidarity with Lauterbach: "*Emden* Officer, Kaiser Wilhelm, Enver Bay, Islam. Hurrah!"[305] Not all, however, were ready to be seduced. Approached by Germans who tried to make small talk, the loyalist Colour-Havildar Rahmat Khan pointed his rifle at them and said: "If you talk to me I will shoot."[306] He was left alone after that.

But the Germans were getting their message across to the others. One guard, Lance Naik Fateh Mohamed, a Pathan of F Company in the left-wing of the 5th, wrote home that the daughter of "Haji Mahmood William (Wilhelm) Kaiser" had married the heir apparent to the Turkish throne. Another guard, Sepoy Taj Mohamed of C Company, walked past a portrait of the German Kaiser painted by a German internee named Hanke and saluted it. When Hanke, who spoke some Malay and Hindi, remarked in Malay: "Are you mad?", Taj replied: "He is my King."[307] Some of the credulous sepoys were led to believe that the Germans had converted to Islam. A few German prisoners allegedly even went to the extent of pretending to pray to Allah. Hanke often heard the sepoys greet his fellow Germans: "*Salaam Aleikum* (Peace be unto you)."

Imtiaz Ali also fed news to an information-hungry Lauterbach, bringing him Singapore newspapers like the *Singapore Free Press* and *The Straits Times*. They talked in depth about the war's progress and the German claimed that he had taught the Indian to read between the lines of the news. With his focus not so much on mutiny but on creating confusion to assist his escape, Lauterbach told Imtiaz Ali:

> Naturally the English never will tell you what has happened to your men. They wouldn't dare. Your Indian regiments in France have lost nearly all their men. It is very cold in France. And your brothers from the Punjab plains cannot stand that kind of climate; they get consumption, and pouf! they are gone. The English newspapers say that the Indian soldiers are dying bravely in battle, mowed down by German machine-gun fire. That is a lie. They do not die gloriously in battle. They die like sick dogs. That is what the English papers say between the lines.[308]

Under Lauterbach's influence, Imtiaz developed an appetite for breaking news. He visited a British volunteer Gordon Lawson who was jobless and lived on camp to make ends meet. Stopping by the 24-year-old's bunk, he would ask for his copy of the *The Daily Graphic*, attracted to the war cartoons of the first daily illustrated newspaper.

As Imtiaz's mind was being turned, the noose was tightening on Kassim Ismail Mansoor who had entertained the sepoys in Pasir Panjang. On 28 December, Kassim foolishly sent an incriminating letter to his son in Rangoon, instructing him to contact the Turkish Consul Ahmed Madani to secure a warship to get the sepoys out of Singapore. He also enclosed a note allegedly written and signed by two men of the Guides, Osman Khan and Sikander Khan, who were in the Texan-born Maclean's unit of Guides artillery. Sikander Khan had refused to serve overseas and was sent back to Taiping. Both *naik*s (corporals) signed off as higher-ranking *havildar*s (sergeants) to inform the Turkish Consul: "There is a regiment here belonging to the English in Singapore called the Malay States Guides. In it there is a mule battery and all the members of this artillery are Mohammedans."[309] This was not true as the battery Nawab Khan once belonged to consisted of Sikhs too, but the letter was clearly appealing to the pan-Islamic sentiments of the Ottoman Turks. It continued:

The whole regiment does not desire to go and fight in Europe.... They say "we want to join the Turkish forces, and we want someone to be kind enough to enable us to join the Turkish forces. We have money to meet our travelling expenses and we do not want one pie even for expenses: but we want someone to show us the way whereby we may reach Turkey. That is all we want." Therefore this letter is written to you as on your side Ahmed Madani is the Turkish Consul, so as to enable that gentleman to write to the Turkish Consul at Bombay or direct to Stamboul in order that a man-of-war may be sent to Singapore. Then the Sepoys here can join the Turkish man-of-war and are all ready to fight in the battles in Europe.[310]

Early in January 1915, British censors in Rangoon found the treasonous letter, which included instructions that a reply be forwarded to "Bengali baker Mr Ismail."[311] Mansoor's cover letter to his son had clumsily warned that the sepoys' note to the consul should not be linked to them. Kassim seemed to have overlooked that in a time of war, the British would have ejected the Turkish consul as an enemy state's diplomat. Moreover, curiously, both letters were written in Gujarati, a language foreign to the Pathans and Punjabi Muslims of the Guides who would use Urdu. As an afterthought, the letter had a postscript scrawled in Urdu.

In mid-January, the Guides CO Lees chaired a meeting in Kuala Lumpur with officers from the police and security forces. They met to get a better grip on the threat posed by the Northern Indians in the Federated Malay States. The meeting agreed that the causes of local unrest were external influences, the *Komagata Maru* incident, war with Turkey, the attitude of the Guides, Germans in parole in the FMS and a "peculiar perverse feeling of hostility for which no special reason can be assigned."[312] It was assessed that "in the case of disaffection that half of the available Sikhs and Punjabi Mohamedans in the MSG and Police would openly resist, the others while giving no trouble themselves would not actively assist us against their own countrymen."[313] The meeting thought that an "Indian rising" was unlikely and "remote"[314] but one recommendation was to pay more careful attention of the disposal of ammunition to prevent it falling into the wrong hands. The report of the meeting was sent to General Reade in Singapore. He forwarded it to Young with the assessment that the forces could not deal with "a general rising of Northern Indians"[315] although that scenario was itself considered remote. No further action appeared to have been taken apart from closer guard over the ammunition which ironically would make it more difficult for relief guard units to have fully loaded weapons when the time came to resist a mutiny.

A week after the meeting in Kuala Lumpur to assess the threat from Northern Indians, Kassim Mansoor was arrested in Singapore on nine charges of treason. The internment of the Northern Indian Muslim trader was a bombshell for the men who habitually visited him. The news spread across the Indian community. Mansoor was seen as a harmless eccentric by those who knew him. But his indulgence in intrigue and sport as a *jihadi*-socialite figure for the sepoys was too dangerous to ignore. The British acted to face down the local threat and even the possibility of a regional conspiracy. British censors in Rangoon, where Mansoor's son was based, had also discovered over 100 envelopes with copies of the *Ghadar*. Mixed in were copies of the 20 November 1914 issue of the Turkish pan-Islamist *Jahan-i Islam* (Islamic World) newspaper, run by the Turkish war office. In Paris, at his revolutionary comrade Madame Cama's urging, Har Dayal had travelled to Constantinople in September 1914 and met with Abu Saiyad, editor of *Jahan-i Islam*. He spent several months in the Ottoman capital and understood the importance of Constantinople as a base for operations against the British.[316] Reflecting Har Dayal's personal influence on its propaganda slant, the Turkish paper reported on a call to arms speech by the Ottoman War Minister, Enver Pasha:

> This is the time that the Ghadar should be introduced in India, the magazines of the English should be plundered, their weapons looted and they should be killed therewith. The Indians number 32 *crore*s at the best and English are only 2 *lakh*s, they should be murdered, they have no army.... Hindus and Muhammedans, you are both soldiers of the army and you are brothers, and the low degraded English man is your enemy; you should become *ghazis* by declaring *jihad* and by combining with your brothers to murder the English and liberate India.[317]

Har Dayal's vision of mutiny promoted in the *Ghadar* newspaper had blended with concepts of *jihad*. Enver Pasha's speech almost seemed to provide a script for events in Singapore – a *jihad*-mutiny in the offing. The lethal cocktail mix was coming together, an Ottoman-ordered *jihad* made in Germany, and an Indian mutiny movement made in San Francisco.

[XIX]

EDGE OF AN EXPLOSION

Oblivious to the gathering storm around him, Governor Young was prepared to dispense with all the sepoys in Singapore. It was not clear if his stance reflected confidence in the overall security situation or a concern over the reliability of the sepoys. The lesson of the Guides could not have been forgotten so soon. The general view was that Singapore only needed the most minimal garrison now, protected as it was by its crack Sikh Police, Volunteers and the Royal Garrison Artillery. Moreover, the Anglo-Japan Alliance ensured that Japanese cruisers and Japanese volunteers in Singapore could assist if required. Only enemy agents could cause trouble now. Writing to the Secretary of State of the Colonies on 19 January 1915, Young offered a strange and rather muddled assurance that would become deeply ironic in the light of coming events: "It is held that should an internal disturbance arise caused by Northern Indians, the Garrison as at present composed would not be able to cope with it. The occurrence of any such disturbance is not anticipated by me: my opinion is that the garrison should be reduced: and even if there is a small risk, I hold that the risk ought to be taken."

A month earlier, Major-General Reade made his annual inspection of the 5th at his headquarters in Tanglin Barracks. It would also be his last. Addressing the battalion's Indian officers at the parade on 22 December, Reade declared: "I am sure you will all do well when the time comes for you to go on service."[318] As Lieutenant-Colonel Martin translated the GOC's speech into Hindustani, he heard Major Cotton whisper to him: "You have forgotten the part about active service Sir."[319] Double Company Commander Captain Hall was stung by the put-down from Reade's Aide-de-Camp Lieutenant W T Torr: "You fellows don't seem to be agitating very much to get on service. I suppose though you are all keen."[320] Reade's verdict in his inspection report on the battalion stated that its discipline and drill were "satisfactory" and its physical appearance were "good".[321]

After the inspection, the men returned to Alexandra Barracks to rest and unwind. It had been a long and tiring day for the already overworked and underfed sepoys. Twenty-one of them had fainted during the inspection at Tanglin or on the march back to their barracks. The only company with a 100 percent rate of sepoys remaining on parade was the Ranghar D Company, led by the red-bearded Subedar Wahid Ali Khan. Possibly on the instigation of his clique member and D Company Jemadar, Chiste Khan, the B Company Jemadar Abdul Ali Khan confronted Wahid Ali and asked why he had not gone easier on the men. Wahid Ali shot back: "Do not talk to me like that or I will tell the Colonel."

Later that evening, Cotton was in the company lines counting waterproof sheets when he saw Lieutenant-Colonel Martin draw up in his car with his wife and daughter. Martin was concerned about the 5th's morale after the parade. He had come to check on the men. Apart from the medical cases, he had noticed many unhappy looking faces after the parade. Martin was questioning Cotton when more than a dozen sepoys came up the road and stopped about ten steps away. The squad of men were led by the regimental hot-head and star of the hockey team, Lance Naik Feroze Khan. He appeared white with rage. The tall and black-bearded sepoy, a close "caste brother" of Imtiaz Ali, told Cotton he had a petition to make. Noticing the approach by the sepoys, Martin called the men over. Feroze complained that they had been unfairly assigned grass clearing duties. This was after they had fainted at the inspection parade and had been sent to the hospital for rest. They had also not eaten all day. Furthermore, they had also lost face when other sepoys jeered them as they did coolie work clearing the grass near the quarter-guard hut. Feroze complained that the adjutant Strover was nowhere to be found and they had to appeal directly to Cotton and now to Martin. Martin made it a point to show his sympathy as all the men looked ill to him. Even Lieutenant-Colonel Ridout of the Royal Engineers who had attended the parade thought the men had "fainted genuinely." Martin told them: "As you can't get your food in a hurry you can have some milk at my expense." He let off the men with a tin of Nestle milk each and a day off parades.

Isolated from his fellow officers, Martin may have found affirmation in being kind and supportive to the sepoys. This was in line with the British Indian army's paternalistic scheme where the officer was supposed to be *ma-bap* or parent to his men. For some of his fellow officers, however, this coddling was considered dangerous. They thought that Martin too often gave the men the benefit of the doubt. The 5th's medical officer, Lieutenant Morrison, feared that the outcome of Martin's appeasement would only encourage malingering. Feroze, a big and burly athlete who practised bayonet fighting and was on the 5th's hockey and tug-of-war team, had much excess energy to burn. Morrison judged him to have "a very excitable fanatical temperament" and to be "a dangerous character."[322] The long-serving Captains Hall and Ball and the ambitious Adjutant Strover also preferred a less indulgent approach to the sepoys. Their attitude was shaped by the then standard views promoted by British Indian Army General Sir George Younghusband:

> It is never wise to stand studied impertinence, or even the semblance of it, from any Oriental.... the moment there is a sign of revolt, mutiny, or treachery, of which the symptoms not unusually are a swollen head, and a tendency to incivility, it is wise to hit the Oriental straight between the eyes, and to keep hitting him thus, till he appreciates exactly what he is, and who is who.[323]

When Ball, the Australian, approached Martin later and argued that Feroze and the men were not ill, Martin disagreed. He called over the skinniest Sepoy Yusaf Khan to the Orderly Room. The Subedar-Major Khan Mohammed Khan, the Adjutant Jemadar Rehmat Khan and several Indian officers were present. Martin ordered Yusaf to unbutton his coat and expose his malnourished-looking body. Pointing to the man, he told the Indian officers in Hindustani: "Look how thin this man is. He ought not to be put on fatigue." Martin thought he looked like a "living skeleton."[324] In the medical officer Morrison's last report the corpulent Subedar-Major Khan Mohammed Khan was noted to have shown a marked tendency to obesity. However, the Subedar-Major had no qualms replying to Martin in a matter-of-fact way: "This man has always been thin and I ha(ve) many men in the regiment who looked thinner and weaker but nevertheless did their work properly without falling out."[325]

When Ball suggested punishing the hot-head Feroze, Martin told him icily, "I am the law in this regiment."[326] He also reprimanded Strover over the incident in front of the sepoys. It was therefore no surprise when Rehmat Khan heard the men grumble that officers like Ball and Strover took no interest in them, but the Colonel at least gave them a hearing. Ball and Strover soon found themselves shunned on Christmas Day by their sepoys who traditionally came to offer a *salaam* (greeting) to their company commanders. Both had lost hold over their companies. A few days after Christmas, Ball and Strover handed in requests for immediate transfer. The Australian Ball had been with the 5th since 1903 and was the longest-serving officer in the battalion.

After the protest over unjust fatigue duties led by Feroze, Martin drafted a letter to Reade. He wrote that the men of the 5th were unfit for active duty because of inadequate rations combined with heavy mobilisation duties. Indeed, when the Guides were sent back to Taiping, the 5th had to pull a double shift to cover for them. Young and Reade seemed to have overlooked the strain this had placed on the sepoys. At one point, three quarters of the battalion were out on post, leaving the lines ragged and everyone stretched with no relief. Moreover, Martin recognised that the men were unhappy about their rations. Instead of 8 ounces (225 grams) of goat-meat twice a week, they received live chickens with feathers at the same scale. This brought down the meat ration to a mere 2 ounces (55 grams) a week. Martin believed he had felt the pulse of the men and was concerned about pushing them too hard. So, he made a request that they should be returned to India for three months to recuperate and regain their stamina.

Reflecting his usual diffidence and eagerness to win over his officers, Martin showed the draft letter to Captain Hall and asked him, "Do you think this is alright?"[327] Hall told him to take out any mention of India or it would look as if they were trying to avoid combat service. Martin mumbled something about avoiding the fiasco of the Guides refusal to serve overseas. He decided to send the draft letter without changes to the office of his Adjutant Strover to be typed up. As soon as he read its contents and the mention of India, Strover rushed off to see Cotton to convince Martin to withdraw the letter. This was hardly obeying orders. The ever ambitious, ceaselessly politicking and self-profiling Strover was desperate to go on active service. As the son of a retired Colonel who had served as British Political Agent in Burma, Strover may have feared that the letter would ruin his chances of seeing action and further advancement.

Finally, on Cotton's insistence and at Strover's quiet bidding, Martin agreed to revise the draft. The chain of command was completely inverted. Martin took out the request to have the 5th returned to India but asked for more rations. One can only speculate if Reade would have agreed to send the men to their homeland for recuperation, but if he took Martin's initial advice, and if the men knew for certain they were returning home, it is highly unlikely that they would have risked mounting a mutiny. Around or just before New Year's Day, Cotton congratulated his portly Subedar Dunde Khan. He believed that the Guides' withdrawal from service increased the 5th's chances of deployment. But Cotton had misread Dunde. Getting wind of Martin's draft letter from the typing pool, Dunde asked Cotton point-blank if it would not be better for the 5th to return to India. They could recuperate after the poor rations and heavy work they had done. He had quoted almost verbatim the words of Martin's early draft. Cotton disagreed, pointing out that the men were completely fit, which was simply untrue. In Cotton's recollection, Dunde agreed with him, or at least gave the impression that he did. Both men had lied to each other.

Dunde Khan's diplomatic response masked his true feelings. In January 1915, he was already closing accounts and preparing for some kind of action, striking some discordant notes in the battalion. He disparaged his old rival the Subedar-Major Khan Mohammed Khan. He told his sepoys that the senior Indian officer was opposed to the Turks and was only getting his own friends and relatives promoted. Rumours on the progress of the war in Europe were also fed to the sepoys. While eating in the lines, Sepoy Arshad of C Company heard Chiste say: "German has taken certain places, Austria has done likewise and Turkey has taken certain places. You people remain watchful."[328]

By the end of January, Cotton heard worrying news from the departing regimental *maulvi* (religious teacher), Faiz Ali Hassain. In a farewell conversation, Hassain had remarked casually that a sepoy he met in the bazaar told him that his successor was urging the sepoys not to fight the Turks. Chiste had, in fact, given the men the same advice each night before they turned in. Hassain also cautioned Cotton that if the 5th were sent to Egypt to fight Turks, the men would kill the Subedar-Major Khan Mohammed Khan who was no friend of Dunde or Chiste. But the *maulvi* considered this practically impossible since the ammunition was safely locked up.

Cotton comforted himself that the stray rounds spotted around the camp had yet to be used in anger. But he was conscientious enough to report to Martin the departing *maulvi*'s disclosures. Unfortunately, Martin had other things on his mind. His wife and beloved daughter were sailing back to England on the P&O liner *Nankin*. The *Emden* was no more but the Germans were preparing to launch unrestricted submarine warfare against British ships to counter a British blockade. On 27 January, the day after their departure, Martin heard from Reade that the 5th was moving to Hong Kong to replace the 40th Pathans. Their time in Singapore was up. Expecting that Martin wanted the 5th to go into combat, Reade apologised for the poor luck and assured Martin that he was doing his best to send the regiment on active service. Martin did not push the point of active service. Nor did he suggest that they be sent to India to rest. Taking a diplomatic line, he told Reade that there was probably good reason for the 5th to be ordered to Hong Kong, and assured Cotton that he would look into the *maulvi*'s warnings once they were in their new post.

The departure date was set for 18th February, just after the Chinese New Year holidays, but events were moving quickly ahead. Unknown to the British, Lauterbach and the Germans had started digging an escape tunnel in the prison camp in Tanglin. Then at the end of Friday prayers on 5 February, Manowar Ali from the Pathan left wing in 3rd Section, E Company, turned to face the assembly in the regimental mosque. He brazenly cried out: "*Din Islam Ki Lashkar ki waste fateh ke dua mango*" (Say a special prayer for the success of the armies of Islam).[329] Still a sepoy after 15 years of service, Manowar had long been a headache for his Company Commander, Subedar Bahadur. Bahadur checked Manowar and reported the issue to his Subedar-Major Khan Mohammed Khan who informed Martin and Strover. However, for some unknown reason, none of the Indian officers reported the matter immediately to Manowar's Double Company Commander, Lieutenant Harold Elliott.

That Friday, as Sepoy Manowar cheered for the victory of Islam, a change took place in the command of the troops in the Straits Settlements. The ailing Reade handed over the baton to Lieutenant-Colonel Dudley Ridout. A few days earlier, Ridout had been given control of an Indian secret agent brought in by Reade from India as Young had instructed. The agent, a Punjabi Muslim, was sent in to gauge the political views of the sepoys after the Guides' refusal to serve. For some reason, Reade prohibited the agent from working among the men of the 5th, and Ridout was not told about this during the handover. When Ridout asked about the condition of the 5th, Reade told him to look at his Inspection Report for December which, despite the high number of men falling-out, showed his satisfaction with the regiment.

On the day of the change in command, yet another canary toppled in the mineshaft. The long-serving A Company Commander, Subedar Mohammed Yunus Khan of Cotton's own double-company, demanded immediate discharge from service. When Cotton turned him down, the old Subedar replied plaintively that his family had served the government of India for over 60 years. He said that he himself had also put in many years' service and had always been "faithful to the British Raj and his salt" but had to go now because his "heart was like water".[330] Pressed by Cotton, Mohammed Yunus gave no reason for his resignation. Desperate to get to the heart of the matter, Cotton asked his battalion Adjutant Strover to find out more. Strover, who claimed to be close to Mohammed Yunus, also drew a blank. That the Subedar wanted to go so urgently suggested to Cotton that something serious was afoot. He summoned Mohammed Yunus to his bungalow again a few days later and questioned him in a private room. Avoiding a showdown with Cotton, Mohammed Yunus merely repeated that his "heart is like water." A frustrated Cotton retorted if he knew the English proverb about "rats leaving the sinking ship."[331]

It was insensitive of Cotton to use a proverb involving sinking ships.

There were rumours among the sepoys that the ship taking them to Hong Kong would be sunk on purpose by the British. Lance Naik Maksud of D Company often heard his fellow sepoys comment grimly in the cook-house, "eat your food and enjoy your pipe for in a few days we shall all be drowned."[332] Many of the sepoys would have recalled the miserable bouts of seasickness on their way to Singapore and hardly looked forward to another sea voyage other than to home. Others speculated that the battalion was not going to Hong Kong, but to Egypt or somewhere else to fight the Turks.

After five years of service as a cavalryman and 11 years in the 5th, Mohammed Yunus wanted out. At wit's end, Cotton warned the Subedar that if something did happen and he got away, he hoped that the responsibility would "crush him as he lay asleep on his bed."[333] Mohammed Yunus was already feeling crushed between the pair of Subedar-Major Khan Mohammed Khan and his friend Wahid Ali Khan on one hand and the trio of Dunde Khan, Chiste Khan and Abdul Ali Khan on the other. He had pleaded with Wahid and Chiste a year before to stop their fighting. Trapped between the rock of salt the Raj provided and the hard place of the sepoys, Mohammed Yunus had remained tight-lipped when interviewed by Martin.

The 5th was already struggling to maintain cohesion and discipline amid covert attempts to turn the sepoys. Hall's servant, Bahadur Khan, had heard from some sepoys at the end of January that there would be trouble in the regiment. Others denied the gossip. Amid the confusion, Cotton was sufficiently concerned to address rumours that they were not going to Hong Kong. He showed his Indian officers a telegram from Colonel Frederic Hill of the 40th Pathans in Hong Kong which had mentioned accommodation arrangements for him and Mrs Cotton in Hong Kong. But the sepoy rumour mill continued to churn, fed by the lack of clear and unambiguous directives from the British military command.

Despite the growing turmoil in the garrison, Ridout seemed blissfully unaware of the level of dissatisfaction among the sepoys. And nothing seemed amiss in Singapore's elite social scene. The terror of the *Emden* had receded into distant memory and was now an object of entertain-ment. On 6 February, the Girl's Friendly Society held a charity sale in a Grange Road residence graced by Lady Young. Among the various funfair stalls, the key attraction was a model of a battleship cruiser with the challenge "Try to sink the Emmed-in", a pun on the *Emden* being hemmed in.[334] A seven-year-old played the game so exuberantly that he had to be warned off from breaking all the crockery in sight in his efforts to smash the toy ship. The once menacing raider which had been no laughing matter just a few weeks before was now part of the fun and games in the settlement.

Also providing entertainment at this charity fete were two young lady friends, Miss Still, daughter of the legendary editor of *The Straits Times*, Alexander Still, and the recently married amateur actress, Marjorie Michie, now Mrs B. M. Woolcombe. The charming actress had previously acted alongside Captain Hall and Lieutenant Strover in the Victoria Theatre. Now the two young ladies delighted the audience with their duologue, "The Crystal Gazer"[335] with Michie playing the role of a sorceress peering into the future. If she could, in reality, predict what was ahead, she would have known that she would be dead in nine days' time, the sole female fatality of the Sepoy Mutiny.

As the European community laughed and played in the sun, Alexandra Barracks was on the edge of an explosion. It was a spark in a broader pattern of planned fireworks. Over in Lahore under Rash Behari Bose's leadership, the Ghadar Party agreed on 12 February to launch the general mutiny against the British Raj on 21 February. Ghadar emissaries were sent to several military cantonments in the Punjab to announce the impending rising. Bombs, arms and flags were prepared, with a declaration of mutiny drawn up. As per the standard plan, sepoys in barracks in Northern India would mutiny, murder their British officers, join with Ghadar revolutionaries, seize magazines and ammunition and detonate a general rising. Each of these moves was reported in detail by an Indian police spy named Kirpal Singh to the Department of Criminal Intelligence.

In Singapore, events moved with the force of their own logic and momentum. Everything was being rushed and compressed ahead of the 5th's departure to Hong Kong. There were some ominous signals during this time. Some of the 5th's carriage and gharry drivers had fled, fearful of what lay ahead. On 12 February, Subedar Suleiman Khan, commander of the Pathan G Company, returned from Pulau Brani. His family hailed from Rohtak and had served the British for a century. The former enlisted cavalryman of the Bengal Lancers had been brought into the 5th as an officer. He was absolutely certain that he owed his salt to the British Raj. Back in Alexandra Barracks, he had heard news that the Ranghar right wing had doubts about going to Hong Kong and that their ship would be sunk. When he came across his fellow Ranghar Subedar Mohammed Yunus whose heart was like water, Suleiman told him that his Pathan double company were ready to go on active service. He found a depressed comrade who told him: "I have not volunteered." When Sulaiman replied: "This is very funny thing. What is the reason for it?"[336] Yunus shared that he had applied to be discharged. But he refused to explain why.

On 13 February, the majority Chinese population in Singapore were gearing up to usher in the Year of the Rabbit the following day. The extra-long weekend began with 15 and 16 February being public holidays. The Swimming Club promised a "Sunday Atmosphere" for both days. The 5th Light Infantry band played its last social engagement at the special dinner and dance at the Sea View Hotel in Katong. The Casino cinema off Beach Road had a special programme at the same time. Advertised to "scare away all thoughts of war in Europe", it was screening *The Great Python Robbery* which was "full of hairbreadth adventures."[337] The next morning, as the Chinese celebrated their New Year with firecrackers and loud celebration, detachments of the 5th were summoned back from their mobilisation stations. The sepoys returned from their posts on Pulau Blakang Mati, Pulau Brani, Labrador, Keppel Harbour and Victoria Dock and were replaced by Singapore Volunteers from the European and Malay companies.

To make up for the holidaying Chinese, the Malay volunteer infantry company were deployed in full force, stationing their men in half a dozen active stations. At Keppel Harbour, Lieutenant Farrar and four men of the Malay Company of the Singapore Volunteers relieved the 5th on Sunday, 14 February. As the 5th's sepoys waited by the roadside for their lorry, Farrar, in his car, noticed one of the sepoys breaking away and making a dash towards him. The man was even loading his rifle. At the last moment, he was pulled back and talked to by a pair of his comrades. The menacing sepoy repeated this move twice before a lorry transport drove up and ferried the men away. Farrar did not know what to make of it and whether he was being taunted or threatened.

At King's Dock in Keppel Harbour, Sergeant Abu Bakar bin Haji Arshad led a force of 22 men from the Malay Company. They relieved the sepoys of the 5th at 3 pm without incident. An hour later, a short-tempered and "burly sergeant"[338] of the 5th, quite possibly Imtiaz Ali or perhaps Abdul Ghani, it is not clear who, came around to the Malay post. He asked how many rounds of ammunition they had in reserve. Sergeant Abu Bakar told him that they had 10 rounds per man and no reserve. He concealed the fact that they had 20 rounds per man and 4,000 in reserve.

The "burly sergeant" brought out two boxes of the popular, Swiss-made Roskopf brand of watches. He offered Abu Bakar two dozen at a bargain price of $1.50 each. Abu Bakar waved him off, provoking a torrent of abuse from the hot-headed NCO. He told Abu Bakar that the Malays were actually Christians and threatened that he would soon return and teach them about their religion. The 27-year-old Abu Bakar was a Singapore-born Bugis who received his education at the elite Raffles Institution. He was not easily intimidated and did not need any lessons

246

on his faith. Any fantasies promoted by the Kampong Java preacher, Nur Alam Shah, or the *jihadi*-socialite, Kassim Ismail Mansoor, that Malays would readily join in the adventure were put to rest by Sergeant Abu Bakar.

Earlier that morning, Colonel Martin had summoned all the Indian officers to his bungalow at the top of the hill. He told them of the move to Hong Kong and provided an approximate date of departure. The exact date could not be shared for operational reasons so as to avoid tipping off the enemy. But the understanding was that they would leave on 18 February, according to the Ranghar C Company Jemadar Hoshiar Ali, or a day or two later. Jemadar Ghulam Haidar, a Pathan from Rohtak in H Company, heard Martin say that "it appears to me there is some considerable doubt in the minds of people – as syces have run away, and other things as to our destination. I wish you to reassure your men that there is no doubt as to our destination. We are going to Hong Kong."[339] Dismissing the rest, Martin kept Ghulam and a few other Pathan officers back. These officers had complained to Hall that they could not accept the promotion of Imtiaz Ali, the big-bearded Ranghar. It would eat into their allotted quota of officers. Martin promised them that the promotion would go to the Pathans. He ordered them to assemble their best Pathan candidates at 4 pm that afternoon for a mock examination.

While Martin addressed the Pathan officers, Jemadar Hans Raj and the other Indian officers returned to their lines. Neither Ranghar nor Pathan, Hans Raj was a Muslim Mula Jat from Rohtak promoted from the ranks five years earlier. Hans Raj and three other officers from No 3 Double Company searched for their young Double Company Commander, Lieutenant Elliott, to see if he had any orders for them and if he believed that they should volunteer for service. However, Elliott was away at Pulau Blakang Mati, where he had been inspecting the European volunteers' Maxim gun section. While seeking out Elliot, Hans Raj and his companions bumped into Strover.

The scheming Adjutant, still looking to distinguish himself in active duty, took the opportunity to quietly lobby the Indian officers. He wanted them to make a special appeal to volunteer for combat service instead of the peacetime garrison in Hong Kong. They were told to offer themselves for field service during Ridout's final inspection parade the following day. After their talk with Strover, the Indian officers encountered the Subedar-Major Khan Mohammed Khan. Learning of Strover's request, the Subedar-Major assured them that he would sound out the other officers and check on the pulse of the battalion to see if it was ready to volunteer for service. He knew what happened to the Guides after their Subedar-Major volunteered them for service without first checking with the men. He had already picked up that his rivals Dunde and Chiste had told the sepoys that he had run down Turkey and promoted his own relatives, which weighed heavily on his mind.

After their discussions with Strover and Khan Mohammed Khan, Hans Raj and the other Indian officers redoubled their efforts to find Elliott and consult him. They finally located the baby-faced officer who was still finding his feet in the 5th. Elliott had joined the Indian Army as a green Lieutenant, transferring from the Worcestershire Regiment. The European volunteers considered him an enthusiastic and competent young officer, but he was still learning the ropes. He had kept apart from the politicking and intriguing and this was appreciated by his CO. In his December 1914 confidential report, Martin wrote that Elliott was a "painstaking, hardworking, intelligent officer, keen and willing at all times."[340] Elliott ordered the Indian officers to start packing their kit after the final inspection parade the next morning. He also told them that he wanted their Double Company to fall in fifteen minutes before the start of the inspection parade the next day. He would ask them if they were ready to go on active service.

Just after 10 am, a 190-strong detachment of Johor Military Forces (JMF) led by the Sultan Ibrahim of Johor arrived at Cluny Station.[341] A platoon from the JMF force broke off towards Tanglin Camp, led by their British Captain C H Cullimore, and three Malay officers including Adjutant Captain Abdul Hamid. They would support the inexperienced European volunteers who were replacing the 5th's guards at Tanglin. The Sultan of Johor personally accompanied the group, which carried rifles but no ammunition. To his great consternation, the Acting Camp Commander, Captain Percy Netterville Gerrard of the Malay States Volunteer Rifles (MSVR), told the Sultan that he had assumed they would have come with their own ammunition. When the Sultan pressed the case, Gerrard told him that "being Sunday and Chinese New Year's Day in addition things could not be done as one would wish."[342] His Guard Commander, Second Lieutenant J H Love-Montgomerie of the Singapore Volunteers, was unable to even provide written orders for the incoming JMF men taking over guard duties. The Sultan found a soiled copy of the orders by accident and tried to figure out if the instructions were still applicable.

After the disorderly handover, a British medic orderly at Tanglin Barracks hospital heard the 5th's sepoys shout "Islam, Islam" as they left the German prisoner's camp. He recalled seeing 15 to 20 sepoys on a lorry waving their turbans and rifles and shouting "Islam" as they were driven away to Alexandra Barracks. Another British volunteer remembered a lot of noise and jeering directed at the European volunteers as the 5th were being relieved. Private Robertson of the Volunteers would later tell the court of inquiry on the mutiny that: "they appeared to be very *sombong*, high and haughty and insolent. They rather looked down on us. It was generally noticed by our men that they looked upon us very contemptuously."[343] The lawyer Roland Braddell, also a Volunteer guard, noticed that the men of the 5th were "insolent" and "laughed at us when we had to move their furniture."[344]

Just before sundown on Sunday, the Sultan of Johor returned by train to his palace. At about the same time, the conspirators Dunde and Abdul Ali arrived in the lines of B Company. They ordered all the Non-Commissioned Officers to fall in. B Company sepoy Lance Naik Maksud was related to the Subedar-Major Khan Mohammed Khan as well as Wahid Ali. He cautiously stood some distance away as their rival Dunde told the men: "You must obey my orders, pack up your baggage and bed and tomorrow when the General comes I will report that my Company is ready to go anywhere." After conveying the official instructions, Dunde shared his plans, declaring "we intend to raise a disturbance and we have no intention of going on service. The Subedar-Major and Subedar Wahid Ali will not allow us full liberty at prayers, and run down Turkey, but we are spreading a net over them which will mean their downfall."[345]

At about 7 pm, Jemadar Rehmat Khan, the native Adjutant in charge of administrative affairs made his way up to Major Cotton's bungalow. Major Cotton had summoned them to check if the sepoys knew for sure they were headed for Hong Kong and that everything was in order before departure. Accompanying Rahmat were three No 1 Double Company officers, Mohammed Yunus of A Company and Dunde and Abdul Ali of B Company. The two B Company officers were in close league with D Company's Chiste. On the narrow, uphill road (today's Royal Road) leading up to Cotton's bungalow, Mohammed Yunus stopped and addressed the others: "Without doubt we are reporting our companies as all well today, but what about the future?"[346]

Rehmat was troubled by his remark which seemed to be hinting at some dark thoughts. Dunde chimed in: "What about the future?" as did Abdul Ali, who oversaw Imtiaz Ali and the guard detachment at the German camp in Tanglin. The group stood in silence for what seemed like a long time before Rehmat broke the silence: "It is no good for us to stay here like this. People will begin to suspect we are up to some mischief."[347] He told the others to get on with it since, as Muslims, their fate was preordained anyway. Rehmat added: "Are you able to say whether we will be alive tomorrow or not?"[348]

The Indian officers had tarried a little too long on their way to see Cotton. When they finally reached his residence, his orderly told them that the Major was out for dinner. They agreed to return later. At about the same time, Khan Mohammed Khan was conferring with Ball in the Mess Hall. Ball noticed that the Subedar-Major seemed to be in fear of his life. He whispered to him: "Come into a dark place to talk". They went down the road below the Mess. The Subedar-Major knew by then that he had lost control of his men. Earlier that day, he had called all the NCOs from C Company to check if they would volunteer for service. The hot-headed Lance Naik Feroze, who was from Khan Mohammed Khan's own village, shot back rudely: "Why don't you volunteer?"[349] When the Subedar-Major said he gladly would, Feroze told him he was ready as well to go on active service himself. Then he added defiantly: "I am not going with the regiment to Hong Kong."[350]

As soon as Ball had finished hearing the Subedar-Major's complaint, Rehmat Khan approached the Australian to raise the promotion issue. He maintained that if the Ranghar Imtiaz Ali was promoted, there would be trouble among the Pathans. But Ball had heard from Hall that the promotion matter was settled. His Pathan Colour Havildar Mohammed Hussain was going to be examined the next day and would be promoted if he passed the test. The consequences on Ranghar morale of Imtiaz Ali being passed up again seemed to have been overlooked by the British officers.

After dinner time at about 9 pm, Rehmat regrouped with the other three Indian officers to see Cotton. They had better luck this time. As the senior Indian officer present, Mohammed Yunus reported to Cotton that the sepoys knew of the move to Hong Kong and had been instructed to pack their kit. Cotton appeared tense and uncertain and quite annoyed. Cotton had, in fact, already given up on Yunus, telling the Indian officer just two days earlier that he was free to go ahead and quit. Yunus duly submitted his resignation the night before to Martin who had agreed to wire it on to headquarters. Wary of Yunus' hollow assurances, Cotton pressed the others to speak their minds.

In a ham-fisted effort to break the awkward silence, Cotton told the Ranghar officers that Imtiaz Ali's promotion was going through, which was untrue. The skittish second-in-command had just learnt from Ball that both he and Strover had real concerns about being shot by the sepoys. If Martin was considered too sepoy-friendly, Ball and Strover were at the other end of the spectrum. Cotton feared being seen in a similar light as Ball and Strover. He asked the men point-blank: "Is anybody going to shoot me?"[351] They told him what he preferred to hear and not what he needed to know for the sake of the battalion.

Early the next morning, on Monday, 15 February, Acting General Ridout arrived in Alexandra Barracks to carry out the final inspection.

The weather was fine but he was in less than perfect health. Ridout was feeling the effects of a malarial fever and needed to get over with the formalities quickly. Just before the start of the inspection at 7 am, Elliott ordered the men of his E & F Double Company to fall in. His Indian deputy Subedar Bahadur asked him if the men were going to be asked to volunteer for combat. But someone, possibly Martin or Cotton, had whispered in Elliot's ear the night before that one of his sepoys had uttered seditious words. He had lost face when he appeared unaware of the incident. Pulling aside Bahadur, he said that it was not the right time to ask the question. He added angrily that he had just learnt of Sepoy Manowar's outburst in the mosque the previous Friday. Chewing out Bahadur and the other Indian officers for failing to report this to him, Elliott said that henceforth he was to be informed about everything that happened in his Double Company.

Ridout did not sense the unhappiness rippling through the lines of sepoys paraded before him. Not wanting to prolong matters, Ridout said the correct things for a British general to say in time of war, not what the frustrated, confused, divided and unhappy sepoys needed to hear. He mentioned the front but did not state explicitly that their final destination was Hong Kong. Instead, he waffled that although it was not their good fortune to go to Europe, they were going where there was need of their services as "It is the duty of all of us to go where we are ordered – no matter what our own feelings are. The Empire is vast and the duty of guarding it great… it may soon be their luck to go to Europe and fight side by side with the Indian troops against our powerful enemy."[352]

After the speech, Colour Havildar Rahmat Khan felt fairly sure that their destination was Hong Kong. However, the loyal Pathan NCO who spurned advances by German prisoners was always ready to do and say the right thing. He was among the minority. This was not the case for many of the Ranghars. Rahmat heard several Ranghar sepoys commenting loudly after the speech that they were not going to Hong Kong but were being sent off to combat. Over the past few days, Lieutenant Strover's orderly, Sepoy Arshad, had to deny rumours that they were being despatched as cannon-fodder to the front. With Ridout's ambiguous speech as translated by Martin, even Arshad harboured doubts about their destination.

With the inspection now over, the men on parade were dismissed, except the selected NCOs from the Pathan left wing who prepared to undergo the promotion examination. As the Ranghar right wing moved off the parade ground, they swung by the left wing of Pathans. A few of the Ranghar sepoys yelled, making derisive noises like jackals. Ridout and the British officers were some distance away and may not have registered their disdain.

The promotion examination took about an hour. A Pathan Colour Havildar named Mohammed Hussain was quickly examined with several other NCOs who were all put through a test drill. After the examination, a telegram was sent to the GOC's headquarters at Fort Canning cancelling Imtiaz's promotion. News of the cancelled promotion was somehow leaked to Imtiaz. It was Strover's office that looked after all the telegrams and someone in his staff had earlier leaked to Dunde the cancelled letter drafted by Martin to propose recuperation for the 5th back in India.

Officially on medical leave for an unspecified ailment, Imtiaz Ali skipped parade on 14 and 15 February. He had had more than enough time to stew over the humiliation of being snubbed again by the promotion board. Imtiaz had lost *izzat*, his dignity. The Pathan G Company Commander, Subedar Suleiman, thought that this disappointment could have pushed him to mutiny, considering Imtiaz Ali: "a man of strong character, a great talker, and had great influence with the men, although not a highly educated man."[353] The crafty Lauterbach had already spent a fortnight with Imtiaz in Tanglin and boasted about putting ideas in his head. Imtiaz had also joined Chiste for prayers at the pro-Ottoman Kampong Java Mosque where the preacher and Ghadar operative Nur Alam Shah remained active. Imtiaz's anger and disappointment had become an instrument in the hands of others.

[XX]

DO IT

Two hours after the final parade, Bahadur and Hans Raj of E Company entered the regimental office to speak to Lieutenant Elliott. Troubled by the normally polite and well-mannered Elliot's early morning rebuke, they wanted to clear the air over Sepoy Manowar's prayer in the regimental mosque. Bahadur blamed the Subedar Major Khan Mohammed Khan for ordering them to hush up the episode. By now, Elliott was back to his usual unruffled form and reassured the Indians: "I am not (in) the least bit angry about it."[354] At 2 pm, after taking his lunch, Elliott walked towards the ammunition magazine next to the quarter-guard hut. He had less than two hours left to live. The boyish looking officer was accompanied by Naik Mahomed Sadiq Ahmed who witnessed him unlock the magazine padlock. A dozen store-men were standing by to transfer 33,327 rounds of small-arms ammunition from the magazine to a waiting motor-lorry. Among the fatigue party was Sepoy Mahboob Khan, a Pathan storeman with 18 years of service and Sepoy Mauzuddin, a rifleman of C Company.

The ammunition had to be returned to the central stores at Fort Canning before the 5th sailed for Hong Kong. The transfer was originally scheduled for the following day but had now been pushed forward. Chiste had uncovered the change possibly only late that morning. At noon, Lance-Naik Ghaffur Khan of C Company saw Chiste confer with Imtiaz Ali under the shade of a large tree on the path to the quarter-guard hut. Careful not to get too close and arouse suspicions that he was eavesdropping, Ghaffur overheard Chiste say: "The ammunition will go away at 3 o'clock today."[355] This meant that the mutineers had to bring forward their own time-table. Seizing the ammunition in the store was the first move to give teeth to the mutiny. Everything else hinged on that first step.

With the ammunition transfer underway, the mutineers put their plan into operation. Sepoy Maizhar Khan of C Company was on duty at the quarter-guard hut under the command of a Pathan Guard Commander, Havildar Jamalludin Khan from F Company. Maizhar noticed his fellow C Company Ranghar guard Sepoy Ismail Khan heading to the lines with his *chilum* (tobacco pipe). Ismail had been part of the Tanglin POW Camp guard detachment under the command of Abdul Ali and Imtiaz. After half an hour, Ismail returned with his tobacco and some news. Maizhar overheard him telling the Guard Commander what Imtiaz and Feroze Khan had said while he was in the lines: "It is better to die than to stay in his gaol."[356]

Near the quarter-guard hut, Sepoy Ali Nawaz of C Company spotted Imtiaz with Feroze Khan and a B Company Ranghar Sepoy named Shamsuddin at Q Block. Imtiaz was complaining to Shamsuddin: "They have made a native officer in the left wing; they have not given it to the right wing... they were going to make me a Jemadar. Why have they made a left wing man? I will make the sentry attack the magazine, or I will break it somehow."[357] Suddenly noticing Ali Nawaz, Imtiaz warned him: "You have better not say a word of what you have heard."[358] Despite Strover's firm insistence later on that he had ensured that news of Imtiaz's cancelled promotion would not leak, Imtiaz already knew all about it.

Standing just a few metres away, Elliott had little inkling of the approaching storm. Satisfying himself that everything was in order, he ordered the Quartermaster Havildar Mohamed Yar to complete the rest of the loading. Then he sauntered off to Ball's bungalow to check on the afternoon's recreation. Elliott found Ball in his quarters lying down and reading. Eager for a distraction, he asked if there was a chance they could have a game of hockey. The weather was good, and since it was a public holiday, most of the Europeans had gone swimming, picnicking or to play golf, cricket or tennis or were simply enjoying a snooze. Ball told him that he could not muster enough players for a game because of the earlier parade. So, for sport, the pair of British officers agreed to go out later that afternoon on a "ratting expedition" – hunting the rodents that infested the barracks.

Before the British officers could start their fun, the mutiny ring-leaders began the operation to seize the ammunition. Ghaffur Khan emerged from the latrine just in time to see Shamsuddin leaving Jemadar Abdul Ali's quarters. Shamsuddin walked towards the quarter-guard hut, presumably to check on the progress of the ammunition unloading. The ideal time to strike was when the ammunition was laid out on the lorry and just before it was driven away. Returning to the native officers' quarters, he called out Imtiaz Ali's name. Imtiaz replied, "What do you want?"[359] Shamsuddin conveyed Abdul Ali's terse order: "*Kar deo*" (Do it).[360] With the command given, Imtiaz strode with purpose towards the quarter-guard hut accompanied by Naik Karim Buksh. Entering the guardroom, he first said his prayers while a group of co-conspirators from A and B Companies stood close by ready for action.

Looking forward to the planned rat-hunt later in the afternoon, Elliott left Ball's quarters at a quarter to three. The fatigue party had by then loaded all the ammunition on to the motor lorry. Mahboob Khan and his fellow storemen were now loading oil drums in the spaces between the ammunition crates. The air was still apart from the sound of the loading. It was not a windy day. The desultory sound of afternoon fire-crackers may have been in the air. And then the first shot of the mutiny was fired. The storeman Mahboob heard the round go past his left ear. He looked up and saw Ismail Khan holding a smoking rifle with bayonet fixed and charging straight for him, shouting "Do you mean to take that motor away?"[361] Mahboob and his Quartermaster Yar Khan ran for their lives. Mahboob dashed through the nearby lines yelling: "The sentry ran amok and is firing" and "The Ranghar sentry has run amok."[362]

Those who heard the gunshot and were not in the plan dismissed it as a Chinese New Year firecracker. The Chinese cracker assumption was made throughout the island whenever mutinous shots were heard. This may have slowed down the reaction time or confused matters. Lance Naik Maksud of D Company was reading the Qur'an in the quarter-guard hut when he heard the commotion. He thought he heard the Guard Commander Havildar Jamalluddin order a turn-out. (Jamalluddin claimed to be in the latrine when the shot was fired.) Peeking outside, Maksud saw an agitated Ismail standing on the ammunition lorry. Imtiaz and Karim Baksh were running around the lorry instructing their companies to form up on the double. Imtiaz ordered rebel sepoys from A Company to unload the ammunition.

Jamalluddin, who was on the quarter-guard hut verandah, hesitated, apparently unsure of what he should do. One of his guards, Sepoy Kandha from E Company, had loaded his weapon and had Ismail in his sights. Jamalluddin stopped Kandha from shooting Ismail, telling him "O you fool Jat, stop that." The Guard Commander was reluctant to assert his powers. It did not take long for Feroze to appear on the scene. Entering the guard room in search of Ismail, he asked: "Where is the lion, he has done very well."[363] Imtiaz appeared next. He challenged Jamalluddin who went through the motion of despatching Maksud to alert the Subedar-Major Khan Mohammed Khan before fleeing the scene. He would quietly return later to the quarter-guard hut to smash open and loot a locked chest containing $900 of private funds.

Mutineers were seizing pickaxes from the quarter-guard hut verandah

*The star makes the spot of the guard-house
and ground zero of the mutiny.*

*House of Commanding Officer,
Lt Col Edward Victor Martin.*

to smash the magazine locks. In the C Company lines, Ghaffur Khan saw Feroze enter and shout: "If any man now has not got a rifle and ammunition he must be shot."[364] Ghaffur ran out without his rifle and was fired upon several times. Feroze took pot shots at him, but he managed to escape into the jungle. Others were not as quick or lucky. Sepoy Mauzuddin who had earlier helped load the ammunition now watched as men from B Company freely looted the magazine. As he tried to flee, he was shot in his knee and chest and crawled away to his quarters. The ever-loyal Colour Havildar Rahmat Khan who had warned German prisoners not to speak with him heard Munshi Khan calling out to the men of his B company to "come and take the magazine."[365] To his horror, men from his own D Company were also freely picking up ammunition. And there was nothing he could do.

When Wahid Ali Khan came on the scene and ordered the men to put down the ammunition, he was ignored. Rahmat noticed Wahid's old nemesis, Chiste, signal for them to carry on. Someone told Wahid to go away. Others threatened, "Get out of this or we will kill you."[366] A sepoy took aim at Wahid but another sepoy pulled the rifle down. That was signal enough for Wahid and Rahmat to take to their heels. The men of Ismail's C Company had also joined the mutiny. Sepoy Taj Mohamed, who had saluted the painting of the Kaiser in Tanglin, was collecting as much ammunition as he could carry in his haversack. The Ranghar sepoys were not acting alone. Fifteen minutes after the first shot, some men from the Guides Battery joined in. Dunde was also seen handing out ammunition to about forty men from his D Company. For now, at least, the Singapore Sepoy Mutiny was following the planned script of the general uprising in India. Sepoys were rising, seizing ammunition, and preparing to kill their officers who taken completely by surprise.

When the first shot was fired, Strover was out at Punggol beach hobnobbing with Sir Evelyn Ellis, an influential lawyer and senior member of the Legislative Council of the Straits Settlements. Major Cotton was lying down in his bedroom, which faced the road leading up to Colonel Martin's house. Martin was at home, having fallen asleep while composing a letter. Subedar Sharaf-ud-din was in his H Company lines talking to a sepoy and checking on the pre-departure packing of kit when he heard the general alarm sounded by a bugler. He gave orders to issue arms to his Pathan No 4 Double Company and post sentries at four corners of the lines to prevent defections. This kept his Pathans more or less intact as Subedar Suleiman Khan joined him. Both Indian officers had a long record of family service to the British Raj stretching back a century. Sharaf-ud-din was always proud to say that his grandfather had served loyally during the 1857 Mutiny.

At 3 pm, Cotton also heard the bugler blow the general alarm, and then the sight of the fat Subedar-Major Khan Mohammed Khan jogging up the hill to Martin's house. As he passed Cotton's bungalow, Khan called out to Cotton that a shot had been fired in the lines. Cotton quickly dressed, grabbed his sword and ran as hard as he could across the parade ground towards the Double Company lines. Elliott had already alerted Ball who quickly put on his boots and also ran to the lines. Passing Cotton's house, he cried out "Major!" and heard Mrs Cotton reply: "Willie has gone on, what is the matter?"[367] Ball said he did not know.

Martin did not have any ammunition for his revolver, so he took his sword and four iron tent pegs and placed these weapons at the ready at the top of the stairs of his house. Clattering into Martin's house, the heavy-set Subedar-Major ran panting up the stairs and told his Commanding Officer: "You had better run away as there has been firing in the lines."[368] He explained that the right wing had mutinied and that he did not know friend from foe as everyone was running off in all directions. As he stood in the upper verandah, he saw a sepoy moving across the parade ground. The sepoy stopped, turned, and fired directly at the bungalow. The Subedar-Major heard the ping of the bullet near him. Martin was telephoning his headquarters in Fort Canning, telling the operator to inform Ridout of the mutiny. He tried calling Normanton Camp but neglected to alert Tanglin Camp or the Central Police Station.

After warning Ball, the young Lieutenant Elliot alerted Hall who was billeted in their shared quarters. The pair ran toward the company lines but were separated near Cotton's bungalow. Hall was watching his Australian colleague and friend Ball as he made haste towards the Indian officers' quarters. Elliott had decided to head to Normanton Camp after trying to settle some of the sepoys and telling his men to keep their wits. He never made it. He was hunted down by a group of mutineers and was cornered and killed by Sepoy Shamsuddin, who had moments earlier passed on Abdul Ali's instructions to Imtiaz to start the mutiny. Elliott's body was found later between 5.25 and 5.5 milestone of Pasir Panjang Road in the ditch opposite the *jihadi*-socialite Kassim Mansoor's property. One of Kassim's Dutch tenants, E F Boode, found the young lieutenant's body. The burns on his uniform suggested that he had been shot through the chest at close range.

Now on his own, Hall decided to get his Pathan No 4 Double Company to fall in. Subedars Sharaf-ud-din and Suleiman had kept them together until his arrival. But the 120 Pathans he gathered only had their rifles and bayonets with no ammunition. When in doubt and pushed against a corner, the infantry officer can resort to cold steel. Telling the sepoys to steady themselves, he ordered them to fix their bayonets and said, "Well, we can charge."[369] But the charge of the Pathans of the light infantry against the Ranghar light infantry was not to be. Hall's men scattered under heavy gunfire, ducking under the rounds whizzing overhead. Only 50 remained with him after the fusillade of shots. The rest had fled in different directions.

Cotton had made it by then to the Indian officers' quarters, where he found Yunus Khan, Dunde Khan and Abdul Ali. With the wavering Yunus Khan, the two ring-leaders did not appear to be openly leading the mutiny at the time. Instead, they acted as if they had nothing to do with it. Feigning innocence, they shared with Cotton what was pretty obvious to all – that there was firing in the lines. The ring-leaders may have been holding back to see how the situation evolved. As Cotton ran out to investigate the situation, they implored him to stay under cover. Cotton heard one of them say: "For God's sake don't go down or you will be killed. You can do nothing. Look there."[370] It was not clear if they were protecting him for now or trying to prevent him from taking charge of the situation. Peering outside, Cotton saw a group of armed sepoys heading towards Tanglin Barracks. Others were skirting around Cemetery Hill just north of Alexandra Barracks. Yet another group were helping themselves to ammunition. Then a bullet whizzed past him.

Like the British officers, the Indian officers who were not in on the game were trying to get a fix on the rapidly unfolding situation and place themselves accordingly. By now, a distraught and flummoxed Major Cotton had been placed on a chair by Dunde and Yunus Khan. It did not help his composure when Captain Ball burst into the Indian officers' quarters and fired off a volley of questions at the already stunned Cotton: "What is the matter? Where is the Commanding Officer? What are the orders?" Cotton's response was a weak: "I don't know."[371] Ball tried to look outside but was pulled back by Hoshiar Ali from C Company with a warning: "The Regiment appears to me to have mutinied. I am alone here and no man with me. I cannot allow you to go in that direction."[372] As he said this, three shots were fired at Ball. Crouching, Ball spotted up to 50 armed sepoys scattered around the parade ground.

Jemadar Hoshiar Ali was a Ranghar from Hissar with 16 years of service. He had only been promoted to officer rank 16 months earlier. Like Yunus, he had tended to vacillate between the Subedar Major Khan Mohammed Khan's clique and that of Dunde and Chiste. He had narrowly missed being killed when a bullet snipped his *pagri* (turban). Despite torn loyalties, his efforts at physically restraining Cotton and Ball from heading towards the confused lines probably saved their lives. Hoshiar Ali watched as Chiste emerged from around the corner of the neighbouring block of officers' quarters. Chiste walked calmly towards Cotton and Ball. As Chiste's Company Commander, Ball had given Chiste an excellent annual report at the end of 1914, and had even favoured him as a possible future Subedar-Major over his own Subedar Wahid Ali. Pulling Chiste aside, Ball told him to do what he could to stop the mutineers. Chiste said he could do nothing.

Feeling let down badly by Chiste, Ball rejoined the flustered Cotton. Next on the scene was Captain Perceval Boyce, who arrived hot and panting in the Indian Officers Quarters. The 28-year-old was the only one of the three officers who had the presence of mind to arm himself. In the thick of it, Cotton said in Boy's Own fashion: "Well, Ball, we are in for it, and we may as well take it decently". Ball replied: "Very good!" A former Old Bedfordian, a school which had produced its share of Victoria Cross winners, Boyce yelled out amid the firing: "Well, I'll take one of the swine with me if I have to go."[373] He lay down on the grass and started firing off shots at the mutineers with his revolver. The reports attracted notice and, before long, the mutineers were returning fire. Some started to manoeuvre towards them. Boyce's shooting checked the sepoys for a while as the British officers beat a hasty retreat.

Dunde and Chiste swung into action after the British officers left the Indian officers' quarters. Dunde led a group of Ranghars over to the Malay States Guides Battery encampment at the southern end of Alexandra Barracks where HortPark is today. After the alarm was sounded, the Guides Battery's Muslim and Sikh gunners were told to fall in by their Sikh NCO, Havildar Sohan Singh. He had also sent a bicycle orderly to fetch instructions from their Commanding Officer, Captain Moira F A Maclean. The Texas-born artillery officer decided to make his way from his quarters to the lines.

Sohan Singh saw Maclean approaching. He was between the F and E Blocks of the barracks, about where the Plant Introduction Garden of HortPark is sited. A body of mutineers lurked to his right in the jungle in the vicinity of today's Google Headquarters and Alexandra Technopark. Spotting them suddenly, Maclean wheeled away but was trapped by another group of mutineers who emerged from between Blocks D and E. They were heard shouting what sounded like "Ali, Ali" or perhaps "Allahu Akbar"[374] as they rushed towards Maclean. The artillery officer was soon overwhelmed. Several shots were fired at Maclean who fell dead south of the left centre of E Block, around the HortPark's Balinese Garden.

Watching Maclean fall dead, Sohan Singh ordered his sepoys to disperse and head for safety in the city. Dunde, in white pantaloons, khaki coat and white turban, appeared and stopped them. He was heard saying: "You people have signed on for serving the Sirkar and you had better get out of this or I will shoot you…."[375] These people are faithless; they have signed on to fight for the Government against Turkey and the Germans. Shoot them first."[376] Dunde forced arms and ammunition on the men with stern threats. At least 11 of the 98 Guides joined the mutiny, some willingly, perhaps, while most waited for a chance to bolt. Bizarrely, the mutineers overlooked the Guides' 10 pounder guns. If pressed into service, the guns could have been used to devastating effect. At Sohan's rushed orders, a gunner removed and hid the breech blocks to disable the cannons.

Pushed back by the intense gunfire outside the Indian officers' quarters, Cotton, Boyce and Ball were taking the long route to the neighbouring Normanton Camp. A company of British volunteers from the Kuala Lumpur-based Malay States Volunteer Rifles (MSVR) were in the camp, which lay across Ayer Rajah Road, for a month's training. To get there, the trio took the longer but safer route that looped behind Martin's bungalow. It was a wise choice as Elliott had lost his life trying to take the shortest route for help. Boyce continued to provide covering fire, until a bullet grazed his head just before they rounded Martin's house. Then the shooting stopped for a while as they disappeared from the sights of the mutineers. The sea and Pasir Panjang Beach stretched out to their left. It was humid and their minds raced as adrenalin pumped through their sweaty bodies. Ball was the first to reach Normanton, followed by Cotton. The wounded Boyce straggled behind. It was every officer for himself. Boyce, who had protected their rear, now lost contact with the pair. The old Bedfordian was finished off later by a band of mutineers who riddled his body with bullets. Three officers were now already dead.

Elsewhere, also separated from his brother British officers, Hall ordered his 50 remaining Pathans to follow him to Normanton Camp to link up with the MSVR. As they approached, Sharaf-ud-din noticed with alarm that the MSVR Volunteers were lined up and ready to shoot them. A friendly-fire disaster was averted when Hall signalled at them with a white handkerchief. As Hall came up in the midst of the MSVR ranks, he found the hapless Cotton throwing up, either out of fear or over-exertion or a combination of both. When Hall tried to supply his men with pouch ammunition from the MSVR, Suleiman warned him against it. Nobody was certain where any of the sepoys stood, not even their own Pathan officers.

The motley group collected itself into some sort of order. Along with the men of the MSVR, the 5th's officers and the Pathan sepoys somehow made it back to Martin's bungalow without a single casualty. On the way up, they passed Cotton's bungalow. His wife was hiding in the space under the house raised on concrete stilts. The nervy Cotton did not make the effort to personally retrieve his wife. Mrs Cotton had crawled under the floor-boards when she heard the firing. She spotted mutineers hiding among trees near the parade ground and heard bullets whizzing past. Just before dusk, Sharaf-ud-din took a volunteer and went down the road to the house. Ignoring the firing from the lines, the slightly tubby and broad-whiskered Pathan extracted Mrs Cotton from 6 Royal Road. Together they made a dash for Martin's bungalow to rejoin her husband "Willie".

Martin, Cotton, Ball and the Subedar-Major prepared the hill-top bungalow for a prolonged siege. The 80 British volunteers from the MSVR took positions within the bungalow and manned pickets on four sides of the adjoining land. Hall's Pathans stacked their rifles upstairs and helped to barricade the verandah. Others were sent down to the Mess to collect food, drinks and servants. The colonial *sahib* could not be expected to fight without victuals and domestic help. The Pathans were told to wait in the lines and keep out of the fight. The Subedar-Major Khan Mohammed Khan, Colour Havildar Rahmat Khan, Pathan Subedars Sharaf-ud-Din and Suleiman, another Havildar and a sepoy were permitted to remain in the bungalow. These half-dozen token Indians were not given weapons nor responsibilities.

As for the mutineers, if they had a clear plan, it was not obvious to anyone at the time. After Imtiaz supervised the ransacking of the ammunition magazine, the mutineers broke up into several groups to carry out various tactical objectives. It was a leaderless revolt as no overall mutiny leader appeared to take operational command. In addition, the strategic intent was not at all defined, other than resisting getting on the British troop ship SS *Nile* which lay in port and waiting instead for a German ship to magically appear. Nevertheless, the mutiny showed some rudimentary organisation.

The majority of mutineers stayed in Alexandra Barracks, with some preparing to assault Martin's bungalow. About 100 men went across to Tanglin Barracks to free the German POWs, arm them, and get them to join the mutiny. They would later return to Alexandra Barracks. Another band, under Dunde's command, had got the Guides to mutiny. Joined by Chiste, some of these men took up position on Labrador Heights off Pasir Panjang Road. Their intent may have been to secure the road leading to Keppel Harbour, either in anticipation of the arrival of a German warship or to repel reinforcements from the city. Part of this group was likely to have been responsible for the killing of British civilians along Pasir Panjang Road.

Another group headed for New Bridge Road, possibly to see if they could free Kassim Ismail Mansoor, the *jihadi*-socialite, from Outram Prison or to make their way to Government House. This detachment split into twos and threes taking pot shots at the Central Police Station and any British officers they encountered. Mingled among these roving bodies of men were stragglers, frightened sepoys on the run and lone wolves who may have enjoyed a killing spree.

The first few killings of civilians were on or around Pasir Panjang Road, opposite and just south-west of Alexandra Barracks. Other killings were around the Sepoy Lines and Chinatown. It was believed that most of the killing was done in a bloody period between 4 to 4.45 pm on the first day. The sepoys deliberately attacked English civilians. Cars were a good target as most were driven by the British governing class; nearly everyone else travelled by horse, carriage, rickshaw, train, tram, bicycle or on foot. A Scully, an Irishman, was driving with an Englishman named Joseph Evans along Pasir Panjang Road. Just past the Keppel Golf Links, the pair found themselves suddenly forced off the road by a large group of sepoys. They were ordered to exit the car at gunpoint. One of the sepoys raised his rifle and was about to shoot when an NCO from the 5th, Karim Buksh, told him to lower his weapon. Another asked, "Are you English?" Evans replied: "What do you take us for" while Scully added "I'm Irish."[377] The mutineers threw stones at their Malay driver before telling the men they were free to go. The relieved pair and their driver got into the car and sped off to the Keppel Harbour Police Station.

Others were not so fortunate. Scully saw a car passing them in the opposite direction. The owner of the car was C V Dyson, a District Judge, with Mr and Mrs D J Marshall who were visiting from up north along with another lady friend and her baby daughter. They had driven from Dyson's house along Orchard Road and were heading to a seaside bungalow at 191 Pasir Panjang Road. They had planned to spend a month enjoying the healthy sea breezes, but it would prove a fatal choice. As they passed the junction of Alexandra Road and Telok Blangah Road towards Pasir Panjang Village, they were flagged down. One sepoy tried to wave them off. Mrs Marshall remembered that the "little Sepoy was quite young, smooth faced. He had a white turban with something red in his hat, conical shaped. He had rather a clean fair skin, was a few inches over 5 feet high, and particularly handsome."[378]

This was likely the 15-year-old Ranghar bugler Nur Mohammed Khan from Gurgaon – the youngest mutineer. But a group of mutineers stopped them. Dyson made the mistake of brandishing his authority, announcing that he was a "Tuan Magistrate." At that moment, his Malay driver fled and the little sepoy sprang back. Dyson was shot in the leg and then through the chest and crumpled against the car, dead. Marshall was shot next. His wife watched him fall over the side of the car with a long sigh, his face buried in his hands. The women and the baby were spared.

The smooth-faced, sepoy bugler physically pushed them to get away.

The newly married Mr and Mrs Belfield Woolcombe were motoring in their two-seater along Telok Blangah in the direction of Pasir Panjang. As it was a public holiday, quite a few motoring enthusiasts were out to experience the thrill of The Gap, known today as South Buona Vista Road. With 99 curves and turns, The Gap passed from Pasir Panjang Road to Dover Road through the inclines of Kent Ridge. The sea would suddenly come into view from the downward slope of the ridge, which offered an additional thrill. The couple had been warned earlier by civilians to get off the road, but they had foolishly continued their joy-ride.

Mutineers stopped them just before the road leading up the Keppel Golf Club links at Bukit Chermin. An A Company Ranghar Lance Naik named Ahmed Khan took aim at Mr Woolcombe. The crack shot had already killed two other drivers as their cars passed by Alexandra Barracks. Taking aim at the moving target, Ahmed Khan fired about six shots. Mrs Woolcombe, the amateur actress who had acted alongside Captain Hall and Lieutenant Strover and recently played the fortune-telling sorceress, was mortally wounded as she tried to shield her husband. Described as "such a sweet, pretty young bride", she had been married only six months earlier in London in "a gown of white, embroidered with pale pink rosebuds and white lace, and a picture hat trimmed with rosebuds."[379] Now her husband was slumped dead over the steering wheel, and she lay bleeding to death on Telok Blangah Road, opposite today's Soka Peace Centre.

Malay Volunteer Infantry Sergeant Abu Bakar bin Hadji Arshad was at his post in the guardroom at Keppel Harbour when a badly wounded Mrs Woolcombe was brought in by sailors from the British naval vessel HMS *Cadmus*. She weakly asked for water. There was not much the sergeant could do for her other than to send for a doctor from the cable-ship, the *Recorder*, which belonged to her dead husband's employer, the Eastern Extension Telegraph Company. Abu Bakar recorded in his diary: "Wounded woman, Mrs B M Woolcombe, arrived in car, shot, asked guard for water. Took inside. Sent for Medical Officer. She and driver said, "shot by Bengalis." Woman died. Crowds coming saying "Bengali amok". Telephoned Fort Canning, no answer. Guard in order."[380]

Three Englishmen working for Guthrie and Company were taking their leisurely afternoon tea on the verandah of The Nest, a bungalow at 474 Pasir Panjang Road. Donald McGilvray, T B Dunne and E D Butterworth had just spent the morning drinking gin slings and smoking in the bathing *pagar* (fenced area) of Mr and Mrs H Knott's bungalow 30 yards down the road. Herbert Smith, Acting Manager of Alexandria Brickworks, who had joined the men recalled "a very jolly and happy party."[381] The three bachelors had returned to Dunne's bungalow for tiffin

Mr and Mrs Belfield Morel Woolcombe

and their after-tiffin snooze when his Hainanese cook, Han Lim Tun, saw four or five sepoys come up the drive.

McGilvray, a corporal in the Volunteers, challenged the mutineers and was shot and killed for his troubles. Han saw Dunne dodge one bullet, run up the hill and take a few more shots. Running away in fear, Han did not see what happened next to his *tuan*. Nor did he see what happened to Butterworth, who had been resting on his long chair on the verandah. Herbert Smith, who had stayed on in the Knotts' bungalow, watched sepoys walking by and then noticed Malays and Chinese from a nearby kampong rushing into their homes, grabbing their children as they went. He did not hear shots but was alerted to Dunne's killing by his house-boy. Walking over to Dunne's home to investigate, he spotted Butterworth on the long chair. Going up the verandah stairs, Smith called out "Get up, you lazy blighter, here's trouble. Where's Dunne?"[382] Butterworth did not budge. He was dead from a stomach wound. Smith also found McGilvray dead, crumpled up in a drain.

Smith went back to the Knotts and told them what he had seen. Mrs Knott became very anxious about her little son Harold who was out with their Hainanese cook. Smith agreed to look for the boy and walked down Pasir Panjang Road towards Alexandra Road. On the way, he passed the body of Lieutenant Elliott. He also passed sepoys, both armed and unarmed. None challenged him. Just before he reached Alexandra Brickworks at the junction of Pasir Panjang Road and Alexandra Road, a sepoy appeared out of the jungle. He raised his rifle to shoot at Smith. In the nick of time, a Chinese passer-by stepped between the sepoy and Smith and told the mutineer that the Englishman was a "Chinaman and a relative of theirs."[383] After this close shave, Smith gave up the search and made his way back to his house in Alexandra Road. He was fired on twice from Labrador Road but got home safely.

Panicked European residents were now fleeing their homes in Pasir Panjang and seeking refuge. Mutineers were very active in the area, moving around and searching houses. Some took pot-shots at any European they saw. Men of the 5th who had not joined the mutiny warned a number of Europeans to hide. Some of these streamed towards the Malay Volunteer Infantry post manned by Sergeant Abu Bakar while others looked desperately for refuge from among their Asian neighbours.

A 59-year-old produce broker named Yeo Bian Chuan was celebrating the Chinese New Year with his family in his home at 155 Pasir Panjang Road, a stone's throw from Kassim Ismail Mansoor's weekend property. The Chinese in the area knew that Kassim had entertained sepoys and was imprisoned. Yeo had by now heard about the mutiny. He had many British neighbours whom he considered friends and he feared the worst:

I had not long to wait before my worst fears were realised. English ladies and their husbands began to arrive, terribly upset, asking if I could give them shelter, as they had seen friends shot, and the Mutineers were already on their track. It was an awful moment for me as I knew that if the Mutineers came and found that I was sheltering Europeans then all I could except (*sic*) for my children, wife and friends would be death. As for myself it would not matter much as I was an old man and Tuan Allah would look after me.[384]

About 20 British civilians took refuge at Yeo's seaside home. Among them were the Knott family who had just entertained the three bachelors who had been killed. Yeo ordered his servants and relatives to "take all the Europeans to the top of the House to the highest room, and to keep on the festivities and illuminations, and act and speak as if nothing had happened."[385]

While looking after his frightened guests, he heard gunfire but tried his best to remain calm. His Malay gardener appeared to warn him that mutineers were approaching the house and "were looking for white people to kill."[386] Yeo went out to face them, noticing that they were "fully armed with rolling eyes and I could see murder in their faces."[387] When interrogated by the sepoys, he just about kept his nerve:

The leader accosted me, saying, Towkay we are driving all the white people into the sea, but the Chinese and Malays have nothing to fear as long as they help us. Have you seen any white soldiers or men this way? We have been told that some have been seen to come towards your grounds.

I replied (seeming very brave, but my knees knocking together).

This is our Chinese New Year and I have been busy entertaining my relations and friends as you can see, and of the trouble I know nothing. This seemed to satisfy the man and giving orders, the Black soldiers left to the number of about eight. In my heart I thanked Tuan Allah without whose help I could have done nothing.[388]

It was not just Europeans in the area who were in fear of their lives or desperately seeking refuge. Dunde's nemesis, Wahid Ali Khan, turned up at the Pasir Panjang Rubber Works with a large group of sepoys. He was not in uniform, but in white *kurta* and traditional trousers with *juttis* (turned up shoes) and white turban. He had with him men from A, C, D, F, G and H companies, an assorted group of Ranghars and Pathans. Questioned by the Rubber Works' watchman Sunder Singh, Wahid Ali told him: "I am not a bad man, I am a good man; and I am afraid of our men. If I return there I may be shot."[389] Wahid had a lot to lose. He was the richest man in the 5th, withdrawing the princely sum in sepoy terms of $264.77 from the savings bank in Singapore two days before the mutiny. He had just escaped from Chiste's posse.

The mutineers' major tactical success took place at Tanglin Barracks, the site of the biggest single massacre of British forces. An estimated 100 mutineers moved up in loose formation from Alexandra Barracks, hiking the three kilometres to the German prisoners' camp at Tanglin. Presumably to avoid detection, the mutineers had avoided using the main roads. Leading this group was Havildar Ibrahim, a Ranghar from Hissar. But the real engine was the hot-headed Feroze Khan. Also in his group was Taj Mohamed who carried a pack full of ammunition. The mutineers swept down through the valley past what is now Queenstown. Splashing through swamps, they had skirted a village and had climbed the grassy incline of Cemetery Hill. They headed towards their objective without stopping.

The action started just as the mutineers moved past today's Pierce Road and got to the rifle range between rubber and coconut plantations. Feroze stood at the top of the bank of the range and shouted orders. To his right was the Tanglin Barracks Hospital at Loewen Road, and straight ahead was the German camp at Blocks 15, 17, 18 and 26 of today's Dempsey Road. The camp guardhouse was located in Block 13, its stairs leading straight down to Barracks Road (now Harding Road). Feroze knew the camp intimately, having guarded it just three weeks earlier. The mutineers planned to take the guardroom manned by British Volunteers next to the entrance to the German camp. First, they prepared to disable three crow's nest observation posts around the camp's recreation field off Barracks Road. Then, the external perimeter, guarded by soldiers of the Johor Military Force (JMF), had to be secured.

Captain Percy Netterville Gerrard of the MSVR was in command of the camp, having succeeded Cotton. In civilian life, Gerrard was a doctor in the Colonial Medical Service based in Selangor and Kuala Lumpur. The intense-eyed, 45-year-old had compiled the first vocabulary of Malay medical terms as well as a study of the symptoms and treatment of the tropical disease Beri-Beri. But the doctor was not an experienced military man. The JMF guards patrolling the camp's external perimeter and the observation posts only had five rounds of ammunition each, scrounged grudgingly from the Volunteers,[390] the result of his administrative slip-up. Now they were about to be outgunned and overrun.

When the attack began, more than 50 of the 300-odd German internees were at the fenced off recreation ground taking their daily exercise. The corporal of the guard, A H Todd, had just left them there with a sentry. The shooting came from the higher ground near the camp hospital (Block 71 Loewen Road today). JMF Private Yaacob bin Salleh was shot and killed in the initial exchange of fire. He was stationed in one the crow's nest boxes overlooking the recreation ground. One of his comrades was wounded in the chest but got away. Hearing the gun-fire, Todd came out to investigate and learnt from a JMF soldier that the "*orang* Bengali" were attacking the sentries. He notified his Guard Commander, 2nd Lieutenant J H Love-Montgomerie of the Singapore Volunteer Rifles, and then ran to the recreation field and told the Germans to lie low. As the JMF sentries were overrun or ran away, Todd found himself quickly becoming a target and decided to retreat from the recreation ground to a safer area.

Also in Tanglin Camp at the time was a detachment of sepoys of the 36th Sikhs. They were in Singapore in transit from Hong Kong to British-leased Weihaiwei in north-west China. The Texan-born Maclean who supervised them had already been killed in Alexandra Barracks. A platoon of the famed Sikh regiment had fought to the last man at Saragarhi on the Indian-Afghan frontier. But in Tanglin, their Lance Havildar Nand Singh told them to keep their heads down when the first shots were heard. With 15 men on leave in the town and six in Alexandra Hospital, he only had 21 rifles for 39 men. He distributed ammunition and told his men to take cover in their barracks (today's Block 9).

Off-duty JMF Second Lieutenant Ungku Aziz had a close shave. As the firing got hot, he left his barracks in today's Block 11 Dempsey and came across his mortally wounded comrade Captain Abdul Jabbar. He tried to help the badly limping man but Jabbar lay down and said no more. Ungku Aziz glanced at four sepoys of the 36th talking in the kitchen of their barracks and then found himself in the cross-fire. He dodged bullets as he ran between Blocks 8 and 9 down towards the valley and on to the rifle range. This was the direction from which the mutineers had approached the camp. His JMF Commander, Captain H Cullimore was shot down on the road between Blocks 9 and 11. He was wounded first in his leg, then shot in the chest.[391]

The mutineers had moved fast from the rifle range taking pot-shots at Loewen Road Hospital as they passed it on their right. They had already overcome the JMF sentries patrolling the perimeter. After disabling the sentries in the crow's nests, they made a pincer movement around the recreation ground, rushing through the British soldiers' quarters at Block 10 is today. The jobless 24-year-old volunteer Gordon Lawson who had shared his *Daily Graphic* newspaper with Imtiaz Ali had his brains blown out in his bunk. Some mutineers made their way towards the guardroom while others approached the back of the German camp. The Guard

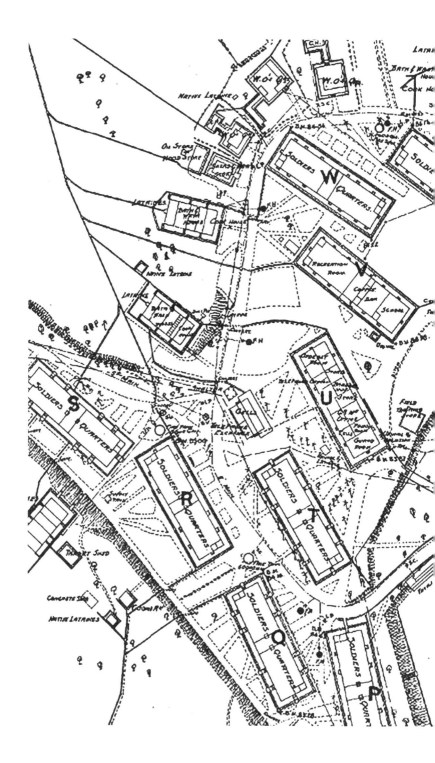

Map of Tanglin Barracks, 1915.
Block U is the guardroom.
A bungalow behind W (today's Block
17) is where Lauterbach was housed.

Commander Love-Montgomerie was now desperately seeking relief.

The previous April, the 27-year-old Scotsman had been a guest at the military wedding down the road in St George's Church with Ridout and his family. Now he was frantically calling Ridout's home to speak to the GOC of the Troops. Answering the phone was Dudley Ridout Junior, the 8-year-old who had held up the bride's train at the wedding. Hearing Love-Montgomerie's agitated voice, he quickly passed the receiver to his mother. Mrs Ridout had already spoken to Love-Montgomerie a little earlier to pass along her husband's warning and to get JMF troops to guard her house. She assured him that help was on the way. But it was too late for Love-Montgomerie and most of the guards. Feroze and his men were now right next to the guardhouse. Love-Montgomerie's last words on the phone before he was shot in the back were: "They are absolutely out of control. The situation is desperate. I must have assistance at once."[392] Also shot while on the phone was the Camp Commandant Captain Gerrard. He took a bullet to the temple and was then shot several more times. The phone lines were then cut.

Many of the badly trained volunteers had a single moment of glory, madness or panic before they were cut down. 25-year-old Volunteer Private Bernard Cameron was shot and killed under a tree at the top of the stairs leading to the guardroom. Frozen in fear and standing unarmed on Harding Road in full view of the mutineers' guns, 36-year-old Private A J G Holt is remembered today by a nearby side-road named after him. Lance-Corporal J G E Harper put up a bit more of a fight as the mutineers occupied the canteen. With Corporal Todd and Private Robertson, the 28-year-old Lance Corporal put up a fight from the cover of an oil shed behind the canteen (now demolished) by Harding Road. As he peeked out to take a shot at the mutineers, he was killed instantly. A road in the Macpherson area is named in his memory. Todd managed to escape with Robertson who was wounded in the neck. R L D Wodehouse, a Singapore cricketer and brother of the comic novelist P G Wodehouse, was hit in his sentry-box outside the German camp. Four or five shots were aimed at the 22-year-old who also took a bullet right through the helmet. Left for dead, he miraculously survived.

Some of the mutineers now blew open the locked gate of the German camp. Inside, the German amateur artist Hanke was at work on a sketch when he heard what he thought were firecrackers. Looking out of the window he saw sepoys shooting at the sentries. The surviving JMF soldiers had beat a hasty retreat. Hanke soon found his former sepoy guards mingling jubilantly with his fellow prisoners, shaking their hands. Taj Mohamed, who had saluted his painting of the Kaiser, burst in and declared: "*Hamdulillah! Hazur, abi usko dejeiga*. (Praise be to Allah, Sir, we will go out), English go, come on!" Hanke replied: "*Hum nay manta*" ("I can't do so). Trying to make sense of the situation, the sarong-clad German made the excuse that he had to get changed, with Taj grinning encouragingly and saying, "Good, good."[393]

The *Emden*'s Prize Officer Julius Lauterbach was in his bungalow behind today's Block 17 Dempsey playing a game of chess when he heard the storm of fire. Lauterbach was a notorious storyteller and it is hard to know how much of his account can be trusted. Nevertheless, he offered his perspective on the mood of the moment. He recalled in his memoirs that the mutineers hoisted him on their shoulders and yelled: "Here is our leader," and when he was put down, he quickly said: "We Germans can do very little to help you. We have no guns." He also recalled that one of the sepoys then put his turban on his head, probably making him look like a "fat drunken sultan". Summarising the situation in his telling, Lauterbach said: "If I should be caught by the British in that turban and as the acclaimed leader of the mutineers, I should have made a fine target, tall and broad, for a firing squad. Moreover, a German officer does not fight without his uniform or in the rank of mutineers. At least he doesn't unless he is a renegade."[394]

A few Germans given weapons by the mutineers returned them saying they had no experience of shooting. One of the mutineers told Lauterbach: "We will bring you arms tonight. You can defend yourselves."[395] Lauterbach told him he only knew about sea and not land warfare. Of course, the wily Lauterbach and the German community leader Diehn were only interested in escape, not in helping in the mutiny. The mutineers may have realised by then that they had pinned too much hope on the Germans. Although the military men among them and quite a few of the more stout-hearted Teutonic types seemed quite happy to incite the others, a half hour of persuasion failed to commit the Germans to their cause. This came as a blow for the sepoys. Their high expectations were dashed.

Most of the civilian internees were fearful. They had been taken by surprise with two of their numbers shot by accident, with one dying from his wounds. The artist Hanke heard several German internees claim that all the forts in Singapore were taken and that a German ship was on the way to Singapore. They may have been encouraged by the butcher's bill racked up by the sepoys. In half an hour, the attackers had killed 14 and wounded several others – three British officers and one Malay officer, seven British and two Malay NCOs and men, with one German POW mortally wounded in the cross-fire. An hour after their blitzkrieg attack on Tanglin Camp, the mutineers left the same way they had come. Before their departure, one of the raiding sepoys told Lance-Havildar Nand

Singh of the 36th Sikhs that they would return later with weapons for the Germans. He warned the Sikhs that they should join the mutiny or face the consequences. Nand Singh and his men stayed at their post. They would later be used in coordination with the Sikh Police Contingent to mount guard at the Central Police Station. But not before running the gauntlet of suspicious and keyed up British volunteers ready to shoot on sight.

On the other side of Tanglin Barracks, at the officers' quarters where the Australian High Commission, US Embassy, British High Commission and Chinese Embassy converge today, Lieutenant W N Sneesby of the Royal Engineers saw Mrs Ridout at his bungalow. She had come from her home nearby to warn her fellow Royal Engineers spouse of the attack and tell him to leave the barracks immediately. Scouting around after sending his family to the Hotel L'Europe, Sneesby bumped into Vice-Admiral Jerram. The Commander-in-chief of the China Station seemed quite lost on land. He was walking by an officer's bungalow where today's Australian High Commission is sited. Conspicuous in his white naval uniform, Jerram asked Sneesby to take him to the German camp.

Moving down Middlesex Road (now Sherwood Road), the pair passed the Married Quarters, now demolished. They could see the German camp with prisoners milling around the entrance. A panicked JMF soldier was running away from the guardroom towards Holland Road. The admiral and the army engineer headed for the barrack guardroom with its stairs leading down to today's Harding Road past the recreation field. On top of the stairs, near a tree, lay the corpse of Private Bernard Cameron of the SVC. Jerram went on to inspect the prison camp and observe the men of the *Emden*. He told Sneesby that they seemed to be behaving themselves. Having satisfied himself with the state of affairs, Jerram decided to go to Government House and report to Young.

Later that evening, Lauterbach stole out of the camp with several German internees and crew members of the *Emden*. The big, blond Diehn, one of the escape party, even had time to go home, bathe and change before sneaking off to Pasir Panjang beach in the dark. Hiring a fishing boat operated by Ceylonese fishermen, the Germans made for the Dutch-controlled Karimun Island off Sumatra. When they landed 14 hours later, the Germans wired a cheeky message to Young that they had arrived safely. The men of the *Emden* had bested Jerram one final time, this time on land.

[XXI]

THE RESCUE AND THE ROUND UP

After receiving Martin's SOS message and getting more details during an anxious follow-up phone call, Ridout shrugged off his fever and got to work immediately. He called the units at Pulau Brani and Blakang Mati to mobilise all available men, the Engineers and the Gunners on the islands' forts. They were to mobilise near the Jardine Steps at the P&O Wharf. This became the rallying point for re-securing Singapore. The Singapore Volunteers' CO Lieutenant-Colonel G A Derrick was ordered to turn out all available men at Drill Hall in Beach Road. They assembled to collect their rifles, belts and bandoliers. Tanjong Pagar Dock Company Manager J R Nicholson was one of the first volunteers to arrive and was sworn in as a Special Constable.

The British naval vessel HMS *Cadmus* was in Keppel Harbour, the only allied naval ship in port at the time. The *Cadmus* had earlier visited Direction Island in November to retrieve the bodies of Lauterbach's comrades from the stricken *Emden* and had just returned again after searching the wreck for documents. A French battleship the *Montcalm* had departed Singapore 24 hours earlier after several weeks of repair in the dock. Captain H D Marryat of the HMS *Cadmus* received orders from Jerram to immediately land a detachment at Jardine Steps. After arranging for guard pickets in strategic points around the city, Ridout got into a car and made his way to Jardine Steps. There, he encountered 30 sailors from the *Cadmus* armed with a Maxim machine gun and sent them in a motor-lorry to Telok Blangah Road to stop any mutineers advancing to the city. Sometime after 5 pm, Sergeant Abu Bakar of the Malay Volunteers Company witnessed the blue-jacketed sailors of the *Cadmus* arrive in their motor-lorry at his post in King's Dock, Keppel Harbour.

Over at Alexandra Barracks, C Company Jemadar Hoshiar Ali had bumped into Dunde and Chiste. Dunde was back in the lines from the

Guides encampment and appeared to be reflecting on the next move with Chiste. Unlike the British, they had not considered how to muster transport or telephone to co-ordinate their mutiny. The conflicted and frightened Hoshiar had been hiding for some time in the Malay States Guides' camp and was even seen crying. He claimed that he tried to talk his fellow Ranghar officers Dunde and Chiste into stopping the mutineers and helping the British officers. "The men who can make peace now will be first in the world,"[396] he told them. But the pair remained unmoved, striding instead towards Alexandra Road.

Hoshiar and his Company Colour Havildar Mahboob trailed Dunde and Chiste at a slight distance. They arrived at a small hill in front of a Chinese shop at the junction of Alexandra, Pasir Panjang and Telok Blangah Roads. Hoshiar and Mahboob saw about 25 men from A and D Company with rifles taking cover in an old practice trench on the hill. It was not clear whether they were waiting to intercept British reinforcements or welcome what some were led to believe would be a German ship. Hoshiar said his prayers. Right after he finished, he heard the sound of a motor-lorry. It came close to the Chinese shop, packed with the men of the *Cadmus* and their machine-gun.

Walking down the hill towards the motor-lorry, Hoshiar raised his hands to show he was unarmed. Mahboob walked alongside him. Dunde and Chiste, who were both unarmed as well, also came forward. Accompanying the four was a pair of armed sepoys, Jallal Khan and Immamuddin of A Company. Under the impression that the sailors were from the much anticipated and discussed but ultimately mythical German warship, Dunde made the mistake of asking the sailors if they were German. He received his reply from the barrel of a gun. Wounded in the shoulder, Chiste scrambled away with Dunde as the Maxim machine gun on the lorry started firing.

Sepoys Jallal Khan and Immamuddin resisted and were machine-gunned. In the short battle, Mahboob was hit twice and fell to the ground wounded. Hoshiar dashed to a side road for cover where he came across a stunned Dunde. They managed to escape and made their way to Mount Faber where a group of the 5th, some armed, had gathered. The sepoys started collecting around Dunde to ask for instructions, but he had no real plan other than finding a way to get to Johor. He hoped that the Muslim Sultan – the very same Sultan whose military force had been shot at and routed in Tanglin by the mutineers – would look on them favourably and protect them. It was not much of a plan.

It would appear that the arrival and action of the *Cadmus* sailors had caused the mutineers in the area to disperse, abandon their weapons and accoutrements to blend among the civilians. However, another group of mutineers had earlier made their way to the Sepoy Lines and China-town through Alexandra Road and Outram Road. Sepoy Rasullulah of Chiste's D company and his companion were the most notorious of the group. Both men were tall and thin 6-footers and stood out. The beard-ed Rasullullah was wearing half of the 5th uniform, khaki jacket and turban with yellow fringe while his companion wore white *kurta* and *dhoti* and a white turban. They made for Outram Road Criminal Prison. It is not clear if their objective was to get Kassim Ibrahim Mansoor released or if they even knew where the *jihadi*-socialite was being held. Carrying rifles with fixed bayonets, they tried to convince a Sikh sentry at the pris-on to hand over the keys. They then threatened an Indian sub-warder who alerted his British supervisor who arrived to investigate. After firing a half-dozen shots in anger at the warder and sub-warder, the pair made their way down Outram Road past Sepoy Lines.

Major Reginald Galwey and Captain F V Izard of the Royal Garrison Artillery had just wrapped up their golf game in the Sepoy Lines Golf Links. Galwey was playing a final round of golf before his scheduled de-parture for Europe in a few days to command a heavy artillery unit. Upon hearing of the mutiny, both men, still in golfing clothes, rushed back to Pulau Blakang Mati to report for duty. Izard was in a rickshaw while Gal-wey travelled in a gharry. Sepoy Rasulullah spotted Izard, pulled the trig-ger and the artillery officer tumbled out of the rickshaw, dead. The Chi-nese rickshaw puller rushed away to safety. Rasullullah and his comrade then took pot-shots at a golfer on Sepoy Lines Links who ran to safety.

The sepoys calmly walked down North Bridge Road with their weap-ons. Chinese shopkeepers and residents ran into their homes, fearing they had gone amok. At New Bridge Road, the mutineers spotted a Hupmo-bile car driven by a Malay chauffeur named Hassan Ketchil with three British men and a woman. They were headed for Sea View Hotel in the Katong area by the seaside. When Ketchil refused to slow down and ploughed on, the mutineers shot at the car. Ketchil was killed instantly and the car swerved into the drain. Two of the male passengers were picked off by the mutineers. The third feigned death while the woman was allowed to escape. A short while later, Major Galwey was shot in his *gharry* and received a serious stomach wound. Rasullulah spotted Straits Settlements Police Inspector R W Meredith assisting the mortally wound-ed Galwey and fired six shots, missing the policeman but killing his horse instead. Meredith ducked and dodged in and out of trees to escape as the 42-year-old Galwey breathed his last.

Dr Edward Whittle of the Colonial Medical Service was making a turn in his car at the junction of Outram and North Bridge Road when the vehicle started taking shots. The 32-year-old doctor had been in charge of Tan Tock Seng Hospital and was the general surgeon at the Singapore Hospital at Outram Road. Known in his younger days as a daredevil, he routinely took high dives in all kinds of weather from a pier in Brighton and practised an early form of parkour, jumping between the ledges of multi-story buildings. But the daredevil doctor had run out of luck behind the wheel of his car. He took several bullets to his abdomen while his wife tried to scramble away. A European warder from the nearby prison came to her assistance and was shot dead. Several Chinese civilians who were celebrating the New Year in the area were caught in the cross-fire.

Rasulullah and his companion next made their way to the Central Police Station and fired at the Sikh police. Two constables were wounded in the leg. As a result, any Sikh constable or family member with any sympathy for the Ghadar movement now rallied against the mutineers. With reports of mounting civilian casualties, Governor Arthur Young gave orders for all European women and children to be escorted by the police and billeted and guarded in hotels – Raffles, Adelphi, Van Wyck and the de L'Europe – or put under protection in the steamers berthed offshore. There were about 2300 European and American women and double that number of Eurasian women, whom the European women resented having to share quarters on board the refuge ships. Ironically, one of the steamers was the troop-ship *Nile* which had been prepared for the journey of the 5th to Hong Kong.

Young conferred with Ridout at Government House. A quietly desperate message was dashed off by Young to the Viceroy in Calcutta: "I regret to have to state that the 5th Native Light Infantry has mutinied, the country near their Barracks now being held by the bulk of the regiment… situation (which is grave) is being met… Brigadier Commanding urges that reinforces of One European Battalion be sent here… Can you do this?"[397] Jerram had by then arrived from the slaughter at Tanglin where the Volunteers had established a strong picket at Tanglin crossroads and Cluny Road. His presence and experience were of great comfort and help to Ridout. Jerram sent off wireless messages to all nearby allied warships along with a telegram to the Viceroy of India requesting help. The Sultan of Johor had despatched 150 men by special train and personally accompanied them down to Singapore. Ridout personally welcomed him at Tank Station just after sundown. Ridout took a look at the Sultan's Afghan platoon from Kabul and asked if they were trustworthy. The Sultan assured him they were, having been in Johor for a long time.

Crucially, Lieutenant-Colonel Brownlow, the CO of the Royal Garrison Artillery (RGA) from Pulau Blakang Mati, was put in charge of a scratch relief force of about 180 men. At his disposal were 80 sailors of the *Cadmus*, at least 50 volunteer infantrymen including the Chinese company and the European Maxim-machine-gun section and 25 armed civilians. There were also 21 gunners from the RGA under his command, including Acting General Staff Officer (GSO) Lieutenant Cecil Olliver, son-in-law of the previous GOC, and groom at the Tanglin military wedding. The irrepressibly striving Lieutenant Strover had now reported for duty at the P&O Wharf from his day at the beach with Sir Evelyn Ellis. He was now keen to be appointed as Brownlow's General Staff Officer instead of Olliver.

By 6.30 pm, martial law was declared. Intelligence was received later that evening that the mutineers were setting out to attack the city and police headquarters. The men in Government House deliberated and decided to send an urgent message to Brownlow, who was putting his experience as a seasoned campaigner from the Indian-Afghan northwest frontier wars to good use. To help relieve the besieged Martin, he had placed his relief force at the junction of Paris Panjang and Alexandra Roads. Brownlow was preparing for the final move on Alexandra Barracks when Captain Edwin Brown of the Singapore Volunteer Rifles Chinese Company appeared on the scene. He found the old warhorse conferring with his staff officer Olliver in a hut at the corner of Alexandra Road and Pasir Panjang Road, close to where Dunde and Chiste had been thwarted by the men of the *Cadmus*. Brown passed on the message from Ridout in Government House.

In his note, Ridout had ordered Brownlow to withdraw from his position and redeploy around the General Hospital and Outram Prison. Brownlow squinted at the message by the flickering light of a smoky oil lamp. He assessed the intelligence from Government House that 700 mutineers were advancing on the city from Alexandra. Ridout, Brownlow's contemporary, was an experienced intelligence officer who had just received his official promotion to substantive Colonel (he remained an Acting General) that evening. He now officially outranked Brownlow. But as the warrior on the ground, Brownlow felt that it would be better off holding position than retreating. Looking straight at Brown, he pointedly asked: "You have never seen this message have you?" Brown promptly replied: "No, sir."[398] So, without further fuss, Brownlow tore up the orders from Ridout. He held the shredded paper to the flaming lamp and declared: "That is over then, we shall attack from here as soon as there is light enough."[399]

Brownlow had taken matters into his own hands and had cut off Young, Ridout and the others in Government House. The warrior did not want the bureaucrats and the professional staffers to get in the way of his doing his job. Lieutenant Olliver was sent back to Government

House and Strover took over sometime that evening as his Staff Officer. Confirming Brownlow's suspicions about the panic and confusion in Government House was the unsettling scene that greeted a young Straits Settlements police cadet named Arthur Harold Dickinson who had been ordered to report to Government House at midnight to check on the police guard. The 23-year-old cadet with striking looks reported:

> There all was quiet. The Colonial Secretary, Mr R J Wilkinson, and the Governor, Sir Arthur Young, were on the verandah alone. Both looked extremely grave. The Governor called me up and spoke a few words. I felt that little more was known at Government House than anywhere else. I expected a hive of activity; I found silence and what seemed to me a rather helpless sense of waiting – understandable in the absence of information as to what eight hundred mutinous Indian troops might be contemplating, with little to oppose them.[400]

Young was in a desperate situation. Just before Dickinson's arrival at Government House, Young had spoken to the Japanese Consul, Fujii Minoru. According to Minoru's account, Young had admitted that the battle was against them and they could not cope with the situation without help. He requested the diplomat to get the Japanese community to furnish special constables. The Japanese agreed to form a special volunteer corps on the conditions that they would guard the town only, be treated in the same way as British volunteers under command of their own officers and would serve until a Japanese warship arrived in Singapore. By 6 am the next morning, near 130 Japanese volunteers had been recruited. Koji Tsukuda, a Japanese journalist for the *Nanyo Shimpo*, reflected proudly on the new status acquired by the Japanese, who in the eyes of the rest of the settlement had only filled the roles of prostitutes and barbers. He crowed that the "British until recently so arrogant now also had their tails down and their wings clinched in, had come to greatly value us."[401]

Meanwhile, over at Martin's bungalow, the defenders were dealing with on and off sniping. Hainanese houseboys calmly served the defenders tea under Mrs Cotton's supervision. As bullets pinged, the MSVR men shouted obscenities, only to earn a sharp rebuke from the very proper hostess. Close to midnight in Towkay Yeo's house in Pasir Panjang, one of the young British men who had sought refuge there appeared to have lost his bottle.

> I heard crashing of glass and furniture and a great noise from above and running up stairs in haste I found an awful sight. One of the European men, alas that I should have to say it, was drunk, and was

breaking up my glasses, mirrors, furniture and treasures generally and waving a revolver at the same time and shouting that he didn't care for all the Mutineers in Singapore. He threw open the window and fired off his revolver and at last had to be overpowered by his friends, gagged and bound and laid on the floor.[402]

When a group of mutineers returned to investigate the disturbance, Towkay Yeo endured the nerve-wracking experience of explaining the sudden racket and gunshot:

Going down the steps I saw them approaching, many more than formerly and some stained with blood. The leader, a big man, said, "Towkay, we know that you have seen white people, and have heard shouting and guns from this way. Tell us the truth and you shall me left alone; but if we find you are double-faced then we will shoot you and all your family." Then did I feel that death was very near, but having always lived under the English Flag and enjoyed happiness and wealth among its laws, I put my trust in Allah and defied them.[403]

The *towkay* was no Muslim but had put his trust in Allah, also invoked by some of the mutineers. While Towkay Yeo talked the mutineers away from his home and British guests, over at Martin's bungalow, the mutineers continued to take pot-shots at the besieged officers. Ridout called and told Martin that a relief force was at hand. Martin had also arranged for a searchlight from Pulau Brani to light up the area around the house. This was to deter the mutineers from sneaking up under cover of darkness. In the otherwise pitch dark, the sweeping searchlight created an eerie effect around the bungalow. Meanwhile, in the lines at Alexandra Barracks, elements of the 5th that had stayed loyal or at least neutral spent a jittery night.

At about 5.30 am, Olliver was ordered to convey an urgent request to the Sultan of Johor to put all his available forces in pickets around Government House, as the mutineers were reported to be approaching in force. The Sultan personally took command of the detachment. This time, his men had about 40 rounds apiece, a little more ammunition than his hapless guards had at Tanglin. They would try to put up more of a fight guarding the seat of power in the Straits Settlements. But the mutineers never came. Reading the situation correctly, Brownlow had made the right call to keep his relief force at Alexandra Road and prepare to take the fight to the enemy.

However, constant sniping by the mutineers through the night gave

Brownlow's relief force little rest. A few men jumped into a road-side drain to try and get some sleep. Others climbed into cars and squeezed together for warmth and security. Close by were the cold and stiff corpses of Sepoys Jallal Khan and Immamuddin, killed earlier in Dunde's encounter with the *Cadmus* sailors. Waking before dawn, Brown stole a glance at Brownlow. The old gunner was sitting on a stone coping over a drain, smoking a cigarette and looking "supremely happy... the old man was in his element in the field."[404] With his faithful wire fox terrier by his side, Brownlow explained his plan to Brown, Olliver and the officers around him. The key objective was to relieve the men in Martin's bungalow, but in order to make their approach, the barracks had to be cleared. The mutineers' stronghold across the road in the Southern Ridges also had to be broken down. The mutineers would then be driven towards the bungalow where Brownlow hoped they would be "caught between two fires, and generally messed up."[405]

At 5.15 am, Brownlow ordered his force to mount the attack. Brownlow's column moved down Alexandra Road with the *Cadmus* sailors spearheading the assault. As soon as they passed the bodies of two European civilians, the *Cadmus* sailors started taking fire. At about 5.30 am, as the *Cadmus* sailors dodged sniper fire, Jemadar Ghulam Haidar of H Company and some of his men tried to rejoin their Double Company Commander, Hall, in Martin's bungalow. A desperate Ghulam called out for his Subedar, Sharfuddin Khan, and heard Ball yell from the upstairs verandah "Who are you?" Ball knew that Brownlow's force had begun their attack. He warned Ghulam that an engagement was about to take place and instructed him and the men to take cover behind the hill with a lone palm tree. With the counter-attack underway, Ghulam's men dispersed to avoid getting caught in the cross-fire. Spotting Ghulam, Hall pulled the Indian officer into the safety of the bungalow. When a grateful Ghulam volunteered to defend the house, Martin said that reinforcements were on the way and they were not needed.

The *Cadmus* men put their machine gun under cover of a tree on Hyderabad Road and started firing at the barracks. After softening up the defences, Brownlow's force swept through towards the bungalow. The mutineers ran and returned fire. Adding to the confusion, other sepoys of the 5th or the Guides emerged from their hiding places and started to surrender. Some of them, including loyalists, were not given the benefit of the doubt and were gunned down as they moved towards the bungalow. From the upper verandah, Hall noticed Brownlow's men advancing towards him in successive lines. He could see muzzle-fire of mutineers coming from the south. He grabbed a megaphone and shouted to the advancing force to pivot to the left to deal with the threat.

There was a half-hour long exchange of fire. One of the *Cadmus* men, 23-year-old Stoker Charles Anscombe, was shot in the forehead and died instantly as the sailors made the advance. Another three Volunteers or armed civilians were wounded, with a completely inexperienced 38-year-old contracting clerk, F Geddes, succumbing to his wounds later. It is estimated that between a dozen to two dozen mutineers were killed. Mutiny ring-leader Jemadar Abdul Ali was killed during this encounter and buried under Hall's direction. The sepoy who had fired the mutiny's opening shot, Ismail Khan, was also believed to have been killed in this battle as the sailors and Volunteers made a full-throated charge. By 8.15 am, the bungalow was relieved. Retreating mutineers as well as loyalists escaped into the jungle behind Martin's house towards Bukit Chandu and other sea-side hills.

An adrenalin-pumped Brownlow was upset that Martin had not led an advance from the bungalow to trap the mutineers as his own force came forward. Martin insisted it was all a mistake. Captain Brown reflected later:

> For some reason or other, never actually fathomed, those 80 to 100 men remained "doggo" in the bungalow, and allowed 300 to 400 mutineers to stream past on either side and get away into the thick country at the back. I think Colonel Brownlow could have died. He had managed his art of the business so well, and when he saw his men going forward in the final charge, must have had visions of rounding up all the mutineers in one fell swoop, and it must have been terribly hard for him to see the indecision of the men in the house... they could almost have jumped on the mutineers from the verandahs.[406]

Brownlow returned the compliment in his official account of the capture of the barracks: "Capt Brown, Chinese Company, SVC... showed himself to be an exceptionally capable and valuable officer. He was in command of the untrained troops in a very hot little piece of fighting, and but for his good and cool leading, it is quite possible that his command might have had to retire, thus disorganising and delaying the whole operation."[407]

After the battle for the bungalow, Brownlow retired his force to the P&O Wharf at Keppel Harbour. He ordered Brown to send the 90 captured mutineers to Outram Prison. As they passed Keppel Golf Club, a mutineer took pot-shots at them from a hill. By the afternoon, the back of the mutiny was broken despite occasional sniping from wandering mutineers. As the volunteers returned to the Drill Hall on Beach Road for further orders, a funeral was held at Bidadari cemetery that afternoon. Laid to rest were about two dozen British victims, military and civilian, including the Woolcombes, the trio of bachelors from Pasir Panjang, the volunteers killed at Tanglin, and the officers shot in Chinatown. The Bishop of Singapore officiated. The ever-reliable Anglophiles Tan Jiak Kim and Seah Liang Seah and the Chinese nationalist Tan Boo Liat represented the Chinese community. The penny pinching colonial government sent individual bills for the cost of the civilian burials to the employers of the slain or to executors of their last will and testament.

Near Keppel Harbour, in the meantime, a Eurasian reported to Sergeant Abu Bakar that five mutineers were hiding behind a store about a kilometre and a half away from the Harbour guardroom. Abu Bakar gathered 15 of his men and converged on the store from three points, firing and advancing. Fire was returned, and the Malay volunteers charged. When they reached the store, they found that the mutineers had dispersed. They searched the area and found a trench covered with leaves with 11 rifles and 2000 rounds of ammunition. As they returned to Keppel Harbour they found a mutineer's body stretched out in a nearby drain.

The atmosphere in Government House remained tense and uncertain that evening. The Sultan of Johor had withdrawn most of his forces earlier that afternoon after reports were received of a large body of mutineers landing in Johor. Government House now lacked a guard. Captain Brown was ordered to report to Ridout at Government House with his Chinese volunteers. Brown and his men arrived after nightfall. Young was in his private office deep in conversation with the Secretary of the Malay States, William George Maxwell, who had rushed down from Kuala Lumpur to discuss the emergency situation. Brown called out in the dark, saying it was unsafe to leave the doors open. His voice startled Maxwell who slipped on the polished floor and fell into a waste-paper basket. Young and Brown had to struggle to extricate the hapless bureaucrat from the bin.

By dawn of 17 February, the British had extricated themselves more generally from the hole they had allowed to form through complacency and neglect. At 6.45 that morning, Ridout had cabled the War Office that the situation was in hand after a serious disturbance broke out in the 5th, chiefly among the Ranghars. He also reported that the primary cause was obscure. The lead editorial of *The Straits Times* that day pronounced that the position had very greatly improved and that it was thoroughly well in hand. The Alhambra cinema in Beach Road advertised a screening for that evening of *Blue Pete's Escape* starring Sam De Grasse, but the British were not going to allow anyone to get away in reality. The French ship *Montcalm* sailed into port after Jerram's call for help the previous day. Two

machine guns and 150 men from the French ship were sent straight to
Seletar where a large body of mutineers had been seen. Late that afternoon, the Japanese cruiser *Otawa* entered port with 100 armed men. A
wounded Chiste Khan was caught a few hours later. His arrival at Outram Prison was witnessed by the wife of a British official who had sought
refuge in the jail along with her two infant children:

> Some of the officers kept him and a few of his pals in the courtyard
> just below our windows while they decided what to do with him.
> He is a native officer, an awful looking beast with a fierce face and
> wuffy black beard. He had been wounded in the shoulder and his
> picturesque white draperies and turban were soaked with blood. The
> English officer says he is a very bad character and hopes he will be
> shot or hung. At present he is in a cell just below us and is spending
> his evening reciting the Koran in a monotonous sing-song voice.[408]

The previous evening, over a dozen mutineers had visited Chiste's
mentor, Nur Alam Shah, in Kampong Java Mosque. The preacher gave
them clothes to disguise themselves as Malays. Imtiaz, who was among
the men, shaved off his beard and wore sarong, *baju* (shirt) and *songkok*
(cap) to blend in. A British secret agent heard him tell the mutineers that
they should have coordinated with him instead of acting as they had
done. Another agent would testify later that Nur Alam Shah had told the
distressed mutineers that he could have got Indians and other Muslims
to join in. As the noose closed on Nur Alam, one agent reported that he
made his escape to a Pathan-run hotel in Rochor Road. Another said he
was taken prisoner. History and the available British archives are silent on
Nur Alam Shah's fate apart from those reports. It is entirely possible that
he was quietly executed and buried.

At about 9.30 pm on 17 February, Imtiaz Ali was walking along Bukit
Timah Road when he was spotted by Police Corporal Busoh bin Ahmat
of Kandang Kerbau Police Station. Busoh noticed something amiss. Despite his Malay costume, the hulking Imtiaz did not resemble a Malay in
gait or appearance. Busoh raised his rifle. The unarmed Imtiaz had no
fight left in him. He immediately put his hands above his head and said:
"No Sir, no Sir. Me Colour-Sergeant, 5th Number, Alexandra Road Barracks."[409] The next morning, Dunde and seven other sepoys were arrested
at Kulai Railway Station in Johor by local police. Dirty and dishevelled,
they carried neither weapons nor ammunition. None resisted arrest. Over
in Singapore, the Japanese sailors from the *Otawa* had now linked up with
Brownlow's men at Keppel Harbour. With the reinforced unit, Brownlow
secured Alexandra Barracks and the Japanese sailors raised the flag of the

Rising Sun in the British military camp.

The Russian naval ship *Orel* arrived the following day and landed 50 armed marines to help out. The European and Eurasian women and children quartered offshore on ships had begun to return to their homes where they found their possessions generally untouched. On the evening of 19 February, a second Japanese ship, the *Tsushima*, arrived with 75 men. By then, most of the mutineers had been rounded up except for scattered bands in Singapore and a group of 61 who had crossed into Johor.

The next morning, the Provost-Marshal of Singapore issued a proclamation requiring that "(a)ll Indians of whatever race will report to the Police Station of their district for the purpose of obtaining passes to protect them from arrest. Each man must produce substantial evidence that he is not a soldier."[410] That evening, six companies of the 4th Shropshire Light Infantry (Territorials) dispatched from Rangoon disembarked from the SS *Edavana* just as a Court of Enquiry into the mutiny was established. The regular Saturday dinner was served at the Sea View Hotel in Katong, but this time without music from the band of the 5th Light Infantry.

In Johor, the last large group of mutineers were cornered by 20 February. They had landed in Johor after making their crossing from Seletar. As the HMS *Cadmus* patrolled further down at the mouth of the Johor River, 45 tired, ragged and hungry mutineers under Naik Munshi Khan were seen hiking up the road to Kota Tinggi. Every now and then, they moved into the jungle and then back on the road to throw off the scent. Munshi had been part of Dunde's B Company and was among the first to raid the magazine at Alexandra. Tracking him was Major Daud Sulaiman of the JMF with about five officers and 28 men in two lorries. They caught up with the mutineers two miles away from Kota Tinggi.

Major Daud approached them with his Hindustani interpreter, Second Lieutenant Alladar. Daud was a seasoned and cool customer. He had accompanied the Sultan to the Tanglin wedding and was a trusted intermediary of the Johor royal. He told Naik Munshi that the Sultan of Johor had personally sent him to speak with them. Munshi replied: "Please don't interfere with us, as we wish to pass through and besides we have done no harm to the Sultan's people, either in or outside his territory."[411] The mutineers had trudged through jungle, swamps and rubber plantations and were in a foul mood. Intending to peacefully disarm the mutineers, Major Daud did not mention the killing of the JMF soldiers in Tanglin. Munshi added: "I would like to see your Sultan and at present we are very hungry."[412] Major Daud promised them food if they accompanied him to Kota Tinggi.

Nearby, a 35-year-old English rubber planter named Jacques Alfonse

Le Doux was warned of the mutineers' arrival in Kota Tinggi by his assistants who ran towards him shouting, "*Orang jahat sudah datang*" (the bad men have arrived).[413] Another of his assistants, a Eurasian, had ridden his bicycle past the mutineers. Fortunately for him, a Hindustani-speaking Pathan policeman at the Kota Tinggi police station told the mutineers that he was a Eurasian and not to shoot. Settling down, Munshi and his fellow mutineers played with the local boys near the station but hung on to their rifles as they ate. The mutineers appeared lost, spent and quite prepared to surrender if handled properly and with respect.

After being fed in Kota Tinggi, Major Daud told Munshi: "You wish to see the Sultan, but I cannot take you before him armed with rifles."[414] Munshi replied: "No, I must retain my arms. If I had the heart to shoot, you would be dead men by now."[415] Daud was persuasive: "Are you sure you are a Mohamedan? Will you take an oath in your own language that you will surrender your arms to the Sultan, if I take you with him?"[416] Munshi swore to do so. Holding out the possibility that they might be taken into service with the Sultan, Daud then marched them down to a waiting launch on the river. Everything was going well until they arrived at the mouth of the Johor River.

Suddenly, the navy sloop HMS *Cadmus* loomed into view. Sultan Ibrahim, mindful of his men's safety, had earlier wired the *Cadmus* with instructions to let his forces handle the sepoys. Instead of gunboat diplomacy he had confidence in Major Daud's abilities. But the mutineers did not know this and started loading their rifles. Snatching a pair of binoculars from the captain of the launch, Munshi asked Daud: "Where is Johore?" Daud replied calmly: "Johore is on our right and Singapore on our left and that boat has nothing to do with us. She is always there guarding day and night."[417] At the same time, Daud frantically waved away the *Cadmus*, and it mercifully slid from view. This calmed the situation on the launch.

Rounding the Johor Strait, the launch chugged into the Skudai River towards the Sultan's Istana Besar (palace). When they arrived, Daud took the mutineers to see Sultan Ibrahim. They were marched in military formation in fours with sloped arms. As soon as Munshi saw the Sultan, he put his rifle down at his feet, just as he had sworn to Daud that he would do. The rest of the mutineers did the same. In total, 40 rifles with 2625 rounds of ammunition were surrendered. Advising the mutineers to trust in the laws of the British government and the fairness of its judicial process, the Sultan said, "Be not afraid… if you are innocent." He assured them that "the British Government will do you no harm if you have done nothing wrong."[418] The sepoys told him that since they had come to a country with a Muslim ruler, it was their duty to obey his command. They were put in half a dozen motor cars and sent off to prison. Major Daud had used skilful diplomacy to contain and neutralise the mutineers and to avoid bloodshed in Johor.

The Singapore-born Sultan Ibrahim, whose mother was Eurasian, was a committed Anglophile. For her own safety, Lady Young was staying with his English advisor, Douglas Graham Campbell. The Sultan was beginning to tire of the nosy Campbell, but he would still put his relations with the British over and above a band of ragged Muslim sepoy mutineers. The following day, Munshi and the other mutineers were handed over personally to Young by their fellow Muslim, the Sultan of Johor. Young had come over to personally take charge of Munshi and the captured mutineers from the Sultan. They were brought back to Singapore on the *Cadmus*, which fired a salute of 17 guns as it left Johor. In total, the Sultan and his forces rounded up 180 men of the 5th Light Infantry.

On 22 February, the first of many courts-martial was held and presided over by Brownlow. Ridout reported to the War Office at 3 am the following morning that the "situation is thoroughly well in hand still."[419] However, Ridout faced a new threat and intrigues of a different kind. His counterpart commanding the Troops in China, Major-General Francis Ventris, telegraphed the War Office recommending that the Straits Settlements be brought under his direct command. When asked for his reasons, Ventris declared: "I have no personal wish for the change but suggest it on imperial grounds."[420]

Alluding to Ridout's inexperience with infantry and Indians, Ventris said that the officer in command had to understand Indian infantry. Ventris complained to the War Office that since the war began, the situation had not been taken sufficiently seriously in Singapore. In a blistering attack on Young and Ridout's leadership, Ventris noted that the Volunteers Corps were not mobilised until after the mutiny took place. He also recalled that Young and Ridout had been prepared before the mutiny to let Brownlow to go home, leaving an officer with no experience of managing Indians, which the War Office fortunately did not take up. Ventris' gaslighting followed by his offer to run Singapore was ignored. The very next day, the first two mutineers were executed.

On 25 February, two Russian sailors from the *Orel* were wounded by a roving band of mutineers in an outlying area of Singapore. With Dyak tribesmen employed to track down the remaining mutineers the residential districts were finally declared safe. The loyal Pathans of the 5th were packed away out of sight in the quarantine station of St John's Island where some succumbed to disease or committed suicide in the spartan surroundings. The cumulative effect of the mass surrenders, execution, reinforcements and the return of British infantry to the garrison underlined that order was effectively restored. Ridout was pleased to receive a commendation on 2 March from Lord Herbert Kitchener, the imposing and domineering Secretary of State for War. Kitchener had wired Ridout expressing his "approval of the manner in which you have handled and successfully dealt with the difficult situation which has recently arisen in Singapore."[421]

Not to be outdone, Young took pains to demonstrate that he was in charge of the situation. A few days earlier, the Governor had quietly arranged for 200 dollars hush money and compensation to be paid to the family of a Malay fisherman from Pulau Brani named Omar bin Kapitan Ahmed.[422] He had been shot in his boat by a trigger-happy British sentry on entering Keppel Harbour at dawn. On 11 March, Young sent a telegram to his superior in London, the Secretary of State for the Colonies: "A deputation from the most influential Singapore Moslems presented to me today a resolution passed on March 6 at a mass meeting of over 3,000 Moslems to be placed before His Majesty the King. Translation is as follows: - "We, the Moslems at Singapore, have from first to last been constant in our allegiance and in our loyalty to the Throne."[423]

The mass meeting had been organised at Victoria Hall by the prominent notables of the Muslim community, led by Syed Omar bin Mohammed Alsagoff. Thousands of Malays, Javanese, Indians, Parsees and Malabaris and other Muslims attended the session in the presence of Young's deputy, R J Wilkinson. Anglophile Alsagoff was aligned with the Hashemites in Arabia who would join with Lawrence of Arabia in the Arab Revolt against the Ottomans. It was almost business as usual, except for the business that remained unfinished.

[XXII]

CRIME AND PUNISHMENT

As the *jihad*-mutiny in Singapore unravelled, the uprising in the Punjab was not going so well. The Punjabis from America and Asia lacked the discipline and secrecy of the Bengal revolutionaries like Jatin Bagha and Rash Behari Bose or the Marathi Veer Savarkar. The British secret police had penetrated the inner circle of the Ghadar uprising before the revolt began. A police spy named Kirpal Singh had spilled every detail of the plan to his handlers just as Rash Behari Bose arrived in Lahore in the Punjab for its denouement. Bose had recovered from his bomb injury and was keen to get matters underway. Under Bose, the Ghadar uprising, set for 21 February, was brought forward to the 19th after Kirpal Singh's behaviour attracted suspicions.

By then, more than 3,000 returning Punjabi revolutionaries had been screened by the police at Ludhiana and Calcutta. Nearly 200 were interned in high-security prisons, and about 700 were restricted to their villages. Many members of the Sikh community across farms in Punjab were policed by the notables in their villages. With their help, the revolutionaries had been chased away or tracked down. Pan-Punjab organisations like Khalsa Diwan pledged support for the British war effort, channelling thousands of young Sikh recruits to fight. For their efforts, the old notables and recruiters won awards and grants of land.

Despite the setbacks, Bose recognised the potential of using Punjabi and Sikh revolutionaries to link up with the Sikh sepoys. He had long planned with Bagha Jatin to foment an uprising in Fort William in Calcutta, but the so-called martial races in the Bengal cantonments were not of his caste or creed. He saw his chance to put into practice a long-cherished aim in Punjab – but it was already too late. Before the rising could take place on 19 February, the police raided Bose's headquarters near the Mochi Gate in Lahore's walled city. The Ghadar uprising was crushed at about the same time the Singapore *jihad*-mutiny fizzled out.

Mutinies in the 12th and 23rd Cavalry, the 26th Punjabis and the 28th Pioneers were forestalled across cantonments in India. A British Punjab Police report investigating the planned uprising concluded that a "(l)ack of organisation, bad leadership, incapacity to maintain secrecy, and the Indian habit of regarding the ideal as the fact accomplished, no doubt played their part in defeating the revolutionaries; but on more than one occasion their designs were dangerously near fulfilment and disaster was narrowly averted."[424]

There were mass arrests. As usual, Bose slipped away and made it back to Varanasi. The fat Bengali disguised himself as a Sikh. As he changed trains, he came across a loyalist Indian officer whom he had known from his days of service in the Forestry Institute in Dehra Dun. The former colleague stared right past him and pretended not to recognise the arch-terrorist. But even Varanasi was not safe and he had to make his way to the French-administered territory of Chandernagore where he had taken refuge previously. Kartar Singh was also hunted down but kept his composure. The police were searching a house in a village near Ludhiana when he passed by on a bicycle. He knew that if he tried to bolt, the police would have got him quite easily, so he walked into the house and coolly asked for a glass of water before getting back on his bicycle and pedalling away calmly. With his companion Harnam Singh Tundilat, the one-armed former sepoy and poet, Kartar headed for the border with Afghanistan. The two men were a world away from their first meeting in the House on the Hill in San Francisco where they had once worked on the *Ghadar* press. Everything had fallen apart.

But the ever ebullient and resilient Kartar was not discouraged. Stopping to rest in a way-station, Kartar recited to Harnam lines from a poem:

Paa Laiyee Shaeedi singh sher gajj ke,
bunee sir sheran de kee jaana bhajj ke
(Let's achieve martyrdom, roaring like a lion;
when the lions face a challenge why run away [from the field]).[425]

A true believer in his mission, Kartar always had a line ready to boost flagging spirits. But poetry was no substitute for good field-craft and insurgent tactics when a revolt was underway. Heading back towards the Punjab to find weapons to renew the insurgency, Kartar and Harnam's days were numbered. Their capture was a matter of time. The Lieutenant-Governor of the Punjab, Michael O'Dwyer, efficiently and methodically tracked down the dispersed insurgents and revolutionaries. Betrayed by a Sikh acquaintance, Kartar and Harnam soon found themselves bundled into Lahore Central Prison.

Also in jail with them was Kartar's mentor and Har Dayal's old friend, Bhai Parmanand. The Arya Samaj missionary, former college lecturer and pharmacist cum revolutionary was upset. He bitterly blamed a single traitor for the unravelling of the conspiracy. The Judas of the Ghadar Party was none other than Nawab Khan. Parmanand believed that the round-up began early soon after the return of the American Ghadar party revolutionaries:

> When they began to be caught some among them turned approvers. The first among these was a man named Nawab (Khan), the only Muslim who had come in this set from America. All his expenses, too, had been met by them out of their common fund. He had already acted as a spy in America and seemed to have come back with a special motive.[426]

Parmanand was convinced that Nawab had carefully kept in mind all the details of what had taken place on the voyage, which included the stop-over in Singapore. As soon as he arrived in India, he began to divulge all the details while pretending to operate as a loyal Ghadarite. Parmanand was also certain that it was Nawab who shared details of his fellow revolutionaries with the police. The information was used to turn more of them into approvers in what eventually became known as the Lahore Conspiracy Case of 1915. Nawab's handlers used him and offered him protection but showed him little respect: "The view we take of him is, that he is a vain and boastful adventurer, at times carried away by the fascination of a Hindu and Muhammadan union; another time he sees things going in such a way as to make him suspect that the ostensible union of interests has beneath the surface only the advancement of Hindus."[427]

In prison, Parmanand asked the teenaged revolutionary, Kartar, why he had chosen the path of revolt. He had lived in comfort in America. He had a bright future ahead of him studying chemistry along with an interest in airplane construction. Kartar confided to Bhai Parmanand that life in America was actually a burden to him. His heart burned when he heard abuse directed at him as a "damned Hindu" from the moment he stepped on American soil. He reminded his fellow Punjabi that it was he who had been partly responsible for his awakening and for grooming his revolutionary outlook. To jolt his memory, Kartar recalled their conversation one day in the United States when Parmanand asked if he knew the history of India and asked him to reflect: "how it was that the nation had become so dead and slavish that a steady stream of invasions had flowed on to it from the north-west for over 700 years."[428]

Kartar told Parmanand that that particular conversation had spurred him to reflect deeply on the question of India and its national strength. Parmanand had also cited to Kartar the martial example of the tenth Sikh Guru Gobind Singh who placed in his followers "seeds of fearless courage by which death once (and) for all lost for them its terrors."[429] Kartar admitted that he had become drawn to the idea of becoming a *shaheed*, a martyr. Despite the threat of capital punishment, Kartar offered perverse encouragement: "Let us be hanged quickly so that we may the sooner by re-born to take up our work where we dropped it."[430] This was an echo of the words at the gallows by Savarkar's young Punjabi protégé, Madan Lal Dhingra, who had carried out the assassination of William Wyllie in London.

After the usual legal due process, their sentences were ready to be passed. Bhai Parmanand, Kartar Singh, Harnam Singh and the other prisoners were led into a circular enclosure in the jail. They were let out in twos or three to hear their doom. Sohan Singh Bhakna, arrested early in October 1914, and Jowala Singh also joined them. With a bare handful of Ghadarites acquitted, the majority were either sentenced to death or transportation for life on the infamous Andamans penal colony. Bhai Parmanand, Harnam Singh, Sohan Singh Bhakna and Kartar Singh found themselves funnelled through a passage towards the death chamber while Jowala was led over to another yard.

A prisoner sentenced to transportation for life begged to be given the death sentence. The judge told him that he could still appeal for capital punishment. Parmanand heard a prisoner say defiantly, "So, that's all"[431] when sentenced to death. Kartar Singh had pleaded guilty to all charges and told the others in a matter of fact way: "I know the consequences – either transportation for life or death sentence. I shall prefer to be executed, for, that would give me an opportunity to be reborn to serve my country. Should I be born as a woman in my next birth, I would wish to give birth to rebel children."[432] When he received the death sentence, he merely said, "thank you" like a polite schoolboy.

Also facing execution, Parmanand regretted that he was going to miss the "fun"[433] of the ongoing world war and its eventual outcome. He had been sentenced to death on two key charges. First, for providing material help and counsel to revolutionaries. Second, for publishing his revisionist *Tarikh-e-Hind* (History of India), which he had researched and written in London. But Parmanand would get his wish to see out the war and tell the tale. His, Sohan and Harnam's sentences were eventually commuted to transportation for life by the Viceroy Lord Hardinge. But transportation for life was another form of death sentence on the dreaded Andaman penal colony where the death rate between 1910 and 1919 was 37.65 percent. Of the 279 revolutionaries tried in the cluster of cases around the Ghadar uprising conspiracy in Lahore, 46 were executed, 69 condemned to transportation for life, and 125 to other sentences. This was about the punishment toll of the Singapore *jihad*-mutiny.

When Kartar Singh's beloved grandfather came to see him before his execution, he asked the teenager: "Kartar, for whom are you accepting this death sentence? They are all disowning you."[434] Taken aback by the prospect of being disowned, Kartar soon recovered his composure. He reeled off the names of his dead relatives and asked his grandfather: "Tell me, *dadaji*, where are they?" His grandfather said, "They are dead!" To which Kartar Singh replied, "And we are also going to die. What is there to bother about?"[435] Kartar's wish for martyrdom was granted and he was hanged.

In Singapore, the captured mutineers reflected on their own approaching fate. E Company Pathan Sepoy Manowar Ali cried out once in jail: "The fault I have committed will surely mean that I shall be shot."[436] Manowar had prayed for Turkey's victory a week before the mutiny and was warned by his Indian officers. His Company Commander Lieutenant Elliott had been hunted down and murdered. Manowar himself had left the barracks with a loaded rifle which he tried to hide in a Malay hut. Imtiaz Ali, with ample time in prison to reflect on his actions, told the court-martial that he had nothing to do with the mutiny. To escape the death sentence, he even pinned the blame on Chiste. He swore that after the final inspection, Chiste told the men that the regiment was not going to Hong Kong but would be put on a ship and drowned. Even Dunde declared his innocence to evade capital punishment.

Of the 212 sepoys tried by court-martial, only one won an acquittal, while 48 mutineers were sentenced to be shot and 1 was to be hanged. Another 64 received transportation for life, 8 were given 20 years of transportation, 26 had 15 years of transportation, 30 were slapped with 10 years of transportation and 9 were to be transported for 7 years. The 11 men of the Guides got off easily with between 1 to 2 years of simple imprisonment. Of the death sentences, ten were later commuted to transportation for life. Dunde and Abdul Ali's B Company alone accounted for close to 60 percent of all the death sentences. No. 4 Double Company under Hall and the loyalist Pathans Suleiman Khan and Sharaf-ud-din Khan received barely any punishment.

After the 22 March execution of Dunde, Chiste and Abdul Ghani along with two other sepoys, Ridout wrote to the War Office to inform them that:

(o)pinion among the natives shows that they consider justice has been done. Only among a few Sikhs of the watchman class did there appear to be any resentment, which is, however, considered as mere bravado. There was a certain amount of sympathy among Punjabi Mahometans, as was to be expected.[437]

Two days later, Singapore witnessed the largest legally sanctioned public execution in its history on 25 March. The condemned men were part of the large group captured on 20 February near Kota Tinggi and handed over by the Sultan of Johor.

On the afternoon of 25 March, 15,000 people turned up to watch this mass execution outside Outram Prison. To secure a good view of the scene below, they were packed closely together on the slopes of the Sepoy Lines Golf Course on the western side of Outram Road. A square of British soldiers from the regulars and volunteers formed a human cordon around the execution ground. Over a hundred volunteers formed the in-dustrial-strength firing squad. Colonel G A Derrick of the Singapore Vol-unteers took charge of the very large firing party, with help from Captain Tongue and two Lieutenants. Brought out first were 45 mutineers under the escort of the Sikh Police Contingent. As the prisoners were paraded, Derrick proclaimed the official version of events to justify their execution:

These 45 men of the 5th Light Infantry have been found guilty of joining in the mutiny. They escaped from Singapore to Johore and refused to surrender there, except under certain conditions, and after surrender some of them prepared to offer resistance to the HM ship.... they have broken their oath as soldiers of His Majesty the King-Emperor and have been untrue to their salt.[438]

Each of the 45 stepped forward as their names were read out, sen-tences promulgated and translated into Malay, Chinese and Hindustani for the benefit of the spectators. They were then marched back to the prison. And then the condemned men were brought out. At 5.25 pm, Naik Munshi Khan, son of Mazkhar Khan of Hissar and his 21 com-rades were placed against stakes four feet apart. These were 10 men from Hissar, four each from Rohtak and Gurgaon with three others from other parts of Haryana. The police cadet A H Dickinson stood close to the pris-on wall near the last of the 21 execution posts. He noticed that compared to the previous executions, the bearing of the condemned men was not nearly as impressive.

Kota Tinggi planter Jacques Alfonse Le Doux had specially come down to Singapore to witness the execution. He was surprised to see that the Volunteers had been chosen for the job. He assumed that this allowed them a dose of vengeance since a number of their men had been killed by the mutineers. Le Doux wrote later:

> In front of me was a dense crowd of spectators. I could only see the heads and shoulders of the condemned. Someone read out the sentence of the Military Court in English. It was intended to give versions in several other languages, but this intention was abandoned after some minutes, as the attendant doctor warned the officer in charge that the condemned men were showing signs of fainting under this refined mental torture. Whilst all this was going on, there issued from the gaol terrible howls and cries from the condemned men's comrades.[439]

Dickinson heard one man cry out, infecting the others with his fear. The whole line of prisoners then swayed and prayed and shouted. Le Doux recalled that the officer commanding the firing party was told to carry on, while Dickinson thought he acted on his own initiative. But Captain Tongue gave the orders too quickly, "T'chun, present, load, aim, fire". Dickinson thought that Tongue's orders could not have been heard by all the soldiers in the 100-strong firing squad.[440] Le Doux remembered that "only desultory, and intermittent bombardment of the poor wretches followed."[441]

The firing party was flustered and had fired messily with scattered shooting. Some of the prisoners pitched forward or slid down to the ground in a crumpled heap. Some lay writhing, and others remained upright at their posts. Dickinson saw some men from the firing squad re-load and fire individually. Some even stepped forward out of their line to administer second shots. For Le Doux it seemed quite some time elapsed before the last of the prisoners "swayed and fell." Le Doux noticed with lurid fascination that "many were not mortally wounded, so the European gaolers went round and polished off the recumbent and still-living victims with their revolvers."[442]

The execution was a cruel and inhumane way to mete out justice. Prolonged wailing was heard from within the prison walls. The medical officer present admitted later to Colonel Derrick that in eight cases, it was doubtful whether they were killed outright and in two cases it was certain that the initial hail did not kill them. Two men nearest Dickinson and furthest away from Captain Tongue were not killed outright. Finally, instead of Chinese prisoners as done for Dunde and Chiste, Muslim prisoners from the jail emerged as the stretcher party to remove the bodies.

A strange silence prevailed amongst the large crowd. The firing party

The botched execution.

were badly shaken by the experience. However, Ridout reported with some pride to the War Office later that evening that the "execution today is reported to have impressed the crowd with the fact that justice was being done, and they remarked that any other nation would have executed wholesale. Evidently the waverers amongst Indian civilian population are being deterred by the action taken."[443] The War Minister Lord Kitchener, who led a scorched earth policy and concentration camps to cow the rebellious Boers in Britain's Boer War, would have approved.

On 17 April, another large batch of mutineers received their sentences. Most were given varying periods of transportation, including Manowar Ali who had brazenly yelled his support for the victory of Islam in the regimental mosque. Instead of being shot as he feared, he received transportation for life, a sentence shared with Havildar Jamalluddin, the slack Guard Commander on the day of the mutiny. Three of the mutineers in this batch were sentenced to death. Among the trio was the regimental hot-head Lance-Naik Feroze Khan who led the assault on Tanglin. The 5th's medical officer Lieutenant Morrison noted that before his execution, Feroze made faces, winked, pointed to the sky and then to the warders. Spotting Morrison, he straightened himself and started to make a speech. He declared that the British government was a most unjust and lying Government. Crying out that it was not his Government, he declared: "I am a German soldier."[444]

Defending his actions to Morrison, Feroze declared that he had been convicted on lies and injustice and scorned his impending execution. His death was absolutely nothing, and no one should think that his plans had been frustrated. He told Morrison to let both the Subedar Major Khan Mohammed Khan as well as his friend Wahid Ali know that their lying evidence which convicted him had made no difference. Arrangements were made whereby his children and children's children would be hunting down all of their children and relatives. They would pay for their lying evidence with their last blood. Morrison thought that he had lost his mind, but the doctor himself seemed conflicted as he noticed both a "slight squint and bulging eyes" on Feroze's face which "was cringing up" as "he was winking his eyes."[445]

To make up for the botched job on 25 March, a perfectly synchronised execution was overseen by Colonel Arthur Newson Bruff Garratt of the Shropshires. Inside the prison, Lance-Naik Fazal Ali, who had been wounded in a Chinatown shootout with Assistant Superintendent of Police L A Thomas, was tied to a chair for his execution as he could not even stand up. The volley inside and outside was coordinated by flag signal. By the time of the last firing squad execution on 26 April, public interest had dwindled. But there was one more execution, to be done in the strictest privacy.

Awaiting his own trial, Kassim Ismail Mansoor the *jihadi*-socialite heard each shot fired outside the prison walls over those two months. He heard the groans and curses of the men inside waiting their turn to face the firing squad or have sentence passed on them. He did not show undue worry. He was, after all, a civilian and had retained three defence counsels including the young and gifted Vincent Devereux Knowles. The pint-sized but bubbly Knowles was a 30-year-old criminal lawyer specially requested by Mansoor. At age 24, Knowles had successfully defended several pirates from the death penalty by arguing that the Colony had no jurisdiction to impose capital punishment for piracy. He was to become a specialist in removing the Damoclean sword hanging over the heads of accused and knew how to win over judge and jury. Calm, quiet but persuasive, Knowles was the ideal defender of last resort. He fenced for sport and knew when to parry and thrust in court.

However, it did not bode well that Mansoor was the first civilian defendant in Britain's Eastern Empire to be tried before a Field General Court Martial instead of before judge and jury. The hearings began in the last week of April. The court focussed on the letters Mansoor had written to Ahmed Madani, the former Turkish Consul in Rangoon, and his own son in Rangoon to help the Guides connect with Turkish forces. The prosecution case hammered home the fact that it was impossible to dissociate Mansoor's actions from the mutiny. He was charged with entertaining men of the 5th and the Guides at his plantation in Pasir Panjang when he had no business mixing with them as they came from another part of India. This was a classic projection of the colonial fantasies of martial races and divide and rule. Knowles dismissed as quite ridiculous the charges levelled against his client of mere socialising.

But it was Mansoor's letter to the Turkish Consul that would do him in. The court found him guilty of one of the eleven charges of treason by forwarding the letter and attempting to wage war on the King. Expecting an acquittal, Mansoor slumped forward as he heard the verdict. The court's unanimous decision was that he should be hanged and that the sentence would be carried out a week later on Monday, 10 May. There was some deliberation in official circles on whether to conduct the execution in public or private. It was decided that it would be done behind the prison walls. Kassim was not a sepoy, even if he had been court-martialled. A public execution of a Muslim civilian could become fodder for enemy propaganda. After a stay of execution of three weeks, Mansoor was told his sentence would be carried out on the morning of 31 May.

The night before his execution Mansoor asked to see Knowles. He had become very fond of the young defence counsel. Speaking to him on death row, he said candidly that he was guilty. He knew he had been foolish but had not understood the seriousness of what he was doing. However, he expected some sort of reprieve because he could not fathom that what he had done would warrant the death penalty. His own cousin, Mahomed Kassim Mansoor, a diamond merchant and land speculator who lived beyond his means and went bankrupt, had testified against him. His testimony was accepted even after he had admitted to being on bad terms with Mansoor after he refused to loan him money. The court prosecutors were scraping the bottom of the barrel.

The next morning, Mansoor stood blindfolded on the gallows with a noose around his frail neck. It appeared that he was struggling to say something, possibly a final plea for a reprieve. Before he could voice the words, the trapdoor swung open with a loud creak and a muffled boom was heard as his body reached the end of its tether and the scaffolding vibrated with a life snuffed out. *The Straits Times* pronounced it a fitting end for an infamous traitor.

On 8 July, a few days after the rehabilitated elements of the 5th had departed for East Africa, 143 of the convicted mutineers filed up the gang-plank to the HMT *Ellenga*. Ridout reported not without some pleasure to Young that: "(i)t was noticed as they left the Jail that they were depressed, and appeared in a disturbed state as if apprehensive as to their ultimate disposal. They had not been told they were to be transferred to India."[446] The prisoners were told in Hindustani in doom-laden terms: "No one but God knows what may happen tomorrow, but remember that everything will depend upon your own behaviour now and hereafter."[447] It was a form of psychological torture. Even Ridout acknowledged that "they had feared being taken to sea and sunk – for they had had this fear prior to 15th Feby."[448] Most of the 143 prisoners were left thinking it was going to be a repeat of what had made some of them join the mutiny in the first instance. They did not learn their ultimate destination until the very last minute. It was an exquisite form of torture in retaliation for the shame and humiliation their British masters had suffered.

Three mutineers, Taj Mohammed Khan, Ismail Khan and Feroze Khan, the latter two namesakes of two of the most infamous mutineers, somehow managed to make their way to Bangkok. They escaped punishment or retribution. The British authorities received reports of their sighting but were never able to apprehend them.

[XXIII]

LIES, SEX AND SPIES

Prior to the outbreak of the *jihad*-mutiny in Singapore, the young Straits Settlements police officer cadet A H Dickinson declared that a "happier, more tranquil place than Singapore it would be difficult to imagine."[449] After the revolt of the 5th, he noted that the "more imaginative conjured up pictures of the Indian Mutiny… (t)he Civil Community knew nothing of the 5th Light Infantry beyond the fact that it was an Indian regiment and the one regular unit left to defend the Island. Now it had mutinied."[450] Dickinson's unpublished account, prepared for the Royal Commonwealth Society, captured the confusion and fear on the night of the mutiny. The young cadet had just arrived from India after two years of training and language learning with the Indian police. Thrown into the thick of it, he listed the questions racing in many minds that night:

> And what would be the effect on the Indian population of the whole country? Hindu and Mohammedan? Further, the Malays were a Mohammedan race. Would the Mohammedans support a jehad – a holy war? Had the Army failed or the Police failed in their intelligence work? Had German money and Indian seditionists combined to subvert the Regiment? Rumours of large sums of money found on mutineers were rife in the ensuing few days. These were the questions gestating in many minds that first night.[451]

The young cadet would go on to become Inspector-General of the Straits Settlements Police twenty years after the mutiny. But more than a century later, many of the questions he raised have not been satisfactorily answered. It did not help that ten days after its outbreak, the official British proclamation issued by acting Brigadier-General Dudley Ridout resolutely dismissed any political motives behind the mutiny:

> Any rumours that these men were shot for refusing to go to fight in other parts of the empire are untrue. The Regiment was to have proceeded to Hongkong on Tuesday, the 16th, to form part of the Garrison there. The men had expressed no objection to that, but it is known that there was jealousy in the Regiment concerning promotion. The Government recognises with gratitude the steadfast behaviour of the Detachment of the 36th Sikhs which happened to be here and of the Sikh and Malay Police and of the General Public of all classes.[452]

With the memories of the Great Indian Mutiny of 1857 still in mind, the dreaded M word could not be mentioned in an official release. This caused a little confusion. Across the Straits of Johor in Kota Tinggi, Jacques Alfonse Le Doux, the English rubber planter with a French sounding name but with no knowledge of French had come across a copy of *The Singapore Free Press* which mentioned an "*emeute*" of the 5th. He had to look up the term in the dictionary to discover that it meant a "popular rising or uproar". Dickinson recalled that the "Authorities in all official communiques preferred to call it an "*emeute*." The Gallic euphemism sounded perhaps less alarming than the more horrific, more brutal "mutiny."[453] For colonial officials, it was important that the official account highlights loyal Sikhs and Muslims and a general public who had kept apart from the fray. Also to be avoided was any mention of *jihad* or holy war or an Islamic state.

However, the diplomatic community in Singapore was not convinced. The Ottoman Empire's Consul-General in Batavia (Jakarta) had a different assessment. In his dispatch home, Consul-General Rifaat Effendi wrote: "(T)he truth is that an Indian Muslim, in (Singapore), and Indian Muslim soldiers have declared major Jihad for the greater Islamic state against the British also including the Hindu soldiers arriving from Singapore as well as those Muslim civilians according to the intelligence that I have received."[454] In a secret cable, Russia's Consul in Singapore, N A Rospopov, reported that the mutiny was a consequence of a "Muslim movement",[455] despite British assertions to the contrary. Based on information from a pair of Japanese barbers in Tanglin Camp, the Japanese Consul Fujii Minoru in Singapore reported to Tokyo that "the Indian Muslim soldiers took their final decision in consideration of their religion, and responded to the German instigation." He dismissed suggestions that it could be ascribed to reasons like "non-promotion."[456]

A British cypher cable sent by Sir Arthur Young to Hardinge, the

Viceroy of India, on 20 February 1915 echoed this line in private:

> Among the mutineers caught to-day there is one Jellal Khan (No.
> 2200) - this man's village is 16 miles from Delhi: he stated to member
> of the Civil Service (by name Seth, who understands Hindustani)
> that the Mulvi had told them although it is true that they had fought
> against Moslems previously, the present war is on a different footing,
> as it entails fighting against the head of their Religion i.e. the Sultan
> at Stamboul. Also state that now that the Germans are allied to
> the Turks, the moslem Indians in France – although they may not
> directly fight against us – will not fight for us. "We receive letters and
> we know the real feelings". This man was unaware of who the Aga
> Khan was, as he said "I know my last hour has struck but what I say
> is the truth."[457]

But this was never repeated in public by the British, giving rise to various conspiracy theories. The MSVR volunteers in Normanton Camp, invited to dinner by the officers of the 5th on the evening of the mutiny, reconstructed the mutineers' possible plan of action several months later:

> The mutineers had not intended to rear up at 3.30 pm. Their little
> game was to murder their officers at mess at 8 pm.... (T)he muti-
> neers were then to descend in full strength upon us, as we sat in our
> mess tent at dinner, unarmed, our rifles in barracks... and massacre
> us to a man.... (A)fter that they were to go to Tanglin, murder the
> guard, proceed down Orchard Road, kill the police and take the
> station. Then on to Government House to transfer His Excellency
> to a better world than this. The whole to wind up with an orgy of
> murder in Singapore.[458]

The MSVR's melodramatic reconstruction featuring the mutineers as pantomime villains more or less stuck to the preferred official script. The sepoys were a mob gone amok. They were on an "orgy of murder." A more sophisticated version of this assessment was offered by a British military scholar who believed that the "Singapore Ghadar could have taken a very serious turn. It failed because the mutineers had no goal, no plan and no revolutionary guidance. They were filled with resentment against their alien masters but lacked the spirit of political revolution and the local population also did not sympathise with them."[459]

The Court of Enquiry set up in Singapore just five days after the mutiny completed its work in May 1915. The report claimed that the principal cause of the mutiny was "the very unsatisfactory state of disci-

REPORT

IN CONNECTION WITH

MUTINY OF 5TH LIGHT INFANTRY AT SINGAPORE 1915

PART I.—Proceedings of Court of Enquiry.

PART II.—Report by His Excellency the Governor of the Straits Settlements and the General Officer Commanding at Singapore.

SIMLA
GOVERNMENT CENTRAL BRANCH PRESS
1915

The report on the mutiny of the 5th Light Infantry.

pline which had prevailed in the 5th Light Infantry apparently for some time."[460] According to the final report:

> To sum up the situation, the British officers were at sixes and sevens. The Indian officers of the right (or mutinous) wing were divided up into two camps. This state of affairs was bound to be, and was, reflected amongst the rank and file with the result that the discipline of the regiment was undermined and weak. This unfortunate state of affairs furnished a ready and fertile field for the sowing and growth of fanatical and seditious ideas which were carefully planted and fostered by cunning agencies, resulting in the lamentable outbreak which occurred.[461]

The report would not be released for public consumption for another half-century. However, in 1918, the India Sedition Committee made public its own report known as the Rowlatt Report. Chaired by the English judge Sidney Rowlatt, the Committee had been formed towards the end of the First World War to analyze political terror in India, particularly in the Punjab and Bengal, its impact and links with Britain's enemies. The report's objective was to justify tough measures against nationalists and freedom fighters whom the British considered seditionists and political. The legislation enacted in the wake of the Rowlatt report allowed for trials without jury and detention without trial. It would end up inspiring Gandhi's civil disobedience movement after the massacre at Jallianwala Bagh in Amritsar.[462] Rowlatt's final report conceded that "the 5th Infantry Regiment which raised an insurrection in February 1915 had undoubtedly been contaminated by Mohammedan and Hindu Conspirators belonging to the American Ghadr Party."[463]

It did not help the British effort that all sorts of rumours and reports were flying around. One bizarre conspiracy theory even connected the mutiny to Singapore as a hub of prostitution. Three months after the last of the mutineers was sentenced, an activist and social reformer named J E Cowen visited Singapore in October 1915. After his visit to Singapore's brothel areas, he sent a letter to the London-based Association for Moral and Social Hygiene enclosing his 25-page study of prostitution in Singapore. The Association was Britain's most well-known organisation dedicated to the control of sexual disease, regulating prostitution and promoting sexual education and abstinence to curb social ills.

Cowen's report noted that other than the port of Canton, no other city in Asia could match Singapore for its open display of European, Indian, Japanese and Chinese prostitution. He observed that the two brothel areas of the Malay Street Quarter and Smith Street Quarter respectively were as prominent features of Singapore as St Andrew's Cathedral, its law courts or Tanjong Pagar Dock. Like a moth to light, Cowen walked from his accommodation in the Sailor's Home down North Bridge Road following the brightest part of town to Malay Street where he counted 24 public brothels, with European and Japanese prostitutes accosting men of every colour. On Malay Street, he noticed a "Fuji Restaurant" where British sailors in naval uniforms drank with brothels on either side of the establishment. He also observed a young English merchant ship's officer misbehaving with Japanese prostitutes in full public view, and expressed his alarm to see two young Englishmen "mauling" a Japanese woman complaining about payment.[464]

According to Cowen, nowhere was "race hatred" more bitter than in the brothel area where "English, German (before the war), Dutch, Mahomedan, Ceylonese and others, jostle each other in the street and rival one another in the brothels."[465] He claimed that English soldiers or sailors entering a brothel and finding "niggers", who could be educated Malay or Indian youths, would kick them out. If these locals were cavorting with European prostitutes, they would also lock the doors to the Englishmen and jeer at them from the balconies. Derided as "nigger", they would reply "white pig."[466] Cowen made the startling assertion that:

> I think it is not too much to say that the mutiny of Mahomedan troops of Singapore, resulting in the indiscriminate murder of Europeans… and the threat of a similar occurrence at Rangoon, were directly connected with the ill-feeling and bitter antagonisms bred in the European and Indian brothel quarters. Both at Rangoon and Singapore the trouble was attributed to German machinations. This theory is easily accepted, but the fact is that racial animosity is bred and fostered day by day and night by night in the brothels….[467]

On Smith Street in Chinatown, he saw an advertisement of "Wrigley's Spearmint Pepsin Gum" displayed at on establishment of easy virtue. He described the picture and its effect on Asians who could not read:

> a large, gaudy-coloured picture of British officers in full dress uniform, dancing with women, presumably English also, in flimsy clothing, the upper part of their bodies exposed, skirts very short and limbs displayed: this attracted much attention from the people in the street… the exhibition of the picture in this street could only bear one meaning for them and seemed calculated, along with the stupid behaviour of English soldiers and other Englishmen in these streets to bring the British name, and especially the army, into contempt.[468]

The report was sent to the Association of Moral and Social Hygiene, which forwarded it with its full endorsement to the Secretary of State for Colonies in London. Officials in London noted that the report "records a very bad state of affairs" but also that some of his "statements are rather wild" like his "fantastic theory on the origins of the Singapore mutiny."[469] The report was sent to the Governor in Singapore to hear what he had to say about it. Young had bigger things on his mind. The mutiny in Singapore was clearly a result of a different kind of intercourse and as-signations and transmissions of a variety other than Cowen imagined. As a major stop-over port, Singapore was open to all sorts of agents of influence and propaganda efforts. The deeper issue faced was the lack of effective intelligence capabilities in Singapore.

While the Inquiry into the Singapore Mutiny was wrapping up its work, Rash Behari Bose slipped out of India and was on his way to a new life in Japan. He posed as a gentleman relative of the Nobel Prize winner Rabindranath Tagore. Stopping over in Penang on a Japanese steamer, he learnt about the Singapore mutiny and its outcome. An Indian hawker told him that all Indians passing through Singapore were being carefully screened. Bose decided to take his chances when the steamer arrived in Singapore two days later. Anchored in the Singapore harbour, a launch approached with a dozen policemen. One of them took his finger-prints which was mandatory for all Indian arrivals in Singapore. But none of them recognised the revolutionary dressed as an Anglophile student en route to higher studies in Japan.[470] In Japan, Bose stumbled across the wrestler-preacher Bhagwan Singh Jakh who was also on the run from the imperial police. The two men conspired to use Japan as a base for revolu-tionary activities against the Raj.

Meanwhile in Singapore, there were public recriminations over the mutiny. At the end of June, with claims that the Government in Singa-pore had "long warning of a mutinous feeling in the regiment and failed to take such cognisance of it as would have secured the safety of the community",[471] as *The Straits Times* put it, Young had authorised the issu-ance of a special communique. The communique denied any knowledge beforehand of mutinous feelings in the 5th, but admitted only to anxiety about the discipline of the Malay States Guides. *The Straits Times* editorial of 22 June supported the government's position but also made the point that "German agents had a hand in this (mutiny) we do not doubt" and that four months after the mutiny, "we are still a long way from the ide-al condition of readiness to meet any similar trouble."[472] While defend-ing his position in public, one practical outcome was that behind closed doors, Young was rushing measures through the Legislative Council. Two new measures that were introduced were the Reserve Force and Civil

Guard Bill and the Seditious Publications (Prohibition) Bill. The Government had noted with embarrassment that many of the volunteers and special constables mustered during the mutiny mishandled their weapons because of lack of training, posing a greater danger in some instances than even the mutineers.

Young gave carte blanche to General Ridout in his thrust to develop an intelligence service in Singapore. On 4 March 1915, Young wrote a secret cable to the Viceroy of India complaining about the lack of information sharing. After the mutiny, Ridout had shown him a secret pamphlet issued by the Army HQ India offering an abstract of information gleaned from open sources on "political and religious movements" in India. Young requested that such information should be shared with the Governor and not just the GOC.[473] Having subtly shifted away some of the blame for not anticipating the outbreak of the mutiny, he allowed Ridout room to improve schemes of intelligence collection.

Ridout worked overtime to establish Singapore as a secret intelligence hub and clearing station for reports on seditionists, political criminals, terrorists and revolutionaries. Both had drawn lessons from the complacent attitude towards foreign intrigues and influences in Singapore and the Straits Settlements. After the failure of the rising in Punjab, the Germans took greater control of Indian revolutionary activities in the America and East Asia, including Singapore. To counter German activities, Ridout started to recruit agents and to establish a network of eyes and spies based in Singapore. He brought over a formidable Parsi Police Inspector from Bombay named Hector Kothavala. The 32-year-old had worked his way up from the rank of constable. He had a photographic memory and was said to be able to remember the tiniest details with just a glance.

Kothavala first come to Singapore to interpret at the trial of a revolutionary. Dudley Ridout would later pay tribute to Kothavala as a "perfect staff officer and in the matter of intelligence dealing with intrigues is my right-hand man."[474] Kothavala became Ridout's key weapon against the revolutionaries and Indo-German plotting, credited for the successes of the anti-Ghadar and Indo-German operations in Singapore and Far East theatre. He was one of the few men who could handle the Indian secret agents in Singapore and also carry out interrogations. Some interrogations of Ghadarites in Singapore could involve torture and highly coercive methods, but Kothavala's bosses thought them effective. The various Ghadarites he interrogated in Singapore included Jowala Singh the "potato king" from Stockton who was held in a military brig in Singapore before being transferred to India. He also interrogated Ghadarites later sent on to San Francisco as approvers in the Indo-German trials to testify against men like Bhagwan Singh Jakh and Taraknath Das.

Kothavala missed Rash Behari Bose's stopover in Singapore, but he caught one of the revolutionaries' emissaries Avani Nath Mukherjee while he was in transit on a Japanese steamer through the port. In his baggage, Kothavala found secret letters from Bose. After interrogating Mukherjee, it was discovered that Bose had passed through Singapore under the assumed identify of P N Tagore, a nephew of Rabindranath Tagore. Kothavala ferreted out Bose's address in Japan from Mukherjee and the British telegraphed the Japanese government excitedly to request his arrest. He could be easily identified by the scar on his hand from the bomb accident in Varanasi. The Japanese slowed things down. This began a period of prolonged cat and mouse games between British detectives and Bose in Japan. He evaded captured because of sheer luck and thanks to his links to an ultranationalist, pan-Asianist secret society in Tokyo.

Kothavala pressed on. He played a key role in breaking and then managing a German agent named Vincent Kraft, who became a British double agent with the codename of Agent "X" on a pay of £2 per day.[475] Kothavala personally accompanied Kraft on a dangerous undercover assignment from Singapore to Shanghai and Peking. This was part of a German plot to use German nationals from the Dutch East Indies to attack the Andamans. Kraft assisted in the plot, which Kothavala used to draw out and expose German operations in the region. The attack itself was supposed to be launched on Christmas Day 1915, which the British would have been prepared to disrupt and repel with advance notice. Although the plot was called off at the last minute, Kothavala's monitoring helped the British seize weapons in Shanghai meant for revolutionaries in India.[476]

The details of these missions were shrouded in secrecy. Ridout appreciated that the Parsi officer carried them out with discretion. The Germans considered Kothavala a serious menace and their legation at Hankow in China put a price of half a million marks on his head. The former Bombay detective also proved very useful in ferreting out a plot by the Germans to send a Chinese named Sing Kwie through Singapore with $10,000 in Straits dollars transferred through a Singapore bank to buy the loyalty of an Indian regiment in Calcutta.[477] Kothavala left Singapore in 1919 to return to work in India, after assisting Ridout in the establishment of the Criminal Intelligence Department in the Straits Settlements Police. This was to become a forerunner to Singapore's Special Branch, later on the Internal Security Department and the Security and Intelligence Division.

Ridout departed Singapore in 1921 to a grand send-off including separate farewells from the Chinese community and the Muslim community.

At the farewell party hosted by a trio of Muslim notables of Singapore, the Malay Tengku Ibrahim bin Abdul Jalil, the Arab Syed Omar bin Alsagoff and the Indian Tamil Moona Kadir Sultan, General Ridout was given effusive thanks. His hosts referred to "the *emuete* of 1915" and the "delicate position of our community" when Turkey entered the war.[178] In a prepared statement, his hosts highlighted that the 5th Light Infantry redeemed itself in service thereafter and Muslim soldiers everywhere had laid down their lives for the Raj. They pledged their everlasting loyalty to the King-Emperor. These were wealthy Muslims who had become prosperous in the settlement under British rule. Known as the "Cattle King" for his meat monopoly on the island, the Tamil Muslim Moona Kadir Sultan had just completed a palatial mansion in Katong near the sea. Never mind that his high meat prices added to the discontent of the sepoys, their fellow Muslim from Karikal in South India had men like Ridout to thank for his continued success.

Responding to their effusive declarations of loyalty, Ridout said he was glad that the Muslims of Singapore were: "true to their salt and that they followed the teaching of the Koran in being true to the ruler under whom they were serving."[479] He reassured them that in his own mind and in the minds of others whose opinions mattered there was never any doubt of their loyalty. Pausing for their polite and appreciative applause, Ridout continued: "At the very outset misunderstandings were brushed aside – and in point of fact that period of stress brought them more closely into touch and made them understand each other better. Out of evil came good."[480]

The farewell offered closure for Ridout as he prepared for retirement in England, following in the footsteps of Young who had completed his tenure as Governor in 1919. It was a very different speech from the one he made to the unsettled sepoys of the 5th on 15 February 1915. That speech during the 5th's farewell inspection helped to produce the train disaster of events. Ridout's subsequent, post-mutiny speech to the loyal remnants of the 5th on the eve of their departure for Africa on 3 July 1915 expressed the hope that they would "do well and return with fresh lustre added to your reputation" and exhorted them to "carve out a fresh career and bury the recent past."[481]

The sepoys of the 5th redeemed themselves in subsequent action but were promptly disbanded after the war. As he rewrote the recent past, Ridout also redeemed himself and British prestige for the time being at least. At its lowest moment, the Acting Secretary of the Federated Malay States, W G Maxwell, who had slipped and fallen into Young's waste basket in Government House on the night of the mutiny, reported that as far north as Kelantan: "The Sultan has, ever since the Singapore mutiny, believed that the downfall of the British Empire was at hand.... (S)ince the Singapore mutiny the Kelantan Malays, as a whole, have been far less respectful to Europeans, and have in many cases tended to adopt an insolent and truculent manner."[482]

Just weeks after the Singapore mutiny, a revolt erupted in Kelantan in May 1915. The popular rebellion was led by the mystical chief of Pasir Puteh and required swift action to shore up sagging British prestige. As usual, Brownlow was sent with a relief force to deal with the revolt in the British protectorate. It was put down quickly with a 1,500 strong force. Ridout had showed himself to be firm and decisive in despatching the force and dealing with the threat. Without the challenge of the mutiny and subsequent events, Ridout would not have made his mark in Singapore. Indeed, as he told the Muslims of Singapore, "out of evil came good". But history does not move in straight lines. The intelligence service and network he built lasted only until the eve of the Second World War, when the Japanese Occupation unravelled the whole spool.

Three days after the farewell parties, Ridout and his wife proceeded to Johnston's Pier to catch a launch for the steamer home. A 13-gun salute was fired from the Saluting Battery at Fort Canning while a guard-of-honour from the all-British infantry of the 1st Battalion South Staffordshires and band saw the couple off. It had been a good innings for General Ridout. Out of evil came good, indeed. But to achieve the good, he had had to do some evil too. Men sleep peacefully in their beds at night because rough men stand ready to do violence on their behalf. Ridout of course considered himself an officer and a gentleman. It was the mutineers who were the rough men, and they were now sleeping under the ground – no threat to the Empire or its people. Not on his watch at least.

But even as Ridout sailed back home to his retirement, the Urdu poet and Indian freedom fighter, Maulana Hasrat Mohani was composing *Inquilab Zindabad* (Long Live the Revolution) and demanding complete independence for India in public political meetings. The freedom struggle was transforming itself into a real mass movement. A non-violent, civil-disobedience movement had developed under the Mahatma Gandhi along with growing Hindu-Muslim unity. In the Punjab, anger still seethed over the Jallianwala Bagh civilian massacre of 1919 prompted by draconian post-war policing and repression. A new generation of revolutionaries were emerging from the dragon's teeth sown by the Ghadar Party. The revolutionary Ajit Singh's then 14-year-old nephew, Bhagat Singh, listened closely to the stories of the Ghadar recounted to him by his father Kishin Singh. As he heard the tales of Kartar Singh Sarabha's heroism, he felt a deep surge of pride and inspiration.

The future martyr, Bhagat Singh, would renew the violent revolutionary struggle begun by the Ghadar Party which began in 1912 in San Francisco as the Hindustan Association of the Pacific Coast. Bhagat would help found the Hindustan Socialist Republican Association (HSRA) in 1928. Its manifesto, called "The Philosophy of the Bomb", harked back to the work of Rash Behari Bose and Har Dayal. In 1929, the HSRA member Bhagat Singh made an attempt to assassinate the Viceroy of India 17 years after Bose failed to kill Lord Hardinge. The HSRA defended their violence as complementary to Gandhi's non-violence. Bhagat made *Inquilab Zindabad* (Long Live the Revolution) the rallying cry for the freedom struggle against the British Raj.

It finally took Gandhi's approach of non-violence to break the cycle of violence. Gobind Behari Lal claimed that Har Dayal succeeded in the Ghadarite experiment by "changing nonpolitical Indian minds"[483] and ventured that it "perhaps prepared the way indirectly, for the Great Gandhi Experiment"[484] that led to India's freedom. Gandhi was eventually killed by firebrands of the revolutionary movement who wanted peaceful revolution to be impossible so that violent revolution would be inevitable.

[XXIV]

THE LAST MUTINY

Indian sepoys would play their part in another turning point of Singapore's history. As the Imperial Japanese Army sliced down the Malay Peninsula in 55 days during the Second World War, the sepoys were among the Empire and Commonwealth troops attempting to hold the line. But the speed and force of the Japanese offensive was overwhelming. Bombed, bulleted and bayoneted, the Empire forces pulled back towards the Johor Straits, leaving Fortress Singapore as its last defensive position. The demoralised Empire forces faced the equally bad choices of surrender, desertion or a fight to the death though many sepoy units put up a spirited but hopeless resistance, discovering that their British masters were far from invincible. As the defenders hunkered down, their well-prepared foe probed for weak points while the raw, teenaged recruits from the Punjab who reinforced the crumbling Singapore garrison found themselves cut-off and abandoned.

North of the partially destroyed causeway linking Singapore and its Malayan hinterland, confusion reigned. Among the stragglers in Northern Malaya was a British Indian army officer named Captain Mohan Singh. The wiry Sikh was second-in-command of the 1st battalion of the 14th Punjab Regiment, nicknamed *Sher Dil Paltan* or Band of Lionhearts. He watched his lionhearts fold after brutal combat around Changlun, about 42 kilometres from Alor Setar in the Malayan sultanate of Kedah during the Battle of Jitra. As Japanese tank-fire ripped through the sepoy ranks, many fled into the jungle including the battalion's British Commanding Officer, Lieutenant-Colonel James Fitzpatrick. About two thirds of the unit were wiped out. A wounded Fitzpatrick stumbled in front of Mohan and then disappeared.

But the stubborn Sikh had fight left in him yet. He baited and taunted Japanese tank gunners. They responded with machine gun-fire. A professional soldier, Captain Mohan was not prepared to spend his best years locked up as a prisoner-of-war. Before going into battle, he celebrated his last day of leave with his fellow Indian officers. After a night of hard soldierly drinking, he told his comrades: "I don't know what will happen, but one thing is certain: I'm not going to die, and mind you, don't be surprised if you see me as your liberator coming down fighting the very British whom I'm now going to defend."[185] He was clearly developing nationalist sentiments. Evading the enemy in the jungle for three days gave him plenty of time to think about his past and his future. He thought long and hard about his loyalties, the discrimination he had faced and his prospects in the British Indian army.

Eventually captured with Fitzpatrick and other survivors from his battalion, Captain Mohan found himself standing in a Kedah rubber plantation near the Thai border. Now a prisoner-of-war, the Sikh officer caught the eye of a Japanese military intelligence officer named Major Iwaichi Fujiwara. Polished, charming and ruggedly handsome, Major Fujiwara was on a special mission. He needed a charismatic Indian officer willing to switch sides and lead the captured sepoys in a new free Indian army. He had a test for the Sikh Captain. As the local police had melted away from the town of Alor Setar, Fujiwara put Mohan and his men in charge of security in the Kedah capital. With just truncheons and handcuffs, Mohan earned Fujiwara's trust and respect when he quickly re-established order from chaos.

Fujiwara now began to work on persuading Mohan to do more for him. With only a bit of English and no knowledge of Hindi, Fujiwara used all his charm to win over the sceptical and battle-hardened Sikh infantry officer. Both men were the same age. At 33, they were at that stage in life when experience forms a barrier of certainty, identity is almost nearly crystallised, and minds are quite made up. It was all that much harder to seduce with mere empty rhetoric. Speaking to Mohan through a translator, Fujiwara found himself making little headway with slogans like "Asia for the Asiatics" or removing India's "shackles of slavery."

Mohan suspected that Japan had designs on India. He was a student of history and had digested a book on the French revolution. He knew the Japanese record in Korea, Manchuria and China. The discussions between the East Asian and the South Asian went on for a few days. Fujiwara was making little headway with intellectual arguments. Mohan was not going to be turned so easily. But the Japanese intelligence officer was not a quitter, and he knew that surest way to a Punjabi's heart is a good meal and honest camaraderie. So he hosted a Indian dinner for Mohan and his fellow Indian officers and even joined in in eating with his fingers. Mohan was genuinely moved, telling the Japanese that in the

Major Iwaichi Fujiwara

British army an English officer would never break bread with fellow Indian officers or the men of a defeated army.

Having thus softened his quarry, the intelligence officer reminded the martial Sikh that it was fighting men who shaped history. Fujiwara appealed to Mohan's sense of *izzat* and challenged him to make a decision: "What are you going to do about it? You are a soldier; it is for you to choose. Your old master is dead. If you really want freedom for your country, you must aspire to do something active. You must raise an Indian National Army."[486]

All enterprises, including mutinies and revolutions, are lit by a moment of illumination followed by conversion. After at least half a dozen meetings, Fujiwara had finally struck a spark in Captain Mohan. It dawned on the Sikh that the sepoys had been "fighting merely as deluded, befooled, mercenary heroes at the expense of poor India for the sole benefit of Britain."[487] He found himself nudged into action, reasoning that if "the British were not prepared to free us, what right they had to ask us to fight for them, when their own freedom was being threatened?"[488] Mohan and his comrades would have to fight for India's independence – and Japan could provide the support they needed. He agreed to Fujiwara's proposal to command an Indian nationalist army drawn from the ranks of the captured sepoys. The sepoy revolt of the Second World War had begun.

Major Fujiwara could thus take the credit for personally winning over Captain Mohan to the Japanese side. Before the Pacific War began in 1941, his superiors had tasked him to lead an intelligence operation to support Asian freedom movements fighting British rule. In reality, Japan had its eye on the region's lucrative natural resources, but Fujiwara knew that Japan had to show real sympathy for regional liberation movements. Fujiwara believed that successful Japanese-Indian co-operation in the Malayan sector could have a positive demonstration effect on the Indians and other Asians fighting British rule.

Fujiwara's special action cell was based in Bangkok, an important regional listening post and hub for spies. He soon became friendly with a pair of Indian freedom fighters; a young Sikh missionary named Pritam Singh Dhillon and his wispy-white-bearded mentor, Amar Singh. Pritam led the Bangkok branch of the early Indian pro-freedom movement, the Indian Independence League (IIL). His older companion, Amar, had been working as a railroad company surveyor in Thailand since the turn of the century. He was also a veteran of the IIL's revolutionary predecessor, the Ghadar Party.

When the old Ghadar revolutionary, Baba Amar Singh, stood before him, hands clasped and fire still burning in his eyes, Fujiwara felt the emotion he carried. Amar had spent a decade in prison, much of it either on death row or on the harsh Black Water penal colony on the Andaman Islands. He spoke to Fujiwara with passion and anger about the inhumanity of British rule. The old, fiery-eyed Amar Singh had reason to be emotional. He was a living ghost of the failed Ghadar Party Siamese-Burmese scheme to invade India as the as well as the larger revolt in the Punjab set for 21 February 1915. After the twin Ghadar plots were uncovered, the Sikh was rounded up with several other comrades who were also implicated in the Singapore mutiny of 1915. While Amar festered in prison on a suspended death sentence, the others were executed.

Fujiwara was impressed by the venerable revolutionary's fervour and courage, but decided to work with the younger Pritam who carried far less baggage. Even before the opening shots of the Pacific War were fired, Pritam had already organised his men to distribute propaganda leaflets among the Indians in Malaya. Fujiwara told Pritam to prime his Indian contacts across the Thai-Malayan border after Japan's attack on Pearl Harbour. As Japan launched its invasion of Malaya, Pritam flew to Southern Thailand with Fujiwara. The Sikh quickly established an outpost of the Indian Independence League across the border in Kedah, unfurling the Indian tricolour national flag. Eventually the pair would adjoin with Captain Mohan Singh.

Soon after Fujiwara secured Mohan's co-operation, the defenders in Singapore began to buckle under Japan's relentless onslaught. Pritam and Mohan worked together on propaganda leaflets, distributed by Mohan's unit of ex-sepoys to their former comrades. The Battle for Singapore did not last long as the Japanese outfought British, Commonwealth, Indian, Malay and Chinese troops. On 15 February 1942, exactly 27 years after the Sepoy Mutiny, Empire forces surrendered in Singapore, many without firing a shot.

Two days later, Major Fujiwara strode into Singapore's Farrer Park Race Course. The grounds were packed with 45,000 captured sepoys. Just before Fujiwara spoke, a Lieutenant-Colonel from Britain's Malayan Command told the sepoys: "Today, I on behalf of the British Government, hand you over to the Japanese Government whose orders you will obey henceforth as you have done ours."[489] The sepoys were riled by the arrogance shown by their defeated former imperial masters. They were being handed over like inferior beings.

Reading the mood of the sepoys, Fujiwara skilfully used the opportunity to recruit as many as he could to his cause. Addressing the men as brothers, the Japanese officer preached Asian solidarity. He asked the sepoys: "how can a brother keep a brother as a prisoner?"[490] The sepoys were invited to join Japan in creating an East Asian Co-prosperity

Sphere and a new liberation army for India. Fujiwara told the Indians that without an independent India, there would be no world peace or independence for Asia. His words roused the sepoys. The race-course resounded with their applause. Taking the floor after Fujiwara, Captain Mohan posed a stark question to his countrymen: "Who will volunteer for the freedom of India?"[491] His words struck a chord. Some of the men raised both hands. Finally, it was Pritam Singh's turn to address the sepoys. By then, the prisoners were rousing themselves with cries of *Inquilab Zindabad!* (Long Live the Revolution!), a line by the Urdu poet Maulana Hasrat Mohani made famous by Ajit Singh's revolutionary nephew Bhagat Singh, who modelled himself after the teenaged Ghadarite Kartar Singh Sarabha.

Spirits lifted by nationalistic fervour, the Indian officers were welcomed up to the racecourse pavilion where Fujiwara offered each a glass of neat brandy. This was another calculated move by the canny Japanese intelligence officer. Indian commissioned officers would not ordinarily drink with their English officers. Now over fortifying Australian brandy, Major Fujiwara assured the officers that they could openly discuss any issue with him. Although not all were convinced, about 25,000 Indian prisoners-of-war eventually enlisted in the Tokyo-sponsored Indian National Army (INA) or *Azad Hind Fauj*. Captain Mohan became their General Officer Commanding. Those who refused to join its ranks were punished, with many tortured or killed under the harsh conditions of Japanese internment.

The newly minted General Mohan Singh had charisma and passion, but he also had an impulsive side. Although he appeared to know his mind, switching sides was a calculated gamble. For the rank-and-file sepoys, they had changed loyalties for a range of reasons, and the conversion was not necessarily the product of reasoned argument. A former colonial official in India offered this construct of the mutineers' motives:

> Among the twenty-five thousand technically guilty of mutiny... motives fall into four classes. Some... joined the INA with the intention of rejoining the British forces when they saw a chance; some – and I would judge the majority – were puzzled, misinformed, misled, and on the whole believe that the course they took was the most honourable open to them. Others were frankly opportunist, some really were fervent nationalists.... (O)f course these categories were not clear-cut; there were men whose motives were thoroughly mixed.[492]

Confused minds need beacons of light. Renamed Syonan or Light of the South by Japan, Singapore provided the headquarters for the newly established INA. But it would not be all smooth sailing. The following month, Pritam Singh was killed in an air-crash en route to Tokyo. Soon after, the veteran Bengali revolutionary, Rash Behari Bose, tried to take charge and issued orders to Mohan. Bose believed he had the support of his Japanese sponsors. After fleeing to Japan following the failed 1915 mutinies, Bose had gained support from right-wing nationalist politicians and pan-Asianist groups. He identified closely with Tokyo's interests. He married a Japanese and the son from their union had even joined the Imperial Japanese Army.

General Mohan began to seriously resent his situation and reassessed his position when the old revolutionary Bose pulled rank on him. The Sikh officer suspected that he had been duped by the Japanese. They appeared uninterested in liberating India and keener to use the ex-sepoys as fodder in their harsh Burma campaign. He discovered that not only was Japan's mantra of "Asia for Asiatics" rhetoric, the reality was that he had exchanged a European master for an Asian one. The INA was beginning to fragment as its leaders squabbled and confronted their Japanese patrons. Not without his own faults, Mohan was viewed as an inflexible disciplinarian by a number of INA officers. His criticisms of the Japanese became more severe as he continued to clash with Rash Behari Bose. It was the older Bengali revolutionary who finally called the Sikh officer into the Japanese spy headquarters in Singapore to tell that he had been fired as Commander of the INA. Mohan was packed off to prison on Singapore's Pulau Ubin island by the Japanese *Kempeitai* (secret police).

In a final meeting with Fujiwara before Mohan's internment, the two men wept and hugged each other. Retaining a special affection for his work with Indian revolutionaries like Mohan, Fujiwara had consciously styled himself after Colonel T E Lawrence. His operational methods paid tribute to the English officer who had led an Arab insurgency against Ottoman power during the First World War. Britain's "Lawrence of Arabia" had exploited Arab tribesmen during the earlier global conflict with promises of independence in exchange for fighting the Ottomans. While skilfully building close but ultimately transactional relations with men like Mohan, Fujiwara cynically used the Indian sepoys to achieve Japan's broader Second World War aims.

Mohan's arrest and the collapse of the first Indian National Army took its toll on the movement. Rash Behari Bose soon fell ill. He contracted tuberculosis and his diabetes flared up. The stress was getting to him.[493] Whole factions of the INA who were close to Mohan refused to engage him. The hulking, veteran revolutionary lost weight and looked like a spent force. Even he agreed that another man was needed to lead the INA. The Japanese turned to another Bose – Subhas Chandra Bose who made his way from Germany to Singapore in July 1943 to renew the struggle and revive the Army. In Singapore, Subhas was introduced to members of the Indian Independence League by Rash Behari and then made an energetic speech to members of the League to renew the fight, exhorting them, "*Chalo* Delhi" (Let's go to Delhi).[494]

Rash Behari did not think the INA could take Delhi. It would be better off training soldiers and inspiring the movement. But he was too sick to argue his case and made his way back to Tokyo for treatment. He was proven right. After two years of fighting, thousands of INA soldiers perished in futile, pitched battles in Manipur, Assam and especially on the Burmese front. The remains of many of those killed in action were never recovered or buried. On 8 July 1945, a chastened and fatigued Subhas Chandra Bose laid the foundation stone of the INA War Memorial at Singapore's Esplanade on Connaught Drive. In his speech, Bose paid homage to the martyrs of the INA remarking that "through temporary failure they paved the way to ultimate success and glory."[495] The memorial would commemorate the INA's "Unknown Warrior".

Bose's tribute was almost an epitaph to the sepoy mutineers. Inscribed on the memorial completed a month later was the motto of the Indian National Army (INA) – *Etihaad, Etmad, Kurbani* or Unity, Faith, Sacrifice. But unity was not to be as the army of mutineers crumbled in a series of camp mutinies at the close of the Second World War. By the middle of August 1945, Subhas Chandra Bose declared the INA's end in a radio broadcast in Singapore. Three days later, he was dead in a plane crash. Rash Behari had been taken away earlier in the year after a cerebral haemorrhage. After atomic bombs on Hiroshima and Nagasaki compelled Japan's surrender on 14 August 1945, Britain negotiated a peaceful handover of Fortress Singapore. Upon his return to the island, Lord Louis Mountbatten, the Supreme Allied Commander of the Southeast Asia Command, ordered the INA Memorial destroyed. The memorial to the Unknown Warrior of the INA had stood for less than a month when preparations were made to demolish it.

On 4 September 1945, under the late afternoon sun, sepoys from Britain's 5th Indian Division took up position near the memorial.[496] The sepoys were hardened veterans of several anti-Japanese campaigns. One of them, a big and burly Naik with a sten gun, observed the operation underway with some satisfaction. The sepoys of the British Indian Army were encouraged to see the INA soldiers as Japanese Inspired Fifth Columnists, or JIFC which simply became "Jiffs". A Malay policeman kept a crowd of civilians at a safe distance. Indian army sappers positioned their guncotton charges while a British Major of the Royal Engineers checked the fuses. The fuse was lit without ceremony and the charge detonated, demolishing the memorial's foundation. Sepoys from the 17th Dogra Regiment of the 5th Indian Division used long poles to topple the monument with its largest face marked *Etmad* (Faith) pushed over to wild clapping just before 6 pm.

Mountbatten wanted to get rid of every physical trace of revolt and rebellion against the authority of the British Empire. The memorial was a reminder of sepoy defiance and the spirit of freedom against British rule. Mountbatten would not allow it to stand lest it give ideas to other independent minded subjects. But a fuse had already been lit under the base of the fast unravelling Empire as forces of communalism, rising Asian nationalism, the clashing ambitions of its leaders and the fear and confusion of the masses interacted in unpredictable ways.

Mountbatten, great-grandson of Queen Victoria, Empress of India, went on to become the British Empire's last Viceroy of India and the first and only Governor-General of Independent India. He would oversee India's transition to independence and facilitate the tragic and bloody partition of Punjab. Under his tutelage, the long-standing British policy of divide and control became a destructive, short-term goal of divide and quit. In negotiations over India's independence, Mountbatten insisted that INA soldiers could not be re-integrated in the British Indian Army. Amid communal carnage that tore apart homes of British Indian Army as well as INA sepoys, the British Empire made a rushed and embarrassed exit. Much of the violence was the work of demobilised sepoys who found themselves dragooned into mobs.

Mountbatten, the last bureaucratic incarnation of the British Raj, felt little compunction about ensuring an orderly departure in 1947. His priorities were to protect narrow British strategic and pecuniary interests, which demanded a hasty "Brexit" from the Crown Jewel of the British Empire. Never mind the human cost or the mayhem of multiple mutinies the policy would unleash. 1947 would pay back for 1857 and the redux of the mutiny started in 1907. And 1915 and its failed uprisings would be forgotten. And so it goes, until we remember not to forget.

EPILOGUE

Today's headline warnings on the dangers of inter-national terrorism are part of the background noise of our media-saturated world. The sense of chronically heightened risk to cities and global infrastructure has become wired into our neural circuits. We accept the need for stepped-up security measures and surveillance to ensure our safety and well-being. But we often fail to pause to think about the taproot triggers of terrorism or populist, anti-globalist violence.

A century after Veer Savarkar's 1907 manifesto calling for a second great mutiny, former US National Security Advisor Zbigniew Brzezinski penned a slim, prescient volume called *Second Chance*. Writing after the geopolitical disaster of the Iraq war and on the eve of the Global Financial Crisis, Brzezinski warned of declining US influence. He emphasized the risk to US standing if seen to be inheriting the mantle of British imperialism:

> Nothing could be worse for America, and eventually the world, than if American policy were universally viewed as arrogantly imperial in a postimperial age, mired in a colonial relapse in a postcolonial time, selfishly indifferent in the face of unprecedented global interdependence, and culturally self-righteous in the face of a religiously diverse world. The crisis of American superpower would then become terminal.[497]

As US President Jimmy Carter's security consigliere, Brzezinski was instrumental in mobilising Muslim *mujahideen* forces against the Soviets in Afghanistan to help win the Cold War. Just like the British and German/Ottoman rival *jihad*s politicised Islam as a proxy weapon during the First World War, the American victory paved the way for the global terror-

322

ism of Al Qaeda and Da'esh. Brzezinski might not have admitted to this complex legacy but he did discern in 2007 the emergence of a worldwide political awakening. He sensed the burgeoning of a global movement, fully aware of massive disparities, now yearning for human dignity. In Brzezinski's telling, the drive of the politically awakened masses for dignity was far stronger than their search for freedom. This was not unlike the quest for *izzat* by the men and women of the Mutiny Movement who rose up against an unjust order maintained by British imperialism.

Preserving *izzat* and dignity had roused Indians in California and North America in 1913 to start the Ghadar Party and then launch a revolt against the British Raj. Their transactional and entrepreneurial instincts notwithstanding, businessmen like Gurdit Singh and Hussain Rahim were deeply affected by the indignities of their situation and that of their fellow Asians. Why should a certain race or nationality or power have the right to enforce a tiered system of human class? The differences in race and class grated on these men. It even pushed women like Gulab Kaur and Madame Cama to join the fight for equal rights, freedom of movement and liberty.

In countering the institutionalised racism of the Raj and its tactics of religious divide and rule, the Ghadar Party or Mutiny Movement ultimately strove to remain a secular party. However, it was ideologically diverse, taking on various shadings of Marxism, anarchist and syndicalist strains over the years. With the preponderance of Sikh Punjabis among its rank and file, the Ghadar ran the risk of being seen exclusively as a Sikh organisation. To manage perceptions, some of its Hindu leadership and even Sikh notables of the revolutionary network like Ajit Singh posed as Muslims. The leadership was determined to attract a broader following and win support from the movement of geopolitical Islam. Religious identities were fluid and these markers were used for political convenience, cover or concealment. For example, the Hindu Socialist, Chagan Khairaj Varma, better known as Hussain Rahim was perfectly at ease mobilising Sikhs in their Vancouver temple while posing as a Muslim. In the case of revolutionaries like "Sufi" Amba Prasad, wearing the mantle of mystical Islam felt even more comfortable as he led ex-sepoys in forays against British troops in Persia during the First World War.

But Hindu leaders of the movement like the Marathi Veer Savarkar and the Punjabi Har Dayal could not sit comfortably or for long working with the mobilising power of Islam. While imprisoned in the Andamans, Veer Savarkar established by 1915 the basic rudiments of the revivalist Hindu nationalist movement known as the Hindu Mahasabha. Following Savarkar's lead, the Bengali Hindu roving revolutionary, Rash Behari Bose, believed that even Indian Muslims should be classified as cultural

Hindus. For the Tokyo-based Bose, men like Savarkar were patriots shoring up India's cultural independence, a prerequisite for political independence. Bose praised Savarkar for building an anti-British independence movement far more powerful than the Indian Congress Party. The results of this are now apparent today.

Equally clear is the denouement of the Ghadar Party. The last surviving member of the Ghadar, Bhagat Singh Bilga, passed away in 2009. Bilga was born when Savarkar published his 1907 manifesto on the second great mutiny. The Punjabi Sikh took a fairly typical route of an overseas Ghadar member after World War I, moving from Calcutta to Rangoon to Singapore, Hong Kong and then to Argentina. In Buenos Aires, he became friendly with Ajit Singh and ended up leading the country's Ghadar Party. Bilga was among a platoon of Mutiny Movement members sent to Moscow to study after the Soviet Union assumed patronage of part of the Ghadar Party. Returning to India to spread a Marxist-infused message of mutiny, Bilga's homeward route took him through various European capitals under the assumed name of Milky Singh before arriving in Kanpur, site of a key episode in the 1857 Mutiny. He organised strikes, an underground press and supported revolutionary communism. Bilga joined the Indian Socialist Congress Party and aligned himself with Subhas Chandran Bose in his call for armed struggle against the British.

After a lifetime of rabble-rousing, Bilga eventually helped to found a Ghadar Party Martyrs Memorial (Desh Bhagar Yaadgar) in his hometown of Jullunder, in Punjab, India. Sitting on the Grand Trunk Road, the memorial building includes an exhibition hall, a conference and reading room and a library with 17,000 books and 2,000 rare photographs. Before passing away at the age of 102, after medical treatment in England, Bilga insisted that the revolt against the Raj had been a success. Defiant until the end, he wanted it remembered as a Ghadar victory not a triumph of Gandhian civil disobedience and politics:

I have dedicated myself to this museum which has 35 other freedom fighters as its members. It traces the life of each and every Ghadari along with their photograph. We have collected them from their villages, relatives and friends, in India and abroad. And all this to tell the world that Englishmen didn't leave India because a handful of Indians threw salt into their eyes. The left because we sent them packing.[498]

The sepoys of the 5th Light Infantry in Singapore and the revolutionaries in the Punjab in 1915 did not achieve the success they envisioned. But they were carried along by a bigger tide that they may have felt in full but perhaps only half understood.

The spirit of rebellion and the demand for human dignity in the face of oppression and injustice is a universal emotion. Love and hatred can both unite, and when love is gone and hatred is no more, what remains is a shiver of a sensation, mutterings of a mutiny made into museum momentoes. Or a saga of sepoys and revolutionaries whose hidden histories I have tried to tell. Faces lost to time and the strange bends and curves of the past, but part of the broader story of the human spirit that one hopes no autocrat algorithm can master or crush.

Appendix I

The route of *Komagata Maru* and other significant places

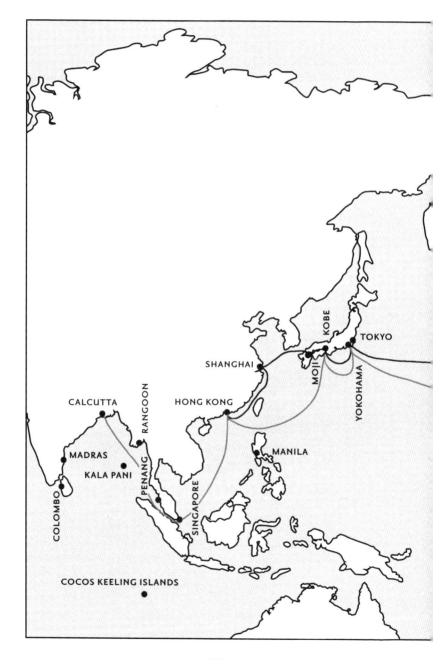

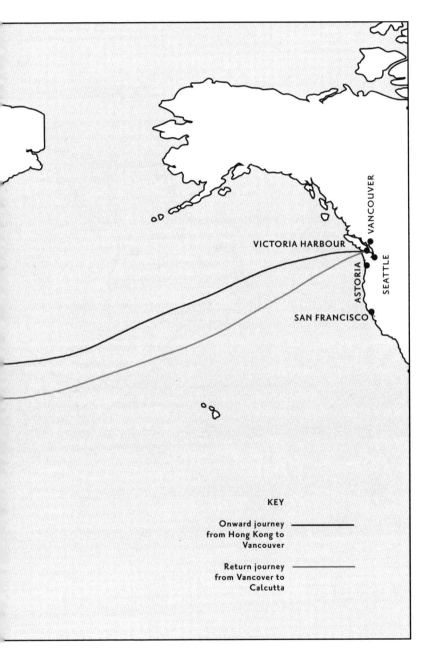

VANCOUVER

VICTORIA HARBOUR

ASTORIA

SEATTLE

SAN FRANCISCO

KEY

Onward journey
from Hong Kong to
Vancouver

Return journey
from Vancover to
Calcutta

Significant points in the Singapore Mutiny

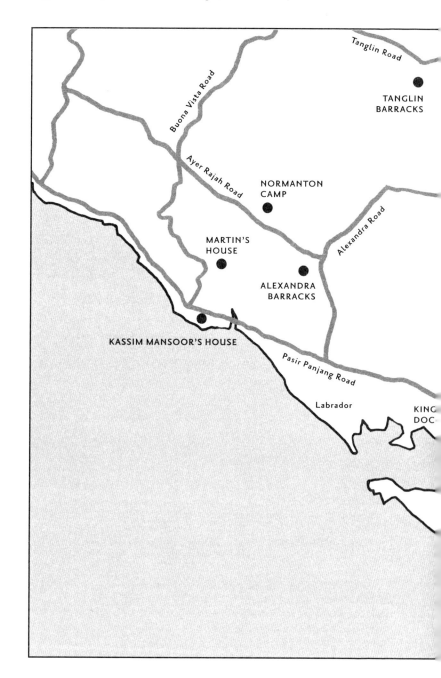

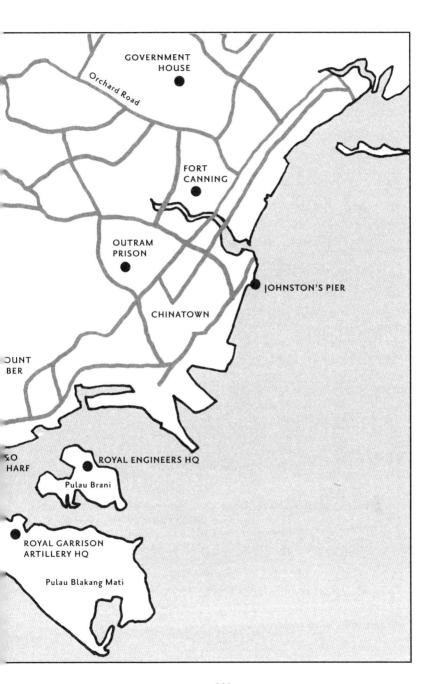

GOVERNMENT
HOUSE

Orchard Road

FORT
CANNING

OUTRAM
PRISON

JOHNSTON'S PIER

CHINATOWN

OUNT
BER

ROYAL ENGINEERS HQ

Pulau Brani

O
HARF

ROYAL GARRISON
ARTILLERY HQ

Pulau Blakang Mati

329

Appendix III

British Indian Army Rank System

VICEROY COMMISSIONED OFFICERS

Subedar-Major = Captain-Major
Risaldar-Major = Captain-Major in Cavalry
Subedar = Captain
Jemadar = Lieutenant

NON-COMMISSIONED OFFICERS

Havildar-Major = Sergeant-Major
Colour-Havildar = Colour-Sergeant
Havildar = Sergeant
Lance-Havildar = Corporal First Class
Naik = Corporal
Lance-Naik = Lance-Corporal
Sepoy = Private
Sowar = Private in Cavalry

Eight Viceroy Commissioned Officers commanded companies of men, lettered from A to H with four pairs of British-commanded double-companies numbered from one to four. Double Companies 1 and 2 formed the Ranghar right-wing of the battalion while 3 and 4 were the Pathan left-wing.

Appendix IV

5th Light Infantry Chain of Command

COMMANDING OFFICER
Lieutenant-Colonel Edward Victor Martin

DEPUTY COMMANDING OFFICER
Major William L Cotton

Ranghar Right Wing
No. 1 & No. 2 Double Company

A & B COY COMMANDER
Major William L Cotton

C & D COY COMMANDER
Captain Lionel Plomer Ball

Pathan Left Wing
No. 3 & No. 4 Double Company

E & F COY COMMANDER
Lieutenant Harold Seymour Elliott

G & H COY COMMANDER
Captain William Draper Hall

BATTALION ADJUTANT
Lieutenant Wyndham G Strover

SUBEDAR-MAJOR
Khan Mohammed Khan

A & B Companies	*C & D Companies*	*E & F Companies*	*G & H Companies*
Subedar Dunde Khan	Subedar Wahid Ali Khan	Subedar Bahadur	Subedar Sharaf-ud-din
Subedar Mohd Yunus Khan	Jemadar Chiste Khan	Jemadar Aziz-ud-din	Subedar Suleiman Khan
Jemadar Abdul Ali Khan	Jemadar Hoshiar Ali	Jemadar Hans Raj	Jemadar Ghulam Haidar
Jemadar Rehmat Khan (also Acting Native Adjutant)			

INDIAN REVOLUTIONARIES

Abdul Hafiz Mohamed Barakatullah Islamist Ghadar Party revolutionary who won the first converts to Islam in Japan, worked briefly for the Ghadar in San Francisco and became the first Prime Minister of the Indian revolutionary government in exile in Afghanistan in 1915.

Ajit Singh Leader of 1907 Punjab Pagri Sambhal Jatta movement and later itinerant revolutionary, also paternal uncle of Kartar Singh Sarabha. Ajit Singh alias Mirza Hassan Khan alias Marshall Antonio Farias escaped the British dragnet in Persia. He made it to Geneva under the assumed name of Mirza Hassan Khan. He left Paris in 1913 and went to Argentina to support the Ghadar party efforts. By 1929, he settled in Brazil after chicken farming in Argentina for eight years. In 1930, after his nephew Bhagat Singh's hanging for his revolutionary activities in India, the Ghadar party tried to get Ajit to California to boost their profile. An avid reader, he donated 5,000 books to the Ghadar party library in Buenos Aires. Traveling on a Brazilian passport he was in Berlin at the start of the Second World War and extended his wide contacts through business in Italy to INA leader Subhas Chandra Bose. After 38 years in exile, he returned to India a year before independence. He died in August 1947, with his last words recorded: "Thank God, my mission is fulfilled and I am leaving this world."

Bhagwan Singh Jakh Wrestler-Preacher and Ghadar Party revolutionary who worked in Malaya, Hong Kong and North America. After a sojourn in Japan where he linked up with Rash Behari Bose followed by Korea, Bhagwan was arrested by the British in 1916. He was tried in 1917 in the Indo-German conspiracy trial in San Francisco when he was indicted of conspiracy against the United Kingdom. Bhagwan served eighteen months of prison time at the McNeill Island Federal Penitentiary. He later founded institutes in the US and in India to promote his personal development philosophy. Although written with the benefit of historical hindsight, a key lesson Bhagwan took with him from the Malay States was "to concentrate on organising and awakening Indians abroad and leave the military alone, save premature mutinies, needless sacrifices and outline a pattern of future activities." Bhagwan wrote these words with an eye to his legacy, and the full knowledge that the mutinies of 1915 had gone nowhere.

Bhai Parmanand A roving Punjabi Hindu revolutionary, loyal friend and supporter of Har Dayal believed to be mentor to Kartar Singh Sarabha. Bhai Parmanand was released from penal servitude in 1920 and remained loyal to his friend Har Dayal despite his conversion. He remained extremely bitter about Nawab Khan's betrayal in particular.

Bhikaji Cama Socialist and Parsi Indian Freedom fighter based in Paris and close associate of Veer Savarkar and other pre-World War One Indian revolutionaries in Europe. She was a strong supporter of gender equality. She died in 1936.

Ghulam Hussain aka Thakur Das Indian revolutionary who was an associate of Ajit Singh and Sufi Amba and a mentor to Nawab Khan after he fell out with his first mentor Hussain Rahim.

Gobind Behari Lal Relative of Har Dayal and early Ghadar revolutionary who would later become first Indian American to win the Pulitzer Prize for journalism.

Gulab Kaur Female Indian Ghadarite who left Manila to join the insurgency in the Punjab. Gulab Kaur was arrested in Nauda Singh Wala village not long after her return to India where she posed as the wife of a returning undercover insurgent. She was tortured in Lahore's Shahi Quila prison and died in 1931.

Gurdit Singh Sikh businessman and Ghadar revolutionary based in Singapore and Malayan States who chartered the *Komagata Maru* steamer to challenge Canada's exclusionary immigration laws. Gurdit Singh escaped after Budge Budge and was a fugitive for seven years before he surrendered himself and served a five-year term. He turned again to political activism after his release and was arrested several times in the 1930s. A British intelligence bureau report in 1932 described him in disparaging terms thus: "Gurdit Singh is a man of little intelligence and he suffers from an inflated idea of his own importance and that of his "Komagata Maru" venture, but his lurid past has given him a position among Sikh extremists. He is an irreconcilable opponent of Government and more or less involved in every form of extremist agitation in the Punjab. Description: Age about 65 years (1932); medium height; strong build; wheat complexion; white beard; wears khaddar clothes and a black pugree." Gurdit Singh stood for elections in the Punjab Assembly, lost and then dedicated himself to shaping his legacy. Gurdit pushed for a memorial to the passengers of the *Komagata Maru* in Budge Budge, Calcutta, completed in 1952 and unveiled by Nehru. He died aged 95, just twenty days after a final reunion with his fellow passengers.

Har Dayal Delhi-born Punjabi, anarchist, Ghadar Party revolutionary and early Indian freedom fighter. Chief among the Indian revolutionaries of the Ghadar party, Har Dayal would be the most prominent one to recant his support for toppling the British Raj. He grew disillusioned first with Turkey and then with Germany. He made his away to Sweden by the end of the First World War. Giving up his German passport, he started learning Swedish to add to his portfolio of thirteen languages. In March 1919, a month before British forces carred out the Jallianwala Bagh massacre in Amritsar, he sent an open letter to a London-based journal entitled "Mr Har Dayal's Confession of Faith." In his letter, he swore his conversion to the principle of imperial unity and loyalty to the British Empire. He attacked the Germans as arrogant megalomaniacs and uncultivated barbarians while affirming that "England has a moral and historical mission in Asia." After repeated attempts, he was given permission to return to London where he arrived in 1927. He was accompanied by the Swedish Agda Erikson and settled down to academic work. He marred the Swede while still legally married to his Indian wife Sundar. In 1938, he returned to the US to lecture. He had failed to get a full amnesty from the British but had applied to be allowed to return to India to see his first wife and daughter, Shanti, whom he had never seen. In the US, he went to see his old friend Professor Van Wyck Brooks who recalled that he: "came out to Connecticut to spend a day, sitting upright in his chair with a bunch of red roses in his hand for my wife and with the white teeth still gleaming in his dusky face. That week the British government had given him permission to go home again and he murmured, half incredulously, over and over, 'The road to India is open.' Ten days later, however, he was dead. At that moment he was only fifty-four years old, but his heart stopped in Philadelphia."

Harnam Singh 'Tundilat' Ex-sepoy, poet and bodyguard of Har Dayal and insurgent after departing Oregon for India. The one-armed Harnam Singh served six years in the Andamans followed by nine years in other jails in India. In 1930, like Sohan Singh Bhakna, he won freedom on medical grounds but served another jail term during the Second World War. In 1947, just before the bloody Partition of the Punjab, the Sikh revolutionary helped Muslims from his village get to safety in refugee camps. He published three acclaimed books of poetry in Punjabi and Urdu and died in 1962.

Hauswirth, Frieda Swiss writer, painter and traveler who attracted Har

Dayal and Taraknath Das and who would marry another Indian revolutionary, Saranghadar Das. She and her husband were called as witnesses to the Indo-German trials in San Francisco in 1918. In later life, she wrote a biography of her experiences and the challenges she encountered in a mixed marriage, *A Marriage to India*. She became a noted painter and spent her last years in California where she died in 1974.

Hussain Rahim aka Chagan Varma Gujarati businessman, Socialist and revolutionary who settled in Canada and headed the *Komagata Maru* Shore Committee. Hussain continued to stay active in socialist and radical politics in Vancouver until his death in 1937.

Jowala Singh Ghadar revolutionary and wealthy businessman in California known as the "Potato King" who also established the first Sikh temple in the United States. Returned with the Ghadar revolutionaries to India in 1914. On arrival in Calcutta he was arrested, spent some time in prison in Singapore where he was interrogated and eventually served 18 years in jail in India. Released in 1933, he took up the rights of farmers and started a newspaper. He was arrested again in 1935 and jailed for a year. He returned to activism and, enroute to a conference for representatives for farmers, his bus met with an accident. He died from his injuries in 1938.

Kanshi Ram Punjabi Hindu labour contractor who was a founding member of Ghadar party and who was executed in India in 1914.

Kartar Singh Sarabha Teenaged revolutionary, Ghadar press worker and University of California in Berkeley Chemistry student who returned to India to become an insurgent and was later executed.

Nawab Khan A Muslim Ghadar founding party member who would play a key role in the destiny of the 1915 revolt in India. It is not clear what happened to Nawab Khan. He survived an assassination attempt while giving evidence at the Indo-German trials in San Francisco, then disappeared from the historical record whether on witness protection or for his own safety.

Rash Behari Bose Bengali and revolutionary leader of underground Bengali network known as Yugantar (new era) and mastermind of assassination attempt on British Viceroy Lord Charles Hardinge in India. Rash Behari Bose alias Taguchi Yutaka alias William Dull alias Ichiro Hayashi alias P N Thakur lived a life full of twists and turns, escaping the British dragnet in 1915 and stopping over in Singapore on the way to his exile in Japan. He evaded British agents who tried to harm him. He sought refuge in a bakery in Shinjuku, Tokyo, when chased by British intelligence in 1915. He eventually married the Japanese daughter of the owners of Nakamuraya Bakery who were supporters of pan-Asianism, and had a son and a daughter with her. The ultra-nationalist Toyama Mitsuru, the leader of the Black Dragon secret society, gave Bose complete protection from any extradition by the British. Bose became a Japanese citizen in 1923, and his wife died a year later. Bose remained close to this father-in-law and introduced Indian curry to Japan – Indo Karii Nakamuraya – which was served and continues to be served at the bakery with his recipe. He continued with his revolutionary activities against the British. One of the author's great-granduncles, Harbaksh Singh, a Ghadarite, was part of his broad network and corresponded with him. Bose returned to Singapore to shape the early INA but handed over the movement to Subhas Chandra Bose. His son was killed fighting for the Imperial Japanese Army on Okinawa, and he received the Order of the Rising Sun, Second Class in 1945. A few days later on 21 January 1945, Bose died of tuberculosis. He spoke his last words during an American air-raid on Tokyo, calling out the names of his two children.

Sohan Singh Bhakna First President of the Ghadar party in San Francisco. Sohan was transferred from the Andamans in 1921 but spent another nine years in prison. He did not give up agitating for India's freedom, was jailed during the Second World War and drifted towards Communism. He was arrested twice after Indian independence before given amnesty by the founding Indian Prime Minister Jawaharlal Nehru. He died of pneumonia in Amritasar, aged 98.

"Sufi" Amba Prasad The one-handed Hindu revolutionary who became a Sufi and fought the British in Persia. He worked closely with Ajit Singh and, after Ajit's departure, he worked with the Indian revolutionaries of the Berlin Committee in Iraq and Iran. He spread anti-British propaganda among sepoys fighting in Iraq. Captured sepoys were assembled in a special force under his charge making forays into the western border of India from Iran right up to Punjab. The rebel sepoys harassed British troops throughout the First World War until Baghdad was captured by the British. Sufi Amba and his rebel sepoys were defeated in Shiraz in 1917 and it was said that he killed himself before capture or died during battle. His writings influenced Kartar Singh's nephew Bhagat Singh. A memorial stands in his memory in Iran.

Taraknath Das Emissary of a Bengali revolutionary leader, anti-British revolutionary. Taraknath was indicted in the Indo-Germany Conspiracy Trial in San Francisco in 1917, along with 16 other Ghadar Party members and 17 German-Americans or German diplomats. He was labelled a most dangerous criminal by the jury, almost lost his American citizenship and just about avoided being handed over to the British. He was sentenced to 22 months in Leavenworth Federal Prison. After his release, he married his long-time companion Mary Keatinge Morse, who was a founding member of the

National Association for the Advancement of Colored People. He became a professor of political science at Columbia University and started an educational trust for Indian students in Columbia with his wife.

Vinayak Damodar 'Veer' Savarkar Maharashtrian born Indian revolutionary who was a member of the Abhinav Bharat secret society, started the Free India Society in London and popularised the concept of a new Indian mutiny and, later, Hindutva, an ideology seeking to establish the hegemony of Hindus and the Hindu way of life. Veer Savarkar made several petitions for release from the the Kala Pani in the Andamans and was finally transferred to a mainland jail in 1921 after serving 11 years in the penal colony, and then released altogether in 1924. He became an implacable opponent of Gandhi and what he considered appeasement of the Muslims. After independence, the main airport on the Andamans was renamed Veer Savarkar International Airport. Veer Savarkar's shaping of political Hinduism as he suffered in the penal colony of the Andamans has stood the test of time. It forms part of the creed of the current Indian ruling party, with the paramilitary group Rashtriya Swayamsevak Sangh co-founded by Veer's brother Ganesh. A half century after its dissolution by Veer, the Abhinav Bharat Society was revived by right wing Hindu ex-army officers in 2006. The secret society became part of the wave of so-called "saffron terror" defending Hindu rights. Its acts of violence against Muslims led to its designation in India as a terror group. In 2010, a full-size replica of London's India House where Veer plotted against the Empire was built in Gujarat to honour him.

MALAYAN AND SINGAPORE RESIDENTS

Abu Bakar bin Haji Arshad Sergeant of the Singapore Malay Volunteers Infantry. Abu Bakar retired after 25 years of service as a Captain and a Member of the British Empire (MBE). After the Singapore *jihad*-mutiny, he took part in the expedition to put down the Tok Janggut uprising in Kelantan.

Braddell, Roland Lawyer, prosecutor in mutiny court-martials.

Brown, Edwin A (Captain) Entrepreneur and Company Commander of Chinese Singapore Volunteer Company. Wrote a joint memoir of his experiences of the Singapore Mutiny with his wife Mary.

Chan Chon Hoe The boy from Chinatown, Chan Chon Hoe, who witnessed the mutiny executions of 1915, went on to live a full life. A life spanning Singapore's history into the early years of the 21st century. The life-long Boy Scout maintained his vigour and fitness into his nineties, completing 10-

km walks right up to the time of his passing. The memory of a mutineer's calm and dignified face seconds before his execution had stayed with Chan Chon Hoe - a reminder of composure in the face of extinction. When the pioneer Singaporean succumbed to pneumonia in 2003, his family also had to keep a brave face. No funeral wake or last rites were performed for his funeral because Singapore was in the grip then of the Severe Acute Respiratory Syndrome (SARS) crisis.

Daud Sulaiman Major of the Johor Military Forces.

Ibrahim of Johor, Sultan The Sultan was deeply upset that, in the words of his private secretary, "no recognition whatever has been accorded either to the Officers or men (of the Johor Military Force)" for their work done during the mutiny. No recognition had been given to any of the local officers or men "though Decorations were awarded to a British Officer in the Johor Military Service who in fact never left the State at all during the War." In 1930, the Sultan had a 70-page memorandum prepared on the work of the JMF and sent it to the War Office in London. His secretary received a polite thank you letter a week later stating that the material would form a "valuable addition" to the record on the work of the JMF. But it was decided that the memorandum would be "closed until 1966" to the public. The report makes for embarrassing reading for the British authorities, highlighting the woeful lack of preparations for hand-over duties when the JMF took over duties at Tanglin Barracks guarding the German camp.

Jagat Singh, Dr Influential Sikh and Punjabi community leader in Perlis and the Malay States, and Ghadar sympathizer. Dr Jagat Singh was tried on four serious charges including abetting the waging of war against the King and seditious comments amounting to treason in Penang in June 1915. His role in many ways eclipsed that of Kassim Ismail Mansoor among the Sikhs and Punjabis. However, such was his influence and clout in the Malayan Sikh community that it was felt better not to make a martyr of him during war-time. He was made to pay 2,000 dollars security to avoid banishment from the Straits Settlements. He even attended the farewell party held by the Sikh community in Queen Street gurdwara in January 1916 for the Colonial Secretary R J Wilkinson. He returned to Punjab in 1918 and was confined to his village until he was allowed to return to Perlis the following year. He ended up becoming the largest landowner in Perlis before independence and a leader of the Malayan Sikh community. He owned large tracts of land in Kedah and Penang as well. He died in 1956.

Kassim Ismail Mansoor Wealthy Gujerati businessman who entertained Malay police officers and Muslim sepoys in his Pasir Panjang bungalow and was accused and convicted of sedition.

Knowles, Vincent Devereu Defence Lawyer for Kassim Mansoour.

Le Doux, Jacques Alfonse British planter in Johor.

Nicholson, John Rumney Chairman of Tanjong Pagar Harbour Board.

Nur Alam Shah Kampong Java Mosque preacher and suspected Ghadar revolutionary.

Tan Boo Liat Singapore community leader and supporter of Chinese republican revolutionary leader Dr Sun Yat Sen.

Tan Jiak Kim A leader of Singapore Chinese community and great-grandfather of future Singapore President Tony Tan.

Woolcombe, Mrs Belfield Morel *nee* **Michie, Marjorie** Only female killed in Singapore Mutiny.

Yeo Bian Chuan Singapore Chinese businessman living in Pasir Panjang Road. Towkay Yeo continued to press the Government in Singapore to recognise his effort to protect the 17 British who sought refuge in his Pasir Panjang home during the mutiny. The Chief Secretary of the Federated Malay States W G Maxwell supported his endeavours in 1920, writing that he "behaved very well indeed in sheltering a number of Europeans" and that his action ought to be recognised by the Colonial and not the Imperial government. However, other colonial officials felt that he was exaggerating his role. He was finally offered a choice of $5,000 or a commemorative medal. He was not after money but due recognition. He chose the medal but it was never presented to him. For some British colonial officials, it may have been too much to stomach that it should be formally acknowledged that an Asian subject of His Majesty had to protect 17 British from harm or death. General Ridout was the key obstruction to Towkay Yeo's official recognition. According to correspondence between the Straits Settlements Government and the Colonial Office, Ridout "was strongly opposed to any further recognition on the ground that there were numerous other acts of self-sacrificing help performed by Asiatics at the same time and that it would be invidious to give special prominence to this occurrence." Yeo died in October 1929, without formal recognition, and just two weeks after the death of his wife to whom he was deeply attached.

BRITISH OFFICIALS AND SOLDIERS

Brownlow, Charles William (Lieutenant-Colonel) Commanding Officer, Royal Garrison Artillery Hong Kong and Singapore Regiment on Pulau Blakang Mati. Brownlow was appointed President of the court-martial proceedings for the mutiny. After the mutiny, he led 160 King Shropshire Light Infantry soldiers, 50 Royal Garrison Artillery, the Malay company of Singapore Volunteers and the Malay States Guides to help put down the rebellion of Tok Janggut, chief of Pasir Puteh in Kelantan in the Malay States. He retired from the military in 1919 and stayed on in Singapore. He died in 1924, shunning publicity and living quietly with his wife and daughter.

Dickinson, Arthur Harold Straits Settlements Police Cadet Inspector. The young police cadet went on to become acting director of criminal intelligence and acting director of the Political Intelligence Bureau by 1928. He focussed his attention on the Communist threat in the region. Appointed in 1939 as Inspector General of Police, Straits Settlements and Civil Security Officer, he was interned during the Japanese Occupation and remained with the police until three weeks after his release from Changi Prison. The mutiny he experienced as a young cadet had a formative experience on his outlook and shaped his later police and intelligence work. He died in 1978.

Hopkinson, William Charles Vancouver Immigration Inspector, Calcutta Police and interpreter for Hindi and Punjabi, headed British secret intelligence activities in North America monitoring Indian revolutionaries.

Jerram, Martyn (Vice-Admiral) Commander of Royal Navy China Station and based in Singapore during the First World War.

Kothavala, Hector Bombay Parsi police officer who helped set up British Intelligence network in Singapore and Far East after the mutiny.

Lees, Charles Henry Brownlow (Lieutenant-Colonel) Commanding Officer, Malay States Guides.

Maxwell, William George Secretary of Federated Malay States, Sir Arthur Young's deputy in Malaya.

Mclean, Moira (Captain) Texan-born Commander of Malay States Guides Mule Battery.

Olliver, Cecil Orme (Lieutenant) Son-in-law of GOC of Straits Settlements General Stephenson and a Royal Garrison Artillery officer under Lieutenant-Colonel Brownlow.

Ridout, Dudley (Brigadier-General) Commanding Officer of Royal Engineers detachment on Pulau Brani and later General Officer Commanding Troops Straits Settlements. General Ridout retired to Richmond in Surrey. His home was bombed during the Second World War and he lost all his records of the Singapore Mutiny, as he reported. He died in 1941, aged 75, from a heart attack.

Wilkinson, Richard James Colonial Secretary of Straits Settlements, Sir Arthur Young's overall deputy. Wilkinson left Singapore in January 1916 to take up the position of Governor of Sierra Leone.

Young, Arthur (Sir) Governor-General of Singapore and Straits Settlements and High Commissioner of Federated Malay States (FMS). Arthur Young died in 1938 aged 84.

5TH LIGHT INFANTRY

The remnants of the Fifth Light Infantry were reconstituted by adding a Hindu wing of Ahirs to replace the Ranghars, but was organised as a smaller force of only six instead of eight companies. It arrived in West Africa (German Cameroon) in August 1915 to fight the Germans and redeem itself under its newly promoted Commanding Officer Lieutenant Colonel William L Cotton. The Fifth Light Infantry ceased to exist after 1922.

British King's Commissioned Officers

Ball, Lionel Plomer (Captain) Originally Australian and Ranghar No. 2 Double Company Commander. Ball continued with a long military career and received Distinguished Service Orders for action in combat in East Africa.

Cotton, William L (Major) Second-in-Command, 5th Light Infantry. Cotton handed over command of the battalion in 1917 and saw action in East Africa. He retired in 1926 and died in 1963, aged 92 years.

Hall, William Draper (Captain) Pathan No. 4 Double (G and H) Company Commander. Hall won Distinguished Service Orders for actions in combat in East Africa and continued with a long military career. He led repeated bayonet charges in Lutende in German East Africa to extricate his unit.

Martin, Edward Victor (Lieutenant-Colonel) Commanding Officer, 5th Light Infantry. Lieutenant Colonel Martin cut a sad, tragic and lonely figure after the mutiny. The 5th's officers were all stationed at the Hotel De

L'Europe during the court of inquiry hearings. He was rebuffed by all his officers and treated rudely even by junior men. After the 5th left Singapore, he returned to England to command an infantry recruiting depot in its southeast for a few months during the war until his retirement in December 1915. He retired to an elegant Georgian Palladian style home on 45, Rouge Bouillon Parish of St Helier in the Island of Jersey. He got as far away as it is possible to get from mainland UK while remaining on British territory. On 11 August 1927 he made his will, bequeathing his entire property to his daughter Kathleen Muriel Martin. He died in 1935.

Morrison, R V (Lieutenant) Medical Officer.

Strover, Wyndham G. (Lieutenant) Battalion Adjutant and son of a former British Political Agent in Mandalay. The ambitious Lieutenant Strover served under William Cotton in German Cameroon where Strover had an indifferent campaign with no accolades. He served with the 50th Kumaon Rifles, and then the 16th Punjab Regiment, reaching the rank of Major. Strover died in a freak drowning accident in July 1930 at the age of 43. He was watching a Sailing Cup Race from a yacht at the Secunderabad (Hyderabad) Boating Club. Strover was with an experienced ship captain and the boat's pilot. A sudden gust of wind capsized the yacht and Strover and the two men swam for shore. The ship's captain made it but Strover and the boat's pilot were entangled in weeds and drowned. It took four days to find and release his body which was caught fast in the weeds.

Indian Viceroy-Commissioned Officers

Ali, Hoshiar (Jemadar) Ranghar C Company Deputy Commander who wavered between factions.

Khan, Abdul Ali (Jemadar) Ranghar and mutiny ring-leader, guard commander at Tanglin German POW camp, regimental scouts officer.

Khan, Chiste (Jemadar) Mutiny ring-leader. Ranghar D Company Deputy Commander, rival of Wahid and follower of preacher Nur Alam Shahid.

Khan, Dunde (Subedar) Mutiny ring-leader. Ranghar B Company commander.

Khan, Khan Mohammed (Subedar-Major) Native Regimental Sergeant Major and Ranghar. He was censured for his cowardice during the mutiny and cashiered out.

Khan, Muhammed Yunus (Subedar) Ranghar A Company Commander close to both Ranghar factions.

Khan, Rehmat (Colour Havildar) Native Adjutant from A Company. Khan was promoted to Jemadar and served under the Mula Jat Subedar Hans Raj. As Jemadar, he won the Indian Distinguished Service Medal.

Khan, Sharaf-ud-din (Subedar) Pathan H Coy Commander. British loyalist.

Khan, Wahid Ali (Subedar) Ranghar D Company Commander and rival of mutiny ringleaders. Wahid Ali became the Subedar Major of the 5th Light Infantry and earned a citation for conspicuous gallantry in action on 30 June 1917. According to the citation: "He commanded his platoon with great gallantry and skill against a superior enemy force at close range. Though exposed to very heavy rifle and machine-gun fire he beat off numerous enemy attacks and counter charged them. Throughout the action he displayed great courage and devotion to duty. He was mentioned in dispatches." Wahid Ali was the only Indian officer from the Ranghar right-wing to survive the mutiny and consequent purge.

Raj, Hans (Jemadar) Mula Jat. Pathan E Company Deputy Commander.

Indian NCOs and Other Ranks

Ali, Manowar (Sepoy) Pathan E Company sepoy and Ottoman enthusiast.

Khan, Feroze (Lance-Naik) C Company Ranghar and regimental hothead, regimental scout, athlete and hockey player.

Khan, Imtiaz Ali (Colour Havildar) A Company Ranghar denied promotion thrice and deputy guard commander at German camp.

Khan, Ismail (Sepoy) Ranghar from C Company who fired the first shot of the Singapore Mutiny.

Khan, Jamalludin (Havildar) Pathan from F Company and Guard Commander on the day of the Singapore mutiny.

Khan, Munshi (Naik) Ranghar B Company NCO who led mutineers to Johor and was among the largest group executed.

Khan, Rahmat (Colour Havildar) Loyalist Ranghar from D Company.

GERMANS

Diehn, August Leader of German community in Singapore and Head of Diehn, Meyer and Company.

Hanke German internee in Singapore and amateur artist.

Lauterbach, Julius (**Leutanant**) Prize Officer of SS *Emden*. Julius Lauterbach escaped from Singapore to Sumatra and then finally back to Germany from Sumatra after an epic journey. He was hailed as a hero and given the Iron Cross First Class and became the subject of a popular biography called *Lauterback of the China Sea* by Lowell Thomas, the man who made Lawrence of Arabia famous. He commanded another raider and had a distinguished naval career. He died in Germany in 1937.

Von Müller, Karl (**Captain**) Captain of SS *Emden*. Karl von Müller was a prisoner of war for the duration of the First World War after his capture at the end of 1914. The "gentleman of war" who insisted on chivalric conduct wrote a prescient letter to his parents as a POW towards the close of the war in 1918. It is worth quoting at some length:

> I fear for our times. The Great War has cut down the Russian monarchy, and it will fell both of our allied empires too. Later they may be reestablished and united, but it will surely happen under the evil banner of nationalistic fanatics who will trigger another great war that will scourge Europe and the world and inflict far higher human cost. And when that second great world war comes to an end the terrible weapons it will surely spawn – weapons much worse than our already terrible killing machines – will certainly grip the entire world in fear.

Müller knew all about sowing fear and confusion. He was prepared to accept Germany's responsibility for the cataclysm of history triggered by First World War. He looked into the future and saw a pile-up of potential disasters in the making: "There will never be peace in our time. Alas, we played our role in starting all of this in 1914 – we were so naïve and unexpecting. But all of us in every country opened this terrorizing Pandora's Box."

Bibliography

ARCHIVAL SOURCES

Imperial War Museum, London
India Office Records, British Library, London
Library and Archives Canada
National Archives of Singapore
Singapore National Library Board online archive (NewspaperSG)
The National Archives, Kew
CO 273/435, Colonial Office: Straits Settlements original correspondence, Offices: war and miscellaneous 1915, parts 1 and 2.
CO 273/564/6, Towkay Yeo Bian Chuan's account of what took place at his Bungalow on the night of February 15th, 1915.
CO 60716, Prostitution in Colony, 19 December 1916, pp 481-512.
FCO141/16054, Singapore: Proposed reduction of the Singapore garrison; Unrest among Northern Indians in the Federated Malay States.
FCO 141/16205, Singapore: possible redeployment of Major General Reade, general officer commanding the troops.
FCO141/16530, Singapore: Mutiny of the 5th Native Light Infantry (Singapore Mutiny); execution of 22 mutineers on 25 March 1915.
FCO 141/16534, Singapore: Mutiny of the 5th Native Light Infantry (Singapore Mutiny); Future and Disposal Of The 5th Native Light Infantry.
FCO 141/16535, Singapore: Mutiny of the 5th Native Light Onfantry (Singapore Mutiny); record of sentences passed on mutineers.
FCO 141/16537, Singapore: Mutiny of the 5th Native Light Infantry (Singapore Mutiny); report on unaccounted men on the regiment's departure for the Cameroons.
FCO 141/16538, Singapore: Mutiny of the 5th Native Light Infantry (Singapore Mutiny); unaccounted men reported to be in Bangkok.
FCO 141/16539, Singapore: Mutiny of the 5th Native Light Infantry (Singapore Mutiny); Cypher Messages Between the Governor of The Straits Settlements And The Viceroy of India.
IOR/L/MIL/7/17023, Collection 405/17, Confidential review reports on Indian Army units for 1913-1914; despatch regarding unfavourable reports on certain British officers.
IOR/L/MIL/17/19/48, Report in Connection with Mutiny of 5th Light Infantry

BIBLIOGRAPHY

at Singapore 1915.
WO32/3630, Straits Settlements. Memorandum on The Work of Johore Military
Forces During Disturbances at Singapore in 1915, 26 July 1930.
WO 95/5451, War Diaries of 5th Light Infantry.

NEWSPAPERS, PERIODICALS

Malaya Tribune
The New York Times
San Francisco Call
The Singapore Free Press and Mercantile Advertiser
The Straits Times
http://komagatamarujourney.ca/newspapers/32
http://www.saadigitalarchive.org/

SELECT SECONDARY SOURCES

Ban Kah Choon, *Absent history: the untold story of Special Branch operations in Singapore 1915-1942*. Singapore: Raffles, 2001.
Barooah, Nirode K., *Chatto: The Life and Times of an Indian Anti-Imperialist in Europe*. Delhi: Oxford University Press, 2004.
Beckett, Ian F. W., 'The Singapore Mutiny of 1915.' *Journal of the Society for Army Historical Research*, Vol. 62, No. 251, 1984, *JSTOR*, www.jstor.org/stable/44226425.
Bernhardi, Friedrich von, *Germany and the Next War*. New York: Longmans, Green, and Co., 1914.
Bhatti, F. M., 'East Indian Immigration Into Canada, 1905-1973', Thesis presented for the degree of Doctor of Philosophy at the University of Surrey, 1974, http://epubs.surrey.ac.uk/847163/1/10797541.pdf, retrieved on 1 May 2019.
Bird, Isabella, *The Golden Chersonese*, Vol 11. London: Konnemann 2000 reprint.
Bose, A. C., *Indian Revolutionaries Abroad, 1905–1927: Select Documents*. New Delhi: Northern Book Centre, 2002.
Braddell, Roland St. John, *The Lights of Singapore*. London: Methuen, 1934.
Brown, Emily C., *Har Dayal, Hindu Revolutionary and Rationalist*. Tucson: The University of Arizona Press, 1975.
Brown, Giles, 'The Hindu Conspiracy, 1914-1917', *Pacific Historical Review*, Vol. 17, No. 3, August 1948.
Brooks, Van Wyck, *An Autobiography*. New York: E. P. Dutton, 1965.
Campbell, Peter, 'East Meets Left: South Asian Militants and the Socialist Party of Canada in British Columbia, 1904-1914.' *International Journal of Canadian Studies*, 9/1/1999.
Chandler, Edmund, *The Sepoy*. London: John Murray, 1919.
Cowen, John, 'Extracts From A Report Upon Public Prostitution in Singapore', *The Shield*, 3rd Series, 1, 1916.
Das, S., *India, Empire, and First World War Culture: Writings, Images, and Songs*. Cambridge: Cambridge University Press, 2018. DOI:10.1017/978113996324.
Dharmavira, Lala, *Har Dayal and Revolutionary Movements of His Times*. India Book Company, 1970.

346

Dickinson A. H., 'The Mutiny of the 5th Light Infantry', unpublished typescript prepared for Royal Commonwealth Society, London, Imperial War Museum Library Papers.

Dignan, Don K., 'The Hindu Conspiracy in Anglo-American Relations During World War I' in *Pacific Historical Review* Vol. 40, No. 1, 1971.

Fecitt, Harry, 'Atonement – The 5th Light Infantry Regiment in German Kamerun August 1915 to February 1916.' April 2015, http://gweaa.com/wp-content/uploads/2013/08/Atonement-5LI-in-German-Kamerun.pdf.

Fecitt, Harry, "The 5th Light Infantry in East Africa." April 2015. Accessed via http://gweaa.com/wp-content/uploads/2012/02/5LI-in-East-Africa.pdf

Gill, Singh Naranjan, *Story of the INA*. New Delhi: Publications Division, Ministry of Information and Broadcasting, 2001.

Gould, Harold, *Sikhs, Swamis, Students and Spies: The India Lobby in the United States*. Thousand Oaks: Sage Publications, 2006.

Greenhut, Jeffrey, "Sahib and Sepoy: An inquiry into the Relationship between the British Officers and Native Soldiers of the British Indian Army." *Military Affairs*, Vol. 48, No. 1, January 1984.

Green, Nile, *Islam and the Army in Colonial India, Sepoy Religion in the Service of Empire*. Cambridge: Cambridge University Press, 2009.

Guha, Ranajit, 'The Small Voice of History', in Amin, Shahid and Chakrabarty, Dipesh, eds., *Subaltern Studies: Writings on South Asian History and Society*, Vol. 9. Delhi: Oxford University Press, 1997.

Gupta, Manmath Nath, *History of the Indian Revolutionary Movement*. Bombay, New Delhi: Somaiya Publications, 1972.

Hardayal, Lala, *Forty-five Months in Turkey*. London: P. S. King & Son, 1920.

Hardinge, Lord of Penshurst, Baron Charles, *My Indian Years, 1910-16*. London: J Murray 1948.

Harper, R. W. E. and Miller, H., *Singapore Mutiny*. Singapore: Oxford University Press, 1984.

Harper, Tim, 'Singapore, 1915, and the Birth of the Asian Underground.' *Modern Asian History*, Vol. 47, No. 6, 2013.

Harper, Tim and Sunil Amrith, Sunil, eds. *Sites of Asian Interaction: Ideas, Networks and Mobility*. Delhi: Cambridge University Press, 2015.

Hopkirk, Peter, *Like Hidden Fire: The Plot to Bring Down the British Empire*. Tokyo: Kodansha International, 1994.

Horne, Charles F, ed., *Source Records of the Great War*, Vol. III, National Alumni 1923.

India Intelligence Burea, Compiled by the Director's Intelligence Bureau, *The Ghadr Directory: Containing the Names of Persons who have Taken Part in the Ghadr Movement in America, Europe, Africa and Afghanistan as well as India*. New Delhi: Government of India Press, 1934

India Sedition Committee Report, Calcutta, 1918.

Irvine, Andrew Alexander, Ellis, Thomas Peter, and Narain, Sheo, *Ghadr Party's Lahore Conspiracy Case, 1915 Judgement*. Meerut: Archana Publications, 2006.

Isemonger F. C. and Slattery J., *An Account of the Ghadar Conspiracy*. Lahore: India Government Printing Office-Punjab, 1919, Meerut: Archana Prakashan, 1998 reprint.

Johnston, Hugh, *The Voyage of the Komagata Maru: The Sikh Challenge to Canada's Colour Bar*. Toronto: UBC Press, expanded and fully revised edition, 2014.

Johnston, Hugh, 'The Surveillance of Indian Nationalists in North America.'

BC Studies, No. 78, Summer, 1988.

Josh, Sohan Singh, *The Hindustan Ghadar Party: A Short History*, Vol. 2. New Delhi: People's Publishing House, 1977.

Josh, Sohan Singh, *Baba Sohan Singh Bhakna. Life of the Founder of the Hindustani Ghadar Party*. New Delhi: People's Publishing House, 1970.

Kealey, Gregory S., *Spying on Canadians: The Royal Canadian Mounted Police Security Service and the Origins of the Long Cold War*. Buffalo, N. Y.: University of Toronto Press, 2017.

Kumar, Anuradha, *Subhas Chandra Bose – The Great Freedom Fighter*. New Delhi: Penguin Random House India, 2010.

Kumar, Raj, 'Empire, The Punjab And The First World War', Thesis submitted to Faculty of Arts and Social Sciences for the award of the Degree of Doctor of Philosophy in History, Department of History, Guru Nanak Dev University, Amritsar, 2016.

Kuwajima, Sho, I*ndian Mutiny in Singapore 1915*. Calcutta: Ratna Prakashan, 1991.

Kuwajima, Sho, *The Mutiny in Singapore: War, Anti-War and the War for India's Independence*. New Delhi: Rainbow Publishers, 2006.

Lal, Gobind Behari, 'The Gadar – at U.C. Berkeley: Thoughts Presented by Gobind Behari Lal.' South Asians in North America Collection, BANC MSS 2002/78, The Bancroft Library, University of California, Berkeley, 1981.

Lal, Gobind Behari, "A Journalist from India, at Home in the World." An oral history conducted in 1981 by Suzanne B. Riess, Regional Oral History Office, The Bancroft Library, University of California, Berkeley, 1983.

Lebra, Joyce, *The Indian National Army and Japan*. Singapore: ISEAS, 2008.

Lüdke, Tilmann, *Jihad made in Germany: Ottoman and German Propaganda and Intelligence Operations in the First World War*. Munich: Lit Verlag, 2001.

MacMunn, Sir George, *The Armies of India*. London: Adam & Charles Black, 1911.

Mason, Philip, *A Matter of Honour: An Account of the Indian Army, its Officers and Men*. London: Cape, 1974.

Mawani, Renisa, *Across Oceans of Law: The Komagata Maru and Jurisdiction in the Time of Empire*. Durham: Duke University Press, 2018.

Mosbergen, Rudolf William, 'The Sepoy Rebellion: a history of the Singapore Mutiny, 1915.' Academic exercise, Department of History, University of Malaya, 1954.

Mukherjee, Prithwindra, *The Intellectual Roots of India's Freedom Struggle (1893-1918)*. London: Routledge, 2017.

Murfett, Malcolm H., Miksic, John, Farrell, Brian and Chiang, Ming Shun. *Between Two Oceans: A Military History of Singapore from 1275 to 1971*. Singapore: Marshall Cavendish International Asia, 2nd ed., 2011.

Nakajima, Takeshi, Motwani, Prem, trans., *Bose of Nakamuraya – An Indian Revolutionary in Japan*. Delhi: Promilla, 2005.

Ogden, Johanna, 'Ghadar, Historical Silences, and Notions of Belonging Early 1900s Punjabis of the Columbia River.' *Oregon Historical Quarterly*, Vol. 113, No. 2, Summer, 2012.

Omissi, David, *Indian Voices of the Great War: Soldiers' Letters, 1914-18*. New York: St. Martin's Press, 1999.

Omissi, David, *The Sepoy and the Raj: The Indian Army, 1860-1940*. London: Macmillan Press, 1994.

Parmanand, Bhai, *The Story of My Life*. Delhi: 1934, 1982 reprint.

Pati, Budheswar, *India and the First World War*. Delhi: Atlantic Publishers, 1996.

Paul, Jaiwant E. and Paul, Shubh, *Har Dayal: The Great Revolutionary*. Delhi: Roli Books, 2003.

Plowman, Matthew Erin, 2013, 'The British Intelligence Station in San Francisco during the First World War', *Journal of Intelligence History*, Vol. 12, No. 1, DOI:10.1 080/16161262.2013.755016.

Popplewell, Richard J., *Intelligence and Imperial Defence: British Intelligence and the Defence of the Indian Empire, 1904-1924*. London: Frank Cass, 1995.

Puri, Harish, *Ghadar Movement: Ideology, Organization, and Strategy*. Amritsar: Guru Nanak Dev University Press, 1983.

Ramnath, Maia, *Haj to Utopia: How the Ghadar Movement Charted Global Radicalism and Attempted to Overthrow the British Empire*. Berkeley: University of California Press, 2011.

Reith, G. M., *1907 Handbook to Singapore*. Singapore: Oxford University Press, reprint, 1986.

Robertson, J. R., *The Battle of Penang: World War One in the Far East*. France, Kuala Lumpur: Editions Intervalles, 2012.

Rogan, Eugene, 'Rival jihads: Islam and the Great War in the Middle East, 1914–1918', *Journal of the British Academy*, Vol. 4, pp 1–20, 2016, DOI: 10.85871/jba/004.001.

Roy, Kaushik, *Brown Warriors of the Raj: Recruitment and the Mechanics of Command in the Sepoy Army, 1859-1913*. New Delhi: Manohar, 2008.

Sahwney, Savitri, *I Shall Never Ask for Pardon, A memoir of Pandurang Khankhoje*. Delhi: Penguin Books, 2008.

Samanta, Amiya K., ed., 'Terrorism in Bengal: Terrorists outside Bengal deriving inspiration from and having links with Bengal terrorists', *Terrorism in Bengal: A Collection of Documents on Terrorist Activities from 1905 to 1939*, Vol. 5. Calcutta: Government of West Bengal, 1995.

Sareen, Tilak Raj, *Indian Revolutionaries Abroad*. New Delhi: Sterling, 1979.

Sareen, Tilak Raj, *Select Documents on the Ghadar Party*. New Delhi: Mounto, 1994.

Sareen, Tilak Raj, *Secret documents on Singapore Mutiny, 1915*. New Delhi: Mounto, 1995.

Savarkar, Vinayak, *Inside the Enemy Camp*. CreateSpace Independent Publishing Platform, 2016, http://www.satyashodh.com/Inside%20the%20enemy%20camp1.htm.

Savarkar, Vinayak, The Indian War of Independence of 1857. London, 1909. http://savarkar.org/en/encyc/2017/5/22/2_03_34_24_the_indian_war_of_independence_1857_with_publishers_note.v001.pdf_1.pdf.

Singh, Fauja and Datta, Lal Chaman, *Who's who: Punjab Freedom Fighters*, Volume 1. Punjabi University, Department of Punjab Historical Studies, 1972.

Singh, Gajendra, *The Testimonies of Indian Soldiers and the Two World Wars: Between Self and Sepoy*. London: Bloomsbury Academic, 2014.

Singh, Gurdit, *Voyage of Komagata Maru of India's Slavery Abroad*. Chandigarh: Unistar, reprint, 2007.

Singh, Harnam 'Tundilat', *Ghadar Party, A Personal Memoir*. 1959, http://legacy.sikhpioneers.org/famous.html.

Singh, Inder, *The Gadar Heroics: The Forgotten Saga of Overseas Indians who Staked their Lives to Free India from the British*. India Empire Publications, 2013.

Singh, Jasbir. *Escape from Singapore*. New Delhi: Lancer Publishers, 2015.

Singh, Khushwant and Singh, Satindra, *Ghadar 1915: India's First Armed Revolution*. New Delhi: R&K Publishing House, 1966.

Singh, Khushwant, *History of the Sikhs*, 2 Vols. Delhi: Oxford University Press, 1996.

Singh, Sunit Sarvraj, 'Echoes of Freedom: Radical Indian Thought and International Socialism, 1905-1920', Dissertation submitted to the Faculty of the Divinity School in candidacy for the Degree of Doctor of Philosophy by University of Chicago, Illinois, March 2018.

Snow, Karen A., "Russia and the 1915 Indian Mutiny in Singapore." *South East Asia Research*, Vol. 5, 1997.

Sohi, Seema, *Echoes of Mutiny: Race, Surveillance, and Anticolonialism in North America*. New York: Oxford University Press, 2014.

Streets-Salter, Heather, *World War One in Southeast Asia: Colonialism and Anticolonialism in an Era of Global Conflict*. New York: Cambridge University Press, 2017.

Tan, Tai-Yong, *The Garrison State: The Military, Government and Society in Colonial Punjab, 1849-1947*. New Delhi, Thousand Oaks, and London: Sage Publications, 2005.

Tarling, Nicholas, '"The Merest Pustule" The Singapore Mutiny of 1915.' *Journal of the Malaysian Branch of the Royal Asiatic Society*, Vol. 55, No. 2, 1982.

Thomas, Lowell, *Lauterbach of the China Sea: The Escapes and Adventures of Seagoing Falstaff*. New York: Doubleday, Doran & Company, 1930.

Toye, Hugh and Mason, Philip, *The Springing Tiger: A Study of a Revolutionary*. London: Cassell Publishers, 1959.

Van Cuylenburg, John Bertram, *Singapore: Through Sunshine and Shadow*. Singapore: Heinemann Asia, 1982.

Van der Vat, Dan, *The Last Corsair: The Story of the Emden*. London: Hodder & Stoughton: 2000.

Waraich, Malwinder Singh and Singh, Harinder, eds., *Ghadar movement original documents – Soldiers' Revolts*. Chandigarh: Unistar Publishing, 2012.

Waraich, Malwinder Jit Singh and Puri, Kuldip, *Tryst with Martyrdom – Trial of Madan Lal Dhingra*. Chandigarh: Unistar Books, 2003.

Yong, C. F. and McKenna, R. B., 'Sir Arthur Young and Political Control of the Chinese in Malaya and Singapore, 1911-1919', *Journal of the Malaysian Branch of the Royal Asiatic Society*, Vol. 57, No. 2, 1984.

Zweig, Stefan, *The World of Yesterday, An Autobiography*. Nebraska: Viking Press, 1943.

Endnotes

1 Braddell, Roland St. John, *The Lights of Singapore*. London: Methuen, 1934, p 96.

2 MacMunn, Sir George, *The Armies of India*. London: Adam & Charles Black, 1911, p 216.

3 Primary Documents - Ottoman Issuance of Fetva, November 1914 from Horne, Charles F., ed., *Source Records of the Great War*, Vol. III, National Alumni 1923, retrieved from https://www.firstworldwar.com/source/ottoman_fetva.htm.

4 Rogan, Eugene, 'Rival Jihads: Islam and the Great War in the Middle East, 1914–1918', *Journal of the British Academy*, Vol. 4, 2016, DOI 10.85871/jba/ 004.001, p 2.

5 Lal, Gobind Behari. May 9, 1973. 'The Gadar – at U.C. Berkeley: Thoughts Presented by Gobind Behari Lal.' South Asians in North America Collection, BANC MSS 2002/78 cz, The Bancroft Library, University of California, Berkeley, 1981.

6 Cited in Kuwajima, Sho, *Indian Mutiny in Singapore 1915*. Calcutta: Ratna Prakashan, 1991, p 93.

7 Harper, Tim and Sunil Amrith, Sunil, eds. *Sites of Asian Interaction: Ideas, Networks and Mobility*. Delhi: Cambridge University Press 2015, p 15.

8 Tarling, Nicholas. '"The Merest Pustule' The Singapore Mutiny of 1915", *Journal of the Malaysian Branch of the Royal Asiatic Society*, Vol. 55, No. 2, 1982, pp 26-59.

9 Green, Nile, *Islam and the Army in Colonial India, Sepoy Religion in the Service of Empire*. Cambridge: Cambridge University Press, 2009, p 4.

10 Guha, Ranajit, 'The Small Voice of History', in Amin, Shahid and Chakrabarty, Dipesh, eds., *Subaltern Studies: Writings on South Asian History and Society*, Vol. 9. Delhi: Oxford University Press, 1997.

11 Rajagopalan, Manasi, 'Man, 91, scarred by sepoy execution'. *The Straits Times*, 13 April 2000.

12 Sareen, Tilak Raj, *Secret documents on Singapore Mutiny, 1915*. New Delhi: Mounto, 1995, p 717.

13 Ibid, p 720.

14 Ibid, p 729.

15 Ibid, p 731.

16 Ibid, p 847.

17 Ibid.

18 *The Straits Times*, 13 April 2000.

19 Ibid.

20 Robson J. H. M., *Records and recollections 1889-1934*. Kuala Lumpur, FMS: Kyle, Palmer & Co, 1934, p. 22.

21 Ibid, p 21.

22 Reith, G. M., *1907 Handbook to Singapore*. Singapore: Oxford University Press, reprint, 1986, p 19.

23 Ibid, p. 19.

24 La Motte, Ellen N., *The Opium Monopoly*. Macmillan 1920, http://www.druglibrary.org/schaffer/history/om/ommenu.htm.

25 Gupta, Manmath Nath, *History of the Indian Revolutionary Movement*. Bombay, New Delhi: Somaiya Publications, 1972, p 42.

26 La Motte, 1920.

27 Ibid.

28 Ibid.

29 'A Presentation'. *The Straits Times*, 26 August 191, p 9.

30 'The King's Dock'. *The Straits Times*, 27 August 1913, p 10.

31 'The Colony's Budget'. *The Straits Times*, 4 October 1913, p 8.

32 Cited in Mansergh Nicholas, *The Commonwealth Experience*. London: Weidenfeld and Nicolson, 1969, p 256.

33 Dutt, Romesh Chunder, *The Economic History of India in the Victorian Age: From the Accession of Queen Victoria in 1837 to the Commencement of the Twentieth Century*. Psychology Press, Reprint, 2001, p 140.

34 Pathak, Rahghunath Prasad, *Teachings of Swami Dayanand: Talks and Sermons*. Hoshiarpur: Vishveshvaranand Vedic Research Institute, 1973, p 72.

35 Paul, Jaiwant E. and Paul, Shubh, *Har Dayal: The Great Revolutionary*. Delhi: Roli Books, 2003, p 55.

36 Ibid, p 15.

37 Brown, Emily C., *Har Dayal, Hindu Revolutionary and Rationalist*. Tucson: University of Arizona Press, 1975, p 19.

38 Regional Oral History Office, 'Gobind Behari Lal: A Journalist From India, At Home in the World,' an oral history conducted in 1981 by Suzanne B. Riess. Berkeley: The Bancroft Library, University of California, 1983, pp 16-17.

39 Paul and Paul, 2003, p 27.

40 Har Dayal, Dharmavira, ed., *Letters of Lala Har Dayal*. Indian Book Agency, 1970, p 14.

41 Sen, N. B., *Punjab's Eminent Hindus: Being Biographical Sketches of Twenty Hindu Ministers, Judges, Politicians, Educationists & Legislators of the Punjab – both Living and Dead – by Some Well-known Writers of this Province*. New Book Society, 1944, p 125.

42 Ibid, p 125.

43 Paul and Paul, 2003, p 28.

44 Ibid, p 29.

45 Ibid, p. 29.

46 Sareen, Tilak Raj, *Select Documents on the Ghadar Party*. New Delhi: Mounto, 1994, p 25.

47 Paul and Paul, 2003, p 29.

48 Hopkirk, Peter, *Like Hidden Fire: The Plot to Bring Down the British Empire*. Tokyo: Kodansha International, 1994, p 46.

49 Barooah, Nirode K., *Chatto: The Life and Times of an Indian Anti-Imperialist in Europe*. Delhi: Oxford University Press, 2004, p 14.

50 Dharmavira, Lala, *Har Dayal and Revolutionary Movements of His Times*. India Book Company, 1970, p 23.

51 Savarkar, Vinayak, *Inside the Enemy Camp*. CreateSpace Independent Publishing Platform, 2016, p 73.

52 Dharmavira, 1970, p 335.

53 Paul and Paul, 2003, p 64.

54 Savarkar, 2016, p 76.

55 Ibid, p 77.

56 Savarkar, Vinayak, *The Indian War of Independence of 1857*, London, 1909, http://savarkar.org/en/encyc/2017/5/22/2_03_34_24_the_indian_war_of_independence_1857_with_publishers_note.v001.pdf_1.pdf, author's introduction, p. vii, retrieved on 1 May 2018.

57 Brown, 1975, p 34.

58 Paul and Paul, 2003, p 41.

59 Brown, 1975, p 36.

60 Ibid.

61 Singh, Harnam 'Tundilat', *Ghadar Party, A Personal Memoir*. 1959, http://legacy.sikhpioneers.org/famous.html, retrieved on 5 May 2018.

62 Paul and Paul, 2003, p 42.

63 Ibid, p 43.

64 Brown, 1975, p 53.

65 Ibid, p 56.

66 Ibid, p 19.

67 Ibid, p 59.

68 Waraich, Malwinder Jit Singh and Puri, Kuldip, *Tryst with Martyrdom – Trial of Madan Lal Dhingra*. Chandigarh: Unistar Books, 2003, p 17.

69 Gandhi, Mohandas Karamchand, *Collected works of Mahatma Gandhi: (23 July, 1908 - 4 August, 1909)*, Vol. 9. Delhi: Ministry of Information Publication, 2000, p 428.

70 Bose, 1971, p 26.

71 Gandhi, 2000, p 428.

72 Ibid.

73 Nayar, Kuldip, *Without Fear: The Life and Trial of Bhagat Singh*. Delhi: Harper Collins, 2012, pp 75-76.

74 Bose, A. C., *Indian Revolutionaries Abroad, 1905-1922, in the Background of International Developments*. New Delhi: Bharati Bhawan, 1971, p 26.

75 Brown, 1975, p 79.

76 Ibid, p 80.

77 Hopkirk, 1994, p 47.

78 Brown, 1975, p 80.

79 Safdar Hashmi Memorial Trust, *The Savarkar Controversy*. Safdar Hashmi Memorial Trust, 2004, p 64.

80 Library and Archives Canada. RG7-G-21, Vol. 201, File 332, Vol. 5, http://komagatamarujourney.ca/node/11900, retrieved 7 May 2019.

81 Bhakna, Sohan Singh, *Jiwan Sangram [Life's Struggle]*, Jalandhar: Youth Center, 1967, p 27 cited in Singh Sunit Sarvraj, 'Echoes of Freedom: Radical Indian Thought and International Socialism, 1905-1920', A Dissertation Submitted To The Faculty Of The Divinity School In Candidacy for The Degree Of Doctor Of Philosophy by University of Chicago, Illinois, March 2018, p 164.

82 Husain Rahim ed., *The Hindustanee*, Vancouver, monthly, Jan.-June, 1914, retrieved from http://komagatamarujourney.ca/node/14693.

83 Ibid.

84 Ibid.

85 Ibid.

86 Singh, Harnam, 1959.

87 Singh M. K., *Encyclopaedia Of Indian War Of Independence (1857-1947)*, 19 Vols. Delhi: Anmol Publications, 2009, p.35 and http://www.cpiml.net/liberation/2007/10/sardar-ajit-singh-hero-pagdi-sambhal-jatta-movement, retrieved on 7 May 2019.

88 Ibid, p. 36

89 Calcutta High Court, The Englishman Limited vs Lala Lajpat Ra, 11 March 1910, 6 Ind Cas 81, https://indiankanoon.org/doc/1774194/, retrieved on 2 May 2019.

90 Brown, 1975, p 89.

91 Ibid.

92 Gompers, Samuel and Gutstadt, Herman, *Meat vs. rice; American manhood against Asiatic coolieism, which shall survive?* San Francisco: American Federation of Labor and printed as Senate document 137, 1902; reprinted with intro. and appendices by Asiatic Exclusion League, 1908.

93 Singh, Khushwant, *A History of the Sikhs: 1839-2004*, Vol. 2, India: Oxford University Press, 2004, p 169.

94 Sahwney, Savitri, *I shall never ask for pardon, A memoir of Pandurang Khankhoje*. Delhi: Penguin Books, 2008, p 84.

95 Zweig, Stefan, *The World of Yesterday: An Autobiography*. Nebraska: Viking Press, 1943, pp 409-410.

96 Ibid.

97 Ibid.

98 Popplewell, Richard J., *Intelligence and Imperial Defence: British Intelligence and the Defence of the Indian Empire, 1904-1924*. London: Frank Cass, 1995, p 153.
99 Mukherjee, Prithwindra, *The Intellectual Roots of India's Freedom Struggle (1893-1918)*. London: Routledge, 2017.

100 Library and Archives Canada. RG7-G-21, Vol. 201, File 332, vol. 5, http://komagatamarujourney.ca/node/11900, retrieved on 7 May 2019.

101 Kealey, Gregory S., *Spying on Canadians: The Royal Canadian Mounted Police Security Service and the Origins of the Long Cold War*. Buffalo, N. Y.: University of Toronto Press, 2017, p 51.

102 Ibid, p 50.

103 Ibid.

104 Ibid.

105 Johnston, Hugh, *The Voyage of the Komagata Maru: The Sikh Challenge to Canada's Colour Bar*. Toronto: UBC Press, expanded and fully revised edition, 2014, p 29.

106 Gill, Parmbir Singh (2014), 'A Different Kind of Dissidence: The Ghadar Party, Sikh History And The Politics Of Anticolonial Mobilization'. *Sikh Formations*, Vol. 10, No. 1, pp 23-41, DOI: 10.1080/17448727.2014.890800.

107 Bhatti F. M., 'East Indian Immigration Into Canada, 1905-1973'. Thesis presented for the degree of Doctor of Philosophy at the University of Surrey by Department of Sociology, University of Surrey, 1974, and Hardinge of Penshurst Baron Charles, *Speeches of His Excellency the Right Hon'able Baron Hardinge of Penshurst, Viceroy and Governor-General of India: 1913-1916*. India: Thompson & Company at the Minerva Press, 1916.

108 Samanta, Amiya K., ed., 'Terrorism in Bengal: Terrorists outside Bengal deriving inspiration from and having links with Bengal terrorists', *Terrorism in Bengal: A Collection of Documents on Terrorist Activities from 1905 to 1939*, Vol. 5. Calcutta: Government of West Bengal, 1995.

109 Isemonger F. C. and Slattery J., *An Account of the Ghadar Conspiracy*. Lahore: India Government Printing Office-Punjab, 1919, Meerut: Archana Prakashan, 1998 reprint, p 10.

110 Ibid.

111 Har Dayal, 'India in America', *The Modern Review*, July, 1911, p 4.

112 Ibid.

113 Ibid.

114 Ibid, p 1.

115 Parmanand, Bhai, *The Story of My Life*. Delhi, 1934, 1982 reprint, Chapter 8, retrieved via Kindle.

116 Ibid

117 Ramnath, Maia, *Haj to Utopia: How the Ghadar Movement Charted Global Radicalism and Attempted to Overthrow the British Empire*. Berkeley, California: University of California Press, 2011, p 30.

118 Puri, Harish, *Ghadar Movement: Ideology, Organization, and Strategy*. Amritsar: Guru Nanak Dev University Press, 1983, p 67.

119 Parmanand, 1982, Chapter 8.

120 Brown, 1975, p 107.

121 Ibid.

122 Ibid, p 105.

123 Ibid.

124 'Savant Sponsor of Free Love,' *San Francisco Call*, 17 September 1912.

125 Brown, 1975, p 52.

126 Irvine, Andrew Alexander, Ellis, Thomas Peter and Narain, Sheo, *Ghadr Party's Lahore Conspiracy Case, 1915 Judgement*. Meerut: Archana Publications, 2006, p 105.

127 Paul and Paul, 2003, p 84.

128 Ibid.

129 Brooks Van Wyck, *An Autobiography*. New York: E. P. Dutton, 1965, p 210.

130 India Intelligence Burea, Compiled by the Director's Intelligence Bureau, *The Ghadr Directory: Containing the Names of Persons who have Taken Part in the Ghadr Movement in America, Europe, Africa and Afghanistan as well as India*. New Delhi: Government of India Press, 1934, pp 248-249.

131 Ibid.

132 Smith R.V., 'The revolutionary of Chandni Chowk', *The Hindu*, 2 August 2004, https://www.thehindu.com/mp/2004/08/02/stories/2004080200420200.htm, retrieved on 1 May 2019.

133 Lord Hardinge of Penshurst, Baron Charles, *My Indian Years, 1910-16*. London: J Murray, 1948, p 80.

134 'Attempted Assassination of The Viceroy', *Waikato Times*, Issue 12466, 27 Dec 1912, https://paperspast.natlib.govt.nz/newspapers/WT19121227.2.20.

135 Popplewell, 1995, p 92.

136 Brown, 1975, p 131.

137 Dharmavira, 1970, p 176.

138 Ibid.

139 Sanyal, Shukla, *Revolutionary Pamphlets, Propaganda and Political Culture in Colonial*

Bengal. New Delhi: Cambridge University Press, 2014, p 46.

140 Dharmavira, 1970, p 176.

141 Malik, Iftikhar Haider, *US-South Asia relations, 1784-1940: a historical perspective.* Area Study Centre for Africa, North & South America, Quaid-i-Azam University, 1988, p 171.

142 Sareen, T. R., 1994, p 35.

143 Ibid.

144 Ibid.

145 Isemonger and Slattery, 1998, p 13.

146 Ibid, p 13.

147 Sareen, T. R., 1994, p 35.

148 Ibid, p 84.

149 Ibid.

150 Ibid.

151 Dharmavira, 1970, p 176.

152 Singh, Harnam, 1959.

153 Ibid.

154 Sareen, T. R., 1994, p 20.

155 Ibid.

156 *Ghadar di Gunj.* Issue no. 1, poem 4, translated by Khushwant Singh, quoted in Puri, 1983, p 74.

157 Translation adapted from Deol, Gurdev Singh, *The Role of the Ghadar Party in the National Movement.* Punjab: Sterling Publishers, 1959, https://archive.org/stream/in.ernet.dli.2015.460856/2015.460856.The-Role_djvu.txt, retrieved on 4 January 2019.

158 *Ghadar,* 1 November 1913, also quoted in Mukherjee, 2017, p 231.

159 Bernhardi, Friedrich von, *Germany and the Next War.* New York: Longmans, Green, and Co., 1914, p 65.

160 'Bernhardi told plans? Said to have divulged war intentions to San Francisco Germans', *The New York Times,* 29 November 1914.

161 Irvine, Ellis and Narain, 2006, p 73.

162 Sohi, Seema. *Echoes of Mutiny: Race, Surveillance, and Anticolonialism in North America.* New York: Oxford University Press, 2014, p 166.

163 Brown, 1975, p 150.

164 India Sedition Committee Report, Calcutta, 1918, p 168.

165 Ibid, p 146.

166 Sareen, T. R., 1994, p 46.

167 Bird, Isabella, *The Golden Chersonese,* Vol 11. New York: G. P. Putnam's Sons, 1883, London: Konnemann 2000 reprint, p 273.

168 Ibid, p 272.

169 Ibid.

170 Ibid, p 273.

171 Letter from Bhagwan Singh Gyanee to Jagjit Singh, dated 19 August 1956, https://www.saada.org/item/20120805-917, retrieved on 13 May 2019.

172 Ibid.

173 Ibid.

174 Singh, Gurdit, *Voyage of Komagata Maru of India's Slavery Abroad.* Calcutta: 1928, Chandigarh: Unistar, reprint, 2007, p 57.

175 Ibid, p 58.

176 Ibid, p 63.

177 Ibid.

178 Johnston, Hugh, 2014, p 60.

179 Singh, Gurdit, 2007, p 75.

180 Ibid.

181 Ibid, pp 75-76.

182 Ibid, p 76.

183 *China Press*, Shanghai, 12 April 1914.

184 Ibid.

185 Ibid.

186 IOR/L/MIL/7/17023 Collection 405/17, Confidential review reports on Indian Army units for 1913-1914; despatch regarding unfavourable reports on certain British officers.

187 Tarling, Nicholas, 1982, p 27.

188 Ibid.

189 Ibid.

190 Ibid.

191 Ibid.

192 Ibid.

193 Greenhut, Jeffrey, 'Sahib and Sepoy: An inquiry into the Relationship between the British Officers and Native Soldiers of the British Indian Army.' *Military Affairs*, Vol. 48, No. 1, January 1984 as cited in Farwell, Byron, *Armies of the Raj: From the Great Indian Mutiny to Independence, 1858-1947*. London: W. W. Norton, 1989, p 180.

194 IOR/L/MIL/7/17023 Collection 405/17.

195 Ibid.

196 Ibid.

197 'The Bad man of the Brahmans', *The Singapore Free Press and Mercantile Advertiser*, 27 January 1913, p 12.

198 '3rd Brahmans Leave', *The Singapore Free Press and Mercantile Advertiser*, 9 April 1914, p 7.

199 'Brilliant Military Wedding', *Malaya Tribune*, 16 April 1914, p 1.

200 'Military Wedding – Olliver-Stephenson', *The Singapore Free Press and Mercantile Advertiser*, 16 April 1914, p 12.

201 'Military Marriage, Miss Stephenson and Lieut Olliver, A Brilliant Function at Tanglin', *The Straits Times*, 16 April 1914, p 10.

202 Ibid.

203 Ibid.

204 Ibid.

205 Ibid.

206 'Brilliant Military Wedding'

207 Gould, Harold, *Sikhs, Swamis, Students and Spies: The India Lobby in the United States*. Thousand Oaks: Sage Publications, 2006, retrieved via Kindle.

208 Paul and Paul, 2003, p 104.

209 Brown, 1975, p 164.

210 Ibid, p 169.

211 Ibid, p 165.

212 Sareen, T. R., 1994, p 24.

213 Brown, 1975, p 170.

214 Ibid, p 171.

215 Ibid.

216 Ansari, H., 2014, 'Maulana Barkatullah Bhopali's Transnationalism: Pan-Islamism, Colonialism, and Radical Politics' in Nordbruch G. and Ryad U., eds, *Transnational Islam in Interwar Europe: Muslim Activists and Thinkers*. Palgrave Macmillan, pp 181-209, DOI: 10.1057/9781137387042_8, p 190.

217 Ibid.

218 Ibid, p 189.

219 Sareen, T. R., 1994, p 44.

220 Ibid.

221 Singh, Khushwant and Singh, Satindra, *Ghadar 1915: India's First Armed Revolution*. New Delhi: R & K Publishing House, 1966, p 23.

222 Johnston, Hugh, 2014, p 72.

223 City of Vancouver Archives, 'Minutes of a Hindu Mass Meeting at Dominion Hall', http://komagatamarujourney.ca/pa/node/538, retrieved on 1 May 2019.

224 Ibid.

225 Nicol, Janet Mary, '"Not to Be Bought, Nor for Sale": The Trials of Joseph Edward Bird,' *Labour/Le Travail* 78, Fall 2016, p 227, https://journals.lib.unb.ca/index.php/LLT/article/download/25373/29379, retrieved on 2 April 2018.

226 Mawani, Renisa, *Across Oceans of Law: The Komagata Maru and Jurisdiction in the Time of Empire*. Durham: Duke University Press, 2018, epigraph to Chapter 5.

227 'Sir Arthur and the Lady Evelyn, Young', *Malaya Tribune*, 17 June 1914, p 6.

228 'The Governor's Holiday', *The Straits Times*, 17 June 1914, p 9.

229 Ibid.

230 Robson, 1934, pp 179-197.

231 Letter to *The Straits Times* on 'The Governor's Holiday', 19 June 1914, p 10.

232 'Tenure of Office', *The Straits Times*, 20 June 1914, p 8.

233 'Indians in Canada', *The Straits Times*, 23 June 1914, p 8.

234 Ibid.

235 Jasanoff, Maya, *The Dawn Watch: Joseph Conrad in a Global World*. New York: Penguin, 2018, p 291.

236 Johnston, 2014, p 117.

237 Ibid, p 231.

238 Ibid, p 232.

239 Ibid, p 122.

240 Ibid.

241 Ibid, p 128.

242 Ibid, p.134 and Johnston, Hugh, *The Voyage of the Komagata Maru: The Sikh Challenge to Canada's Colour Bar*. Delhi: Oxford University Press. 1979, p 86.

243 Kautsky Karl, *The Guilt Of William Hohenzollern*. London: Skeffington & Son, 1919, p 177, https://archive.org/stream/guiltofwilliamho00kautiala/guiltofwilliamho00kautiala_djvu.txt.

244 Ibid.

245 Home Department, Political-B, Proceedings, GOI, October 1915, File No. 91 cited in Kumar, Raj, 'Empire, The Punjab And The First World War', Thesis submitted to Faculty of Arts and Social Sciences for the award of the Degree of Doctor of Philosophy in History, Department of History, Guru Nanak Dev University, Amritsar, 2016, https://shodhganga.inflibnet.ac.in/bitstream/10603/172252/12/12_chaper%205.pdf.

246 National Archives, Kew, War Diaries of 5th Light Infantry, WO 95/5451.

247 Sareen, T. R., 1995, p 286.

248 Ibid, p 287.

249 'Perak and the Great War', *Malaya Tribune*, 20 June 1931, p 12.

250 Isemonger and Slattery, 1998, p 48.

251 Azad, Prithvi Singh, *Kranti Path Ka Pathik* [Hindi]. Agra: Pragya Prakashan, 1970, p 66.

252 Bhakna, Sohan Singh, 1967.

253 Puri, Harish, *Ghadar Movement, A Short History*. New Delhi: National Book Trust India, 2011, p 106.

254 Ibid, p 106.

255 Ibid, p 112.

256 Isemonger and Slattery, 1998, pp 54-55.

257 Deol, 1959, p 188, https://archive.org/stream/in.ernetdli.2015.460856/ 2015.460856.The-Role_djvu.txt, retrieved on 2 Feb 2018.

258 Isemonger and Slattery, 1998, p 50.

259 Johnston, 2014, p 197.

260 Sareen, T. R., 1995, p 98

261 Ibid.

262 Sareen, T. R., 1995, p 50.

263 Pati, Budheswar, *India and the First World War*. Delhi: Atlantic Publishers, 1996, p 119.

264 Isemonger and Slattery, 1998, p 66.

265 Irvine, 2006, p 266.

266 Ibid, p 134.

267 Isemonger and Slattery, 1998, pp 66-67.

268 Ibid, p 69.

269 Pati, Budheswar, 1996, p 121.

270 Thomas, Lowell, *Lauterbach of the China Sea: The Escapes and Adventures of Seagoing Falstaff*. New York: Doubleday, Doran & Company, 1930, p 69.

271 Robertson, J. R., *The Battle of Penang: World War One in the Far East*. France, Kuala Lumpur: Editions Intervalles, 2012, p 140.

272 Lüdke, Tilmann. *Jihad made in Germany: Ottoman and German Propaganda and Intelligence Operations in the First World War*. Munich: Lit Verlag, 2001.

273 Tucker, Spencer, ed, *World War I: The Definitive Encyclopedia and Document Collection*, 5 Vols, The Definitive Encyclopedia and Document Collection, ABC-CLIO, 2014, p 1865.

274 Ibid.

275 Paris, Timothy J., *Britain, the Hashemites, and Arab Rule, 1920-1925: The Sherifian Solution*. London: Routledge, 2003, p 22.

276 Letter from the Governor of the Straits Settlements to the Secretary of State for the Colonies regarding Court of Inquiry and Causes of Mutiny, August 15, 1915 cited in Sareen, T. R., 1995, p 711.

277 *The Straits Times*, 13 November 1914, p 6.

278 Omissi, David, *Indian Voices of the Great War: Soldiers' Letters, 1914-18*. New York: St. Martin's Press, 1999, p 25.

279 Sareen, T. R., 1994, p 180.

280 'Another Conspiracy Case', *Malaya Tribune*, 31 May 1915, p 5.

281 'Jagat Singh – Enquiry at Penang', *The Singapore Free Press and Mercantile Advertiser*, 22 June 1915, p 3.

282 Sareen, T. R., 1995, p 617.

283 Ibid, p 756.

284 Ibid, p 754.

285 Ibid, p 751.

286 Ibid, p 755.

287 CO 273/435/4564, telegram from GOC Straits Settlements to WO, 27 November 1914, and see Murfett, Malcolm H., Miksic, John, Farrell, Brian and Chiang, Ming Shun, *Between Two Oceans: A Military History of Singapore from 1275 to 1971*. Singapore: Marshall Cavendish International Asia, 2nd ed., 2011, p 130.

288 CO 273/435, Colonial Office: Straits Settlements original correspondence. offices: war and miscellaneous 1915, Report by Commandant, Malay States Guides dated 6 December 1914, , part 1, p 23.

289 Ibid, p 24.

290 Ibid.

291 CO 273/435, p 23

292 Ibid, p 27.

293 CO 273/435, part 1.

294 Ibid, pp 17-18.

295 'Perak and Great War'.

296 FCO 141/16205, Singapore: possible redeployment of Major General Reade, general officer commanding the troops.

297 Sareen, T. R., 1995, p 562.

298 'Jagat Singh – Further Evidence', *The Singapore Free Press and Mercantile Advertiser*, 2 July 1915, p 10.

299 Nakajima, Takeshi, Motwani, Prem, trans., *Bose of Nakamuraya – An Indian Revolutionary in Japan*. Delhi: Promilla, 2005, p 36.

300 Ibid.

301 Thomas, 1930, p 97.

302 Ibid, p 98.

303 Sareen, T. R., 1995, p 562.

304 Thomas, 1930, p 107.

305 Ibid, p 108.

306 Sareen, T. R., 1995, p 168.

307 Ibid, p 210.

308 Thomas, 1930, p 109.

309 'Mansoor Case', *The Straits Times*, 23 April 1915, p 7.

310 Ibid.

311 Ibid.

312 FCO 141/16054, Singapore: Proposed reduction of the Singapore garrison; Unrest among Northern Indians in the Federated Malay States

313 Ibid.

314 Ibid.

315 Ibid.

316 Sareen, Tilak Raj, *Indian Revolutionaries Abroad*. Delhi: Sterling Publishers, 1979, p 222.

317 Kuwajima, Sho, *The Mutiny in Singapore: War, Anti-War and the War for India's Independence*. New Delhi: Rainbow Publishers, 2006, p 41.

318 Sareen, T. R., 1995, p 457.

319 Ibid.

320 Ibid.

321 IOR/L/MIL/7/17023 Collection 405/17, Confidential review reports on Indian Army units for 1913-1914; despatch regarding unfavourable reports on certain British officers.

322 Sareen, T. R., 1995, p 546.

323 Younghusband, George John, *Forty Years a Soldier.* London: Putnam's Sons, 1923, p 5.

324 Sareen, T. R., 1995, p 596.

325 Ibid, p.289

326 Ibid, p. 459

327 Ibid, p.458

328 Ibid, p. 129

329 Ibid, p. 290

330 Ibid, p. 384

331 Ibid, p. 385

332 Ibid, p. 79

333 Ibid, p. 385

334 'Girls Friendly Society', *The Singapore Free Press and Mercantile Advertiser*, 8 February 1915, p 4.

335 Ibid.

336 Sareen, T. R., 1995, p 364.

337 'Singapore Amusements', *The Straits Times*, 13 February 1915, p 11.

338 'How Malays Helped to Rout the Mutineers – Mrs Woolcombe Tragedy', *The Straits Times*, 17 February 1935, p 16.

339 Sareen, T. R., 1995, p 350.

340 IOR/L/MIL/7/17023 Collection 405/17, Confidential review reports on Indian Army units for 1913-1914; despatch regarding unfavourable reports on certain British officers.

341 WO32/3630, Straits Settlements. Memorandum on The Work of Johore Military Forces During Disturbances At Singapore in 1915, 26 July 1930.

342 Ibid.

343 Sareen, T. R., 1995, p 235.

344 Ibid, p 233.

345 Ibid, p 82.

346 Ibid p 371.

347 Ibid.

348 Ibid, pp 371-372.

349 Ibid, p 57.

350 Ibid.

351 Ibid, p 374.

352 Ibid, p 717.

353 Ibid, pp 715-716.

354 Ibid, p 346.

355 Ibid, p 183.

356 Ibid, p 150.

357 Ibid, p 185.

358 Ibid, pp 185-186.

359 Ibid, p 183.

360 Ibid.

361 Ibid, p 63.

362 Ibid, p 63.

363 Ibid, p 150.

364 Ibid, p 184.

365 Ibid, p 167.

366 Ibid, p 168.

367 Ibid, p 420.

368 Ibid, p 573.

369 Ibid, p 462.

370 Ibid, p 420.

371 Ibid, p 339.

372 Ibid, p 421.

373 Ibid, p 674.

374 Ibid, p 676.

375 Ibid, p 683.

376 Harper, R. W. E and Miller, H., *Singapore Mutiny*. Singapore: Oxford University Press, 1984, p 81.

377 Ibid, p 285.

378 http://woollcombe.co.uk/data/getperson.php?personID=I176&tree=Family, retrieved on 26 May 2019.

379 'An Important Part', *Malaya Tribune*, 9 July 1935, p 14.

380 Sareen, T. R., 1995, p 278.

381 Ibid, p 278.

382 Ibid, p 279.

383 CO 273/564/6, Towkay Yeo Bian Chuan's account of what took place at his Bungalow on the night of February 15th, 1915, p 5.

384 Ibid.

385 Ibid.

386 Ibid.

387 Ibid, p 6.

388 Sareen, T. R., 1995, p 283.

389 WO32/3630.

390 Ibid.

391 Harper and Miller, 1984, p 59.

392 Sareen, T. R., 1995, p 206.

393 Thomas, 1930, p 114.

394 Ibid.

395 Sareen, T. R., 1995, p 341.

396 CO 273/435, Colonial Office: Straits Settlements original correspondence. offices: war and miscellaneous 1915, Cypher message from Arthur Young to Office of Viceroy in Calcutta.

397 Brown, Mary and Brown, Edwin A., *Singapore Mutiny: A Colonial Couple's Stirring Account of Combat and Survival in the 1915 Singapore Mutiny*. Monsoon Books 2015, p 125.

398 Ibid, p 125.

399 Dickinson, A.H., 'The Mutiny of the 5th Light Infantry', unpublished typescript prepared for Royal Commonwealth Society, London, Imperial War Museum Library Papers, p 14.

400 Sareen, T. R., 1995, p 779.

401 CO 273/564/6, p 6.

402 Ibid, p 7.

403 Brown and Brown, 2015, p 51.

404 Ibid, p 54.

405 Ibid, pp 65-66.

406 Song, Ong Siang, *One Hundred Years' History of the Chinese in Singapore*. Singapore: Oxford University Press, Reprint 1985, p 514.

407 'The Riot in Singapore. A Woman's Story', *The Times*, 26 March 1915, p 9.

408 Sareen, T. R., 1995, p 625.

409 Ibid, p 822.

410 Ibid, p 625.

411 Ibid.

412 'From Kota Tinggi to the Firing Squad in Outram Road', *The Singapore Free Press*, 14 April 1951, p 7.

413 Sareen, T. R., 1995, p 625.

414 Ibid, p 626.

415 Ibid.

416 Ibid.

417 WO32/3630, Straits Settlements. Memorandum on The Work of Johore Military Forces During Disturbances At Singapore in 1915, 26 July 1930.

418 CO 273/435, Colonial Office: Straits Settlements original correspondence. offices: war and miscellaneous 1915, No. 221, Cipher from General Officer Commanding Ridout to War Office on 22 February 1915, 3am.

419 CO 273/435, Colonial Office: Straits Settlements original correspondence. offices: war and miscellaneous 1915, No. 1, Cipher from General Officer Commanding, China to War Office, 24th February 1915, 2.10 pm.

420 CO 273/435, Colonial Office: Straits Settlements original correspondence. offices: war and miscellaneous 1915, No. 3367, Cipher from War Office to General Officer Commanding, Singapore, 2nd March, 1915, 1.55 pm.

421 CO 273/435, Colonial Office: Straits Settlements original correspondence. offices: war and miscellaneous 1915, No. 268, Cipher from General Officer Commanding, Straits Settlements to War Office, 5th March 1915, 3.30 pm.

422 Sareen, T. R., 1995, pp 843-844.

423 Isemonger and Slattery, 1998, p 44.

424 Puri, Harish, 2011, p 127.

425 Parmanand, Bhai, 1982, Chapter 4.

426 Irvine, Alexander, Ellis and Narain, 2006, p 57.

427 Parmanand, Bhai, 1982, Chapter 10.

428 Ibid.

429 Ibid.

430 Ibid.

431 Gupta, 1972, p 44.

432 Parmanand, Bhai, 1982, Chapter 10.

433 Gupta, 1972, p 44.

434 Ibid.

435 Sareen, T. R., 1995, p 49.

436 CO 273/435, Colonial Office: Straits Settlements original correspondence. offices: war and miscellaneous 1915, No. 284, Cipher from General Officer Commanding Ridout to War Office on 22 March 1915.

437 Sareen, T. R., 1995, p 849.

438 'From Kota Tinggi to the Firing Squad in Outram Road'.

439 Dickinson, A.H., p 22.

440 'From Kota Tinggi to the Firing Squad in Outram Road'.

441 Ibid

442 CO 273/435, Colonial Office: Straits Settlements original correspondence. offices: war and miscellaneous 1915, parts 1 and 2, GOC Telegram, 25 March 1915, 286, in War Office to Colonial Office, 26 March.

443 Sareen, T. R., 1995, p 542.

444 Ibid, p 542.

445 FCO 141/16534, Note from GOC Commanding Troops S.S. to the Governor Sir Arhur Young in Singapore: Mutiny Of The 5th Native Light Infantry (Singapore Mutiny); Future And Disposal Of The 5th Native Light Infantry.

446 Ibid.

447 Ibid.

448 Dickinson, A.H., p 12

449 Ibid, p 12-13.

450 Ibid, p 13.

451 Sareen, T. R., 1995, p 827.

452 Dickinson, A.H., p 23

453 Hammond, Joseph, 'Remembering the Ottoman Empire's forgotten Indian Allies', *Daily Sabah*, 14 February 2015, https://www.dailysabah.com/world/2015/02/14/remembering-the-ottoman-empires-forgotten-indian-allies.

454 Snow, Karen A., 'Russia and the 1915 Indian Mutiny in Singapore', *South East Asia Research*, Vol. 5, 1997.

455 Kuwajima, Sho, 2006, p 71.

456 CO 273/435, Colonial Office: Straits Settlements original correspondence. offices: war and miscellaneous 1915, parts 1 and 2, and FCO 141/16539, Paraphrase of cyber cable from Sir Arthur Young to Viceroy of India, 20 February 1915, p 6.

457 Sareen, T. R., 1995, pp 863-864.

458 Pati, Budheswar, 1996, p 129.

459 Sareen, T. R., 1995, p 36

460 Ibid, p 38.

461 Wagner, Kim, *Amritsar 1919: An Empire of Fear and the Making of a Massacre*. New Haven: Yale University Press, 2019.

462 India Sedition Committee Report, 1918, Calcutta, p 121.

463 CO 60716, p 501.

464 Ibid, p 494.

465 Ibid.

466 Ibid, pp 494-495.

467 Ibid, p 496.

468 Ibid, p 481.

469 Nakajima, 2005, pp 48-51.

470 'Mutiny Matters', *The Straits Times*, 22 June 1915, p 6.

471 Editorial, *The Straits Times*, 22 June 1915.

472 FCO 141/16539, Secret Cable from Sir Arthur Young to Viceroy of India, 4 March 1915, p 9.

473 Biographical Summary and CV of Major H. R. Kothavala, Indian (Imperial) Police (retired) kindly provided by his family and by kind courtesy of his

descendant and namesake, Hector Kothavala.

474 Popplewell, 1995, p 263.

475 CO 273/435

476 Ibid.

477 'Farewells to General Ridout', *The Straits Times*, 23 March 1921, p 9.

478 Ibid.

479 Ibid.

480 FCO 141/16534, Ridout's address to the 5th on eve of departure for East Africa, Singapore: Mutiny Of The 5th Native Light Infantry (Singapore Mutiny); Future And Disposal Of The 5th Native Light Infantry.

481 Cheah, Boon Kheng, 'Hunting Down the Rebels in Kelantan, 1915: The Sultan's "Double Game"'. *Journal of the Malaysian Branch of the Royal Asiatic Society*, Vol. 68, No. 2 (269), 1995, pp 9-32, http://www.jstor.org/stable/41493643.

482 Ibid.

483 ibid.

484 Lebra, Joyce, *The Indian National Army and Japan*. Singapore: ISEAS, 2008, p 16.

485 Toye, Hugh and Mason, Philip, *The Springing Tiger: A Study of a Revolutionary*. London: Cassell Publishers, 1959, p 3.

486 Ibid, p 7.

487 Singh, General Mohan, *Soldiers' contribution to Indian independence*. New Delhi: Army Educational Stores, 1974, pp 65-66.

488 Gill, Singh Naranjan, *Story of the INA*. New Delhi: Publications Division, Ministry of Information and Broadcasting, 2001, Chapter 4.

489 Bakshi, Anil, *The Road to Freedom: Travels Through Singapore, Malaysia, Burma, and India in the Footsteps of the Indian National Army*. Michigan: Odyssey Books, 1998, p 19.

490 Kumar, Anuradha, *Subhas Chandra Bose – The Great Freedom Fighter*. New Delhi: Penguin Random House India, 2010.

491 Toye and Mason, p xiv.

492 Nakajima, 2005, p 284.

493 Ibid, p 292.

494 Bose, Chandra Kumar, 'What I learnt about the adoration of Subhas Chandran Bose in Singapore', *Daily O*, https://www.dailyo.in/variety/subhas-chandra-bose-bose-memorial-singapore-ina/story/1/20100.html, retrieved on 20 June 2019.

495 JIN 104, Imperial War Museum, Demolition of Indian National Army War Memorial at Singapore, https://www.iwm.org.uk/collections/item/object/1060042527 retrieved on 20 June 2019.

496 At Moira in Manipur, India, a replica was constructed of the razed INA Memorial commemorating its Unknown Warrior. See Sushant Singh, 'INA and Indian Army – A History of Conflict, A Legacy of Pride', *Indian Express*, 23 November 2017, https://indianexpress.com/article/explained/ina-and-indian-army-a-history-of-conflict-a-legacy-of-pride-4950146/, retrieved on 18 June 2019.

497 Brzezinski, Zbigniew, *Second Chance: Three Presidents and the Crisis of American Superpower*. New York: Basic Books, 2007.

498 'Red Salute Baba Bhagat Singh Bilga', *Lalkar*, July/August 2009, http://www.lalkar.org/article/773/red-salute-to-baba-bhagat-singhbilga.

Index

INDEX